SHORT STORIES
FOR
MIDDLE SCHOOL

Compiled and Edited by
Teresa Thuel

First Edition

TABLE OF CONTENTS

FICTION

POETRY

FOLKLORE

NONFICTION

FICTION

FICTION

A Horseman in the Sky
Ambrose Bierce

I

One sunny afternoon in the autumn of the year 1861 a soldier lay in a clump of laurel by the side of a road in western Virginia. He lay at full length upon his stomach, his feet resting upon the toes, his head upon the left forearm. His extended right hand loosely grasped his rifle. But for the somewhat methodical disposition of his limbs and a slight rhythmic movement of the cartridge-box at the back of his belt he might have been thought to be dead. He was asleep at his post of duty. But if detected he would be dead shortly afterward, death being the just and legal penalty of his crime.

The clump of laurel in which the criminal lay was in the angle of a road which after ascending southward a steep acclivity to that point turned sharply to the west, running along the summit for perhaps one hundred yards. There it turned southward again and went zigzagging downward through the forest. At the salient of that second angle was a large flat rock, jutting out northward, overlooking the deep valley from which the road ascended. The rock capped a high cliff; a stone dropped from its outer edge would have fallen sheer downward one thousand feet to the tops of the pines. The angle where the soldier lay was on another spur of the same cliff. Had he been awake he would have commanded a view, not only of the short arm of the road and the jutting rock, but of the entire profile of the cliff below it. It might well have made him giddy to look.

The country was wooded everywhere except at the bottom of the valley to the northward, where there was a small natural meadow, through which flowed a stream scarcely visible from the valley's rim. This open ground looked hardly larger than an ordinary door-yard, but was really several acres in extent. Its green was more vivid than that of the inclosing forest. Away beyond it rose a line of giant cliffs similar to those upon which we are supposed to stand in our survey of the savage scene, and through which the road had somehow made its climb to the summit. The configuration of the valley, indeed, was such that from this point of observation it seemed entirely shut in, and one could but have wondered how the road which found a way out of it had found a way into it, and whence came and whither went the waters of the stream that parted the meadow more than a thousand feet below.

No country is so wild and difficult but men will make it a theatre of war; concealed in the forest at the bottom of that military rat-trap, in which half a hundred men in possession of the exits might have starved an army to submission, lay five regiments of Federal infantry. They had

3

marched all the previous day and night and were resting. At nightfall they would take to the road again, climb to the place where their unfaithful sentinel now slept, and descending the other slope of the ridge fall upon a camp of the enemy at about midnight. Their hope was to surprise it, for the road led to the rear of it. In case of failure, their position would be perilous in the extreme; and fail they surely would should accident or vigilance apprise the enemy of the movement.

II

The sleeping sentinel in the clump of laurel was a young Virginian named Carter Druse. He was the son of wealthy parents, an only child, and had known such ease and cultivation and high living as wealth and taste were able to command in the mountain country of western Virginia. His home was but a few miles from where he now lay. One morning he had risen from the breakfast-table and said, quietly but gravely: "Father, a Union regiment has arrived at Grafton. I am going to join it."

The father lifted his leonine head, looked at the son a moment in silence, and replied: "Well, go, sir, and whatever may occur do what you conceive to be your duty. Virginia, to which you are a traitor, must get on without you. Should we both live to the end of the war, we will speak further of the matter. Your mother, as the physician has informed you, is in a most critical condition; at the best she cannot be with us longer than a few weeks, but that time is precious. It would be better not to disturb her."

So Carter Druse, bowing reverently to his father, who returned the salute with a stately courtesy that masked a breaking heart, left the home of his childhood to go soldiering. By conscience and courage, by deeds of devotion and daring, he soon commended himself to his fellows and his officers; and it was to these qualities and to some knowledge of the country that he owed his selection for his present perilous duty at the extreme outpost. Nevertheless, fatigue had been stronger than resolution and he had fallen asleep. What good or bad angel came in a dream to rouse him from his state of crime, who shall say? Without a movement, without a sound, in the profound silence and the languor of the late afternoon, some invisible messenger of fate touched with unsealing finger the eyes of his consciousness--whispered into the ear of his spirit the mysterious awakening word which no human lips ever have spoken, no human memory ever has recalled. He quietly raised his forehead from his arm and looked between the masking stems of the laurels, instinctively closing his right hand about the stock of his rifle.

His first feeling was a keen artistic delight. On a colossal pedestal, the cliff,--motionless at the extreme edge of the capping rock and sharply outlined against the sky,--was an equestrian statue of impressive dignity. The figure of the man sat the figure of the horse, straight and soldierly, but with the repose of a Grecian god carved in the marble which limits the suggestion

4

of activity. The gray costume harmonized with its aerial background; the metal of accoutrement and caparison was softened and subdued by the shadow; the animal's skin had no points of high light. A carbine strikingly foreshortened lay across the pommel of the saddle, kept in place by the right hand grasping it at the "grip"; the left hand, holding the bridle rein, was invisible. In silhouette against the sky the profile of the horse was cut with the sharpness of a cameo; it looked across the heights of air to the confronting cliffs beyond. The face of the rider, turned slightly away, showed only an outline of temple and beard; he was looking downward to the bottom of the valley. Magnified by its lift against the sky and by the soldier's testifying sense of the formidableness of a near enemy the group appeared of heroic, almost colossal, size.

For an instant Druse had a strange, half-defined feeling that he had slept to the end of the war and was looking upon a noble work of art reared upon that eminence to commemorate the deeds of an heroic past of which he had been an inglorious part. The feeling was dispelled by a slight movement of the group: the horse, without moving its feet, had drawn its body slightly backward from the verge; the man remained immobile as before. Broad awake and keenly alive to the significance of the situation, Druse now brought the butt of his rifle against his cheek by cautiously pushing the barrel forward through the bushes, cocked the piece, and glancing through the sights covered a vital spot of the horseman's breast. A touch upon the trigger and all would have been well with Carter Druse. At that instant the horseman turned his head and looked in the direction of his concealed foeman--seemed to look into his very face, into his eyes, into his brave, compassionate heart.

Is it then so terrible to kill an enemy in war--an enemy who has surprised a secret vital to the safety of one's self and comrades--an enemy more formidable for his knowledge than all his army for its numbers? Carter Druse grew pale; he shook in every limb, turned faint, and saw the statuesque group before him as black figures, rising, falling, moving unsteadily in arcs of circles in a fiery sky. His hand fell away from his weapon, his head slowly dropped until his face rested on the leaves in which he lay. This courageous gentleman and hardy soldier was near swooning from intensity of emotion.

It was not for long; in another moment his face was raised from earth, his hands resumed their places on the rifle, his forefinger sought the trigger; mind, heart, and eyes were clear, conscience and reason sound. He could not hope to capture that enemy; to alarm him would but send him dashing to his camp with his fatal news. The duty of the soldier was plain: the man must be shot dead from ambush--without warning, without a moment's spiritual preparation, with never so much as an unspoken prayer, he must be sent to his account. But no--there is a hope; he may have discovered nothing--perhaps he is but admiring the sublimity of the landscape. If permitted, he may turn and ride carelessly away in the direction whence he came.

Surely it will be possible to judge at the instant of his withdrawing whether he knows. It may well be that his fixity of attention--Druse turned his head and looked through the deeps of air downward, as from the surface to the bottom of a translucent sea. He saw creeping across the green meadow a sinuous line of figures of men and horses--some foolish commander was permitting the soldiers of his escort to water their beasts in the open, in plain view from a dozen summits!

Druse withdrew his eyes from the valley and fixed them again upon the group of man and horse in the sky, and again it was through the sights of his rifle. But this time his aim was at the horse. In his memory, as if they were a divine mandate, rang the words of his father at their parting: "Whatever may occur, do what you conceive to be your duty." He was calm now. His teeth were firmly but not rigidly closed; his nerves were as tranquil as a sleeping babe's--not a tremor affected any muscle of his body; his breathing, until suspended in the act of taking aim, was regular and slow. Duty had conquered; the spirit had said to the body: "Peace, be still." He fired.

III

An officer of the Federal force, who in a spirit of adventure or in quest of knowledge had left the hidden *bivouac* in the valley, and with aimless feet had made his way to the lower edge of a small open space near the foot of the cliff, was considering what he had to gain by pushing his exploration further. At a distance of a quarter-mile before him, but apparently at a stone's throw, rose from its fringe of pines the gigantic face of rock, towering to so great a height above him that it made him giddy to look up to where its edge cut a sharp, rugged line against the sky. It presented a clean, vertical profile against a background of blue sky to a point half the way down, and of distant hills, hardly less blue, thence to the tops of the trees at its base. Lifting his eyes to the dizzy altitude of its summit the officer saw an astonishing sight--a man on horseback riding down into the valley through the air!

Straight upright sat the rider, in military fashion, with a firm seat in the saddle, a strong clutch upon the rein to hold his charger from too impetuous a plunge. From his bare head his long hair streamed upward, waving like a plume. His hands were concealed in the cloud of the horse's lifted mane. The animal's body was as level as if every hoof-stroke encountered the resistant earth. Its motions were those of a wild gallop, but even as the officer looked they ceased, with all the legs thrown sharply forward as in the act of alighting from a leap. But this was a flight!

Filled with amazement and terror by this apparition of a horseman in the sky--half believing himself the chosen scribe of some new Apocalypse, the officer was overcome by the intensity

6

of his emotions; his legs failed him and he fell. Almost at the same instant he heard a crashing sound in the trees--a sound that died without an echo--and all was still.

The officer rose to his feet, trembling. The familiar sensation of an abraded shin recalled his dazed faculties. Pulling himself together he ran rapidly obliquely away from the cliff to a point distant from its foot; thereabout he expected to find his man; and thereabout he naturally failed. In the fleeting instant of his vision his imagination had been so wrought upon by the apparent grace and ease and intention of the marvelous performance that it did not occur to him that the line of march of aerial cavalry is directly downward, and that he could find the objects of his search at the very foot of the cliff. A half-hour later he returned to camp.

This officer was a wise man; he knew better than to tell an incredible truth. He said nothing of what he had seen. But when the commander asked him if in his scout he had learned anything of advantage to the expedition he answered:

"Yes, sir; there is no road leading down into this valley from the southward."

The commander, knowing better, smiled.

IV

After firing his shot, Private Carter Druse reloaded his rifle and resumed his watch. Ten minutes had hardly passed when a Federal sergeant crept cautiously to him on hands and knees. Druse neither turned his head nor looked at him, but lay without motion or sign of recognition.

"Did you fire?" the sergeant whispered.

"Yes."

"At what?"

"A horse. It was standing on yonder rock--pretty far out. You see it is no longer there. It went over the cliff."

The man's face was white, but he showed no other sign of emotion. Having answered, he turned away his eyes and said no more. The sergeant did not understand.

"See here, Druse," he said, after a moment's silence, "it's no use making a mystery. I order you to report. Was there anybody on the horse?"

"Yes."

"Well?"

"My father."

The sergeant rose to his feet and walked away. "Good God!" he said.

The Luck Of Roaring Camp
Bret Harte

There was commotion in Roaring Camp. It could not have been a fight, for in 1850 that was not novel enough to have called together the entire settlement. The ditches and claims were not only deserted, but "Tuttle's grocery" had contributed its gamblers, who, it will be remembered, calmly continued their game the day that French Pete and Kanaka Joe shot each other to death over the bar in the front room. The whole camp was collected before a rude cabin on the outer edge of the clearing. Conversation was carried on in a low tone, but the name of a woman was frequently repeated. It was a name familiar enough in the camp,—"Cherokee Sal."

Perhaps the less said of her the better. She was a coarse and, it is to be feared, a very sinful woman. But at that time she was the only woman in Roaring Camp, and was just then lying in sore extremity, when she most needed the ministration of her own sex. Dissolute, abandoned, and irreclaimable, she was yet suffering a martyrdom hard enough to bear even when veiled by sympathizing womanhood, but now terrible in her loneliness. The primal curse had come to her in that original isolation which must have made the punishment of the first transgression so dreadful. It was, perhaps, part of the expiation of her sin that, at a moment when she most lacked her sex's intuitive tenderness and care, she met only the half-contemptuous faces of her masculine associates. Yet a few of the spectators were, I think, touched by her sufferings. Sandy Tipton thought it was "rough on Sal," and, in the contemplation of her condition, for a moment rose superior to the fact that he had an ace and two bowers in his sleeve.

It will be seen also that the situation was novel. Deaths were by no means uncommon in Roaring Camp, but a birth was a new thing. People had been dismissed the camp effectively, finally, and with no possibility of return; but this was the first time that anybody had been introduced *ab initio*. Hence the excitement.

"You go in there, Stumpy," said a prominent citizen known as "Kentuck," addressing one of the loungers. "Go in there, and see what you kin do. You've had experience in them things."

Perhaps there was a fitness in the selection. Stumpy, in other climes, had been the putative head of two families; in fact, it was owing to some legal informality in these proceedings that Roaring Camp—a city of refuge—was indebted to his company. The crowd approved the choice, and Stumpy was wise enough to bow to the majority. The door closed on the extempore surgeon and midwife, and Roaring Camp sat down outside, smoked its pipe, and awaited the issue.

The assemblage numbered about a hundred men. One or two of these were actual fugitives from justice, some were criminal, and all were reckless. Physically they exhibited no indication of their past lives and character. The greatest scamp had a Raphael face, with a profusion of blonde hair; Oakhurst, a gambler, had the melancholy air and intellectual abstraction of a Hamlet; the coolest and most courageous man was scarcely over five feet in height, with a soft voice and an embarrassed, timid manner. The term "roughs" applied to them was a distinction rather than a definition. Perhaps in the minor details of fingers, toes, ears, etc., the camp may have been deficient, but these slight omissions did not detract from their aggregate force. The strongest man had but three fingers on his right hand; the best shot had but one eye.

Such was the physical aspect of the men that were dispersed around the cabin. The camp lay in a triangular valley between two hills and a river. The only outlet was a steep trail over the summit of a hill that faced the cabin, now illuminated by the rising moon. The suffering woman might have seen it from the rude bunk whereon she lay,—seen it winding like a silver thread until it was lost in the stars above.

A fire of withered pine boughs added sociability to the gathering. By degrees the natural levity of Roaring Camp returned. Bets were freely offered and taken regarding the result. Three to five that "Sal would get through with it;" even that the child would survive; side bets as to the sex and complexion of the coming stranger. In the midst of an excited discussion an exclamation came from those nearest the door, and the camp stopped to listen. Above the swaying and moaning of the pines, the swift rush of the river, and the crackling of the fire rose a sharp, querulous cry,—a cry unlike anything heard before in the camp. The pines stopped moaning, the river ceased to rush, and the fire to crackle. It seemed as if Nature had stopped to listen too.

The camp rose to its feet as one man! It was proposed to explode a barrel of gunpowder; but in consideration of the situation of the mother, better counsels prevailed, and only a few revolvers were discharged; for whether owing to the rude surgery of the camp, or some other reason, Cherokee Sal was sinking fast. Within an hour she had climbed, as it were, that rugged road that led to the stars, and so passed out of Roaring Camp, its sin and shame, forever. I do not think that the announcement disturbed them much, except in speculation as to the fate of the child. "Can he live now?" was asked of Stumpy. The answer was doubtful. The only other being of Cherokee Sal's sex and maternal condition in the settlement was an ass. There was some conjecture as to fitness, but the experiment was tried. It was less problematical than the ancient treatment of Romulus and Remus, and apparently as successful.

When these details were completed, which exhausted another hour, the door was opened, and the anxious crowd of men, who had already formed themselves into a queue, entered in single file. Beside the low bunk or shelf, on which the figure of the mother was starkly outlined below the blankets, stood a pine table. On this a candle-box was placed, and within it, swathed in staring red flannel, lay the last arrival at Roaring Camp. Beside the candle-box was placed a hat. Its use was soon indicated. "Gentlemen," said Stumpy, with a singular mixture of authority and *ex officio* complacency,—"gentlemen will please pass in at the front door, round the table, and out at the back door. Them as wishes to contribute anything toward the orphan will find a hat handy." The first man entered with his hat on; he uncovered, however, as he looked about him, and so unconsciously set an example to the next. In such communities good and bad actions are catching. As the procession filed in comments were audible,—criticisms addressed perhaps rather to Stumpy in the character of showman: "Is that him?" "Mighty small specimen;" "Hasn't more'n got the color;" "Ain't bigger nor a derringer." The contributions were as characteristic: A silver tobacco box; a doubloon; a navy revolver, silver mounted; a gold specimen; a very beautifully embroidered lady's handkerchief (from Oakhurst the gambler); a diamond breastpin; a diamond ring (suggested by the pin, with the remark from the giver that he "saw that pin and went two diamonds better"); a slung-shot; a Bible (contributor not detected); a golden spur; a silver teaspoon (the initials, I regret to say, were not the giver's); a pair of surgeon's shears; a lancet; a Bank of England note for L5; and about $200 in loose gold and silver coin. During these proceedings Stumpy maintained a silence as impassive as the dead on his left, a gravity as inscrutable as that of the newly born on his right. Only one incident occurred to break the monotony of the curious procession. As Kentuck bent over the candle-box half curiously, the child turned, and, in a spasm of pain, caught at his groping finger, and held it fast for a moment. Kentuck looked foolish and embarrassed. Something like a blush tried to assert itself in his weather-beaten cheek. "The d—d little cuss!" he said, as he extricated his finger, with perhaps more tenderness and care than he might have been deemed capable of showing. He held that finger a little apart from its fellows as he went out, and examined it curiously. The examination provoked the same original remark in regard to the child. In fact, he seemed to enjoy repeating it. "He rastled with my finger," he remarked to Tipton, holding up the member, "the d—d little cuss!"

It was four o'clock before the camp sought repose. A light burnt in the cabin where the watchers sat, for Stumpy did not go to bed that night. Nor did Kentuck. He drank quite freely, and related with great gusto his experience, invariably ending with his characteristic condemnation of the newcomer. It seemed to relieve him of any unjust implication of sentiment, and Kentuck had the weaknesses of the nobler sex. When everybody else had gone to bed, he walked down to the river and whistled reflectingly. Then he walked up the gulch past the cabin, still whistling with demonstrative unconcern. At a large redwood-tree he paused and retraced his steps, and again passed the cabin. Halfway down to the river's bank he again paused, and then returned and knocked at the door. It was opened by Stumpy. "How goes it?" said Kentuck, looking past Stumpy toward the candle-box. "All serene!" replied Stumpy. "Anything up?" "Nothing." There was a pause—an embarrassing one—Stumpy still holding the door. Then Kentuck had recourse to his finger, which he held up to Stumpy. "Rastled with it,—the d——d little cuss," he said, and retired.

The next day Cherokee Sal had such rude sepulture as Roaring Camp afforded. After her body had been committed to the hillside, there was a formal meeting of the camp to discuss what should be done with her infant. A resolution to adopt it was unanimous and enthusiastic. But an animated discussion in regard to the manner and feasibility of providing for its wants at once sprang up. It was remarkable that the argument partook of none of those fierce personalities with which discussions were usually conducted at Roaring Camp. Tipton proposed that they should send the child to Red Dog,—a distance of forty miles,—where female attention could be procured. But the unlucky suggestion met with fierce and unanimous opposition. It was evident that no plan which entailed parting from their new acquisition would for a moment be entertained. "Besides," said Tom Ryder, "them fellows at Red Dog would swap it, and ring in somebody else on us." A disbelief in the honesty of other camps prevailed at Roaring Camp, as in other places.

The introduction of a female nurse in the camp also met with objection. It was argued that no decent woman could be prevailed to accept Roaring Camp as her home, and the speaker urged that "they didn't want any more of the other kind." This unkind allusion to the defunct mother, harsh as it may seem, was the first spasm of propriety,—the first symptom of the camp's regeneration. Stumpy advanced nothing. Perhaps he felt a certain delicacy in interfering with the selection of a possible successor in office. But when questioned, he averred stoutly that he and "Jinny"—the mammal before alluded to—could manage to rear the child. There was something original, independent, and heroic about the plan that pleased the camp. Stumpy was retained. Certain articles were sent for to Sacramento. "Mind," said the treasurer, as he pressed a bag of gold-dust into the expressman's hand, "the best that can be got,—lace, you know, and filigree work and frills,—d——n the cost!" Strange to say, the child thrived. Perhaps the invigorating climate of the mountain camp was compensation for material deficiencies. Nature took the foundling to her broader breast. In that rare atmosphere of the Sierra foothills,—that air pungent with balsamic odor, that ethereal cordial at once bracing and exhilarating,—he may have found food and nourishment, or a subtle chemistry that transmuted ass's milk to lime and phosphorus. Stumpy inclined to the belief that it was the latter and good nursing. "Me and that ass," he would say, "has been father and mother to him! Don't you," he would add, apostrophizing the helpless bundle before him, "never go back on us."

11

By the time he was a month old the necessity of giving him a name became apparent. He had generally been known as "The Kid," "Stumpy's Boy," "The Coyote" (an allusion to his vocal powers), and even by Kentuck's endearing diminutive of "The d—d little cuss." But these were felt to be vague and unsatisfactory, and were at last dismissed under another influence. Gamblers and adventurers are generally superstitious, and Oakhurst one day declared that the baby had brought "the luck" to Roaring Camp. It was certain that of late they had been successful. "Luck" was the name agreed upon, with the prefix of Tommy for greater convenience. No allusion was made to the mother, and the father was unknown. "It's better," said the philosophical Oakhurst, "to take a fresh deal all round. Call him Luck, and start him fair." A day was accordingly set apart for the christening. What was meant by this ceremony the reader may imagine who has already gathered some idea of the reckless irreverence of Roaring Camp. The master of ceremonies was one "Boston," a noted wag, and the occasion seemed to promise the greatest facetiousness. This ingenious satirist had spent two days in preparing a burlesque of the Church service, with pointed local allusions. The choir was properly trained, and Sandy Tipton was to stand godfather. But after the procession had marched to the grove with music and banners, and the child had been deposited before a mock altar, Stumpy stepped before the expectant crowd. "It ain't my style to spoil fun, boys," said the little man, stoutly eying the faces around him, "but it strikes me that this thing ain't exactly on the square. It's playing it pretty low down on this yer baby to ring in fun on him that he ain't goin' to understand. And if there's goin' to be any godfathers round, I'd like to see who's got any better rights than me." A silence followed Stumpy's speech. To the credit of all humorists be it said that the first man to acknowledge its justice was the satirist thus stopped of his fun. "But," said Stumpy, quickly following up his advantage, "we're here for a christening, and we'll have it. I proclaim you Thomas Luck, according to the laws of the United States and the State of California, so help me God." It was the first time that the name of the Deity had been otherwise uttered than profanely in the camp. The form of christening was perhaps even more ludicrous than the satirist had conceived; but strangely enough, nobody saw it and nobody laughed. "Tommy" was christened as seriously as he would have been under a Christian roof, and cried and was comforted in as orthodox fashion.

And so the work of regeneration began in Roaring Camp. Almost imperceptibly a change came over the settlement. The cabin assigned to "Tommy Luck"—or "The Luck," as he was more frequently called—first showed signs of improvement. It was kept scrupulously clean and whitewashed. Then it was boarded, clothed, and papered. The rosewood, cradle, packed eighty miles by mule, had, in Stumpy's way of putting it, "sorter killed the rest of the furniture." So the rehabilitation of the cabin became a necessity. The men who were in the habit of lounging in at Stumpy's to see "how 'The Luck' got on" seemed to appreciate the change, and in self-defense the rival establishment of "Tuttle's grocery" bestirred itself and imported a carpet and mirrors. The reflections of the latter on the appearance of Roaring Camp tended to produce stricter habits of personal cleanliness. Again Stumpy imposed a kind of quarantine upon those who aspired to the honor and privilege of holding The Luck. It was a cruel mortification to Kentuck—who, in the carelessness of a large nature and the habits of frontier life, had begun to regard all garments as a second cuticle, which, like a snake's, only sloughed off through decay—to be debarred this privilege from certain prudential reasons. Yet such was the subtle influence of innovation that he thereafter appeared regularly every afternoon in a clean shirt and face still shining from his ablutions. Nor were moral and social sanitary laws neglected. "Tommy," who was supposed to spend his whole existence in a persistent attempt to repose, must not be disturbed by noise. The shouting and yelling, which had gained the camp its infelicitous title, were not permitted within hearing distance of Stumpy's. The men conversed in whispers or smoked with Indian gravity. Profanity was tacitly given up in these sacred precincts, and throughout the camp a popular form of expletive, known as "D—n the luck!" and "Curse the luck!" was abandoned, as having a new personal bearing. Vocal music was not interdicted, being supposed to have a soothing, tranquilizing quality; and one song, sung by "Man-o'-War Jack," an English sailor from her Majesty's Australian colonies, was quite popular as a lullaby. It was a lugubrious recital of the exploits of "the Arethusa, Seventy-four," in a muffled minor, ending with a prolonged dying fall at the burden of each verse, "On b-oo-o-ard of the Arethusa." It was a fine sight to see Jack holding The Luck, rocking from side to side as if with the motion of a ship, and crooning forth this naval ditty. Either through the peculiar rocking of Jack or the length of his song,—it contained ninety stanzas, and was continued with conscientious deliberation to the bitter end,— the lullaby generally had the desired effect. At such times the men would lie at full length under the trees in the soft summer twilight, smoking their pipes and drinking in the melodious utterances. An indistinct idea that this was pastoral happiness pervaded the camp. "This 'ere kind o' think," said the Cockney Simmons, meditatively reclining on his elbow, "is 'evingly." It reminded him of Greenwich.

On the long summer days The Luck was usually carried to the gulch from whence the golden store of Roaring Camp was taken. There, on a blanket spread over pine boughs, he would lie while the men were working in the ditches below. Latterly there was a rude attempt to decorate this bower with flowers and sweet-smelling shrubs, and generally someone would bring him a cluster of wild honeysuckles, azaleas, or the painted blossoms of Las Mariposas. The men had suddenly awakened to the fact that there were beauty and significance in these trifles, which they had so long trodden carelessly beneath their feet. A flake of glittering mica, a fragment of variegated quartz, a bright pebble from the bed of the creek, became beautiful to eyes thus cleared and strengthened, and were invariably put aside for The Luck. It was wonderful how many treasures the woods and hillsides yielded that "would do for Tommy." Surrounded by playthings such as never child out of fairyland had before, it is to be hoped that Tommy was content. He appeared to be serenely happy, albeit there was an infantine gravity about him, a contemplative light in his round gray eyes, that sometimes worried Stumpy. He was always tractable and quiet, and it is recorded that once, having crept beyond his "corral,"—a hedge of tessellated pine boughs, which surrounded his bed,—he dropped over the bank on his head in the soft earth, and remained with his mottled legs in the air in that position for at least five minutes with unflinching gravity. He was extricated without a murmur. I hesitate to record the many other instances of his sagacity, which rest, unfortunately, upon the statements of prejudiced friends. Some of them were not without a tinge of superstition. "I crep' up the bank just now," said Kentuck one day, in a breathless state of excitement, "and dern my skin if he wasn't a-talking to a jaybird as was a-sittin' on his lap. There they was, just as free and sociable as anything you please, a-jawin' at each other just like two cherrybums." Howbeit, whether creeping over the pine boughs or lying lazily on his back blinking at the leaves above him, to him the birds sang, the squirrels chattered, and the flowers bloomed. Nature was his nurse and playfellow. For him she would let slip between the leaves golden shafts of sunlight that fell just within his grasp; she would send wandering breezes to visit him with the balm of bay and resinous gum; to him the tall redwoods nodded familiarly and sleepily, the bumblebees buzzed, and the rooks cawed a slumberous accompaniment.

Such was the golden summer of Roaring Camp. They were "flush times," and the luck was with them. The claims had yielded enormously. The camp was jealous of its privileges and looked suspiciously on strangers. No encouragement was given to immigration, and, to make their seclusion more perfect, the land on either side of the mountain wall that surrounded the camp they duly preempted. This, and a reputation for singular proficiency with the revolver, kept the reserve of Roaring Camp inviolate. The expressman—their only connecting link with the surrounding world—sometimes told wonderful stories of the camp. He would say, "They've a street up there in 'Roaring' that would lay over any street in Red Dog. They've got vines and flowers round their houses, and they wash themselves twice a day. But they're mighty rough on strangers, and they worship an Ingin baby."

With the prosperity of the camp came a desire for further improvement. It was proposed to build a hotel in the following spring, and to invite one or two decent families to reside there for the sake of The Luck, who might perhaps profit by female companionship. The sacrifice that this concession to the sex cost these men, who were fiercely skeptical in regard to its general virtue and usefulness, can only be accounted for by their affection for Tommy. A few still held out. But the resolve could not be carried into effect for three months, and the minority meekly yielded in the hope that something might turn up to prevent it. And it did.

The winter of 1851 will long be remembered in the foothills. The snow lay deep on the Sierras, and every mountain creek became a river, and every river a lake. Each gorge and gulch was transformed into a tumultuous watercourse that descended the hillsides, tearing down giant trees and scattering its drift and debris along the plain. Red Dog had been twice under water, and Roaring Camp had been forewarned. "Water put the gold into them gulches," said Stumpy. "It's been here once and will be here again!" And that night the North Fork suddenly leaped over its banks and swept up the triangular valley of Roaring Camp.

In the confusion of rushing water, crashing trees, and crackling timber, and the darkness which seemed to flow with the water and blot out the fair valley, but little could be done to collect the scattered camp. When the morning broke, the cabin of Stumpy, nearest the river-bank, was gone. Higher up the gulch they found the body of its unlucky owner; but the pride, the hope, the joy, The Luck, of Roaring Camp had disappeared. They were returning with sad hearts when a shout from the bank recalled them.

It was a relief-boat from down the river. They had picked up, they said, a man and an infant, nearly exhausted, about two miles below. Did anybody know them, and did they belong here?

It needed but a glance to show them Kentuck lying there, cruelly crushed and bruised, but still holding The Luck of Roaring Camp in his arms. As they bent over the strangely assorted pair, they saw that the child was cold and pulseless. "He is dead," said one. Kentuck opened his eyes. "Dead?" he repeated feebly. "Yes, my man, and you are dying too." A smile lit the eyes of the expiring Kentuck. "Dying!" he repeated; "he's a-taking me with him. Tell the boys I've got The Luck with me now;" and the strong man, clinging to the frail babe as a drowning man is said to cling to a straw, drifted away into the shadowy river that flows forever to the unknown sea.

Golden Trail
J. Allan Dunn

I

The pool in the creek was still cloudy when the ranger came to it. Someone had passed through within the last few minutes. The current was not very swift and the pool was slow in clearing. The bandit was only a little way ahead of him, if he was still on the bandit's trail.

"Bud" Jones, corporal in Company F, Texas Rangers, checked his roan, Pepper, and allowed it to drink before he started to cross the creek. He sat upright and alert in the saddle, a soldierly looking figure in his ranger equipment.

There was no attempt at regular uniform, but all the troop wore similar sombreros and high-heeled boots with Mexican spurs. All of them wore double-belts of cartridges for six-gun and rifle, and every trooper balanced his revolver at his right hip with the bowie knife on his left. Bud Jones was the youngest member of the troop and its latest recruit, although he was a corporal, promoted for valor and efficiency.

Now he was trailing a man named Morrissey— "Black" Morrissey—leader of a gang of bandits who were on the rangers' list but who had, so far, by frequent moves, dodged arrest. The ranger service was slowly but inevitably rounding up the western section of the State of Texas, ridding it of undesirables and rendering it fit for settlement by worthy citizens.

Some of the outlaws had been shot, others strung up and left swinging to sturdy oaks in the towns where they had been tried and found guilty. Some had been driven beyond the Rio Grande to seek refuge in Mexico.

But Morrissey and his outfit had remained at large. They were known to have a hideout somewhere, but the rangers had never been able to obtain any definite information as to its whereabouts in the mountain fastness.

Bud believed it was not far from Thunder Creek. He hoped that the man he was following— he was pretty sure that it was Morrissey himself— was heading back for this hiding place. It was very likely that there would be other members of the gang there, at any time.

But such odds stimulated Bud rather than checked him. If he had a fault it was what his captain termed his "excess of initiative." Without doubt it often led Bud into difficult situations, but so far he had always extricated himself, though not always without honorable wounds, the scars of which both he and Pepper bore.

Morrissey's last crime had been the daring holdup of a stage and the looting of the express box that held gold specie consigned to the bank at Cedarville. Besides the robbery, murder had been committed, wanton and unnecessary. The driver had held up his hands at Morrissey's command, but the express messenger had made an attempt to get his weapon, checking it when he saw that Morrissey had himself and the driver, both on the front seat, covered.

From then on he had made no resistance but had obeyed the bandit's orders to haul out the box. He had attempted no more than his duty, but his first action seemed to have enraged the outlaw. After taking from the two passengers all that they had in jewelry and money, he put the gold coin in a gunny sack which, after tying it at the mouth with a leather string, he tied again so as to divide it into two compartments. He flung the heavy, jingling burden across his saddle bow, resting in front of him as he mounted, all the time covering the defenseless occupants of the stage, whom he had lined up on one side of the vehicle, hands above their heads, their weapons thrown into the heavy brush. At the last moment he had cursed the messenger for trying to protect the treasure and deliberately shot him between the eyes.

By the time word got to the rangers' camp, Morrissey had a good start. Bud was detailed for the job by Captain Halstead. Pepper, like the horses of all the troop, superior to any other mounts in the vicinity, began to cut down that lead as soon as Bud had reached the scene of the crime and picked up the sign.

It was as clear to him as the printed words in a book. Morrissey had made no attempt to hide his trail in the beginning, but had evidently urged his horse to top speed. Long before the tracks brought Bud to the mountain road he knew that the outlaw's horse was tiring rapidly.

Not only had it been pushed to its utmost effort through a rough country, but it was carrying extra weight, dead weight in the sack of looted gold. The messenger had not known the exact amount in the locked box. That could not be ascertained until the banking concerns were reached, and Bud had wasted no time in starting the pursuit. Judging from previous shipments there might be anywhere between twenty and fifty thousand dollars in gold coin. The probability was that the bandit was carrying at least fifty pounds of the precious metal, a serious handicap.

There had been a good deal of travel on the mountain road, and much of it was recent. One set of tracks turned off to follow a trail down to where Bud now sat in his saddle while Pepper wisely slaked his thirst, drinking with caution, hot and blown from the fast and toilsome pursuit.

There had been nothing particularly distinguishing about the tracks. They were those of a shod horse, of a tired horse going with a shortened stride, but that was all. Other tracks on the mountain road looked much the same. The road led to a ford. The creek could also be crossed at this pool. Bud was acting on a hunch that was not without logical basis.

Morrissey would have seen, or known beforehand, that the mountain road was well traveled. In one way, through confusion of tracks, this would aid him; in another, through the possibility of his being met or otherwise recognized, it imperiled him. He had undoubtedly deliberately meant to mix up his sign, but Bud believed that he would take the first opportunity of a side trail.

His hunch told him that Morrissey had crossed the creek, warned him that even now the bandit murderer might be watching him from the thick cover of the woods, waiting to put a bullet into him from ambush.

Bud had imagination enough, but it did not handicap him. He figured out the moves the men he was after were likely to make, and the conclusion that they were likely to bushwhack him was usually inevitable.

Morrissey's horse was nearly played out. Pepper was still fresh. If the hideout was close at hand the bandit might decide to make for it, where he could join or be joined by his companion outlaws and either put up a stubborn defense or trust to not being discovered.

Or he might elect first to get rid of his pursuer. There was no doubt but that he knew by now that justice was on his trail. If he had not glimpsed Bud before from the advantage of higher ground he had ample opportunity now to confirm the suspicion that the rangers were after him. It was the first time they had ever been directly in pursuit.

Morrissey would know well enough that one ranger meant the ultimate action of the entire troop if it became necessary. If he killed Bud others would take up the chase. He knew that his cause was desperate. But, all in all considered, Bud felt that he was safe at present from a bullet, and that Morrissey was hurrying on as best he could to his hideout.

One of the passengers had stated that the outlaw had a rifle in his saddle sheath. The other had contradicted this, and the driver had frankly acknowledged that he had been too occupied with the muzzle of the bandit's six-gun to notice anything else.

In any event Bud could not change matters. He had his duty to perform, and that to him was paramount. He knew that he was targeted in the open, but every second that Pepper drank peacefully gave credence to his theory that Morrissey was still on the run. If it *was* Morrissey who had crossed the creek. That had to be determined promptly. If Bud's hunch was wrong and the outlaw had continued along the road he would have regained much of his start, might even now be in his sanctuary. And that was not going to be an easy spot to find.

Bud crossed the creek. The trail on the other side was shelving as it led upward from the stream. Then it became rocky. It looked as if it had been deliberately chosen because of its inability to hold sign. It was wide enough so that a horseman would not disturb the brush on either side. The shale ground showed nothing that could be determined, unless Bud dismounted and made a minute search.

He was loath to use the time for this. Someone had gone ahead, and he hoped that it was Morrissey, pushing on. Pepper was a long way from being played out, and made the steep trail nimbly. Bud desired above all things to make sure that he was not after the wrong man. To make certain of this he must catch a glimpse of him or overtake him.

The doubt that began to assail him, to offset his hunch, was persistently unpleasant. He could not afford to make a mistake, and yet, if he *was* on the wrong track he must turn back almost immediately or lose his man. He slid out of the saddle, not to look for sign so much as to listen. He was certain by now that the rider, be he Morrissey or not, had not turned off the trail into the woods.

The click of his roan's hoofs on the rock interfered with hearing. Now he fancied that he caught, far up the trail, the click of steel shoes. That gave him no clue, and it was a long way ahead. The man, whoever he was, was pushing his horse to the limit. It suggested that the animal was not as tired as Bud had imagined Morrissey's mount to be.

It increased the doubt in Bud's mind, and he knew that he had to make a decision. It was in moments like this that Bud invariably fell back on his hunch. He resolved to go on, and, as he swung into the saddle he suddenly saw an object in the trail that arrested his attention.

II.

The sun, shining dappled through the woods, flung bright markings on the path, like little pools of light. In the center of one of these was an object of dazzling brilliance, refracting the sunbeams with such fire as to render its outline vague, though Bud guessed at its character and how it happened to be there in his path. Here was his hunch justified, a break of luck with him at the very moment of his indecision. He had determined to go on, but now that plaguing doubt was dispelled.

Black Morrissey was ahead. There was no doubt as to that. The shining object was a double eagle, a twenty-dollar piece, new-minted gold coin.

Morrissey's fast getaway, the urging of his horse up and down the steep mountain trails with the dead weight of gold in his money bags ever chafing against the saddle above his mount's vigorously moving withers, had frayed the coarse sacking and one of the coins had worked out. The leak was evidently at the top of one of the divided piles, otherwise there would have been a steady shower of gold. The outlaw, fast though he was going, intent upon escape, would have noticed it. Before very long, as the weight of the metal widened the leak, he was bound to do so.

Bud picked up the evidence and pouched it, setting Pepper again to the steep grade, urging him with his voice. It was more effective than spurs, and the roan went up in strenuous cat leaps.

They reached the bench. Now the woods began to thin. What trees there were of larger growth, growing in pockets of soil between the rock masses that everywhere thrust themselves

19

from the side of the mountain. There was one more coin here, and Bud retrieved it by leaning from his saddle, getting it without dismounting.

His hunch had again assumed dominance. Now it whispered to him emphatically that somewhere amid these rocky ramparts Morrissey had taken refuge. It was hard to tell which way the trail ran, to left or right along the stony bench flanked by irregular walls of granite.

"Coin brought us luck once, hawss," said Bud. "Let's try again."

He flipped the second coin into the air, where it spun flittering before it descended into his palm.

"Heads we go right, tails left," he said. It came heads and he swung to the right. A hundred yards and he came across a badly blown horse, practically foundered, evidently abandoned.

Its trembling body, was covered with sweat. The saddle mark was dark upon it. Its flanks were cruelly raked with spurs, red from long, deep cuts. Foam, produced by a heavy bit, was on its sides. It had been stripped of blanket, bridle, and saddle.

Morrissey's horse, beyond a doubt. He had ridden it to its destruction and left it to its fate. Bud's expert glance told him that the horse was ruined. Its knees were badly cut and it would never breathe properly again. If it had not been for the alarm he would have put it out of its misery with a bullet. But Morrissey could not be far off. He was on foot and he was carrying the gold with him. He might have discovered the leak in the sack or he might not.

Bud, casting about for sign, hoped the latter. The way led over solid rock. The brush was scant enough to be easily avoided. There were no grass stems, bruised and bent, to indicate that anyone had gone that way. Here and there were fissures and crevices in the rocky walls, any one of which might lead to the hideout, and in none of them, in the swift but keen inspection that he gave them, did Bud see as much as a scrape or scratch. He could not spare the time for an extended search and he hurried on, hoping to find a better clew.

At last he discovered it. Morrissey was plainly unaware that fate was working against him, that the gold he had stolen and for which he had murdered was fate's instrument. The jolting of his shoulders under his heavy but precious burden had worked out a third coin and it had fallen in the one place where no ring might betray it to the bandit. Some movement of his had caused it to be flung fairly into a patch of lichens that had deadened its fall.

The lichens, really a species of moss, carpeted the surface of an almost flat rock which had been detached by frost and gravitation from the top of the wall and lay, half blocking a narrow passage. A little farther in another fallen mass completely closed the way. A man might climb it, but his horse would have to be left behind.

Bud looked over every foot of the trail. There were signs where men had surmounted the obstacle. It was a cleverly chosen retreat. Back of that rock, one man might keep many at bay. But Morrissey, eager to cache his gold, had gone on, confident that he would not be run to earth.

If this corridor led to the hideout, it was plain to Bud that the horses of the gang were either left in some place outside and close to the entrance, or led up the rocks to the top. He could not risk having followers belonging to Morrissey's outfit discover Pepper. He did not want to take the time to try to discover any trail. He wanted to follow Morrissey directly, to follow the Golden Trail.

But he had to dispose of the roan. At last he found a satisfactory place—a niche in the wall where he could be secreted. It was plainly not in use, and he left Pepper there, knowing that he would find him when he returned and that the well-trained roan would not disclose its whereabouts by any whicker. Then he went back to the entrance, surmounted the telltale rock and kept on up the narrow corridor.

Here and there he found unmistakable signs that the passage was in frequent use. Evidently the men who used it considered themselves safe from observation, from pursuit. Honest men would hardly choose such a route. There were ends of burned matches, stubs of cigarettes.

He came at length to an opening in the shape of an inverted V. It was dark, and he had to stoop to go in. It looked as if it might be the entrance to the den of a wild beast, and it rapidly opened out. He could tell that as he stood inside and slowly straightened up, able to feel nothing on either side of him. He was confident that he was standing in the lair of a brute, of many brutes. But these walked on two legs, though they were fiercer and more dangerous than any bear or puma.

Evidently the entrance angled. Little light came through it to the interior. All about him was pitchy darkness and utter silence. He stood there tense, listening, his six-gun in his hand. He did not breathe and he could hear no sound coming from the cavern.

At last he ventured to light a match, and set the flaring stick of it in a crevice, stepping instantly to one side, expectant of a shot. None came. In the brief flare he saw that he was in a cavern, roughly circular, approximately twenty feet in diameter. He made out a litter of what looked like bedding, evidently unoccupied.

The walls stretched up to a great height, and they showed no exit. But as the light went out he caught the glint of yet another coin. This had fallen upon the dirt floor of the cave, and by the light of a second match he found footprints, plainly recent, that led to the coin and there ended at a blank face of rock.

He was positive that Morrissey had come in here, equally positive that he had not gone out again. There were no returning footprints, save marks that had been scuffed and were old. He picked up the fourth gold piece.

He made a little torch from some paper he had in his pocket and examined the bedding, concluding that it was used by someone who played outer sentinel. There must be *some* exit to the hideout other than by the way he had entered. The paper charred down to his fingers and he had seen nothing but the rough walls, mounting upward into blackness, his light unable to reach the top.

Close to the bedding lay some rough sticks. He picked one of them up. It was a resinous pine knot. These were torches, and he used one of them more boldly, still on his guard, but convinced that the man he was hunting had somehow, somewhere, gone on to an inner chamber.

He burned two of the torches and remained baffled. Of necessity they flung shadows that might conceal some shelf. But if there was one, he could not determine it, though he held the torches high above his head. Nor could he find any means of ascent.

He had just dropped the end of the second torch when he caught the sound of voices. They were hardly to be heard, evidently outside the cave. Undoubtedly their owners were coming in. More of Morrissey's men.

Bud, tense in the darkness, moved to action. He set his foot on the remnant of the torch and extinguished it. His sense of direction was accurate, and the next moment he had hidden himself under the pile of none-too-clean bedding. He was watchful, his gun ready.

He did not worry about his ability to take care of the newcomers. But he hoped that they would not examine the bedding, notice the burned ends of the torches, or otherwise discover him. It made no difference to him that their number increased the odds against him. He did not consider that. Only the fact that he was going to be able to take more of the outfit was in his mind, trusting that they would show him the secret of the cave.

They came in, two of them, bearded men of mountain type, but rascally of features, elated, evidently aware, as their conversation showed, of Morrissey's escapade. One of them bore aloft a blazing pine bough. They were evidently in jovial mood, totally unsuspicious of the presence of the ranger or of any one unconnected with them.

"Blacky sure come kicking back," said one of them. "Ruined a good hawss, but I'll bet he's got enough with him to pay for a thousand hawsses. He's a mighty slick one."

"If he pulled it off," said the other, "we'll be lighting' out. Give him the signal, Bill." Bill set his dirty fingers to his lips and whistled shrilly, two long notes and then a short one. There was no immediate response. It was dark where Bud crouched, and he slightly shifted his coverings to get a better view of the two ruffians.

"Don't see why he don't answer," grumbled Bill. "He must be here. I'll tell you one thing, Jim—I ain't lighting' out until the split's made. I don't trust Blacky none too much. He'd made off with all of it if he thought he could. He's got his saddle with him an' the gray is up there. I believe he's beaten it."

"Try him again," said Jim.

The whistle sounded again, echoing in the vaulted chamber. They waited, and then a faint light began to glow some fifteen feet up, gradually increasing until a figure emerged on a shelf that, cast in dense shadow, was not to be otherwise discerned. The man held his torch so that it lighted up his villainous face, a hook nose projecting like a beak, fiercely glittering eyes, all framed in a tangle of black hair and whiskers.

"Put down the ladder, Morrissey," said Jim.

III.

Morrissey appeared to hesitate, and Bill, with an oath, whipped out a pistol.

"I've got you covered," he said. "Don't try and double-cross us. Shove down that ladder an' do it in a hurry, or you'll be coming' down yourself." It was evident that there was not much trust in the Morrissey gang.

"I'll put it down," said Morrissey in a deep voice. "You want to cut out that sort of talk, Bill Slade. An' you both want to get a move on you. Did you bring up the hawsses? You should have come in that way."

"I'm no kangaroo," said Bill. "You know well the takeoff is bad from the fur side. I ain't risking' no jump across a crack like that when I have to land higher than where I started from. What are you worrying' about? You got the money, didn't you?"

"I got it," said Morrissey sullenly.

Bud came to the conclusion that he was none too pleased to see these two members of his gang, but that he had some use for them. His conclusion was proved in the next sentence.

"They've got the rangers out after us," said Morrissey. "One of 'em trailed me plumb to Thunder Crick, though I reckon I fooled him after that, on the rock. My hawss near went down under me, but I made it. But we may have to shoot our way out yet if we don't hurry."

"It's *you* that's keeping' us," said Jim. "Put down that ladder."

Morrissey laid his flaring torch on the shelf and disappeared, going back into some recess that was not to be seen from the floor of the cave. Then the ends of the ladder projected and it was let down to the ground. The two men climbed it swiftly and it was at once drawn up after them.

23

Bud made no attempt to check them. He knew that he could follow them. He had seen outside, before he entered, a dead tree, evidently swept into the ravine by some storm of several seasons past. Its remaining boughs, most of them broken, would furnish him with scaling equipment.

He waited until the glow died away, then darted to where faint gray light proclaimed the entrance, and went out.

It seemed clear to him that there was some sort of tunnel leading from the shelf to the top of the cliff. Also that, barring the way to the horses, there was a crevice that could be jumped from the left side, but not so easily negotiated from the opposite. He hoped to catch up with them before they reached this place—at least, to get within shooting range.

He wanted to bring in his men alive if possible. It was the rule of the rangers, wherever possible, to secure prisoners who might serve as public examples. A bandit swinging from the bough of the trees generally used as gallows did more to discourage outlaws and weaken their prestige than the mere fact that one of them had been killed in a fight. Such procedure heartened citizens and settlers, and increased the sterling reputation of the rangers.

He got his tree, in which the sap had long since dried, and half hauled, half carried it to the mouth of the cave, thrusting it ahead of him. By the light of another pine knot he reared it against the shelf and rapidly clambered up, bearing the light, discovering what he had expected to see— a gap in the wall.

This he promptly entered. It twisted and turned considerably, for which he was thankful, as the winding served to screen his light from heralding his advance.

There were several things to his advantage. Morrissey believed that the hideout had not been discovered. Though he was anxious to get away, his two partners would insist on dividing the gold, and it was clear enough that Morrissey had not taken it across to where the horses were stationed or he would have known of their arrival. But it was risky work just the same.

From what he had heard, Bud decided that this robbery was to be the final coup of Morrissey's outfit before they left the territory, rapidly getting too dangerous for men of their calling. They knew that the rangers would sooner or later round them up. They were desperate, and Bud knew that he would, in all likelihood, have to shoot it out with the three of them, unless he could succeed in creeping up on them unseen and covering them.

He saw daylight ahead of him, the outline of the side wall revealed at the end of the rift. He flung his torch away and went rapidly but cautiously on to where the end of the tunnel overlooked a tiny glen.

Grass and bushes grew here, with a few stunted trees. Water fell from the cliff into a little pool. It was about ten feet to the floor of the glen, but clefts and ridges made the descent simple enough if he could tackle it without being seen and shot at.

If he was discovered he would undoubtedly be riddled by the three men who were now squatting on the ground with their backs toward him. They were on the near side of a split that extended clear across the glen. It did not look like a particularly lengthy or impossible jump for active men, though Bud surmised, from Bill's remark, that the chasm was deep enough for a slip to kill any man falling into it.

He could see no horses on the far side, but he made out a notch in the cliff which he imagined was a pass to some other basin where the horses would be grazing. He made a careful study of what might turn out to be a battle ground, squatting down in the mouth of the tunnel.

There was a cloth in front of the trio—the blanket from Morrissey's foundered mount. His saddle and bridle lay to one side. He must have made two trips, Bud fancied, to have packed them in as well as the gold.

The latter was in shining evidence on the blanket, glittering heaps of valuable metal. It was impossible to guess at the amount, save that there were many hundreds of the coins, which were divided roughly into three piles, one of which was much larger than the others.

This division was evidently the cause of a discussion that bade fair to terminate in a violent quarrel.

Black Morrissey was claiming the lion's share of the spoils he had collected. And the two others did not fancy their roles of jackals. Their voices came plainly to Bud. First the deep notes from Morrissey, mounting to a bellow.

"We'll share as we always have," he declared. "Them that takes part in the job gets more than the rest. Those skunks that got cold feet an' cleared but last week when we got the tip the rangers had us next on their list leaves all the more to you boys. You're getting' twice as much now as you would ordinary. Close to five thousand apiece. An' that's plenty, seeing' I turned the trick alone, took all the risk. I had to shoot one man as it was, an' that might put my neck in a noose if they ketch me—which they won't."

"I'm not so sure of that," muttered Bud to himself beneath his breath, as he slipped off his boots and prepared to make a silent descent in his socks.

It had to be done swiftly and surely, and he calculated every step so that his six-gun would be clear for action. He knew that they would not be able to hear him unless they turned accidentally, which was not likely, intent as they were upon the loot. But if he was to be a target, he meant to be a moving one.

He was out of pistol range and he wanted to get in closer to them before he announced his presence or started any attack that might be necessary.

Jim's voice sounded in a snarl.

"Aw, to blazes with yore risks! This is the last job, an' we'll share even. We're goin' to separate after we get goin', an' we'll split alike."

"That's right," said Bill, starting to rise to his feet, his hand on the butt of his gun. "I'm either goin' to get a third out of this or I'll get *half*, Morrissey. Understand that."

Morrissey did not move from his position, squatting on his haunches, his big hands on his knees. Bud caught the gleam of his teeth in something that Morrissey may have meant for a smile, for an attempt to suggest a willingness to concede to their demands—anything to blind them to his real purpose. He alone of the three wore two guns. Bud saw that the holsters were open, and his hunch prophesied to him with startling rapidity what was about, to happen.

Even as Bud descended, leaping lightly from a projection to the top of a boulder and then to the ground, the tragedy occurred—if the riddance of such rascals from the world could be so termed.

As he squatted, the open ends of Morrissey's holsters touched the top of the grass stems. Bud himself, by dint of long practice and natural coordination, could draw and fire with such rapidity as to make it impossible for the eye to follow his movement.

But he had never seen such a lightning draw as that made by Morrissey. He did not shift from his crouch, save to turn slightly at the waist, as his two guns streaked out flame and smoke.

They were not the only ones that roared in that little glen. Bill had seen, or guessed, what his defiant statement would bring about. He had practically challenged Morrissey, hinted that he meant to kill him and share the loot with Jim.

Jim was evidently of the same mind, but slower of movement. His gun never got more than halfway from leather.

Bill was the first to fall, shot through the body from hip to hip, knocked down by the blow of the heavy slug. He sprawled backward on the grass, tearing up tufts of it in his death agony.

Bud saw Jim slowly turning, the action ending in his knees crumpling as he pitched forward. Black Morrissey had shot him through the heart.

Now Morrissey rose, his masking smile a grin of savage exultation. He caught sight of the ranger running toward him, and he fired one shot, even as Bud pulled the trigger.

IV.

The ranger saw Morrissey stagger and knew that he had hit the bandit, long though the range was for accuracy. At the same second he was spun about by the impact of a bullet that caught

26

him high up in the left shoulder, breaking or splintering bone with a nerve shock that, despite all his will and courage, temporarily halted him, while his vision blurred.

He caught instinctively at the trunk of a stunted piñon to steady himself, still holding his gun. Through a haze, while he summoned all his powers of recovery, the blood coming fast from his wounded arm, he saw Morrissey stoop and swiftly gather together the corners of the blanket that held the gold.

With an effort the outlaw heaved the heavy bundle over his right shoulder and started for the crevice.

Now Bud saw that his shot had struck the bandit in his right thigh. He ran lamely but made good progress, though once his leg seemed to buckle under him and a dark stain was spreading on his clothing.

Bud got himself together and ran after him, firing a shot that he felt sure would be futile. For the outlaw was once more out of range. But Bud hoped it might halt the man in a surrender. Bud was playing that chance.

It did not, however. The shot and perhaps the whine of the bullet only spurred the bandit on. Bud was conscious of growing weakness from his wound. His knees were none too steady, threatening to give way as he ran, stumbling a little over rough spots hidden by the grass. He was unable to gain.

The outlaw paused on the brink of the crevice, the bag of gold still on his shoulder. He stooped a little as if to gauge a leap.

Then he sprang, with Bud closing in on him, holding his fire. Morrissey had killed three men now, though two of them deserved it, and Bud wanted more than ever to take him in alive, to get him before he reached the horses. Two of these might still be saddled, but mounting would take time, encumbered as the bandit was with the gold he evidently meant to risk everything to keep.

He risked too much. A slope led down toward the brink of the cavern, and now Bud could see the farther side of it, lower. He imagined the space to be some twelve feet. It was a long jump, but not impossible for athletic men. Bud did not mean to stop but to make the most of a running start.

He checked himself after all, digging his heels into the turf when he saw what was happening.

Morrissey's greed was literally his downfall. The weight of the gold, plus the wound in his leg, which must have weakened the driving power of his muscles, was too much for him. Bud saw that he could never make it, that his feet would strike below the edge on the far side. He had overestimated his powers.

Morrissey saw it, too. He let go of the blanket, which fell like a plummet to the bottom of the chasm, the glittering coins showering down. Morrissey let out a roar as he saw that he was doomed. With one last, despairing, prodigious effort, he tried to hunch himself as he struck the rim too low. He strove to clutch at a bush and actually ruffled it with his fingers before he went hurtling down. With a sickening thud he landed, his back broken, his skull smashed on the rocks amid the double eagles.

For a moment Bud gazed down. Then he started to bind up his arm and stop the crimson flow as test he could before he went back through the cavern and the ravine to where Pepper was awaiting him.

The dead men and the gold could wait until he had reported at camp. The buzzards might arrive before the detail reached them, but such matters were a part and parcel of what fate preserves for men like Morrissey and his comrades.

Fool's Peak
Wilson Campbell

Wiggling a bit for more comfortable adjustment in the sand hollow which was to be his bed for the night, Alf Chase drew his blanket closer, about his shoulders, and closed his eyes to the keen, low-hanging stars.

"'Night, Vincente," he said sleepily.

The Yaqui merely grunted.

A lonesome breeze rattled dry pods in the mesquite on the hillside; embers of the supper fire flared in a failing struggle to hold darkness away from the sleepers. An owl hooted sadly. All things seemed well in the quiet of the night.

A rock clattered down a steep slope, and on the heels of the scattered echoes a low moan, weary and hopeless, brought the two from the Z B Ranch to wakefulness.

"Trouble," whispered Alf. "Trouble for someone. We're miles from the nearest ranch."

Guided by the moans which now came regularly, the young rancher and the tall Yaqui hurried down the coulee in which they had made camp. After crossing several small ridges, they came finally to an inert body sprawled on the gravel at the bottom of a steep slope.

Striking a match, Vincente leaned over the figure.

"An Indian boy," he said. "Papago, I think. He is exhausted from long exertion."

The Yaqui swung the lad across his broad shoulders, and with Alf guiding the way, they returned to their camp. Vincente gave the Papago sparing sips of water while the Arizonan replenished and fanned the fire. Fear was in the young Indian's eyes when he opened them, but it quickly faded at sight of his rescuers.

"*Gracias, señores,*" he said. "Like a flame of hope in the dark night I saw your fire. Señores, I beg your help! For the life of my father there is no hope, unless by dawn you have saved him!"

The boy—Alf judged that he was a lad of about seventeen—shuddered, and his face darkened in a spasm of hatred. "There are two men who would kill him!"

The boy told his story quickly. When he had finished, the two from the Z B Ranch looked at each other. There was no doubt in the minds of either of what they would do.

"We will go with you," Alf told the Papago. "Eat and rest in these few minutes while we get ready."

A short time later the three of them were riding due west toward the Sunset Mountains, in the foothills of which they had been camping. The Papago, who said his name was Joe, was mounted on the extra horse Alf had brought as a pack animal. Though they made as good time as possible, the lad was impatient for more speed. "I fear they will kill my father before we get there," he said time and again. "Fools! They think he knows of gold in those mountains. There is no gold in those mountains! Is not the highest of them all called Fool's Peak?"

"That is right," the Yaqui agreed, for his knowledge of that whole country was unsurpassed, "but surely there is some reason for their attack."

For a moment the boy was silent. "Yes," he admitted at length, "something else is there, but the men think it is gold. I cannot tell you now what it is, but if my father—"

He broke off, and they rode in silence for a time, each one busy with his thoughts. Alf was recalling the many adventures he and Vincente had had together, ever since the time—months ago, now—he had saved the Yaqui from misplaced and violent revenge that the cowpunchers of the Z B were about to wreak on him. The Indian's declaration of gratitude had not been empty. Taking a job on the Z B Ranch, which belonged to Alf's father, Vincente had made himself invaluable, for through his knowledge of the country he had saved the ranch countless cattle, to say nothing of the life of young Alf Chase himself, and on more than one occasion.

Alf recalled particularly the time Vincente had dragged him out of Galleon Sink while a desert-maddened prospector raced after him over treacherous, death-hiding sands.

On that occasion Alf had gone with an old desert rat to take minted gold from an ancient Spanish galleon which had lain for countless years not far from the Gulf of Lower California. They found the galleon and the gold, but the expedition came near to tragedy when their horses ran off in a severe sandstorm, and the desert rat went crazy.

Vincente, knowing the dangers of Galleon Sink, had followed; and Alf smiled as he thought of how fine the Yaqui had looked with his great, muscle-corded torso bare to the hot sun, and his blue dungarees flapping about his legs when he came to the rescue. Now, with colder weather, Vincente had put on a shirt, but his black hair still blew free in the winds, and his tough feet knew not the feel of shoe leather.

They had ridden for several hours when Joe stopped them. "We are near the place now," he said. "We go slow and careful."

When the three of them rode over the next divide, they could see the glow of a fire reflected on a rocky hillside a little ahead. The Papago lad was hopeful at seeing the fire, for it gave him reason to believe that his father still lived.

At the bottom of the divide they dismounted, leaving the reins over their horses' heads so the animals would not wander away. Then they crept slowly forward, careful not to rattle even the smallest pebble. It seemed an age before they attained the top of the next hill, but finally they were able to peer cautiously into the next draw.

II.

They were hardly prepared for the sight that met their eyes. Stretched out on the dry gravel, stream bottom, his arms and legs tied cruelly tight to heavy stakes, his clothes ripped off his body, was an Indian who was obviously Joe's father. Near him a fire was burning brightly, flickering luridly on the prone man, making him grotesque in its wavering light. Standing over him were two men—burly, unkempt, brutal-looking fellows—who were preoccupied with their task of extracting the leads from rifle bullets with their teeth. The powder they carefully collected in a tobacco can.

"Guess we got enough tuh make the buzzard squawk a while, Ed," one of them said. "Should I pour it out on 'im?"

"Yeah. Make somethin' fancy—you're purty good at drawin'!"

The first speaker stooped over the inert captive and carefully sprinkled the powder on his bare flesh, talking to him the while.

"Yuh better come across wit' the dope on that gold, Injun," he muttered. "If yuh don't you're goin' tuh be a purty dead redskin!"

The old Papago tensed his muscles and opened his eyes to glare malignantly at his tormentor. "I never tell you," he said in a low, pain-wracked voice. "You kill me, and you find out never, also."

The black-bearded white man swore. "We'll get that kid of yourn," he said. "He slipped away from us once, but he won't be able to, the second time—not if he gets hamstrung!" He snapped out the last word viciously.

Up on the hilltop, Joe clutched the arm of each of his companions, but Vincente warned him to keep quiet.

The other man took a hand in the miserable affair. "One chance more, Injun. We're smart hombres. We'll give yuh a sample of how awful burnin' powder hurts when it burns *on* a guy—an' then yuh can figger out fer yourself what'll happen when we puts it on yore eyeballs!"

He waited a moment, but the Papago Indian shook his head. Then, anger flaming in his cruel face, the black-bearded man suddenly stooped; and before the watchers on the hill realized what he was up to, he touched the coal of his cigarette to the train of powder that wound around the Indian's chest and stomach.

The powder flared into sputtering brilliance, making the firelight seem pale. It sped on its horrible course, burning deep. The Papago, after a moment of silent agony, screamed. The two men grinned. And then, suddenly as it had flared, the powder burned itself out.

"One more time'll fetch him, Scruggs," Ed chuckled. "Where's them extra bullets?"

Alf Chase jumped to his feet. "I've got enough bullets for you fellows," he shouted angrily. "Put up your hands!"

The two men wheeled and faced the young rancher, their arms lifted high above their heads. The six-shooter that pointed straight at them was strong enough argument that the intruder meant business.

"Where the blazes did you come from?" Scruggs wanted to know; and then his eyes widened as the Indian lad and Vincente stood up, one on either side of the Arizonan. He spat disgustedly. "Thar's what yuh get, Ed, fur lettin' that little hellion break loose!"

Ed snarled at his companion out of the corner of his wide, ugly mouth which was too red and too moist; and they might have fought right there had Alf not warned them to keep still.

Vincente hurried down the hill and disarmed them, running his hands expertly over their clothes to make sure that they carried no concealed weapons. At the same time, barely able to hold back his tears, the Papago lad was cutting the thongs which bound his father's arms and legs with Vincente's long dagger. The Indian was gritting his teeth in his determination not to moan.

Alf, looking down on the scene, blamed their folly for not having stopped the two men before the old Papago had been made to suffer so greatly; but he was later to learn that the Indian had already gone through untold agonies. And now, even as Joe severed his father's bonds, and the tortured man tried to lift himself, he fell back with a moan and slipped into unconsciousness.

Vincente found the horses belonging to the men farther up the draw; and making them mount with their hands tied in back of them, the Yaqui whipped the animals into a gallop. They clattered away into the darkness with their helpless riders cursing and shouting back sincerely meant threats.

III.

Toward noon of the next day Alf and Vincente jumped off their horses at the foot of Fool's Peak—a towering, conical mountain that piled up into the sky, a mangled, twisted mass of stone.

32

They stared up the jagged slope, and wondered how it would be possible to climb that cruel surface without being scratched and torn to shreds.

Alf pulled a big nickel watch out of his pocket. "Just in time, Vincente," he said. "We got twenty minutes to get to the end of the shadow of the peak!"

They left their horses where grass grew along the short-lived course of a warm spring, and lost no time in making their way up the steep, hazardous mountainside. There was no lack of footholds on the hard, harsh lava; but they had to be careful lest the sharp stone tear their flesh.

Fortunately, however, the winter sun cast a long shadow from the southern sky, and the shade from the peak reached almost to the foot of the great mountain. By dint of breathless effort they got to the apex of the shadow just two minutes before twelve.

"Where the shadow of Fool's Peak falls at high noon," Alf said thoughtfully, looking about curiously. "See anything, Vincente?"

The Yaqui was staring intently at the point of the long shadow from the mountain above. After a moment he grunted with satisfaction. "Joe and his father spoke the truth," he said. "Here we can enter the mountain!"

As he spoke Vincente reached out an experimental foot and threw his weight on it. A huge block of lava teetered with the pressure; and a moment later the two of them were tugging at it vigorously. With very little difficulty they slid it aside and stared into a hole about four feet in diameter that went straight down for a distance of perhaps seven feet. Its black sides were astonishingly slick and shiny, and at the bottom they could see a passage leading into the mountain.

"A quarter of an hour late, and we wouldn't ever have found the darned place," Alf said. "Well, are we going in, Vincente?"

For answer the tall Yaqui put his feet over the edge and slid into the hole. "Drop the torches to me," he directed. "Then, while I hold you on my shoulders, you shall pull the cover block back in place."

Alf dropped the bundle of torches Joe had given them that morning and grinned down at his friend. "Hot down there, Vincente?" he asked. "That's a fumarole you're in—sort of a safety valve that lava and gas used to come flowing out of. If it isn't hot now, it was once. We can be glad that Fool's Peak has only been playing scenery for the last couple of hundred years."

"You talk much," Vincente said dryly. "When you are inside, this volcano will be active once more."

Astraddle Vincente's shoulders a few seconds later, Alf tugged at the big block of lava which had concealed the fumarole. It was harder to move from this strained position, but after a few moments it settled back into place with a thud.

"I wish," Alf said as they lighted their torches, "Joe had told us what to look for. I'm kind of thinking it would help considerably."

"No," the Yaqui said, "for now we will look at all things and see a great deal more."

The turn at the bottom of the fumarole took them down a gentle slope, and as they traveled along the passage the top got higher, and presently they were able to stand upright. They went forward cautiously, however, for they knew that volcanic formations are often treacherous, and the Papagoes had warned them to be sure of every step they took.

After they had traveled about a hundred yards they came to a large cavern which dropped suddenly to a depth beyond the light glow of their torches. Picking their way carefully, they descended more than a hundred feet. It was a vast place, and the darkness of it pressed close upon their flickering lights. Save for the slow, unvarying drip, drip, drip of water, there was no sound.

They felt their way about cautiously, and came to a growth of stalagmites, black as ebony, and gleaming with the moisture of the unceasing drops of water that spattered on their pointed tops. Most of them were taller than Vincente, and the largest Alf judged to be over fifteen feet high. The young rancher gazed upward, but the companion stalactites were lost in the gloomy darkness of the cavern.

"Golly," Alf said, "this place is big enough to put a city in! Wish we had it on the Z B Ranch."

Exploring thoroughly, they came upon all manner of twisted shapes of lava, and always there were the gleaming stalagmites, pointing up eternally, like so many stony exclamation points. It was a magic, eerie place, with its echoing drops of water; its wild, insane formations, as if here Nature had at last gone mad. They spoke in whispers, and their voices sounded loud and harsh. But they found nothing that could be of any possible value.

"Whatever we have come to find," Vincente said thoughtfully, "must be farther in the mountain, or far down in the earth. There are four passages leading out of this place—and two of them go straight down. I think we better try the others first!"

They went to the largest opening their search had disclosed, and after following it for fully a hundred yards as it wandered up and down in the heart of Fool's Peak, they came to an abrupt halt against a wall of lava, just as they thought they were getting somewhere.

The next passage meandered even more, but it finally gave into a second cavern, even vaster than the first, and, as they had traveled steadily downward, many feet below it. Here again they found stalagmites, but this time they were of purest white, and their myriad crystals gleamed in the light of the torches.

Alf, looking up again, was astonished to see a patch of blue. He moved away from Vincente until he stood under it, and saw that it came through a long fumarole, or chimney, such as they had used in entering the mountain. And as he looked, a head peered down at him, black and unrecognizable against the sky.

Evidently the man above could see the young Arizonan, for the head was quickly withdrawn. Alf still stood there, staring upward, holding his blazing torch in his hand. As he looked, the head and shoulders reappeared, a spurt of flame jumped out from them, and a bullet spattered at Alf's feet. He jumped aside quickly, and heard the rolling echoes of the shot. He drew his own gun and fired into the bottom of the fumarole, but there was no evidence that the random shot was successful.

"What's the matter?" Vincente called across the cavern; and in that moment Alf knew why the head had seemed familiar.

"Scruggs!" Alf shouted back. "They've trailed us here!"

"Umph," Vincente grunted. "Well, they haven't found a way in—yet. Of course, there may be other ways of getting inside the mountain, but if it's gold they're going to all this trouble after, they're going to be two mad hombres, Don Alfredo. There is no gold in all this mountain."

"That won't keep them from making trouble, Vincente. I've got an idea that they don't like us any too well."

"Let them come," the Yaqui replied. "They cannot surprise us, for this place has too many echoes. We shall go on and look for the mysterious wealth the Papagoes told us about."

I□.

The second chamber was even more startlingly beautiful than the first, but it proved to be as bare of anything of value. They wasted little time in it, now that the presence of the men outside gave them a reason for hurry. They followed the first horizontal outlet they came to, but it soon gave into a small but amazingly lovely room. The place was dome-shaped, and wholly covered with a crust of glowing crystals, white as snow save when light fell directly on them, and then flashing fire like myriads of diamonds. The whole place blazed magnificently and dazzlingly, and Alf was reluctant to leave it.

"If we don't find a durned thing," he said in a whisper, "that was worth the trip!"

Back in the large cavern, they immediately turned into the next passage, and trailed along its winding course. They walked until Alf began to think that they had come to a tunnel without end, and still they went on. Above them they could see the smudge of smoke on the stone, and they felt at last they were on the right path. The way was mostly uphill, at times becoming so steep that they had to stop for a breath of air.

Quite suddenly, when Alf had given up hope of ever reaching to the end of the old lava vent, they came upon the most spectacular cavern of all. Its dimensions were staggering, and the place seemed comparatively bright. High above, Alf counted the bottom ends of five fumaroles, and through these the light streamed in long, clear shafts.

On the far side of the gigantic space there was a huge outlet, now blocked by fallen lava and stone. Vincente said he thought it was debris from the crater for they had traveled far enough underground to be near the center of the extinct volcano; and he knew that the crater had fallen in.

But the cavern itself was not the thing that interested the two from the Z B most. In the center of the great natural underground hall was a pile of bones—such bones as neither of them had ever seen before. They hurried over to examine them.

"Looks like a dinosaur's happy hunting ground," Alf commented as he poked with his foot at a huge curved piece of bone that obviously had once been a rib.

Vincente's face was beaming. "We have found the great wealth of which the Papagoes told us," he announced.

Alf stared at him. "Bones! How come?"

"Ivory," said Vincente. "Look at those tusks! A fortune of it is here!"

The Yaqui was right. Mingled with the bones of the scattered skeletons of the prehistoric monsters, were long, darkened tusks. In every case they had fallen out of the skulls to which they had once belonged. Alf picked one of them up. For all the world, with its covering of dust, it looked like some of the smaller stalagmites they had examined.

"A fortune," he repeated. "I'll say. There's enough ivory here to make billiard balls for—"

Vincente held up his hand for silence. "I hear a noise," he said. "Your friends, Scruggs and Ed, have found a way inside."

Alf regarded the pile of bones speculatively. "I've got an idea, Vincente," he told his friend, and his gray eyes sparkled as he outlined the scheme.

Vincente listened, and when Alf had finished, the Yaqui's dark face crinkled into a broad smile. "Then we must get to work," he said, *"muy pronto!"*

Half an hour later not one ivory tusk remained with the pile of bones. From time to time the two could hear noises from Scruggs and his companion as they wandered about in the outer caverns, but every sound was amplified so that it was difficult to follow their progress.

Alf Chase and Vincente concealed themselves behind a cluster of stalagmites and stalactites which had grown to such proportions that they had joined to become monster columns reaching from the floor of the cavern to the vaults above. They made a perfect defense, for nothing less than small artillery could have shattered them, and between the separate columns were openings through which it would be possible to fire at an enemy. They had the farther advantage of being in the darkest part of the vast sub-mountain room.

While they waited—for they had concluded that the best way of dealing with the two overambitious men was to let them do the seeking—the young rancher and the Indian advanced theories as to how the great skeletons might have gotten into the heart of the extinct volcano.

"In Africa," Alf said, "the elephants are supposed to go to a far-distant place, in the jungle when they feel that they are going to die. It is said that all elephants have died there—when death came naturally—for hundreds of years. Maybe the dinosaurs—or whatever they were—came here for the same reason."

"Maybe," Vincente said, "but I doubt it. In this country there may have been a great drought—we know that once there were tall forests here. But inside this mountain there was water, even as there is now, while it is wholly dry outside. The beasts came for water, entering through that wide passage which is now fallen in. Finding water, they drank; and perhaps it was poisoned by salts of arsenic or some such thing, dissolved out of the lava."

Alf nodded. There were any possible number of explanations, and one man's was as good as another's. "I wish those two hombres would happen along," he complained. "I'm getting hungry!"

As if willing to be obliging for once in their lives, the two men who had tortured the Papago the night before appeared on the opposite side of the cavern.

"Halt!"

Alf's voice sent the echoes flying. In that high, vaulted place it sounded like rolling thunder. The men stopped abruptly.

"Who says so?" Scruggs shouted back. His voice was big, but it had a ring of uncertainty. In that echoing place he could not tell where the Indian and the Arizonan were concealed.

"Now," Alf shouted back, "you fellows have looked around, and I guess you are convinced that there is nothing here. What you expected to find when you were torturing that poor Papago is more than I can see. Anyhow, there's no sense in fighting over nothing, is there?"

The two men whispered, and after a time Scruggs shouted back: "Guess you're right, young fella—but we wanta be sure first. Yuh come on out, an' we'll all take a look-see, an' no hard feelin'."

Alf started to show himself, but the Yaqui restrained him. "Those men are no good," he said in a low voice. "You wait."

□.

Taking a match from his shirt pocket, Vincente lighted it. Its flame seemed bright in that gloom—and to the men on the far side of the cave, it flickered behind the stalagmites, making them seem like the shadows of men. While the match still burned, Scruggs whipped out his gun and fired. The bullet pinged away from one of the limestone columns, and Vincente snuffed out the flame.

Alf, in anger at this lack of faith, drew out his own gun and fired. A cry of pain told of some success. He saw Scruggs holding his shoulder as he leaped into the protection of the passageway.

"Keep on firing," Vincente directed. "I'm going over there and get them!"

As Alf fired two more shots, the Yaqui left his hiding place and darted across the irregular floor of the subterranean vault. In that half gloom it was hard to follow his progress, but a shot from Alf's gun now and then kept the two men from seeing him at all.

Alf ceased firing when he saw that Vincente was standing at one side of the passage mouth. After a little bit, Scruggs ventured out, his gun in hand.

Like a striking snake, Vincente's arm flashed out to hit the man a painful blow on the wrist. His gun flew into the air and fell clatteringly out of sight. Ed, his companion, rushed out at the moment of attack, but the Yaqui's ready dagger discouraged him from violence, and he handed over his gun without daring to use it.

A moment later Alf had joined the Yaqui, covering the two men with his six-gun. They were sullen and silent.

"These men can help us carry out the things we gathered," Vincente said to the young rancher. Turning to the prisoners, he directed: "Take off your shirts—we need 'em."

Muttering, they obeyed. "Yuh did find somethin'," Scruggs growled. "We'll get yuh fer this!"

"Only some souvenirs," Vincente said, accepting the reluctantly proffered shirts.

While Alf held the captives, Vincente went to the spot where he had stood the ivory tusks upright, and made a show of breaking them off. One by one he piled them on the shirts, and then he used his own and Alf's. The men looked on contemptuously.

"Shucks," Ed said, "that's what yuh came in here fer, eh?" Alf nodded. "And you are going to help carry 'em out," he said. "They're pretty heavy."

At last they were ready, and each took a bundle, Scruggs getting the lightest on account of his wounded shoulder. The men groaned and complained at having to carry a load of rock like a couple of burros, but the Arizonan reminded them that they had brought all their troubles on themselves.

It was late afternoon when they were out of the volcano's many twisting passages. Scruggs, in a burst of talkativeness, explained how they had found the loose block covering the fumarole. Then he told how they had seen the Papago coming from the mountains many times, and had concluded that he had a hidden gold mine somewhere about the foot of Fool's Peak.

Now that there wasn't any gold, he said, he didn't bear the Yaqui and young Chase any malice. He felt that his wound was about what he deserved for being such a darned fool.

It was late afternoon when they slung the improvised packs which Vincente had made of the shirts over the waiting horses. Alf handed Ed a real stalagmite to examine in the daylight.

"Rock," Ed snorted. "Just plain, purty rock. But it ain't worth nothin'. I'm darned if I see what yuh want with so much of it!" He looked with puzzled eyes at the long, smooth shapes of the tusks showing through the shirts.

"Don't you worry too much about it," Alf advised. "They make fine door weights, or gateposts if they're big enough. I tell you what. We are coming back for bigger ones. I'll give you both a job helping me get them back to the ranch."

"Not on yer life," Scruggs said. "I've had enough carryin' fer a year. Ed an' me is leavin' this neck of the woods anyhow."

Vincente nodded approvingly. "Just as well," he said. "You are lucky. We do not forget things around the Palo Verde Valley. If you come back—be careful!"

The men rode away in silence. After they had disappeared, Alf and Vincente turned their own mounts, heavily laden with a treasure in ivory, southward toward the Z B Ranch.

The Gift Of The Magi
O. Henry

One dollar and eighty-seven cents. That was all. And sixty cents of it was in pennies. Pennies saved one and two at a time by bulldozing the grocer and the vegetable man and the butcher until one's cheeks burned with the silent imputation of parsimony that such close dealing implied. Three times Della counted it. One dollar and eighty-seven cents. And the next day would be Christmas.

There was clearly nothing to do but flop down on the shabby little couch and howl. So Della did it. Which instigates the moral reflection that life is made up of sobs, sniffles, and smiles, with sniffles predominating.

While the mistress of the home is gradually subsiding from the first stage to the second, take a look at the home. A furnished flat at $8 per week. It did not exactly beggar description, but it certainly had that word on the lookout for the mendicancy squad.

In the vestibule below was a letter-box into which no letter would go, and an electric button from which no mortal finger could coax a ring. Also appertaining thereunto was a card bearing the name "Mr. James Dillingham Young."

The "Dillingham" had been flung to the breeze during a former period of prosperity when its possessor was being paid $30 per week. Now, when the income was shrunk to $20, the letters of "Dillingham" looked blurred, as though they were thinking seriously of contracting to a modest and unassuming D. But whenever Mr. James Dillingham Young came home and reached his flat above he was called "Jim" and greatly hugged by Mrs. James Dillingham Young, already introduced to you as Della. Which is all very good.

Della finished her cry and attended her cheeks with the powder rag. She stood by the window and looked out dully at a gray cat walking a gray fence in a gray backyard. To-morrow would be Christmas Day, and she had only $1.87 with which to buy Jim a present. She had been saving every penny she could for months, with this result. Twenty dollars a week doesn't go far. Expenses had been greater than she had calculated. They always are. Only $1.87 to buy a present for Jim. Her Jim. Many a happy hour she had spent planning for something nice for him. Something fine and rare and sterling—something just a little bit near to being worthy of the honor of being owned by Jim.

There was a pier-glass between the windows of the room. Perhaps you have seen a pier-glass in an $8 flat. A very thin and very agile person may, by observing his reflection in a rapid sequence of longitudinal strips, obtain a fairly accurate conception of his looks. Della, being slender, had mastered the art.

Suddenly she whirled from the window and stood before the glass. Her eyes were shining brilliantly, but her face had lost its color within twenty seconds. Rapidly she pulled down her hair and let it fall to its full length.

Now, there were two possessions of the James Dillingham Youngs in which they both took a mighty pride. One was Jim's gold watch that had been his father's and his grandfather's. The other was Della's hair. Had the Queen of Sheba lived in the flat across the airshaft, Della would have let her hair hang out the window someday to dry just to depreciate Her Majesty's jewels and gifts. Had King Solomon been the janitor, with all his treasures piled up in the basement, Jim would have pulled out his watch every time he passed, just to see him pluck at his beard from envy.

So now Della's beautiful hair fell about her, rippling and shining like a cascade of brown waters. It reached below her knee and made itself almost a garment for her. And then she did it up again nervously and quickly. Once she faltered for a minute and stood still where a tear or two splashed on the worn red carpet.

On went her old brown jacket; on went her old brown hat. With a whirl of skirts and with the brilliant sparkle still in her eyes, she fluttered out the door and down the stairs to the street.

Where she stopped the sign read: "Mme. Sofronie, Hair Goods of All Kinds." One flight up Della ran, and collected herself, panting. Madame, large, too white, chilly, hardly looked the "Sofronie."

"Will you buy my hair?" asked Della.

"I buy hair," said Madame. "Take yer hat off and let's have a sight at the looks of it."

Down rippled the brown cascade.

"Twenty dollars," said Madame, lifting the mass with a practiced hand.

"Give it to me quick," said Della.

Oh, and the next two hours tripped by on rosy wings. Forget the hashed metaphor. She was ransacking the stores for Jim's present.

She found it at last. It surely had been made for Jim and no one else. There was no other like it in any of the stores, and she had turned all of them inside out. It was a platinum fob chain, simple and chaste in design, properly proclaiming its value by substance alone and not by meretricious ornamentation—as all good things should do. It was even worthy of The Watch. As soon as she saw it she knew that it must be Jim's. It was like him. Quietness and value—the description applied to both. Twenty-one dollars they took from her for it, and she hurried home with the eighty-seven cents. With that chain on his watch Jim might be properly anxious about the time in any company. Grand as the watch was, he sometimes looked at it on the sly on account of the old leather strap he used in place of a chain.

When Della reached home her intoxication gave way a little to prudence and reason. She got out her curling irons and lighted the gas and went to work repairing the ravages made by generosity added to love. Which is always a tremendous task, dear friends—a mammoth task.

Within forty minutes her head was covered with tiny close-lying curls that made her look wonderfully like a truant schoolboy. She looked at her reflection in the mirror, long, carefully, and critically.

"If Jim doesn't kill me," she said to herself, "before he takes a second look at me, he'll say I look like a Coney Island chorus girl. But what could I do—Oh! what could I do with a dollar and eighty-seven cents?"

At seven o'clock the coffee was made and the frying-pan was on the back of the stove hot and ready to cook the chops.

Jim was never late. Della doubled the fob chain in her hand and sat on the corner of the table near the door that he always entered. Then she heard his step on the stair away down on the first flight, and she turned white for just a moment. She had a habit of saying little silent prayers about the simplest everyday things, and now she whispered: "Please, God, make him think I am still pretty."

The door opened and Jim stepped in and closed it. He looked thin and very serious. Poor fellow, he was only twenty-two—and to be burdened with a family! He needed a new overcoat and he was without gloves.

Jim stopped inside the door, as immovable as a setter at the scent of quail. His eyes were fixed upon Della, and there was an expression in them that she could not read, and it terrified her. It was not anger, nor surprise, nor disapproval, nor horror, nor any of the sentiments that she had been prepared for. He simply stared at her fixedly with that peculiar expression on his face.

Della wriggled off the table and went for him.

"Jim, darling," she cried, "don't look at me that way. I had my hair cut off and sold it because I couldn't live through Christmas without giving you a present. It'll grow out again—you won't mind, will you? I just had to do it. My hair grows awfully fast. Say 'Merry Christmas,' Jim, and let's be happy. You don't know what a nice—what a beautiful, nice gift I've got for you."

"You've cut off your hair?" asked Jim laboriously, as if he had not arrived at that patent fact yet, even after the hardest mental labor.

"Cut it off and sold it," said Della. "Don't you like me just as well, anyhow? I'm me without my hair, ain't I?"

Jim looked about the room curiously.

"You say your hair is gone?" he said, with an air almost of idiocy.

"You needn't look for it," said Della. "It's sold, I tell you—sold and gone, too. It's Christmas Eve, boy. Be good to me, for it went for you. Maybe the hairs of my head were numbered," she went on with a sudden serious sweetness, "but nobody could ever count my love for you. Shall I put the chops on, Jim?"

Out of his trance Jim seemed quickly to wake. He enfolded his Della. For ten seconds let us regard with discreet scrutiny some inconsequential object in the other direction. Eight dollars a week or a million a year—what is the difference? A mathematician or a wit would give you the wrong answer. The magi brought valuable gifts but that was not among them. This dark assertion will be illuminated later.

Jim drew a package from his overcoat pocket and threw it upon the table.

"Don't make any mistake, Dell," he said, "about me. I don't think there is anything in the way of a haircut or a shave or a shampoo that could make me like my girl any less. But if you'll unwrap that package you may see why you had me going a while at first."

White fingers and nimble tore at the string and paper. And then an ecstatic scream of joy; and then, alas! a quick feminine change to hysterical tears and wails, necessitating the immediate employment of all the comforting powers of the lord of the flat.

For there lay The Combs—the set of combs, side and back, that Della had worshipped for long in a Broadway window. Beautiful combs, pure tortoise shell, with jewelled rims—just the shade to wear in the beautiful vanished hair. They were expensive combs, she knew, and her heart had simply craved and yearned over them without the least hope of possession. And now, they were hers, but the tresses that should have adorned the coveted adornments were gone.

But she hugged them to her bosom, and at length she was able to look up with dim eyes and a smile and say: "My hair grows so fast, Jim!"

And then Della leaped up like a little singed cat and cried, "Oh, Oh!"

Jim had not yet seen his beautiful present. She held it out to him eagerly upon her open palm. The dull precious metal seemed to flash with a reflection of her bright and ardent spirit.

"Isn't it a dandy, Jim? I hunted all over town to find it. You'll have to look at the time a hundred times a day now. Give me your watch. I want to see how it looks on it."

Instead of obeying, Jim tumbled down on the couch and put his hand under the back of his head and smiled.

"Dell," said he, "let's put our Christmas presents away and keep 'em a while. They're too nice to use just at present. I sold the watch to get the money to buy your combs. And now suppose you put the chops on."

The magi, as you know, were wise men—wonderfully wise men—who brought gifts to the Babe in the manger. They invented the art of giving Christmas presents. Being wise, their gifts were no doubt wise ones, possibly bearing the privilege of exchange in case of duplication. And here I have lamely related to you the uneventful chronicle of two foolish children in a flat who most unwisely sacrificed for each other the greatest treasures of their house. But in a last word to the wise of these days let it be said that of all who give gifts these two were the wisest. Of all who give and receive gifts, such as they are wisest. Everywhere they are the wisest. They are the magi.

The Open Window
H.H. Munro (SAKI)

"My aunt will be down presently, Mr. Nuttel," said a very self-possessed young lady of fifteen; "in the meantime you must try and put up with me."

Framton Nuttel endeavored to say the correct something which should duly flatter the niece of the moment without unduly discounting the aunt that was to come. Privately he doubted more than ever whether these formal visits on a succession of total strangers would do much towards helping the nerve cure which he was supposed to be undergoing

"I know how it will be," his sister had said when he was preparing to migrate to this rural retreat; "you will bury yourself down there and not speak to a living soul, and your nerves will be worse than ever from moping. I shall just give you letters of introduction to all the people I know there. Some of them, as far as I can remember, were quite nice."

Framton wondered whether Mrs. Sappleton, the lady to whom he was presenting one of the letters of introduction came into the nice division.

"Do you know many of the people round here?" asked the niece, when she judged that they had had sufficient silent communion.

"Hardly a soul," said Framton. "My sister was staying here, at the rectory, you know, some four years ago, and she gave me letters of introduction to some of the people here."
He made the last statement in a tone of distinct regret.

"Then you know practically nothing about my aunt?" pursued the self-possessed young lady.

"Only her name and address," admitted the caller. He was wondering whether Mrs. Sappleton was in the married or widowed state. An undefinable something about the room seemed to suggest masculine habitation.

"Her great tragedy happened just three years ago," said the child; "that would be since your sister's time."

"Her tragedy?" asked Framton; somehow in this restful country spot tragedies seemed out of place.

"You may wonder why we keep that window wide open on an October afternoon," said the niece, indicating a large French window that opened on to a lawn.

"It is quite warm for the time of the year," said Framton; "but has that window got anything to do with the tragedy?"

"Out through that window, three years ago to a day, her husband and her two young brothers went off for their day's shooting. They never came back. In crossing the moor to their favorite snipe-shooting ground they were all three engulfed in a treacherous piece of bog. It had been that dreadful wet summer, you know, and places that were safe in other years gave way suddenly without warning. Their bodies were never recovered. That was the dreadful part of it." Here the child's voice lost its self-possessed note and became falteringly human. "Poor aunt always thinks that they will come back someday, they and the little brown spaniel that was lost with them, and walk in at that window just as they used to do. That is why the window is kept open every evening till it is quite dusk. Poor dear aunt, she has often told me how they went out, her husband with his white waterproof coat over his arm, and Ronnie, her youngest brother, singing 'Bertie, why do you bound?' as he always did to tease her, because she said it got on her nerves. Do you know, sometimes on still, quiet evenings like this, I almost get a creepy feeling that they will all walk in through that window--"

She broke off with a little shudder. It was a relief to Framton when the aunt bustled into the room with a whirl of apologies for being late in making her appearance.

"I hope Vera has been amusing you?" she said.

"She has been very interesting," said Framton.

"I hope you don't mind the open window," said Mrs. Sappleton briskly; "my husband and brothers will be home directly from shooting, and they always come in this way. They've been out for snipe in the marshes today, so they'll make a fine mess over my poor carpets. So like you menfolk, isn't it?"

She rattled on cheerfully about the shooting and the scarcity of birds, and the prospects for duck in the winter. To Framton it was all purely horrible. He made a desperate but only partially successful effort to turn the talk on to a less ghastly topic, he was conscious that his hostess was giving him only a fragment of her attention, and her eyes were constantly straying past him to the open window and the lawn beyond. It was certainly an unfortunate coincidence that he should have paid his visit on this tragic anniversary.

"The doctors agree in ordering me complete rest, an absence of mental excitement, and avoidance of anything in the nature of violent physical exercise," announced Framton, who labored under the tolerably widespread delusion that total strangers and chance acquaintances are hungry for the least detail of one's ailments and infirmities, their cause and cure. "On the matter of diet they are not so much in agreement," he continued.

"No?" said Mrs. Sappleton, in a voice which only replaced a yawn at the last moment. Then she suddenly brightened into alert attention--but not to what Framton was saying.

"Here they are at last!" she cried. "Just in time for tea, and don't they look as if they were muddy up to the eyes!"

Framton shivered slightly and turned towards the niece with a look intended to convey sympathetic comprehension. The child was staring out through the open window with a dazed horror in her eyes. In a chill shock of nameless fear Framton swung round in his seat and looked in the same direction.

In the deepening twilight three figures were walking across the lawn towards the window, they all carried guns under their arms, and one of them was additionally burdened with a white coat hung over his shoulders. A tired brown spaniel kept close at their heels. Noiselessly they neared the house, and then a hoarse young voice chanted out of the dusk: "I said, Bertie, why do you bound?"

Framton grabbed wildly at his stick and hat; the hall door, the gravel drive, and the front gate were dimly noted stages in his headlong retreat. A cyclist coming along the road had to run into the hedge to avoid imminent collision.

"Here we are, my dear," said the bearer of the white mackintosh, coming in through the window, "fairly muddy, but most of it's dry. Who was that who bolted out as we came up?"

"A most extraordinary man, a Mr. Nuttel," said Mrs. Sappleton; "could only talk about his illnesses, and dashed off without a word of goodbye or apology when you arrived. One would think he had seen a ghost."

"I expect it was the spaniel," said the niece calmly; "he told me he had a horror of dogs. He was once hunted into a cemetery somewhere on the banks of the Ganges by a pack of pariah dogs, and had to spend the night in a newly dug grave with the creatures snarling and grinning and foaming just above him. Enough to make anyone lose their nerve."

Romance at short notice was her specialty.

Typhoon Seas
Edgar Anthony Manley

The rasping melody of an untuned piano swelled above the hoarse voices of seamen in Sailor Jack's Retreat, halfway down the odorous Street of Celestial Peace—a name that mocked the crooked lane cutting off sharply from the Hong Kong waterfront.

It was a street of vengeful hatreds, of black, brooding passions. In all the fetid Orient, Bill Hamilton could not have found a more fitting region in which to encounter a foe, the man he had sworn to crush into the bitter dust. Strange how the passing years had cooled his hate.

Hamilton shoved his way arrogantly through the crowd in Sailor Jack's. Two score of eyes stared at him suspiciously through the dense smoke wafted about the room. Ship's officers, chesty with the pride of caste, seldom visited the turbulent dive.

For a few moments Hamilton paused near a vacant table, idly studying the surging mob that hailed from a score of countries. Two Dutch sailors shouted furious oaths at each other, but the skipper of the freighter Black Hawk paid scant attention to them. Hamilton's glance rested for an instant on the painted girl at the piano, and his lips curled derisively.

Fighting his way through the throng came a burly figure. The bronzed-faced skipper turned swiftly as a hand was placed on his shoulder, and glanced at Jim Carey, his chief engineer.

"Seen him tonight?" Hamilton demanded.

"Nope—not yet. But I guess he'll show up. He haunts this place like a spook, they tell me!"

"Sit down and let's swallow a drink. Darned hot tonight! Curse this roasting country! What'll you have, chief?"

"Whiskey and soda."

"We'll make it two. Hey, waiter!"

A slippered Chinaman moved fearfully through the knots of sailors and bowed subserviently as he took Hamilton's order. He vanished among the clouds of smoke and sweating bodies, as the skipper again faced his chief engineer.

It was strange, Hamilton reflected, how he had run across Phil Gordon in Hong Kong. Ten years had passed like winter gales since they had served together in the destroyer fleet far up in the torpedo-menaced North Sea. Gordon's destiny seemed linked with his own. It was Gordon who had wormed him out for appointment as chief petty officer. Three times they had fought bloody fist battles—and Gordon had always won. Back in Brooklyn, Gordon had become his rival in love, and had married Kitty Higgins.

"I was thinking', Jim, what a heckuva proposition life is," said Hamilton as he sipped his liquor. The Chinese boy hovered about the table and Hamilton flung him a silver dollar, then waved him impatiently away. The skipper's eyes grew moody.

"Was this feller, Gordon, a pal of yours, captain?" asked Carey.

"No! Hate him like heck! Worsen any man I know on the globe!"

"He sure sneaked out of here last night when he saw you. I made some inquiries about him today as you told me to, cap'n. Seems like this here guy Gordon has gone native. Just a lousy beachcomber of the rottenest type. Even the birds that hang out around here look down upon him."

"Anything else about him?"

"Yep. This will surprise you. He used to be first officer on a tub running' to Java until about six months ago. Fairly steady feller. Then he took to drink all of a sudden. Went from bad to worse as some bozos seem to do."

"Talking' about the devil, Jim!"

Carey glanced up quickly at a lean, half-starved man who was pushing his way through the mob that loitered about the swinging bamboo doors. The newcomer's face was gaunt, and he wore a native hat of coarse straw. He was clad in a dirty white drill suit, two sizes too small. An English seaman turned on him with a snarl, his loud voice rising above the medley of noise.

"Darn yer, how dare you push me?" he shouted.

"Let 'im be, Hawkins!"

"'Ave a dirty dog like 'im push into me? Like 'ell!"

The Englishmen raised a ham-sized fist and crashed it into the jaw of the derelict. Hamilton half rose to his feet to watch the altercation. He wondered if Gordon still retained enough fighting guts to send him into a hopeless battle.

Gordon scrambled to his feet, rubbing his injured jaw with a filthy hand. He glared at the Englishman and tore in furiously. The Britisher drew back mockingly as Gordon struck him on the chest; then the big sailor's fist swung into action. The blow sent Gordon reeling halfway across the room. The seaman laughed unpleasantly.

"Dirty, filthy scum!" he yelled.

The chief engineer banged his hand on the liquor-stained table. Hamilton raised his glass to his lips, drained the last drop of whisky and soda and encountered Carey's eyes.

"Well, that's that!" Hamilton muttered. A sickly smile distorted his large mouth.

"What's your game, cap'n?"

"My game? Guess I don't get you, Jim. Mebbe I ought to be just contented lettin' Gordon rot to heck in Hong Kong. Still, he's a white man, ain't he, and a former shipmate of mine? I wonder if he's rotten clean through. Except for him, I guess I'd have married the sweetest little girl in America."

Carey nodded, and the freighter captain continued, "You say he used to be chief officer on a steamer in the Java trade? That shows he must have had something in him. Even tonight he showed guts in a scrap. Drink has knocked many a good man to heck."

The rouged girl at the piano lighted a cigarette and puffed on it somberly. Her lips were of an unnatural carmine hue, and two gold teeth gleamed like the beady eyes of a cobra as she turned. For the first time, Hamilton perceived that she was a half-caste. She smiled at him with wanton coquettishness, and his lids narrowed angrily.

"Heck!" he growled.

The girl turned, and her thin fingers spread above the yellowed keys. For a few moments her hands remained poised in the air with thoughtless grace, then crashed upon the keys. The softly melancholy lilt of "Silver Threads Among the Gold" filled the gaudily lacquered front room of Sailor Jack's Retreat.

A lantern-jawed Swede, lured by the music, shambled to his rocking feet and shuffled to her side. The beefy Englishman who had sent Gordon reeling to the dirty floor shouted an oath, and followed him angrily. A swarthy Greek got in the Englishman's way and was knocked aside with a clenched fist.

"Both of them guys has been after her a week. She's kinda sweet on the limey."

"There'll be trouble now!" said a voice that carried the nasal twang of Vermont.

Hamilton crouched back in his chair as an ominous hush fell on the room. Fitful lights cast a bleak yellow cone over the girl at the piano and the two rivals for her love. Through the gloom, Hamilton peered at Gordon, who was huddled over a table at the far corner. The beachcomber's hat had fallen to the floor, and his head was buried in his hands. A glass of whisky was on the table.

Suddenly the girl, filled with the madness of too much liquor, increased the tempo until the old air was distorted into raging jazz. Gordon raised his head and glared angrily. "Play that right, darn you!" he yelled. "Play it with a little sentiment, you—!"

The Englishman wheeled about angrily. "I'll beat you to a pulp!" he shouted.
Growling with rage, the Swede turned on his rival as Gordon leaped around the table. Hamilton wondered if the Swede thought the remark was addressed to himself. The blond head ducked

low and the Swede's fist shot out with fury, catching the Englishman on the temple. For an instant the Britisher paused, half-dazed by the blow. The girl darted from the piano and screamed.

Jing Lee, portly native owner of the Retreat since the lamented death of Sailor Jack in a knife fight two years before, hurried toward the brawling men. The Chinese carried a Colt automatic in his muscular fingers, and stern determination gleamed in his almond eyes. He made two steps through the still mob; then heavy hands seized him. The pistol clattered to the floor.

The events that followed dazed Hamilton by their swiftness. They seemed to melt in each other like scenes in a motion picture. Out of the ground darted a Greek seaman, laughing wildly. The man was beastly drunk, but he still remembered the crack of the Englishman's fist. He picked up the weapon and pointed it at the Britisher. The helpless Chinese proprietor watched him.

"Catchee him!" shouted Jing Lee.
The venomous bark of a bullet tore through the tobacco smoke, and the Englishman clawed at his thick throat. A foolish look of amazement crossed his heavy face. Then, with a gurgling groan, he sagged to the floor. The bullet had plowed its burning way through his jugular vein.

The painted half-caste girl cried out piteously, and fell across the body of the dying man, smothering his lips with kisses. Somebody yelled, "Give him air!" A laugh followed, as tables were overturned by patrons in a mad rush for the door. Hamilton saw Gordon lurch against a table and falter. Seamen smashed the electric lights with vandal fury.

Hamilton leaped across the room and seized Gordon by the collar. The beachcomber glared at him angrily. "Leave me be, darn you!" he shouted.

The skipper struck him across the face. Gordon attempted to resist, but sagged in a drunken stupor. "Come with me, you bloody fool!" Hamilton commanded. He dragged Gordon from a chair, though the other resisted with ferocious determination. The struggle seemed to sober Gordon. Glancing up, Hamilton saw a Sikh policeman, black-bearded and wearing a huge turban, standing in the doorway.

The wails of the half-caste girl filled the room. "He's dead!" she sobbed. "Oh, God, he's dead!"

Hamilton raised his fist and crashed it in a sweeping arc against Gordon's chin. With a sudden spring the Sikh leaped toward Hamilton. He was armed with a stout club. As Hamilton, dragging Gordon, continued to advance, the Sikh raised the club above his head. Had the blow descended on Hamilton's head, it would have fractured his skull. The freighter captain ducked the blow, and the club landed on the flexed muscle of his right arm.

Shouting an oath, Hamilton drew back, gritting his teeth in pain. Carey watched the Sikh narrowly and with a dexterous move of his foot tripped him. Before the turbaned policeman could regain his feet, Hamilton stepped on his wrist, kicked the club out of his grasp, bent over and seized the weapon.

"Hurry!" he shouted.

Gordon darted through the door with Hamilton and Carey at his heels. The ragged American ran up the noisy Street of Celestial Peace for a dozen feet and darted toward a black doorway. Then Hamilton caught up with him. The Sikh's club swung in the captain's hand and crashed into the base of Gordon's skull. The beachcomber's legs sagged under him, and his face fell into the dust.

Hamilton wondered if the blow had killed him. Those fellows who went native and drank themselves half to death hadn't much resistance. He seized Gordon by the collar and turned the limp body over, placing his hand over the other's heart. A faint beat reassured him. Hamilton turned swiftly to his chief engineer.

"Grab him under the arms!" he ordered. "I'll carry him by the legs."

"Takin' him to the ship?"

"Yep!"

The strange procession made its way along the half-deserted street. As it passed the Café of the Three Lanterns, a half-dozen shouting seamen rushed through the door and stared at the group curiously. The sight of a supposedly stupefied seaman, however, was not one to evoke excessive amazement on the part of chance spectators.

"Yer partner drunk?" inquired a Yankee merchant sailor.

"Yep, he passed out," responded Carey.

Eight minutes' hasty walk brought the ship officers and their unconscious burden to the waterfront. The Black Hawk lay out in the roadstead. Hamilton stumbled across a cargo-laden wharf and hailed a small native boat. The unconscious man was flung into the little bark.

Through the junk-filled harbor, the little sailboat made its way to the port side of the Black Hawk. Hamilton's second officer, George Johnson, stood on the darkened deck.
"Here's a new member of the crew," said the master of the freighter.

Johnson bent over the heavily breathing form and muttered a protest. "He's a white man, captain! Say, all the crew we got are Lascars and coolie Chinese"

"This guy is lower in the scale than a Lascar," said Hamilton bitterly. "And, by the way, Mr. Johnson, not a word—"

The second officer nodded. As Hamilton and Carey walked across the deck, with Gordon swaying crazily between them, he muttered, "I'll be darned. So the Ol' Man's gone in for the shanghai racket?" But Johnson knew on which side his bread was buttered. He shook his head dismally, and a crooked smile played about his lips. "What the heck!" he said under his breath. It was none of his business what the skipper did.

Hamilton led the way forward into the well deck and up to the forecastle head of the Black Hawk. He glanced idly over the port bow at the gleaming lights of the city. From somewhere in the darkness near the waterfront came the rasping notes of Chinese music. Voices floated through the still air. Hamilton dropped Gordon's legs.

"Down in the forecastle with him?" asked Carey.

"I wonder if I ought. But I guess not, on second thoughts. Remember he's a white man even if he ain't much to look at. Hey, Li, Togi!"

Two Lascars, dozing on heavy tarpaulins beyond the winches, scampered through the gloom from the starboard side. Hamilton pointed to Gordon. The man who had gone native was coming to. His breath was exhaled in hoarse bursts, and he mumbled incoherently. The Lascars picked him up.

"Put him in the lazaret," said Hamilton gruffly. "Tie his arms and legs. Savee?"

Li nodded and, aided by his companion, dragged the struggling prisoner down into the well deck and on toward the poop. Hamilton made his way to the starboard rail and stared contentedly over the harbor. He lighted a thickly caked pipe and puffed on it reflectively. His air was that of a man at peace with the world.

Shortly after daybreak the Black Hawk weighed anchor and steamed slowly through the bumboats and frowsy junks that cluttered up the harbor. Her whistle sounded shrilly through the haze that hovered over the waterway. Out of the mist swept a steamer toward the port bow of the Black Hawk. The freighter's whistle belched noisily, and Hamilton, standing near the starboard wing of the navigating bridge, swore.

Johnson, in the chart room, clutched the telegraph, and the Black Hawk slowed suddenly. The offending steamer swerved sharply, leaving a clear path for the freighter. Hamilton shaded his eyes with a cupped hand, and watched the crew battening down the hatches. Then he made his way to the chart room.

"Where's Mr. Holmes?" he demanded. Holmes was the chief mate.

"He didn't show up. He's been on a heck of a bat since we struck Hong Kong."

Hamilton's outburst blistered the sultry atmosphere of the chart room. He was pleased in one way to sail without Holmes. The man was a troublemaker if ever there was one. He turned to Johnson and demanded to know why the other had failed to tell him Holmes had not come aboard.

A sickly grin spread across Johnson's face. "Thought he'd show up at the last minute like he generally did. I clean forgot about him when we started to shove off."

"Like the devil you did! Out after his job, eh? Well, you'll do double tricks, Mr. Johnson. Don't forget that. To heck with this lousy drunk, Holmes, anyway! Mr. McMasters, our new third, is around all right?"

"Yes, sir."

The burning glare of full daylight found the Black Hawk well beyond the harbor and headed into the open China Sea toward the Lema Islands. The freighter was bound for Borneo. Hamilton sniffed the clean ocean air delightedly. The foul stench of the native district, in the heart of the treaty port, still oppressed him, lingering in his imagination like something vile.

The treacherous waters of the China Sea were cut by a perverse wind that lashed up heavy waves. Ground swells surged about the Black Hawk, and spindrift dashed against the plates, causing the decks to roll. But the motion of the ship was joy to Hamilton, and the Black Hawk was his first command.

Hamilton called Li and directed him to release Gordon. Twenty minutes later, Hamilton made his way aft and found Gordon huddled over the fantail. An ugly welt disfigured the base of Gordon's closely cropped skull. Hamilton's lips tightened with repulsion as he noticed a layer of filth on Gordon's neck. The fellow would shame a heathen coolie, he reflected, with his lack of cleanliness.

"Gordon!" said Hamilton sharply.

The beachcomber turned around. The fury of a cornered rat crept into his eyes, and his fists clenched. "Goin' to hit me, eh?" demanded Hamilton growling. "Try an' do it, mister, and you'll never forget it! Recognize me, do you?"

"Yes, blast you, I do! An' I want to tell you, Hamilton, you're goin' to face heck for dragging me on your bloody ship. This shanghai business is illegal nowadays!"

Gordon leaned against the taffrail and glared at his old-time enemy. The bitter thought swept his mind that Hamilton had risen like a skyrocket in the world of ships. He thought of his own fall into the abyss, and tears glistened in his eyes.

The skipper turned. With a catlike leap, Gordon sprang toward a hammer which had been left on the poop deck by the ship's carpenter. Murder surged in the heart of the prisoner. If he could crush Hamilton's skull to pulp, he would gladly leap to his own death in the tossing seas.

Hamilton walked toward the starboard rail, his head sunk on his chest. The soft patter of Gordon's bare feet on the deck failed to penetrate his consciousness. The yellow sun beat furiously on the lurching deck, casting a grotesque shadow of the slinking figure behind Hamilton. He turned swiftly and seized Gordon's upraised wrist in an iron grip. Gordon uttered a low cry of pain as Hamilton twisted the wrist until the bone threatened to snap. The hammer fluttered across the deck.

"So you thought you'd kill me, you sneaking cur?" demanded Hamilton. "Darn you for a rat—"

The freighter captain's fist swept in a swift arc that forewarned Gordon of the punishment to follow. The beachcomber attempted vainly to dodge the blow, but Hamilton's fist followed the moving head with unfailing skill. The knuckles tearing into Gordon's jaw caused his teeth to rattle. His eyes glazed as he fell to the deck.

"I'm putting' you on as boss, Gordon!" remarked Hamilton. "Guess I ought to make you sign on as a spud-peeler to the Chinese cook or as a mess boy. You belong with the native crew, all right, but white men can't mix with those birds—not under me. Will you sign?" Hamilton paused with his toes pointed toward Gordon's gaunt ribs. The fallen first officer of the Java route sputtered with hatred, but he shook his head affirmatively as Hamilton's foot drew back.

The second night out found the Black Hawk sweeping into a stiff squall. A howling wind lashed the masts and the wireless antennae hissed under the cutting currents of air. A deadly calm followed. Hamilton stood in the chart room, watching the barometer drop ominously.

"We're in for some dirty weather, Mr. Johnson," he said, turning to his acting first officer, who bent over a chronometer.

A cross-swell set in from the direction of the Strait of Formosa. The dying sun poured leaden heat across the lonely China Sea, and Hamilton, stripped to his undershirt, oozed with sweat. Down in the well deck, he saw Gordon directing a Lascar and three Chinese sailors in the holystone art. The thump of the propeller sounded dully in Hamilton's ears as he walked to the bridge.

The beachcomber had proved himself an efficient boss. For a few moments the skipper idly watched him; then he shouted his name. Gordon left the group of seamen and climbed up the ladder to the bridge. The sickly yellow pallor had been erased from his face by the sun and hard work. Hamilton was surprised at the transformation. Gordon stared at him sullenly.

"You have done good work, Gordon!" Hamilton began fumblingly.

The other laughed unpleasantly. "Maritime laws are strict. Right now I'm a member of your crew. I guess you know me long enough to admit I'm a good sailor."

The skipper nodded. For half a minute his hands fumbled on the rail. The face of Kitty Higgins rose before his eyes.

"When you went to pieces, Gordon, didn't you figure you were sticking a knife into Kitty?" he muttered.

"What the heck is that to you?"

"Remember I wanted to marry her once, myself. You beat me out."

"She's dead. Passed out seven months ago in Seattle. We lived there."

Hamilton's harsh face softened, and he laid his hand on Gordon's shoulder. "I'm sorry, ol' man, sorry as heck. Guess her death shot you to pieces. Any kids?"

"Two—boy and girl. They're with her parents in Brooklyn now."

Hamilton turned on the bridge. The tragedy of Gordon's downfall was pitifully plain. Words of sympathy failed him, and he turned to the boss, his voice hard and matter-of-fact. "Get below and rout out all hands," he ordered. "We're in for a bad storm. Have 'em cover up all the ventilators."

The voice of Johnson came from the chart room. "Which way is the swell coming' from, Mr. Hamilton?"

"Northeast."

He knew that down in the engine room, the temperature was that of a living heck—at least a hundred and fifteen degrees. He saw Jim Carey, a black figure, crawl to the deck for a breath of air. Angry voices rose through the skylight from the stokehold. The stokers were the first to suffer.

Hamilton knew Gordon well enough to realize that he could depend on the man in an emergency. The beachcomber might still harbor bitter hatred toward his old enemy, but the rasping life of the sea had instilled in his mind a spirit of rigid obedience to authority.

The skipper might have voiced amazement, indeed, if he could have read the thoughts in Gordon's mind as the boss scampered down the ladder to assemble the native crew. In the Far East there are two courses open to the white man who goes native. Either he can drop completely into the abyss, or, catching himself in time, he can drag himself figuratively by his boot straps back to solid ground again.

And Gordon, filled with distaste at himself, was determined to force his way back to the ranks of ship officers in the Oriental trade. Hard work had lashed the last of the liquor fumes from his befogged brain.

"Darn him to heck!" he growled under his breath. "I'll beat him to pulp some of these days. I'll—" The boatswain's sour voice died. On ships, sometimes, a whisper carries.

In a way, Gordon welcomed the coming of the typhoon. He was too experienced a sailor not to recognize that a hurricane of unusual violence was about to tear into the Black Hawk. He felt that the fight would restore his long-lost self-respect and stamina.

Hamilton watched his surly boss order the crew into action. He walked toward the chart house and caught Johnson's eyes. "Well, Johnson, our new boss seems to be hitting' his job," he remarked.

"He's just like the usual run of those birds."

"Like heck he is. Gordon holds his first officer's ticket. He's a darn fool. In lots of ways I used to hate him more than any man in the world, but ten years wipe out a lot of memories, Johnson."

The Black Hawk held to her course, not a fraction of a point off. At the wheel, boxed in a little house, stood a tall Lascar, apparently as immovable as the image of Buddha in a jungle temple. A dense bank of clouds scudded across the eastern sky, black and sinister, as the ship floundered forward like an exhausted monster.

"Think we're in for a typhoon, Mr. Hamilton?"

The skipper turned angrily toward the chart house from which his acting chief's voice came faintly. The rising wind made hearing difficult.

"I'll tell the cockeyed world we're in for a typhoon!"

The ship rolled in the heavy cross-swell with startling suddenness, and the bridge tossed under Hamilton's feet. He clutched the rail to keep from falling.

"That was a heavy one!" he yelled. "How is the barometer?"

"Still falling like blazes!"

The Black Hawk swung wildly about, each roll worse than the one before. Hamilton watched the Lascar at the wheel. The Oriental helmsman's arms seemed galvanized into frantic life.

"Hang on to it!" shouted Hamilton. "You must have gone off eight points that last time."

Hamilton made his way with difficulty into the chart room and put on his oilskins, sou'wester and sea boots. A sudden gust of wind filled the little house and the patter of rain swept the deck. The storm had overtaken them, and was lashing the panting Black Hawk with demoniacal strength. Blackness filled the heavens.

The Lascar, nearly crushed by the wildness of the wind, which threatened the destruction of the wheel house, released his hold on the steering gear and fell backward through the open door. He was swept helplessly halfway across the bridge, and the ship tossed about until it dipped into a raging head sea. The decks were awash. Hamilton thanked his stars that the ship carried no deck load. Above the fury of the elements came the shouts of Chinese and Lascars.

The ship swung about despairingly, and her beams shook as she took a breathless plunge from the top of a mountain of waves. Hamilton struggled to reach the wheel. Through the door of the chart house, framed by the light of a swaying lantern, he saw Johnson darting toward the madly racing helm.

The plunge into the abyss seemed everlasting. The frightened cries of the Chinese came faintly to Hamilton's ears. The Orientals, it was evident, believed that the Black Hawk was diving to her doom. Then the freighter hit bottom, in the depths of a valley of restless waters. With startling suddenness the bow rose high, sending both officers against the wall of the chart house. They saw a dim figure dash up the ladder and scurry across the perilously dipped bridge toward the wheel. The ship veered and swept again south.

Hamilton leaped toward the rail and made his way to the wheel house. He recognized the scarecrow form holding the wheel as Phil Gordon, and a glow of surprise filled him. Then the Lascar who had relinquished the wheel returned, on badly shaken sea legs, and took the helm.

Lightning flashed across the sky, illuminating the hills of waves momentarily. Hamilton perceived a low hanging bank of clouds directly above the Black Hawk. Then impenetrable darkness again fell over the China Sea. A great wind tore shrilly through the masts and mountainous waves swept the decks. Hamilton was hurled halfway across the navigating bridge, tossed in great volumes of water. He thrashed about helplessly with his arms and legs.

The skipper regained his feet as a second flash of lightning swept through the heavens. He caught a fleeting glimpse of men crazed with panic in the well deck; beneath him he saw a maze of battered companions, covered winches, a swaying mast and tops of hatches. Two of the boats, he observed, had been swept into the seas.

Hamilton turned toward the chart house. The solitary lantern swayed crazily. He glanced around for Johnson, and his face grew stern at failing to find his aide. Then he peered toward his feet. Johnson lay on the deck, unconscious, bleeding profusely about the skull. He had been flung against a bulkhead as the ship tossed to her beam's ends. Hamilton dipped his handkerchief in sea water and washed the wound.

The skipper made his way to the wheel house and bent over the binnacle, checking up the course. The helmsman's face seemed cold and far away in the faint light.

Returning to the chart room he glanced at his acting chief mate and saw the young officer move. "He'll come through all right," he muttered.

Three Chinese, their faces distorted with fear, darted into the chart room. Behind them came Gordon. The white man's drawn countenance seemed like that of a man of sixty, but his eyes bespoke enraged determination. He seized one of the Chinese by the neck and struggled to force him from the chart house. The other two Chinese leaped toward Hamilton. A knife flashed in the hand of one of the seamen. Hamilton backed toward his desk on the starboard side of the room.

Hamilton flung a chair at the mutineers and opened a drawer of his desk. His fingers clutched an automatic. At the sight of the weapon the Chinese drew back. It was better in their minds to await death in the maddened sea than to encounter certain and immediate extinction in front of the muzzle of Hamilton's pistol.

"What's all this?" shouted Hamilton above the screaming wind.

"Devils get ship!" yelled one of the Chinese. "Turn back China!"

Hamilton turned in surprise toward the Chinese who had spoken. Then he glanced inquiringly at Gordon.

"They saw McMasters swept overboard!" he said. "Big comber got him."

The Black Hawk tossed furiously in a sudden swell, and Hamilton stumbled backward. One of the Chinese leaped on top of him, forcing him to the floor. The mutineer madly attempted to wrest the pistol from his grasp. It was all too evident that the men were crazed with panic and beyond words of reason. With a white crew, Hamilton knew, he might fight his way safely through the hurricane.

Gordon released his hold of the third Chinese and leaped to the aid of the captain. If he still harbored hatred of the man who had shanghaied him, he failed to show it in this mad situation. With a swift blow of his left fist, he knocked the seaman aside and gained possession of the pistol.

"Back, darn you, back!" he shouted.

Confronted by the pistol held in Gordon's determined hand, the three seamen edged toward the door. The Lascar helmsman still clung to the wheel, apparently oblivious of the battle in the chart house.

Hamilton stumbled to his feet and fell upon the table as the ship lurched. "Good work, Gordon!" he shouted. "I have another gun. Keep hold of the one you got!"

The Chinese were in full flight, sweeping unsteadily across the bridge. Shouting an oath, the ragged boss pursued them, and watched them disappear into the darkness of the forward well deck.

Followed by Gordon, Hamilton made his way to the bridge rail. The death of the third officer, McMasters, had whipped the Chinese and Lascars into a frenzy of fear. Truly the sea gods were angry and demanded great sacrifices of human beings.

A grim story of a sea captain, tossed into the raging waves of a typhoon to appease the enraged deities of the deep, crossed Hamilton's mind. The human sacrifice had occurred two months before on the China Sea. He wondered if his own crew had similar designs on his life.

"About McMasters?" yelled Hamilton.

"Caught quick as heck! I managed—save—self. Caught rail. Three—Lascars—drowned!"

The Black Hawk dived from atop a steep mountain, and Gordon was flung against the skipper by the force of the plunge. A flash of lightning, followed by a sharp volley of thunder, illuminated the ship. Crouched in the well deck, a refuge on their way to the forecastle, were the mutineers. Two other men clambered out of the stokehold and joined them.

A pinpoint of flame flashed from the huddled ranks of the five seamen, and a bullet tore into the rail, a bare half a foot from Hamilton's clutching fist. Gordon leveled his pistol swiftly and fired. A yell of agony told him he had wounded one of the mutineers.

"Some of the black gang must tote guns!" he yelled.

Hamilton cupped his hand and placed it against Gordon's ear. "Gotta keep sharp lookout! Birds—ready—heck!"

"They want us—turn back."

"Like heck we will! We're scudding away from the storm!"

Dim shapes were outlined on the port side of the bridge. Gordon rushed to meet the attack. His pistol spat twice. The Lascar with the pistol, one of Carey's stokers, fired. Smoke from the weapon burned Gordon's face. He heard Hamilton utter a cry.

"He got me!" the skipper shouted.

The Lascar pointed his weapon at Gordon and blazed away. Two of his companions attempted to seize Gordon's legs in an endeavor to trip him. The American shook them off. The report of another shot filled his ears. A Chinese had gained possession of Hamilton's gun and fired at him. A bullet tore through Gordon's shoulder and he winced in agony. The steel cut a blazing path through flesh and bone.

Gordon squirmed out of the grasp of brown and saffron fingers, then waited for a flash of lightning to reveal the whereabouts of his assailants. A yellow shaft of light flushed the murky sky, and he caught sight of the man who had seized Hamilton's weapon. Gordon squeezed on the trigger, and the Chinese slid across the deck, wounded.

Again the ship canted, and Gordon felt himself imprisoned under tons of icy water. He grasped a stanchion with iron fingers to save himself from being swept to death. His other hand stretched across the deck, and he felt a foot, clad in the shoes of a white man, pressed against it.

Gordon reached out desperately and seized Hamilton's thick ankle. The pressure of the water was almost unbearable. He felt as if his lungs were bursting, and he struggled to raise his head above the swirling seas. Once he nearly lost his grip on the stanchion. Only by a supreme effort of will did he retain consciousness. Then the giant wave passed over the ship.

Gordon weakly dragged Hamilton by the heels toward the chart house. He wondered if the skipper of the ill-starred freighter was dead. Inside the chart house he felt the other's heart. Hamilton was still alive. Blood flowed from his right arm. The bullet fired by the mutinous Chinese had caught him about three inches above the wrist.

Strangely enough, the terror of the great wave had wiped out all thoughts of the Chinese and Lascar mutineers from Gordon's mind. He recalled them with a start. Peering through the door, he looked about for the five seamen, but they were not in sight. The helmsman also had disappeared. Hamilton opened his eyes and stared at Gordon dazedly. Johnson, half-drowned, huddled in a corner.

"Where are those birds?" Hamilton demanded.

"Down in Davy Jones' locker by now, I guess."

Hamilton leaped to his feet and made his way to the wheel. Gordon shoved him aside. "I'll hold it down," he said angrily. "How in heck, Hamilton, can you work the steering gear when your wrist is shot to pieces?"

The worst of the storm had passed. If it had continued fifteen minutes more, the ship would have had slight chance of keeping afloat. Part of the cargo had shifted, causing the Black Hawk to list perilously.

"Darn it all!" said Hamilton, half to himself.

The ship held fast under Gordon's powerful hands. He swung the wheel sharply in response to Hamilton's shouted commands. After all, he reflected, he could not help but respect the skipper even if he hated his guts. Darned few skippers in the Orient trade could have weathered the typhoon. Most of them, he told himself, should be running bumboats on the Hwang Ho.

The skipper studied the binnacle intently. Carey, black-faced and haggard, made his way to the navigating bridge.

"Turbines all right?" Hamilton demanded.

"Yes, sir. Shipped a lot of water, but it didn't reach the boilers."

"Keep agoin'! We're makin' straight for Borneo."

Carey nodded and disappeared. Li, the Lascar seaman, stumbled up the ladder to the bridge. Hamilton ordered him to relieve Gordon at the wheel. The skipper motioned Gordon to the chart room. Above the plunging ship, the wild wind died down.

"We just caught the tail end of the typhoon," said Hamilton. "Thank God it's over. If we had had to keep going through that heck much longer we'd never have made port."

"I'm afraid not, cap'n."

"And say! Guess I ought to apologize for the two beatings I gave you—in the dive at Hong Kong, and that morning on deck."

Gordon grinned. "That's all right, cap'n. At that, I'm one ahead of you. Remember I cleaned you up three times when we were in the navy."

"So you did. By the way, Mr. Gordon."

"Yes, sir."

"Understand you got first officer's papers. Want a job as first mate on this tub?"

Gordon seized Hamilton's red fist. "I'll tell the cockeyed world, Bill, I want the job!"

A Creeping Terror
Douglas M. Dold

Garry Lloyd lurched into the open, staggered and fell. He was aware that the Terror crept up behind him. He got to his feet, grasping the thorny branch of an acacia for support. He must reach higher ground before it caught up.

His bony, mask-like face set. The flat black mustache bristled stubbornly, his brown eyes grew glassy as the pain pounded and pulsed. He longed to take time to cut the "jigger" from its sac under his toenail. Objects swayed distorted before his eyes; he hoped that it was not the walking fever. Never had he felt such heat. The sky was pale, parched blue. The sun blazed formless and white-hot.

A steamy shroud-like haze gnawed at the horizon. Back of the mist lay safety and the hills. Far to the southwest was the forest beyond the Bahrel Ghazal. To the south where the Mountains of the Moon should have been, was a sooty cloud fading into yellow. Was this the cause of the flood? Could the Mufumbiro volcanoes be at it again? No chance to reach Kota or Wadeli.

About him, vast in its solemn desolation, was the swamp. To his right flowed the saffron flood of the river, lapping, gurgling as it slid silently into its backwaters. From *under* the haze it slipped, coiling, and beyond it slid into the haze, a shape of fear. There was no peace or quiet here, not even when one listened. And death—death was in the air, the morass breathed decay. It was the home of death—this swamp.

Beyond, mile upon mile, the apple-green mop headed papyrus quivered, its bifid filaments glistening, broken here and there by stagnant pools. Lilies of blue, red, and white grew here. Here the razor-billed stork with its red beak and bronzy green, black and white plumage stood a silent sentinel. It was in such a pool of silence that Lloyd had lost both his Somali gun bearers; the only survivors of the rapids.

His mouth set stubbornly, his eyes glowed with dull fury to destroy, his hands clutched at the hot barrels of his Holland. He pulled the battered green Topi further down to protect his neck, shifted the pack on his galled shoulders. There was little time, for the Terror crept higher with dirty little tongues at his very boots.

A flock of cow herons hovering over a matted patch of elephant grass spoke of danger. Probably a herd of buffalo, but it might be elephants.

Lloyd plunged once more into the game trail. The papyrus met over his head. After the glare the shadows seemed purple-black and the air stank, freighted with hot steamy decay. His boot splashed. Snails slimed the black mud. He slapped at the "booma" fly, killed it. To the cloud of mosquitoes that rose he paid no attention. Again he slapped, this time examining the dead fly. It was a tsetse. He prayed to God it was not infected with sleeping sickness.

God! How he hated Africa!

Again he emerged into glare and white heat. A flock of egrets froze into immobility. Beyond them, very still, sprawled five crocodiles, jaws agape, eyes cold and baleful. The sand spit on which they lay was yellow; about its ends curled the yellow current.

The egrets rose with a sighing rustle and floated off like the petals of a white flower. Warily Lloyd crossed the spit. From high overhead floated down the wail of a kite. And never ceasing rustled the papyrus, furtive and sly with hidden life. Never ceasing churred and croaked the frogs, and never ceasing shrilled and buzzed the insects.

Ahead of him, now so near he could see the scarlet midriff of the raphia palm fronds, rose the kana or island of higher ground. Again he paused. A hippopotamus squealed. Hollow, mysterious, the pulsing notes beat into his ears. The Shensi drums beat out their message, boom, boom, boomaroom, boom! From afar beyond the horizon followed silence. Then from the west, nearer, he heard the answer. Boom-a-ranga, boom, boom!

He could almost see the naked black men squatting beside the yellow tree trunks, beating their message. They might be laughing at him—at him—

"Another white man dead. Mjuba, we are glad. It served him right. The river gods were angry. They ate his canoes, his servants, all his belongings, in the rapids it had taken place. The crocodiles were many. Eya, they feasted on those swakilis. He is a great man, but the gods of the river they ate him. Ha! Ha! He was a great hunter—oh, yes, he was a great hunter. The linghas have said it. It was to shoot the white rhinoceros—he of the square lip. Yes, it was so. But he will shoot no more—and we are glad, eya, Mjuba."

The Terror had grown bolder. It lapped at Lloyd's feet, hungry. Suddenly he gasped. Beyond his vision he heard the notes of a launch engine. It would mean rescue. He forgot caution and began to run at a stumbling trot.

Once he all but fell on a crocodile. He *must* reach a vantage point where he could signal the launch. The wooded island in the swamp loomed. There was no mistaking, it was a launch, but the trees and thick bush hid all the sight of it. He waded waist-deep. So far as he could see, the ground was at least sixty acres in extent, and it was now surrounded by water. He had been just in time. He stumbled onto dry ground, but was forced to use his heavy kukri knife, as the jungle was thick. He shouted, wild with anxiety lest the launch should leave. He was about to fire the elephant gun when an explosion louder than a hundred rifles shook the air. Followed splashing sounds, then silence.

Panting and sweating, Lloyd cut his way toward the east side of the island. Here the main river ran close and it was from this direction he had heard the sound of the explosion.

The going was easier. He forgot thirst, fatigue, tortured body. Of the launch he could see nothing. An agony of doubt and fear assailed him. He cried out from beyond a clump of flowering acacias.

He heard a shriek. What in God's name might that mean? From behind massed yellow blossoms fled a white woman! A girl in battered pith helmet, her skirts clinging to her, torn and muddy.

"Hurry, oh, hurry, it's taking Uncle John!" In her hand she held an automatic. "I don't know how to fire it. Oh, God! Hurry!"

Lloyd said nothing, but rushed behind the screen of blossoms. There, littering a sandy beach, was strewn the remains of a steam launch. He arrived just in time to see an old man's face, bloody in death, vanish beneath the swirling saffron flood . . . for a moment above the swirl there was a serrated tail that lashed the water.

Despair seized Lloyd. Was it worthwhile fighting? What was the use? The girl joined him, sobbing. Lloyd snorted. What was a woman doing out here? No sensible *man* would venture into this country.

"Sit down," he said, clumsily patting the heavy shoulders, "here on this crate." Lloyd saw the river rising with terrible rapidity. It might be the sudden damming up things.

"Let's chin, this isn't so bad. Six feet of land yet before the flood gets up—then there are the trees. You need not worry, your uncle was dead before the crocodiles got his body."

Lloyd told her of his predicament, of his misfortunes. She was a weak, helpless little thing, but somehow she gave him courage. Her pale little face with the velvety, soft brown eyes held a poignant appeal. The drooping scarlet lips, the clenched little hands, the dented helmet all touched his manhood.

Watching him as he deliberately cut the jigger from his toe she spoke haltingly:

"I'm Myrtle Tabor, a missionary. We came in a launch from below Lado, on our way to Kota. Mr. Gleason was my uncle. We had to come in here for wood, fuel, you know. We hit something. The *Mercy*," nodding toward the launch, "began to sink. We were getting our things out, she was near shore. I was carrying some kerosene up there by the palm and then the boat blew up and the two Uganda boys—were gone. I pulled Uncle John up, he was all bloody, and ran for the bandages, then a crocodile poked its head out of the water and got his foot. I screamed."

"We must get ready for—anything," he replied. "We aren't the only refugees on this—er— I suppose it's an island now. First we must make a fire and boil some water. I'm dry as the 'Gobi.' Watch out for the flies with crossed wings; they look like small house flies. Don't let them bite you. Put gloves on if you've got them."

Lloyd gathered wood. Never had he seen so many insects. The woods were alive with scorpions and centipedes, driven there by the floods. Cicadas and great blue and red butterflies patched the wild datewood palm fronds; ants swarmed. Myrtle Tabor watched the man work and shuddered at the great gray scorpions.

Soon they had water to drink, and both ate, for Lloyd had insisted on this. The Terror was all about them now, eating away at the bank; a great mapoli tree like an English elm fell splashing mightily into the flood.

Carefully choosing the highest point on which grew a tall borassus palm, Lloyd cleared away the ground. A bloated puff adder lividly chevroned black and white struck from its lurking place beneath the fleshy-mottled aloe leaf. Around the palm bole Lloyd built a strong boma of thorn limbs. The fire was built in there; all the cases that might prove useful he carried here, the girl obeying him mechanically as he directed.

The girl sobbed and often shuddered. The afternoon wore on. Always the creeping Terror licked higher. Always the horror was nearer. Lloyd shuddered at the thought of the night they faced. Hour by hour the island grew smaller as the river rose, only the mop-headed tops of the papyrus rose above the water. Of the shore they could catch no glimpse. Only a swirling, polished saffron flood that lapped and whispered.

Back of them in the gloomy, moving bush there came sound of many living things, restless and afraid. About the island in gathering numbers floated dark objects patiently waiting for the gift of the creeping Terror. Back in the purple-mottled gloom the restless sounds were growing louder, more fearful. A dreadful menace was gathering; these dumb things felt it first. Ever increasing, the crocodiles swam about the doomed island. Slowly, inch by inch, the land was swallowed by the river.

The heat was less tormenting. The insects, however, grew more and more numerous. Life of all kinds was gathering, packed closer and closer by the Terror that crept. Now even the elephant-grass tops only showed here and there. A great sea slid by almost silently. As it touched the haze the sun grew scarlet. It lit the river in a deep, blood color, while the little waves were tinkling, dancing flames. Only ten acres remained above water. The girl moaned; he saw that she gazed at the redheaded, red-tailed lizards that moved restless, at the hordes of beetles and insects of all kinds that wove about on the ground. Above them the slate-gray bats hung feasting with twitching ears. The crocodiles had moved closer, circling.

Lloyd put more wood on the fire and prepared to climb the palm. There was plenty of rope; he thanked God for that fact. Tying his feet together and making a loop, he began to climb. Bracing himself, he hitched jerkily up the trunk. At the top he had to dislodge a horde of ants, who attacked him savagely, until he was able to drive them out with kerosene. Here amid the dark green, fan-shaped fronds would be safety if anywhere.

Never would he forget the girl's cry as he began to lift her by means of the rope to the palm top. She turned and saw the lions! There were three of them, all males. Even as he heaved and strained, he watched their nervously twitching tails, heard the angry snarls. Again and again she shrieked. Now she was up gasping and clinging to him; he tied her so she could not fall. He laced lianas amongst the fronds.

The lions had vanished and in spite of her pleadings he descended to the ground. In place of the lions he saw a monitor lizard and two warthogs grunting and snuffing. A darting mongoose ran hither and thither, barking, strangely excited. Then he saw snakes everywhere. Cobras for the most part, gliding restlessly about, twined in all the lower growth. Around the branch of a Euphorbia which was in the sunset light, he counted six big snakes; one of the largest was almost lemon yellow. Two slim, green mambas, three of the dreaded ringhals breed.

Article after article they pulled into the palm top. As the darkness crept on, the animal life more and more crowded, became articulate as the Terror seized and held them. The huge fig tree branches swayed and trembled with its many refugees. Now the island crawled with life. Once more he was in the palm top. Myrtle's hand sought his and held it. Below them the island slowly changed shape as the river rose. More and more numerous were the black oblong patches. They looked like floating coffins. A myriad of cliff swallows flitted about.

Lloyd endeavored to cheer the girl. "Like Noah's Ark or—or a menagerie, isn't it?" He was surprised at the high, cracked tone in which he spoke. The Terror that crept had now got him in its power. It was terrible to think of that slow, slow rise with those saurian guardians to drag one down, deep down into the mud. It had grown almost dark amongst the trees; so dark that many eyes glowed and winked out; eyes of all shapes and sizes, but all lit with the same Terror.

There was something very unnatural in seeing so many wild things crowded together. Amongst a grove of hyphaene palms Lloyd saw the restless swaying hulks of a herd of elephants; further away at the far end of the shrinking land, a ring of buffaloes pawing and snorting, their bossed horns clicking sharply as their heads met. Along the water line, moving restlessly and gazing toward the hidden hills, stood Kobs hartebeeste, bush buck, oribi and other antelope, and looming larger were a pair of giant elands.

On the top of the raphia palm nearest was perched two marabou storks, hideous heads tucked down into hunched-up shoulders. Over all other tones came an insistent, seething gnawing. A mimosa limb, which shook and trembled like a live thing with the ague, had lost its actual outlines.

Ants by the million were everywhere. Near them they saw a group of scorpions impotently jabbing and striking with their fanged tails, but the ants swarmed over them.

A big hairy spider met the same fate, that of being eaten alive!

Where the light still fell, the ground crawled with insects. Cane rats, hedgehogs and smaller things of all kinds ran hither and thither, covered by the biting plague. Once a hyena moaned. Jackals yapped and howled, furtive shapes snapped at the insects all over them. . . . The antelopes had begun milling. The buffaloes still stood in circular formation, heads and horns forming a barrier.

Now and then they bellowed, stamping to shake off the ants; their protests held a leathery, creaky note. The two in the palm tops gasped as they breathed; there was something frightful in this scene of destruction, something fascinating, too. Below them a warthog barked, screamed and ran amuck. They saw a mamba, its hood spread flat, sway before the warthog's muzzle and strike. They heard the squeals, almost articulate.

All about the crocodile had begun bellowing, long gong-like sounds that had a quality of brainless cruelty. They were triumphant; it was their hour; they would feed well. Above all in a spiraling funnel soared kites and vultures. Then with a spectacular suddenness it was dark. The two tied up in the borassus palm could see nothing, yet they knew the Terror crept up, eating at their safety. The clamor from below became louder, edged with ferocity and all but articulate with the Terror. Pungent, acrid scents permeated the air about them. The odor of crushed insects, the fragrance of mimosa and acacia, the mud and musky reek of crocodiles, civets, and servals all added to the mingled stench. From the trees about came the agonized chatter and squeak of monkeys; the barking of baboons; the occasional whistling trumpet of elephants; the snarling of cats, and filling in the clamor the crepitating, crawling insect horde . . . killing and being killed, but seeking safety.

The moon rose out of a bed of thin ghastly mist. . . . It was immense and crimson in color. All about them was water. Water that glimmered black with silver lacquer. Mist floated about them. From below through a pall of mist arose terrific sounds of combat. Here and there a treetop emerged into the brilliant light of the moon. Their refuge, thought Lloyd, must be awash. Sharp staccato shrieks. Bubbling, gurgling moans, loud splashes, told the end of many creatures. How much longer would their palm stand? Occasionally it shook at the impact of some animal's body. The clamor grew louder; sometimes there was individuality of note as when the lions roared, not low and satisfied as after a kill, but high, snarling, shrieking roars. Or when a leopard coughed and spat from the limb of the fig tree near them. Below them was lust . . .unthinkable slaughter. Once the girl went limp. Lloyd's face was mask-like. Fear gripped him, for he knew the Terror was creeping up!

Beyond them, monkeys danced and chattered; blood dripping from them. Ants were everywhere, hiding in the leaves. A python, lashing and twisting, crashed down, ants raining from its body. Cobras clung to the constrictor like ribbons. The reek of musk and mud grew stronger. Again the mist parted. On limbs of a gambach tree danced and hopped a group of lean baboons. Their white teeth gleamed as they grimaced. Below them in the water were crocodiles that snapped at them with an audible click. It was to avoid the gaping, saw-like jaws that the apes leaped in their dance of death.

Now the clamor had grown into a tortured babel, made up of squeals; the crack of breaking bones; bellowing, hissing, panting breaths; dull, thudding splashes; snapping, tearing limbs; grunting, coughing, roaring, shrieking and monotonously reiterated splashings. Lloyd shuddered and groped protectively for the girl.

Each splash meant another death. Again he caught sight of the scene below.

Almost all of the land was underwater. All the smaller living things had disappeared. Many antelopes were missing, the remainder fought in a frenzy of berserker rage, full to the last with their wish to survive. Always ready, always waiting lay the great lizards, fang-studded, jaws agape at the creeping Terror's edge, their rough bodies lapped by the silver-lacquered flood.

Still the river rose. Tight-packed and jammed the animals fought. Eyes that gleamed red in the moonlight; lolling scarlet tongues; horns wet with blood; teeth that gleamed from foam-flecked lips, drawn back. The herd of buffaloes slowly pushed their way forward as the water drove them back. Their blue-black, hairless hulks gleamed wet. A bull charged at a palm tree, catapulting its monkey refugee out into the water together with the reddish palm fruit. It was terrible to see them sink, for none rose. The elephants, too, had moved nearer to the great fig tree whose denizens, tortured to madness by the ants, were dropping off already half-eaten by the savage insatiable insects. Now the smell of blood rose sickeningly sweet. The mist had thinned. Through its gauzelike veil crocodile eyes ringed the doomed land. Crocodile tails flayed the rising river into yellow foam.

Only an oryx and three elands remained from all the antelopes. These were soon dragged into the flood in spite of their utmost resistance. The buffaloes stood knee-deep in water. Lloyd peered from between two fronds; below there was nothing of their boma left. Not once had he fired his gun. From the water a small shape crawled. Slowly it climbed, tediously and pausing often. The water was not more than forty feet below. The borassus palm vibrated now continually. Lloyd looked down again; the little thing was close, it raised a terrified little face. It was only a small black monkey!

"Save it, oh, the mite," the girl breathed. Lloyd had not seen that she had noticed.

He reached down and grasped the little furry thing. It made no attempt to bite. Myrtle Tabor took the baby simian with a gulping sob and held it close; it cuddled, trembling in the girl's arm.

A splash followed by a roar made Lloyd look down. A porcupine, bristly black and white, had tumbled out of the fig tree; pierced by his quills was a long black mamba. The porcupine had fallen on a lion's haunches. The big cat had been hunched on a fast crumbling anthill near to the fig tree. Rolling off the lion the porcupine spun bobbing in the current; all about it, like a shower of sawdust, floated ants. The lion, maddened by the long, sharp quills, leaped into the midst of the buffalo herd. Here he clawed and bit his way over the blue backs, his tawny body and black-manged head gored by heavy horns till it jetted blood.

The crocodiles, taking advantage of the fight, crawled in and took a heavy toll. The second lion ran amuck, then the third, at the same time joined by the leopard, who sprang clawing at a crocodile, ripping the saurian wide open. Still the reptile turned and crunched the leopard's head. The two sank beneath the water, bubbles and smothered screams arose as a fighting muddy mass reappeared to sink again.

Only the six elephants were left. These huge creatures moved restlessly about, stamping at the enemies who evidently did their best to attack them from beneath the water. With ears cocked out straight and small tails vertical, the little herd trumpeted again and again. Their trunks waved and curled with increasing menace; their wrinkled, gray bodies smeared with debris and blood. Two cows from the herd began butting and pushing the remaining three, as if by this deed they might protect themselves. One palm after another was uprooted in this way, all their unhappy occupants falling into five feet of water which now covered what had been the highest elevation.

Lloyd loaded and sighted his double-barrel crocodile rifle.

"I've got to shoot those two elephants or they will get us."

Myrtle looked at him with wide, almost unseeing eyes. . . . He took careful aim, shot and killed the first cow immediately; she sank to be tugged off by the water fiends.

Still the river rose, but now more slowly. Again the booming thunder of the rifle spoke. The recoil jerked his shoulder back. The cow fell at the smashing impact of the heavy bullet, got up again, bright, arterial blood welling out of the wound. She screamed a terrible note. Lloyd reloaded. He had eighteen cartridges left. . . . If the remaining four elephants charged their palm it meant certain death. Trumpeting shrilly, mouth open, the mortally wounded cow had fallen, recovering, got slowly and ponderously to her knees, fumbled with her trunk under water, grasped something, lifted it out of the water. A twelve-foot crocodile! She swung at the reptile— it clawed futilely at her trunk—Lloyd saw the crocodile's jaws open and close, heard the wet snapping click; saw the crocodile hurled into the fig tree; the shower of insects that fell like hail into the water; heard the cow splash as she slowly toppled; saw the crocodile fall, a broken-headed, lashing cripple, saw them both dragged under water, the four other elephants, one huge bull with curling tusks, charge the fig tree; saw them belly deep attack its branches, heard the branches snap and tear; saw the tree topple, for the river had undermined its roots; it swayed and began to fall. It made a mighty crash. . . .

The moon had nearly set. . . . Its glancing rays gilded the insect snow that followed the great tree as it bobbed and gyrated slowly down the river.

Now there were the three elephants. All about them floated in a ring, the crocodiles, their eyes growing green by the moon's last light. Lloyd waited with cocked rifle. The girl, with bent head low, talked in whispers to the little monkey that whimpered and clung with arms about her neck. Only three palms besides their own topped the current; all swayed alarmingly. The end must be near!

The elephants made no more hostile moves. They stood trumpeting shrilly and stamping at the unseen attackers as they swayed.

Now it was dark again. Centuries of awful suspense seemed to pass. Lloyd waited. Once there was a great splashing, gurgling scream and a terrific pounding thumping, a something that rained water on them as it hurtled over. Again, silence.

Lloyd thought the Terror no longer crept, the current slackened. Dawn broke gray over the ghastly, yellow flood, mist-shrouded. Only one palm was left standing besides their own, only one elephant; the great bull stood swaying and lashing a bloody trunk, now not belly-deep. Suddenly the sun appeared a blazing, scarlet, fiery flower. There were not so many crocodiles, yet the big bull elephant was being attacked. Lloyd admired the lone survivor. What courage! What strength! The elephant stood bathed in ruddy sunrise glory; his trunk felt about and probed where something pulled and tugged at the hind leg. With a jerk the bull grappled and tore his tormentor from the water. It was the largest crocodile that Lloyd had ever seen. The monster was over twenty feet in length, his belly was yellow and scabrous with moss. The creature's jaws were wide, its mouth looked white inside. The bull elephant lifted it, inspected it long, then— pushed it under the water.

With slow, deliberate hate it stabbed with its tusks again and again. Once more it lifted the saurian—its wounds were hideous—this time he lowered it, and putting his ponderous front foot down, pushed. He saw the elephant straining with its tusks. Even at that distance he could see its wild little eyes were lit with the killing hunger. Slowly, with a ripping, hideous note, the big lizard broke and tore. Its great jaws in their death agony had set and cut the big bull's trunk. The bull stood slowly swaying, then with a bubbling trumpet-note of mingled torture and triumph, he turned, trunk curled over his head, ears wide, back deluged by his own blood, and began to walk into the deep water. Over him flew a wailing escort of kites, beside him swam the crocodiles. Now only his back and head showed, soon only the head, finally alone the blood-spurting stump of the trunk rose above the crimson surface of the falling flood. Then it was gone. . . .

Slowly the water fell. Hours of agony passed. Thirst and heat sickened the two in the palm tree. It seemed to them the sun's rays were javelins of fire that quivered bolt-like from the burnished, brassy sky or danced, gauzelike, over the river. Lloyd grew delirious. Far off he distinguished something black that moved. "Delusions. More carnage," he muttered.

The girl stirred and moaned. . . .

For a moment his mind grew clearer. Long, long he looked. It was a launch! He fired his gun. The monkey trembled and the girl shrieked. Again and again until the eighteen cartridges were gone, he fired. From over the water the approaching launch engine puffed.

To Lloyd's fevered senses it was like the drums. He sprang up, gesticulating and shouting curses.

"My God! It's Garry Lloyd! He's raving!" said the D.C., "and if I ain't blind there's a woman and a monkey with him."

Later, as the journey upriver was resumed, the men listened in awed silence to Myrtle Tabor's story. Her face still wore the look of terror, yet her eyes were very tender as they fell on Lloyd who lay on a mat breathing hard. Sitting up suddenly and staring, he said in a hard, cracked voice: "A monkey . . . a girl . . . a man and a couple of palms . . . survival of the fittest. Island, trees, Noah's Ark . . . all gone . . . crocs and creeping terror got 'em. . . . It's Africa's way. . . ."

The Invalid's Story
Mark Twain

I seem sixty and married, but these effects are due to my condition and sufferings, for I am a bachelor, and only forty-one. It will be hard for you to believe that I, who am now but a shadow, was a hale, hearty man two short years ago, a man of iron, a very athlete!—yet such is the simple truth. But stranger still than this fact is the way in which I lost my health. I lost it through helping to take care of a box of guns on a two-hundred-mile railway journey one winter's night. It is the actual truth, and I will tell you about it.

I belong in Cleveland, Ohio. One winter's night, two years ago, I reached home just after dark, in a driving snow-storm, and the first thing I heard when I entered the house was that my dearest boyhood friend and schoolmate, John B. Hackett, had died the day before, and that his last utterance had been a desire that I would take his remains home to his poor old father and mother in Wisconsin. I was greatly shocked and grieved, but there was no time to waste in emotions; I must start at once. I took the card, marked "Deacon Levi Hackett, Bethlehem, Wisconsin," and hurried off through the whistling storm to the railway station. Arrived there I found the long white-pine box which had been described to me; I fastened the card to it with some tacks, saw it put safely aboard the express car, and then ran into the eating-room to provide myself with a sandwich and some cigars. When I returned, presently, there was my coffin-box back again, apparently, and a young fellow examining around it, with a card in his hands, and some tacks and a hammer! I was astonished and puzzled. He began to nail on his card, and I rushed out to the express car, in a good deal of a state of mind, to ask for an explanation. But no—there was my box, all right, in the express car; it hadn't been disturbed. [The fact is that without my suspecting it a prodigious mistake had been made. I was carrying off a box of guns which that young fellow had come to the station to ship to a rifle company in Peoria, Illinois, and he had got my corpse!] Just then the conductor sung out "All aboard," and I jumped into the express car and got a comfortable seat on a bale of buckets. The expressman was there, hard at work,—a plain man of fifty, with a simple, honest, good-natured face, and a breezy, practical heartiness in his general style. As the train moved off a stranger skipped into the car and set a package of peculiarly mature and capable Limburger cheese on one end of my coffin-box—I mean my box of guns. That is to say, I know now that it was Limburger cheese, but at that time I never had heard of the article in my life, and of course was wholly ignorant of its character. Well, we sped through the wild night, the bitter storm raged on, a cheerless misery stole over me, my heart went down, down, down! The old expressman made a brisk remark or two about the tempest and the arctic weather, slammed his sliding doors to, and bolted them, closed his window down tight, and then went bustling around, here and there and yonder, setting things to rights, and all the time contentedly humming "Sweet By and By," in a low tone, and flatting a good deal. Presently I began to detect a most evil and searching odor stealing about on the frozen air. This depressed my spirits still more, because of course I attributed it to my poor departed friend. There was something infinitely saddening about his calling himself to my remembrance in this dumb pathetic way, so it was hard to keep the tears back. Moreover, it distressed me on account of the old expressman, who, I was afraid, might notice it. However, he went humming tranquilly on, and gave no sign; and for this I was grateful. Grateful, yes, but still uneasy; and soon I began to feel more and more uneasy every minute, for every minute that went by that odor thickened up the more, and got to be more and more gamey and hard to stand. Presently, having got things arranged to his satisfaction, the expressman got some wood and made up a tremendous fire in his stove.

This distressed me more than I can tell, for I could not but feel that it was a mistake. I was sure that the effect would be deleterious upon my poor departed friend. Thompson—the expressman's name was Thompson, as I found out in the course of the night—now went poking around his car, stopping up whatever stray cracks he could find, remarking that it didn't make any difference what kind of a night it was outside, he calculated to make us comfortable, anyway. I said nothing, but I believed he was not choosing the right way. Meantime he was humming to himself just as before; and meantime, too, the stove was getting hotter and hotter, and the place closer and closer. I felt myself growing pale and qualmish, but grieved in silence and said nothing.

Soon I noticed that the "Sweet By and By" was gradually fading out; next it ceased altogether, and there was an ominous stillness. After a few moments Thompson said,

"Pfew! I reckon it ain't no cinnamon 't I've loaded up thish-yer stove with!"

He gasped once or twice, then moved toward the cof—gun-box, stood over that Limburger cheese part of a moment, then came back and sat down near me, looking a good deal impressed. After a contemplative pause, he said, indicating the box with a gesture,

"Friend of yourn?"

"Yes," I said with a sigh.

"He's pretty ripe, ain't he!"

Nothing further was said for perhaps a couple of minutes, each being busy with his own thoughts; then Thompson said, in a low, awed voice,

"Sometimes it's uncertain whether they're really gone or not,—seem gone, you know—body warm, joints limber—and so, although you think they're gone, you don't really know. I've had cases in my car. It's perfectly awful, becuz you don't know what minute they'll rise up and look at you!" Then, after a pause, and slightly lifting his elbow toward the box,—"But he ain't in no trance! No, sir, I go bail for him!"

We sat some time, in meditative silence, listening to the wind and the roar of the train; then Thompson said, with a good deal of feeling,

"Well-a-well, we've all got to go, they ain't no getting around it. Man that is born of woman is of few days and far between, as Scriptur' says. Yes, you look at it any way you want to, it's awful solemn and cur'us: they ain't nobody can get around it; all's got to go—just everybody, as you may say. One day you're hearty and strong"—here he scrambled to his feet and broke a pane and stretched his nose out at it a moment or two, then sat down again while I struggled up and thrust my nose out at the same place, and this we kept on doing every now and then—"and next day he's cut down like the grass, and the places which knowed him then knows him no more forever, as Scriptur' says. Yes'ndeedy, it's awful solemn and cur'us; but we've all got to go, one time or another; they ain't no getting around it."

There was another long pause; then,—

"What did he die of?"

I said I didn't know.

"How long has he been dead?"

It seemed judicious to enlarge the facts to fit the probabilities; so I said,

"Two or three days."

But it did no good; for Thompson received it with an injured look which plainly said, "Two or three years, you mean." Then he went right along, placidly ignoring my statement, and gave his views at considerable length upon the unwisdom of putting off burials too long. Then he lounged off toward the box, stood a moment, then came back on a sharp trot and visited the broken pane, observing,

"'Twould 'a' ben a dum sight better, all around, if they'd started him along last summer."

Thompson sat down and buried his face in his red silk handkerchief, and began to slowly sway and rock his body like one who is doing his best to endure the almost unendurable. By this time the fragrance—if you may call it fragrance—was just about suffocating, as near as you can come at it. Thompson's face was turning gray; I knew mine hadn't any color left in it. By and by

Thompson rested his forehead in his left hand, with his elbow on his knee, and sort of waved his red handkerchief towards the box with his other hand, and said,—

"I've carried a many a one of 'em,—some of 'em considerable overdue, too,—but, lordy, he just lays over 'em all!—and does it easy Cap., they was heliotrope to HIM!"

This recognition of my poor friend gratified me, in spite of the sad circumstances, because it had so much the sound of a compliment.

Pretty soon it was plain that something had got to be done. I suggested cigars. Thompson thought it was a good idea. He said,

"Likely it'll modify him some."

We puffed gingerly along for a while, and tried hard to imagine that things were improved. But it wasn't any use. Before very long, and without any consultation, both cigars were quietly dropped from our nerveless fingers at the same moment. Thompson said, with a sigh,

"No, Cap., it don't modify him worth a cent. Fact is, it makes him worse, becuz it appears to stir up his ambition. What do you reckon we better do, now?"

I was not able to suggest anything; indeed, I had to be swallowing and swallowing, all the time, and did not like to trust myself to speak. Thompson fell to maundering, in a desultory and low-spirited way, about the miserable experiences of this night; and he got to referring to my poor friend by various titles,—sometimes military ones, sometimes civil ones; and I noticed that as fast as my poor friend's effectiveness grew, Thompson promoted him accordingly,—gave him a bigger title. Finally he said,

"I've got an idea. Suppos'n we buckle down to it and give the Colonel a bit of a shove towards t'other end of the car?—about ten foot, say. He wouldn't have so much influence, then, don't you reckon?"

I said it was a good scheme. So we took in a good fresh breath at the broken pane, calculating to hold it till we got through; then we went there and bent over that deadly cheese and took a grip on the box. Thompson nodded "All ready," and then we threw ourselves forward with all our might; but Thompson slipped, and slumped down with his nose on the cheese, and his breath got loose. He gagged and gasped, and floundered up and made a break for the door, pawing the air and saying hoarsely, "Don't hender me!—gimme the road! I'm a-dying; gimme the road!" Out on the cold platform I sat down and held his head a while, and he revived. Presently he said,

"Do you reckon we started the Gen'rul any?"

I said no; we hadn't budged him.

"Well, then, that idea's up the flume. We got to think up something else. He's suited wher' he is, I reckon; and if that's the way he feels about it, and has made up his mind that he don't wish to be disturbed, you bet he's a-going to have his own way in the business. Yes, better leave him right wher' he is, long as he wants it so; becuz he holds all the trumps, don't you know, and so it stands to reason that the man that lays out to alter his plans for him is going to get left."

But we couldn't stay out there in that mad storm; we should have frozen to death. So we went in again and shut the door, and began to suffer once more and take turns at the break in the window. By and by, as we were starting away from a station where we had stopped a moment, Thompson pranced in cheerily and exclaimed,

"We're all right, now! I reckon we've got the Commodore this time. I judge I've got the stuff here that'll take the tuck out of him."

It was carbolic acid. He had a carboy of it. He sprinkled it all around everywhere; in fact he drenched everything with it, rifle-box, cheese and all. Then we sat down, feeling pretty hopeful. But it wasn't for long. You see the two perfumes began to mix, and then—well, pretty soon we made a break for the door; and out there Thompson swabbed his face with his bandanna and said in a kind of disheartened way,

"It ain't no use. We can't buck agin him. He just utilizes everything we put up to modify him with, and gives it his own flavor and plays it back on us. Why, Cap., don't you know, it's as much as a hundred times worse in there now than it was when he first got a-going. I never did see one of 'em warm up to his work so, and take such a dumnation interest in it. No, Sir, I never did, as long as I've been on the road; and I've carried a many a one of 'em, as I was telling you."

We went in again after we were frozen pretty stiff; but my, we couldn't stay in, now. So we just waltzed back and forth, freezing, and thawing, and stifling, by turns. In about an hour we stopped at another station; and as we left it Thompson came in with a bag, and said,—

"Cap., I'm a-going to chance him once more,—just this once; and if we don't fetch him this time, the thing for us to do, is to just throw up the sponge and withdraw from the canvass. That's the way I put it up." He had brought a lot of chicken feathers, and dried apples, and leaf tobacco, and rags, and old shoes, and sulphur, and asafoetida, and one thing or another; and he, piled them on a breadth of sheet iron in the middle of the floor, and set fire to them.

When they got well started, I couldn't see, myself, how even the corpse could stand it. All that went before was just simply poetry to that smell,—but mind you, the original smell stood up out of it just as sublime as ever,—fact is, these other smells just seemed to give it a better hold; and my, how rich it was! I didn't make these reflections there—there wasn't time—made them on the platform. And breaking for the platform, Thompson got suffocated and fell; and before I got him dragged out, which I did by the collar, I was mighty near gone myself. When we revived, Thompson said dejectedly,—

"We got to stay out here, Cap. We got to do it. They ain't no other way. The Governor wants to travel alone, and he's fixed so he can outvote us."

And presently he added,

"And don't you know, we're pisoned. It's our last trip, you can make up your mind to it. Typhoid fever is what's going to come of this. I feel it acoming right now. Yes, sir, we're elected, just as sure as you're born."

We were taken from the platform an hour later, frozen and insensible, at the next station, and I went straight off into a virulent fever, and never knew anything again for three weeks. I found out, then, that I had spent that awful night with a harmless box of rifles and a lot of innocent cheese; but the news was too late to save me; imagination had done its work, and my health was permanently shattered; neither Bermuda nor any other land can ever bring it back tome. This is my last trip; I am on my way home to die.

The Ransom Of Red Chief
O. Henry

It looked like a good thing: but wait till I tell you. We were down South, In Alabama—Bill Driscoll and myself—when this kidnapping idea struck us. It was, as Bill afterward expressed it, "during a moment of temporary mental apparition"; but we didn't find that out till later.

There was a town down there, as flat as a flannel-cake, and called Summit, of course. It contained inhabitants of as undeleterious a self-satisfied a class of peasantry as ever clustered around a Maypole.

Bill and me had a joint capital of about six hundred dollars, and we needed just two thousand dollars more to pull off a fraudulent town-lot scheme in Western Illinois with. We talked it over on the front steps of the hotel. Philoprogenitiveness, says we, is strong in semi-rural communities; therefore, and for other reasons, a kidnapping project ought to do better there than in the radius of newspapers that send reporters out in plain clothes to stir up talk about such things. We knew that Summit couldn't get after us with anything stronger than constables and, maybe, some lackadaisical blood-hounds and a diatribe or two in the Weekly Farmers' Budget. So, it looked good.

We selected for our victim the only child of a prominent citizen named Ebenezer Dorset. The father was respectable and tight, a mortgage fancier and a stern, upright collection-plate passer and forecloser. The kid was a boy of ten, with bas-relief freckles, and hair the color of the cover of the magazine you buy at the news-stand when you want to catch a train. Bill and me figured that Ebenezer would melt down for a ransom of two thousand dollars to a cent. But wait till I tell you.

About two miles from Summit was a little mountain, covered with a dense cedar brake. On the rear elevation of this mountain was a cave. There we stored provisions.

One evening after sundown, we drove in a buggy past old Dorset's house. The kid was in the street, throwing rocks at a kitten on the opposite fence.

"Hey, little boy!" says Bill, "would you like to have a bag of candy and a nice ride?"

The boy catches Bill neatly in the eye with a piece of brick.

"That will cost the old man an extra five hundred dollars," says Bill, climbing over the wheel.

That boy put up a fight like a welter-weight cinnamon bear; but, at last, we got him down in the bottom of the buggy and drove away. We took him up to the cave, and I hitched the horse in the cedar brake. After dark I drove the buggy to the little village, three miles away, where we had hired it, and walked back to the mountain.

Bill was pasting court-plaster over the scratches and bruises on his features. There was a fire burning behind the big rock at the entrance of the cave, and the boy was watching a pot of boiling coffee, with two buzzard tail-feathers stuck in his red hair. He points a stick at me when I come up, and says:

"Ha! cursed paleface, do you dare to enter the camp of Red Chief, the terror of the plains?"

"He's all right now," says Bill, rolling up his trousers and examining some bruises on his shins. "We're playing Indian. We're making Buffalo Bill's show look like magic-lantern views of Palestine in the town hall. I'm Old Hank, the Trapper, Red Chief's captive, and I'm to be scalped at daybreak. By Geronimo! That kid can kick hard."

Yes, sir, that boy seemed to be having the time of his life. The fun of camping out in a cave had made him forget that he was a captive himself. He immediately christened me Snake-eye, the Spy, and announced that, when his braves returned from the warpath, I was to be broiled at the stake at the rising of the sun.

Then we had supper; and he filled his mouth full of bacon and bread and gravy, and began to talk. He made a during-dinner speech something like this:

"I like this fine. I never camped out before; but I had a pet 'possum once, and I was nine last birthday. I hate to go to school. Rats ate up sixteen of Jimmy Talbot's aunt's speckled hen's eggs. Are there any real Indians in these woods? I want some more gravy. Does the trees moving make the wind blow? We had five puppies. What makes your nose so red, Hank? My father has lots of money. Are the stars hot? I whipped Ed Walker twice, Saturday. I don't like girls. You dassent catch toads unless with a string. Do oxen make any noise? Why are oranges round? Have you got beds to sleep on in this cave? Amos Murray has got six toes. A parrot can talk, but a monkey or a fish can't. How many does it take to make twelve?"

Every few minutes he would remember that he was a pesky redskin, and pick up his stick rifle and tiptoe to the mouth of the cave to rubber for the scouts of the hated paleface. Now and then he would let out a war-whoop that made Old Hank the Trapper, shiver. That boy had Bill terrorized from the start.

"Red Chief," says I to the kid, "would you like to go home?"

"Aw, what for?" says he. "I don't have any fun at home. I hate to go to school. I like to camp out. You won't take me back home again, Snake-eye, will you?"

"Not right away," says I. "We'll stay here in the cave a while."

"All right!" says he. "That'll be fine. I never had such fun in all my life."

We went to bed about eleven o'clock. We spread down some wide blankets and quilts and put Red Chief between us. We weren't afraid he'd run away. He kept us awake for three hours, jumping up and reaching for his rifle and screeching: "Hist! pard," in mine and Bill's ears, as the fancied crackle of a twig or the rustle of a leaf revealed to his young imagination the stealthy approach of the outlaw band. At last, I fell into a troubled sleep, and dreamed that I had been kidnapped and chained to a tree by a ferocious pirate with red hair.

Just at daybreak, I was awakened by a series of awful screams from Bill. They weren't yells, or howls, or shouts, or whoops, or yawps, such as you'd expect from a manly set of vocal organs—they were simply indecent, terrifying, humiliating screams, such as women emit when they see ghosts or caterpillars. It's an awful thing to hear a strong, desperate, fat man scream incontinently in a cave at daybreak.

I jumped up to see what the matter was. Red Chief was sitting on Bill's chest, with one hand twined in Bill's hair. In the other he had the sharp case-knife we used for slicing bacon; and he was industriously and realistically trying to take Bill's scalp, according to the sentence that had been pronounced upon him the evening before.

I got the knife away from the kid and made him lie down again. But, from that moment, Bill's spirit was broken. He laid down on his side of the bed, but he never closed an eye again in sleep as long as that boy was with us. I dozed off for a while, but along toward sun-up I remembered that Red Chief had said I was to be burned at the stake at the rising of the sun. I wasn't nervous or afraid; but I sat up and lit my pipe and leaned against a rock.

"What you getting up so soon for, Sam?" asked Bill.

"Me?" says I. "Oh, I got a kind of a pain in my shoulder. I thought sitting up would rest it."

"You're a liar!" says Bill. "You're afraid. You was to be burned at sunrise, and you was afraid he'd do it. And he would, too, if he could find a match. Ain't it awful, Sam? Do you think anybody will pay out money to get a little imp like that back home?"

"Sure," said I. "A rowdy kid like that is just the kind that parents dote on. Now, you and the Chief get up and cook breakfast, while I go up on the top of this mountain and reconnoiter."

I went up on the peak of the little mountain and ran my eye over the contiguous vicinity. Over toward Summit I expected to see the sturdy yeomanry of the village armed with scythes and pitchforks beating the country-side for the dastardly kidnappers. But what I saw was a peaceful landscape dotted with one man ploughing with a dun mule. Nobody was dragging the creek; no couriers dashed hither and yon, bringing tidings of no news to the distracted parents.

There was a sylvan attitude of somnolent sleepiness pervading that section of the external outward surface of Alabama that lay exposed to my view. "Perhaps," says I to myself, "it has not yet been discovered that the wolves have borne away the tender lambkin from the fold. Heaven help the wolves!" says I, and I went down the mountain to breakfast.

When I got to the cave I found Bill backed up against the side of it, breathing hard, and the boy threatening to smash him with a rock half as big as a cocoanut.

"He put a red-hot boiled potato down my back," explained Bill, "and then mashed it with his foot; and I boxed his ears. Have you got a gun about you, Sam?"

I took the rock away from the boy and kind of patched up the argument. "I'll fix you," says the kid to Bill. "No man ever yet struck the Red Chief but what he got paid for it. You better beware!"

After breakfast the kid takes a piece of leather with strings wrapped around it out of his pocket and goes outside the cave unwinding it.

"What's he up to now?" says Bill, anxiously. "You don't think he'll run away, do you, Sam?"

"No fear of it," says I. "He don't seem to be much of a home body. But we've got to fix up some plan about the ransom. There don't seem to be much excitement around Summit on account of his disappearance; but maybe they haven't realized yet that he's gone. His folks may think he's spending the night with Aunt Jane or one of the neighbors. Anyhow, he'll be missed to-day. To-night we must get a message to his father demanding the two thousand dollars for his return."

Just then we heard a kind of war-whoop, such as David might have emitted when he knocked out the champion Goliath. It was a sling that Red Chief had pulled out of his pocket, and he was whirling it around his head.

I dodged, and heard a heavy thud and a kind of a sigh from Bill, like a horse gives out when you take his saddle off. A head rock the size of an egg had caught Bill just behind his left ear. He loosened himself all over and fell in the fire across the frying pan of hot water for washing the dishes. I dragged him out and poured cold water on his head for half an hour.

By and by, Bill sits up and feels behind his ear and says: "Sam, do you know who my favorite Biblical character is?"

"Take it easy," says I. "You'll come to your senses presently."

"King Herod," says he. "You won't go away and leave me here alone, will you, Sam?"

I went out and caught that boy and shook him until his freckles rattled.

"If you don't behave," says I, "I'll take you straight home. Now, are you going to be good, or not?"

"I was only funning," says he sullenly. "I didn't mean to hurt Old Hank. But what did he hit me for? I'll behave, Snake-eye, if you won't send me home, and if you'll let me play the Black Scout to- day."

"I don't know the game," says I. "That's for you and Mr. Bill to decide. He's your playmate for the day. I'm going away for a while, on business. Now, you come in and make friends with him and say you are sorry for hurting him, or home you go, at once."

I made him and Bill shake hands, and then I took Bill aside and told him I was going to Poplar Cove, a little village three miles from the cave, and find out what I could about how the kidnapping had been regarded in Summit. Also, I thought it best to send a peremptory letter to old man Dorset that day, demanding the ransom and dictating how it should be paid.

"You know, Sam," says Bill, "I've stood by you without batting an eye in earthquakes, fire, and flood—in poker games, dynamite outrages, police raids, train robberies, and cyclones. I never lost my nerve yet till we kidnapped that two-legged skyrocket of a kid. He's got me going. You won't leave me long with him, will you, Sam?"

"I'll be back some time this afternoon," says I. "You must keep the boy amused and quiet till I return. And now we'll write the letter to old Dorset."

Bill and I got paper and pencil and worked on the letter while Red Chief, with a blanket wrapped around him, strutted up and down, guarding the mouth of the cave. Bill begged me tearfully to make the ransom fifteen hundred dollars instead of two thousand. "I ain't attempting," says he, "to decry the celebrated moral aspect of parental affection, but we're dealing with humans, and it ain't human for anybody to give up two thousand dollars for that forty-pound chunk of freckled wildcat. I'm willing to take a chance at fifteen hundred dollars. You can charge the difference up to me."

So, to relieve Bill, I acceded, and we collaborated a letter that ran this way:

"Ebenezer Dorset, Esq.:

"We have your boy concealed in a place far from Summit. It is useless for you or the most skillful detectives to attempt to find him. Absolutely, the only terms on which you can have him restored to you are these: We demand fifteen hundred dollars in large bills for his return; the money to be left at midnight to-night at the same spot and in the same box as your reply—as hereinafter described. If you agree to these terms, send your answer in writing by a solitary messenger to-night at half-past eight o'clock. After crossing Owl Creek, on the road to Poplar

Cove, there are three large trees about a hundred yards apart, close to the fence of the wheat field on the right-hand side. At the bottom of the fence-post, opposite the third tree, will be found a small paste-board box.

"The messenger will place the answer in this box and return immediately to Summit.

"If you attempt any treachery or fail to comply with our demand as stated, you will never see your boy again.

"If you pay the money as demanded, he will be returned to you safe and well within three hours. These terms are final, and if you do not accede to them no further communication will be attempted.

"TWO DESPERATE MEN"

I addressed this letter to Dorset, and put it in my pocket. As I was about to start, the kid comes up to me and says:

"Aw, Snake-eye, you said I could play the Black Scout while you was gone."

"Play it, of course," says I. "Mr. Bill will play with you. What kind of a game is it?"

"I'm the Black Scout," says Red Chief, "and I have to ride to the stockade to warn the settlers that the Indians are coming. I'm tired of playing Indian myself. I want to be the Black Scout."

"All right," says I. "It sounds harmless to me. I guess Mr. Bill will help you foil the pesky savages."

"What am I to do?" asks Bill, looking at the kid suspiciously.

"You are the hoss," says Black Scout. "Get down on your hands and knees. How can I ride to the stockade without a hoss?"

"You'd better keep him interested," said I, "till we get the scheme going. Loosen up."

Bill gets down on his all fours, and a look comes in his eye like a rabbit's when you catch it in a trap.

"How far is it to the stockade, kid?" he asks, in a husky manner of voice.

"Ninety miles," says the Black Scout. "And you have to hump yourself to get there on time. Whoa, now!"

The Black Scout jumps on Bill's back and digs his heels in his side.

"For Heaven's sake," says Bill, "hurry back, Sam, as soon as you can. I wish we hadn't made the ransom more than a thousand. Say, you quit kicking me or I'll get up and warm you good."

I walked over to Poplar Cove and sat around the post-office and store, talking with the chaw bacons that came in to trade. One whiskerando says that he hears Summit is all upset on account of Elder Ebenezer Dorset's boy having been lost or stolen. That was all I wanted to know. I bought some smoking tobacco, referred casually to the price of black-eyed peas, posted my letter surreptitiously, and came away. The postmaster said the mail- carrier would come by in an hour to take the mail on to Summit.

When I got back to the cave Bill and the boy were not to be found. I explored the vicinity of the cave, and risked a yodel or two, but there was no response.

So I lighted my pipe and sat down on a mossy bank to await developments.

In about half an hour I heard the bushes rustle, and Bill wobbled out into the little glade in front of the cave. Behind him was the kid, stepping softly like a scout, with a broad grin on his face. Bill stopped, took off his hat, and wiped his face with a red handkerchief. The kid stopped about eight feet behind him.

"Sam," says Bill, "I suppose you'll think I'm a renegade, but I couldn't help it. I'm a grown person with masculine proclivities and habits of self-defense, but there is a time when all systems of egotism and predominance fail. The boy is gone. I have sent him home. All is off. There was martyrs in old times," goes on Bill, "that suffered death rather than give up the particular graft they enjoyed. None of 'em ever was subjugated to such supernatural tortures as I have been. I tried to be faithful to our articles of depredation; but there came a limit."

"What's the trouble, Bill?" I asks him.

"I was rode," says Bill, "the ninety miles to the stockade, not barring an inch. Then, when the settlers was rescued, I was given oats. Sand ain't a palatable substitute. And then, for an hour I had to try to explain to him why there was nothin' in holes, how a road can run both ways, and what makes the grass green. I tell you, Sam, a human can only stand so much. I takes him by the neck of his clothes and drags him down the mountain. On the way he kicks my legs black-and-blue from the knees down; and I've got to have two or three bites on my thumb and hand cauterized.

"But he's gone"—continues Bill—"gone home. I showed him the road to Summit and kicked him about eight feet nearer there at one kick. I'm sorry we lose the ransom; but it was either that or Bill Driscoll to the madhouse."

Bill is puffing and blowing, but there is a look of ineffable peace and growing content on his rose-pink features.

"Bill," says I, "there isn't any heart disease in your family, is there?"

"No," says Bill, "nothing chronic except malaria and accidents. Why?"

"Then you might turn around," says I, "and have a look behind you."

Bill turns and sees the boy, and loses his complexion and sits down plump on the ground and begins to pluck aimlessly at grass and little sticks. For an hour I was afraid for his mind. And then I told him that my scheme was to put the whole job through immediately and that we would get the ransom and be off with it by midnight if old Dorset fell in with our proposition. So Bill braced up enough to give the kid a weak sort of a smile and a promise to play the Russian in a Japanese war with him as soon as he felt a little better.

I had a scheme for collecting that ransom without danger of being caught by counterplots that ought to commend itself to professional kidnappers. The tree under which the answer was to be left—and the money later on—was close to the road fence with big, bare fields on all sides. If a gang of constables should be watching for anyone to come for the note, they could see him a long way off crossing the fields or in the road. But no, sire! At half-past eight I was up in that tree as well hidden as a tree toad, waiting for the messenger to arrive.

Exactly on time, a half-grown boy rides up the road on a bicycle, locates the pasteboard box at the foot of the fence-post, slips a folded piece of paper into it, and pedals away again back toward Summit.

I waited an hour and then concluded the thing was square. I slid down the tree, got the note, slipped along the fence till I struck the woods, and was back at the cave in another half an hour. I opened the note, got near the lantern, and read it to Bill. It was written with a pen in a crabbed hand, and the sum and substance of it was this:

"Two Desperate Men.

"Gentlemen: I received your letter to-day by post, in regard to the ransom you ask for the return of my son. I think you are a little high in your demands, and I hereby make you a counter-proposition, which I am inclined to believe you will accept. You bring Johnny home and pay me two hundred and fifty dollars in cash, and I agree to take him off your hands. You had better come at night, for the neighbors believe he is lost, and I couldn't be responsible for what they would do to anybody they saw bringing him back. Very respectfully, "EBENEZER DORSET."

"Great pirates of Penzance!" says I; "of all the impudent——"

But I glanced at Bill, and hesitated. He had the most appealing look in his eyes I ever saw on the face of a dumb or a talking brute.

"Sam," says he, "what's two hundred and fifty dollars, after all? We've got the money. One more night of this kid will send me to a bed in Bedlam. Besides being a thorough gentleman, I think Mr. Dorset is a spendthrift for making us such a liberal offer. You ain't going to let the chance go, are you?"

"Tell you the truth, Bill," says I, "this little he ewe lamb has somewhat got on my nerves too. We'll take him home, pay the ransom, and make our get-away."

We took him home that night. We got him to go by telling him that his father had bought a silver-mounted rifle and a pair of moccasins for him, and we were going to hunt bears the next day.

It was just twelve o 'clock when we knocked at Ebenezer's front door. Just at the moment when I should have been abstracting the fifteen hundred dollars from the box under the tree, according to the original proposition, Bill was counting out two hundred and fifty dollars into Dorset's hand.

When the kid found out we were going to leave him at home he started up a howl like a calliope and fastened himself as tight as a leech to Bill's leg. His father peeled him away gradually, like a porous plaster.

"How long can you hold him?" asks Bill.

"I'm not as strong as I used to be," says old Dorset, "but I think I can promise you ten minutes."

"Enough," says Bill. "In ten minutes I shall cross the Central, Southern, and Middle Western States, and be legging it trippingly for the Canadian border."

And, as dark as it was, and as fat as Bill was, and as good a runner as I am, he was a good mile and a half out of Summit before I could catch up with him.

Crutch Brigade
Raley Brien

Short, fat and forty, Hal Menner, football coach at Southland U, was a martinet to the squad. But to his daughter, Mary, who kept house for him, he was a soft gob of putty that could be molded as she desired.

But Mary Menner was having a tough time molding the putty this evening as her father relaxed after devouring a dinner over which she had purposely taken an unusual amount of time and trouble. For once, a good dinner had not softened the putty.

Nor had her pouts, her coaxing voice, her "verge of tears" attitude, which generally worked because it made her look so like her dead mother. Mary Menner was having a tough time of it.

"You're just stubborn, Dad," she said, as she flopped into an easy chair within a few feet of the one in which her father was sprawled.

"It's not enough that I have professional troubles," Hal Menner complained. "Only one football game this year, by arrangement because of the war. And that with Riggstown College, Southland's hated rival. Played at a little town halfway between the two schools, where the field will be full of bumps and maybe rocks. Not even fit dressing rooms."

"But, Dad—" Mary broke in.

"And that's not enough!" he continued, as if she had not spoken. "What have I got in the way of a team? Boys we wouldn't have used to carry the water a couple of years ago. The halt and the lame, not to mention the blind. Studious lads with theories about football—"

"Which brings us around to Burt Jenks again," she said quickly.

Menner still ignored her. "No, that's not enough! I wish they'd take me into the Army, where it's all quiet and peaceful. A place like Bataan or Tunisia would be a rest cure compared to this. Even in my home, my own daughter—" He ran out of breath and words at the same time.

Mary nodded her pretty head. "If you'd only listen—" she began.

"And this Riggstown team—ha! They have a few real scrubs the Army or Navy didn't take. Scrubs they may have been last year, but compared to the boys I've got, they're candidates for the All-American. They'll mow us down. It'll be the first time in years. They'll smother us with scores. They'll—"

"Maybe they won't, if you'll listen to Burt," his daughter managed to get in.

"I've listened to Burt Jenks. I think he's insane. If you're in love with the lad and want to marry him, you have my blessing. I'm not the one to interfere with love's young dream. It's none of my business. And I don't want anybody interfering in my business. What's sauce for the gander is applesauce for the goose."

"Burt Jenks is all right," Mary cried.

"Sure he is. He'll make a mark for himself in his chosen profession—which isn't football. He'll be a good provider. As a son-in-law, I'll probably like him. But when he comes around with some wild scheme to win the Riggstown game—he's nuts."

"I don't think it's so wild."

"Now, listen!" Menner begged. "As a daughter, you're a darling. No man ever had a better. But as one to judge what is and isn't the thing in football, you're—you're—I can't think of the word."

"I can, and it's not polite," Mary told him. "I asked Burt to drop in this evening, and he's about due. I want you to be nice to him."

"So I can't have a moment of peace, even in my own home," Menner complained. "What a life!"

"If you'll listen to Burt, you'll win that Riggstown game."

"To win that game, I'd listen to anybody. But listening to Burt Jenks won't win it. He's—"

The doorbell rang. Mary jumped up smiling.

"That's probably Burt. Now, you behave."

It was Burt Jenks, all right. He came into the living room of the coach's cottage a moment later. He was a tall, thin, serious-appearing young man who wore spectacles, and of whom his professors expected great things. He and Mary Menner had been engaged for two years. They intended to be married next June, when Burt Jenks was to be given an assistant professorship and a salary.

Coach Menner groaned a little and shifted himself in his chair. Burt Jenks sat down in front of him and opened up.

"I know our team is much weaker than Riggstown's," he said. "So the answer is—wear down the Riggstown team so it is weaker than ours."

"That's a wonderful idea," Menner replied, with some sarcasm. "Would you give them sleeping powders or slow poison?"

"They have been making fun of us," Burt Jenks said. "They call us the 'Crutch Brigade.' So—let's be that."

"Huh?" Menner gulped.

"I have it all worked out. It's two weeks until the game. I have selected from four to six men for each position on the team. It is my intention to train these men so they can be sent in as substitutes. Imagine! A fresh man in almost every position in almost every play!"

"Imagine," Coach Menner echoed.

"The best man I have is Lee Snoddy, and he'll be general field captain."

"And I wouldn't even let him put on a uniform," Menner muttered.

Burt Jenks bent forward earnestly.

"All I ask is that you let us use the old practice field, give us old suits and gear, and take us to the game and put us on the sidelines. Every man is eligible. If the worse comes to the worst, let me send in my men."

"And that'll be worse than the worst," the coach declared. "But, what have I to lose? Bring your men around in the morning, and we'll find some old clothes for 'em. Kick holes in the practice field all you please. Now, take Mary out somewhere and buy her a soda, and let me have a moment's peace."

After they had gone, Coach Menner considered the prospects. Because of the war and the shortage of athletes, not to mention the difficulty of traveling to games, both Southland U and Riggstown College had arranged to play but the one usual game, and take on no other opponents during the season. The schools were about forty miles apart. It was arranged to play the game on the high school gridiron at Portland, a small town about half way between Southland U and Riggstown. Students and others interested would get to Portland in any way possible.

That game was no joke to Menner. He wanted to win it as much as if it had been the usual contest at the end of a full season, and with all his stars in the lineup. He did not like the idea of being defeated by Riggstown under any circumstances.

He began considering what Burt Jenks had told him, and decided there might be something in it. The field officials probably would drop with apoplexy, but what of it? Rules were rules, and if Jenks' boys were eligible they could play. And so long as the rules for substitutes were not broken, the plan could be worked.

So Coach Menner wandered down to the practice field late the following afternoon, after sending his own team of misfits to the showers, and watched Burt Jenks' bunch. They were short and tall, thin and fat. They panted and wheezed when they ran, or rather stumbled, through the formations. Burt Jenks and Lee Snoddy, one of his close friends, were working with the boys in relays.

Jenks had Menner's plays and signals, the signals to be changed before the game, naturally. The players ran through the plays in groups, and then the groups were mixed up, and they started in again. It bewildered Menner, but it didn't seem to bother the boys.

He called Lee Snoddy to him, and told him the details of a few plays Burt Jenks did not know.

"It's great to have you come here and watch us, sir," Snoddy said. "It'll make the fellows feel important. They'll get the idea that they really are a part of the team, and that's good psychology."

"A team of psychologists and scientists," Menner groaned. "Well, keep on working, Snoddy. I'll drop around and watch whenever I can. Don't let any of the boys overtax their strength and drop with heart failure. I don't want the prexy to have me on the carpet and be accusing me of inhuman treatment."

During the following two weeks, Menner worked with his own squad, and went to the old practice field and watched Burt Jenks' outfit whenever he got the chance.

Jenks' gang did not seem to improve any. They knew the plays, but that was about all that could be said. Running through half a dozen formations with no opponents exhausted them. Menner refused to think what would happen if they had another team tearing at them.

Two evenings before the game, Menner ate the especially fine dinner Mary had prepared, and then relaxed in his usual chair.

He could hear Mary singing as she did the dishes. When she finally came into the living room and sat down, Menner frowned at, her.

"Let's have it," he said.

Mary Menner's eyes opened wide. "Have what, Dad?"

"None of that, now. Whenever you cook me an extra fine dinner, with something I like especially, I know you're going to ask for something. The answer probably is 'no' this time, but let's get it over with."

"This time you got that good dinner just because you let Burt do as he wished," she replied.

"I'll admit he's been slaving with that gang," her father said.

"That gang may win the Riggstown game for you."

"It'll take a miracle to do that," Menner declared, gloomily. "Day after tomorrow is the slaughter. About the only even half-man I have on the team is Jim Harlan."

"Oh, him!" Mary said.

"What's the matter with Jim Harlan?"

"He knows Burt and I are engaged, but he won't give up."

"Tenacity makes a good football player," Menner replied, grinning.

"His tenacity won't do him any good when it comes to me. I haven't anything special against Jim Harlan. He's nice enough. But—there's Burt."

"I wish love problems were all I had to worry me," Menner told her, sighing.

An auto horn "honked" in front of the cottage, and Mary sprang to her feet and rushed out. She recognized the sound of the horn of Burt Jenks' dilapidated car as well as she did his voice.

Menner sighed and relaxed again. It was good to be young and in love. He could remember when he had been himself. But just now he was wondering if that new shift play he had been trying to teach the squad would gain yardage or result in such confusion that the enemy would have an advantage.

He kept on wondering about it until high, angry voices disturbed him. Menner sat up straight in his chair. He heard Mary screech, and then heard a sound he knew well—the thud of fists.

Hal Menner jumped to his feet, got through the little front hall in record time, and darted out upon the front porch. His daughter was standing at the top of the steps imploring somebody to stop. Down on the lawn, two young gentlemen were battling in the moonlight, their only weapons being those they had been born with.

Menner almost grinned. They were swinging wild, but now and then connected. It was a rather burlesque battle to him, but he realized it was serious enough for the two fighters. He brushed Mary aside and went down the steps, grabbed the combatants and separated them.

"What's all this?" the coach demanded.

One of the combatants was, as he had expected to find, Burt Jenks. The other was Jim Harlan, captain of the team.

"This—this madman," Jim Harlan said, "should be in custody."

"I'll put you in the hospital!" Bert Jenks squeaked.

"Take it easy, and tell me what started this," Menner said. "I don't like to have prize fights in my front yard by moonlight this late in the season. You talk first, Harlan. And you keep quiet, Mary."

Jim Harlan brushed a hand across a bloody face and gulped to get his breath. He, too, was the studious type. His only pretension to being a football player was that Menner had kept him on the second squad a couple of years.

Harlan looked at the coach in an embarrassed way and coughed.

"I simply came here and asked Mary if she would ride to Portland to the game with me in my' car," Jim Harlan said. "I have a good car, as you know, and she would be comfortable. My sister and her fiancé are going with me, also, so everything would be all right. I always observe the conventions."

"Admirable of you," Menner said. "Go on."

"Before she could answer, this—this maniac who calls himself Burt Jenks, attacked me."

"He knows Mary and I are engaged, but he still pesters around her," Jenks put in.

"I've heard you say that you're engaged, but to the best of my knowledge you're not married to her yet," Jim Harlan observed. "There is always the chance that she may discover your true character in time, and turn against you. Then I'll be at her elbow, so she can realize my true worth—"

"Why, you poor—!" Jenks started for him.

Menner shook them both.

"Listen to me," he said. "I don't like men fighting over my daughter. Mary will ride to the game with me. And you'll both keep away from her until after the game. Is that understood?"

"Mary was going to ride with me," Jenks said.

"You'll never make the twenty miles to Portland in that heap of junk you drive," Jim Harlan said.

"That's enough!" Menner roared. "Get out of here, both of you! Harlan, you drive north, and Jenks will drive south. And don't let me hear of you mixing before the game. Psychologists and scientists, huh?"

He watched them drive away, then went back to the porch to find Mary sitting on the steps weeping.

"I didn't know that scientific sweetheart of yours was such a slugger," Menner said. "Regular brute! Harlan surprised me some, too. They almost hit each other a couple of times. Why don't you give both of 'em the brushoff and get a fine, upstanding man like your father was at their age?"

"Oh, him!" Mary sniffed.

A close check by Menner disclosed that Harlan and Jenks did not engage in fisticuffs again, or even high words. They merely glared at each other in passing. Menner gave the team its last workout, and went to the old practice field to watch Jenks and Lee Snoddy put the 'Crutch Brigade' through their paces.

The players were earnest enough, Menner admitted to himself. They ran the signals smoothly, too. But they had never clashed with opponents. He began wishing he had given them some real practice.

"How do they look?" he asked Lee Snoddy.

"They can go through any of the plays backwards, sir."

"That's what I'm afraid of," Menner admitted.

"From four to six men for every position. Turn the game over to Burt, if you're in a tough spot in the last half, and these boys will do wonders."

"There's no doubt but what they'd make football history," Menner said. "Well, we'll see. Get 'em to Portland somehow, and let 'em take along those old football togs."

The trip to Portland, from Southland U end, looked like the flight of refugees from a war-threatened village. They went in almost every sort of conveyance. Cars whose owners had or could dig up gasoline enough for the round trip, were filled to overflowing. Bicycles were put in use, the riders getting an early start. Even some horse-drawn vehicles were in the parade.

And from Riggstown, in the other direction, came a similar parade to meet in the village of Portland for the annual big game.

This was quite the biggest event in Portland's history, and her citizens had hung up bunting and flags and dressed in holiday attire. The field was a poor one, but it had been marked properly by men from Southland U and Riggstown. There were a couple of rickety grandstands. A private house at the corner of the field had been taken over for dressing rooms. The players could get showers at the town's one small hotel after the game, if they were willing to wait long enough to take turns.

There weren't benches enough, for an ordinary team. So Burt Jenks' men—almost fifty of them—sat on the ground, huddled together. They wore old, torn uniforms and had battered headgear, and the most of the blankets which draped their shoulders were thin or full of holes.

"Crutch Brigade," the Riggstown rooters chanted. "Crutch Brigade." Burt Jenks was walking slowly up and down before his squad, talking to them in low tones.

"Heads up, men. If we get a chance, we'll show 'em. They won't be laughing at you then!"

Southland won the toss, and decided to receive. The Riggstown kick went almost to a corner, and the Southland man who got the ball was nailed on the twenty-yard line. Coach Menner groaned. He had hoped to have the team look good for a few minutes, anyhow.

A moment later, he was on his feet, while the Southland rooters cheered. In some queer and unorthodox manner, Southland had executed a pass, and Jim Harlan had raced down the field for a gain of twenty yards.

Then, the Riggstown team dug in.

Three tries which resulted in a loss of four yards forced Jim Harlan to kick. The kick was a bad one, and the Riggstown player brought the ball back so that the kick netted less than fifteen yards.

Southland battled with a will, but the Riggstown team battered them back yard by yard, making two first downs. The ball was planted in the danger territory. Riggstown tried an end run, and scored as the first quarter ended. They failed to get the extra point.

Good fortune rather than good playing helped Southland in the second quarter. The half ended with Riggstown six points ahead.

It was a torn and battered and dispirited Southland team that huddled together at the end of the field between the halves. Menner tried to cheer them up, but failed. He scorned them. Even that did not bring the fighting spirit to them.

"If you don't snap out of this gloom, so help me, I'll send in the Crutch Brigade," Menner threatened.

Jim Harlan, his face aflame, sprang to his feet.

"Don't do that," he said. "We'll fight. We'll do our best."

"You'll have to do a lot better than your best, if you win this game," Menner said.

Southland kicked to open the second half. Jim Harlan managed to get away a fair kick, and the team charged and nailed the Riggstown ball carrier on Riggstown's forty-yard line.

Then, Riggstown began marching up the field. There were no spectacular gains, but they retained the ball and kept on marching. They were on their way to another touchdown, and Menner knew it.

He glanced to where the Crutch Brigade sat huddled, with Burt Jenks marching back and forth in front of them, talking in low tones.

Menner beckoned Lee Snoddy.

"What's the scheme, if I turn this game over to Jenks?" Menner asked.

"He'll make the substitutions as fast as needed, sir. You'll have to sign the slips for the referee, of course. Maybe you'd better sign a bunch of 'em ahead, sir, because Jenks will work fast."

"I'll get 'em ready," Menner promised, "but I'm not saying yet that I'll use you men. Where do you come in, if I do?"

"I'll be sent in at tackle and stay there as long as I can and brace up the others as they come in."

"Harlan is captain of the team, you know. He'll be giving the orders."

"Oh, that's all right, sir." Howls from the rooters made Menner look up quickly. Riggstown had executed an end run, and the ball was on Southland's twelve-yard line.

"Now, sir?" Lee Snoddy asked hopefully.

Before Menner could reply, Riggstown executed another quick play, in eagerness to put over a touchdown before the Southland team could recover composure. A Riggstown player fumbled, and a Southland linesman got the ball.

"Not yet," Menner said to Snoddy. "Go back to Jenks, and watch to see if I call him."

"Yes, sir." Snoddy hurried away.

But all the cheers from the Southland rooters could not drive the team to victory. They tried a trick play which netted them nothing. They made a yard off tackle. They made another through center, and had to kick out of danger.

Jim Harlan kicked well again, but his teammates were slow getting down the field, and they met the returning ball carrier almost half way. Riggstown began marching up the field again. The third quarter ended with the ball in Riggstown's possession on Southland's forty-yard line.

Menner realized the situation. Riggstown was six points to the good. The team had only to play for time to win, and probably would be cautious. Whereas, Southland had to get a touchdown to and convert for the extra point to win.

Menner beckoned, and Lee Snoddy touched Burt Jenks on the arm and whispered to him. Jenks hurried to the coach.

"Take over, Burt," Menner said. "Send in your Crutch Brigade. Here's a bunch of signed blanks for the referee."

Jenks grabbed the blanks and ran back to his squad. He barked orders, and the men sprang to their feet and tossed aside their frayed blankets. Then began the queerest football game of history.

Jenks sent in four substitutes, and, they reported and went to their positions. Jim Harlan flashed an angry glance toward the bench but Coach Menner was looking the other way. The next Riggstown play was broken up. Jenks sent in three more new men, replacing three of the first four he had sent in.

The wholesale substitution rattled the Riggstown team more than the playing ability of the new men. Southland held again, and the Riggstown captain decided to kick, then hold Southland until the final whistle. Southland had been held at will so far.

Riggstown kicked, and a Southland player was down with the ball on Southland's own thirty-yard line. Burt Jenks sent in four more new players, using the blanks Menner had signed.

A chorus of howls from the stands and a roar of rage from the field made Menner snap erect. One of the four men coming out, with the referee urging him on, was Jim Harlan.

That meant he was out for the rest of the game. Burt Jenks had worked his little trick.

Harlan charged straight at the bench and confronted the coach. "What's the idea of yanking me?" he howled.

"The Crutch Brigade has taken over, Jim," Menner said.

"Even so, why yank me? I'm about the only man who's been doing anything out there. I'm fit to finish the game."

"You did well, Jim. But we have to score to win—"

"I know that Crutch Brigade stuff. I'm still asking why you yanked me."

"I didn't have anything to do with it. Jenks is running the rest of the game with his Crutch Brigade. He's doing all the yanking."

"Oh, he is?"

Howls of glee from the Southland rooters made both of them look at the field. Southland had broken through, and the ball rested on Riggstown's thirty-yard line.

Jenks sent in four more substitutes to replace the men who had been good for not more than two plays. The angry and bewildered referee could do nothing but stop the game until the substitutions were made. Everything was legal and in order.

Southland lined up, and signals were called. It was a run around right end this time. Menner thought he never had seen such a ragged affair. The interference tripped over its own feet. It split and left the runner wide open for attack. But he got through the hole and made his dash, and came down to the enemy's twenty-yard line.

"So Jenks took me out, did he?" Jim Harlan was saying. I'll—"
Menner gripped his arm. "You stay right here and do nothing. We've got a chance to score. Bother Jenks now, and I'll bust you myself—so help me! And I still swing a mean right."

Jenks sent in four more substitutes.
Lee Snoddy tried a line buck and made only one yard. That would never do, with time almost up. So, Jenks sent in four more substitutes. These had orders for Lee Snoddy, who was not

acting as captain. After the first play, which was off tackle and good for only a yard, they reported Jenks' orders to Snoddy in the huddle. Everything still official.

Coming from the huddle, Southland lined up, and the quarter began chanting signals. The desperate Riggstown players prepared to charge. They did not know what to expect.

Neither did Coach Menner. He watched the movements of the men closely. The formation told him they were going to try to pass. He groaned. As he groaned, the play was made. Lee Snoddy faded back, and the fresh substitutes covered him effectually. Snoddy waited until the last possible moment, and hurled the ball. It went straight into the hands of an eligible receiver.

The man turned, ran, dodged. Riggstown had been caught flat-footed. The Southland substitute sprawled over the goal line, and the score was tied.

Above the din could be heard the chant: "Crutch Brigade! . . . Crutch Brigade!" But it was a chant given by the Southland rooters this time.

"Well, we tied 'em," Menner said. "It's too much to hope for the extra point. But this being the day of miracles—"

The teams were in position. A substitute held the ball, and Lee Snoddy kicked. It sailed between the goal posts.

"We've won!" Menner howled. "There's not enough time for another kickoff. Seven to six! That Crutch Brigade idea—"

Coach Menner turned to where Jim Harlan had been standing, to find Harlan gone. He was rushing madly toward Burt Jenks.

"Here, you—!" Menner howled, starting after him.

But he was too late. As he dashed on he saw Jim Harlan stop in front of Burt Jenks. He got close enough to hear.

"Jenks, you skunk. Pulling me out—"

"Snoddy was trained to handle my boys," Jenks cut in, "and I knew you'd interfere—"

Jim Harlan swung. And Coach Menner scarcely could believe his own eyes when he saw Burt Jenks sink his left in Jim Harlan's stomach and double him up, and then straighten him up and down him with a right to the chin. And then Jenks calmly dusted his hands and prepared to send in more substitutes. But the gun cracked to end the game.

Some three hours later, after the men had dressed and everybody had eaten dinner wherever they could find anything in town to eat, Mary Menner faced her father.

"I'm riding home with Burt in his heap of junk," she said, defiantly. "There's a nice moon."

99

"So there is," Menner agreed smiling. "Well, I'll pick up somebody to ride with me. I'll come along behind. If that heap of junk breaks down, I'll give you a lift."

"If it breaks down, Burt probably will be able to fix it," she said.

"Oh, I don't doubt that," Coach Menner confessed. "I don't doubt it for a minute. Seems to me he can do almost anything."

Fumblefist Plays The Game
Johnston Mcculley

The coach's whistle sounded, and the pile unscrambled. As he walked to his position at right end, Hal Lorney had no false ideas about his presence there. He knew well that he was playing on the Denville College first team not because of his exceptional playing ability, but because of the manpower shortage.

Hal Lorney had spent three seasons with the scrubs and second team, being used as a sort of punching bag by the regulars, and had been glad to take the punches if it helped the team get into condition. But, until now, he always had been overlooked when the coach, "Big Ed" Bannis, listed the players for a major game. This had irked Hal considerably, for he had an ambition to play in at least one big game before he quit the Denville campus forever.

He often wondered what made him fall just a little short of qualifying for the first team. He had plenty of weight and speed. He didn't flinch at a collision or slow down before going into a furious scrimmage. He obeyed orders and never had to be disciplined.

But, when an emergency came, he was slow in thought. Sometime before he had been nicknamed "Fumblefist" by some thoughtless friends. The name had stuck to him like a cockle burr to the hide of a burro. A man with a nickname like that was like a baseball player with two strikes against him and a bat broken in the middle when he stepped up to the plate.

Hal Lorney would have been wearing Uncle Sam's Army uniform now instead of football togs except that, when he had been called up for induction, the fussy Army doctors had discovered a little something wrong with him. But a minor operation had corrected the physical fault and he'd been listed as 1-A again. Inside a couple of weeks he was due to report for an examination. He knew he would pass this time.

At least one of his ambitions would be realized before he was inducted into the Army—he would play as a regular in the Denville squad out this afternoon for a last gridiron struggle with Upstate University.

It would be Hal's last chance to distinguish himself on the football field, for this was his senior year at college. When Uncle Sam was finished with him, he would have no time for football.

He would accept the engineering job he had been offered, which would be held open for him until his return, and start his career in the post-war world. Also there would be the little matter of getting married and settling down to a normal and useful life.

It was the last practice before the big game. The Upstate squad had arrived the evening before, acting like a bunch that felt sorry for their opponents. They had used the Denville field for practice that morning. Big Ed Bannis had called the Denville squad out this afternoon for a last warm-up and to have the men run through some new signals.

Hal Lorney crouched now in his position at right end. He turned his head slightly to grin at Joe Piper, the right half-back and Denville's star player. When it came to Joe Piper, Hal indulged in a mild form of hero worship.

Joe Piper was almost a genius at coordinating thought and action. His mind seemed to work like a streak of lightning. His muscles were like steel springs which responded instantly to the orders of his mind. Joe Piper would start for an Army training camp in a few days, too.

The team captain signaled for a play around right end. The second team, composed of players almost as good as the regulars, knew what was coming. But Hal Lorney took out the opposing end without any trouble and cleared a path, and Joe Piper raced around outside him and headed for the distant goal line.

"That was playing it, Hal," Piper yelled as he slowed down to turn back. Hal glowed at the praise. He was wondering again just what fault kept him an ordinary player instead of him being a brilliant flash like Joe Piper.

Given a thing to do, Hal did it properly and methodically, working like a human machine. He had weight and power. When a signal was called, he could be depended on to do what was expected of him.

But the unexpected always seemed to a catch him asleep or astound him into inaction. Confronted with an emergency, he paused to think out a course of action. By the time he had it thought out, it was too late to act.

He had been given the nickname "Fumblefist" because it seemed he never could catch and hold a ball, either from a kick or a pass. He generally juggled it, and while he juggled three or four of the opposing team would fall upon him.

"Hit the showers, boys," Coach Big Ed Bannis was shouting at the squad now.

The players left the field and raced through the stadium runway and into the dressing rooms, shouting and laughing. The men began getting out of their playing clothes. Hal dropped on a bench and grunted as he bent over to unlace his shoes. Joe Piper sank down on the bench beside him. .

"Hal, my lad, something whispers to me that much will be demanded of us tomorrow," Piper told him. "You know how unbalanced the team is. You know the regular right end is in a

Navy uniform and that you're in his place, and that Edwards is laid up, and the old backfield is all shot."

"Yeah," Hal muttered.

Edwards was the regular left half, almost as good on the playing fields as Joe Piper. He and Piper usually divided the ball carrying and kicking, and presented a double threat to the enemy. But Edwards was in the hospital now, waiting for a surgeon to remove his appendix, and a second string man was playing his position.

"We'll probably have the biggest share of the work to do tomorrow at our end when the team's on the offensive," Piper continued. "That's all right with me, as long as I can stand up under it. And you'll be there helping."

"You betcha!" Hal said.

"I never have to worry about you getting signals mixed. You know what to do when you get a signal, Hal, and you time your moves perfectly. But, if the least thing unusual happens, you go haywire."

"I know," Hal said, miserably. "Why?"

"Maybe I've got the answer, Hal. I've been watching you work. Say a kick comes your way. You don't concentrate on getting the ball and tucking it away and starting off. As the ball comes at you, your glance shifts around too much. You try to watch the ball and maybe half a dozen men who're charging you at the same time. You forget you've got team-mates who'll give you all the protection they can while you make the catch."

Hal nodded. "That may be it," he admitted.

"Maybe you're thinking of the crowd, too, and that's always a bad thing. You realize that everybody is watching you, and it makes you nervous. You may have a touch of fear that you'll make a bad play, and worry about what the crowd will think of it if you do. Forget the crowd."

"Yeah," Hal said.

"Think of the ball and nothing else until you have it safe. Grab it and start away, or down it as the case may be. But always grip it, and never let it go. You got your nickname from fumbling, remember."

"I'll do the best I can tomorrow, Joe," Hal said.

"You'll be all right. Play hard, and try to get mad. You never do. I don't mean hot, flaring mad, the kind that makes a man see red and blinds him. I mean cold, fighting mad, the kind that makes a man determined to wipe out all obstacles. This is a big game. But don't let that bother you. It's only another game. Think of it that way."

103

"I heard that Lou Stoman will be in the Upstate lineup," Hal hinted.

"That's right. He came with the squad. Upstate will have their star men," Piper answered. "He goes up for induction in the Navy, but won't have to go to boot camp for a week or so yet, so he can play."

"Since some of the sports writers mentioned him as a possibility for the All-American, he thinks he's the only man in football," Hal said.

"Let him think it, if it gives him fun. He's good, all right, and a triple threat man," Joe Piper admitted. "I give him credit for that. But he's not so good personally. His middle name should be Arrogance. I'd like to tie a few knots in him."

"I don't like the way he sounds off about you sometimes," Hal declared.

"Let Lou Stoman sound off, if he feels like it," Piper said, as they started for the showers. "I can stand it. He's always sounding off about something. Most of his team-mates don't like him, either. But the Navy will take all that out of him soon enough."

They went to the showers. When they finally came out and dressed, they found Big Ed waiting to say a few words to the squad.

"Take it easy until game time tomorrow, boys," the coach ordered. "We'll have a little skull practice before the game."

As they strolled out of the dressing room, Joe Piper linked arms with Hal and walked beside him.

"Hal, we'll both be in the real Big Game in a few days," the star halfback said. "Wish we could go through it side by side, but probably we'll be far apart. Just a little tip, Hal - don't ever play 'fumblefist' with a hand grenade, and never juggle one. I understand they're bad stuff if juggled too long."

Hal Lorney grinned and Joe Piper laughed as they stopped on a street corner.

"I suppose you're going to the Soda Bar now to see Lucy Marks," Piper said. "Lucky lad! Lucy's a fine girl. Going to get married before you go to camp?"

"I haven't asked her yet to marry me," Hal confessed.

"What? Everybody on the campus thinks you two have been engaged for a year or more. You never look at another girl, and Lucy never dates another man."

"Just never got around to asking her."

"You'd better get around to it, my lad, if that's what is in your mind. Don't play 'fumblefist' with your happiness. Things like that should be settled. Get her promise. Tie her down. Make her sign on the dotted line."

Joe Piper slapped him on the back and turned toward one of the frat houses. Hal went along the street toward the Soda Bar, where he knew Lucy would be working at this hour.

The Soda Bar was a favorite hangout of undergraduates. It supplied the student body with soft drinks, sandwiches, candy and magazines. Lucy Marks' father owned it, and he and Lucy operated it. Both "Pop" Marks and Lucy were great favorites.

Hal Lorney's romance with Lucy had been a natural thing. They had become friends and the friendship had ripened into something stronger. No actual words had been spoken regarding love and marriage, but Hal felt they had an understanding. He intended to marry Lucy when he knew how everything stood. He had decided against rushing into marriage before being inducted.

The Soda Bar was crowded when Hal reached it, and some of the Upstate players were there with a scattering of their supporters. Upstate was only a short distance from Denville, and the two groups of students knew each other fairly well. Tomorrow's game being the last of the season, training would be broken, and a dance was to be given in the Denville gymnasium in honor of the teams.

When Hal walked into the Soda Bar, several friends called to him. Lucy was busy at the soda fountain. And Lou Stoman, the Upstate arrogant star, was sitting on a stool at the end of the fountain trying to focus the attention of everybody on himself.

"It'll be a ragged, one-sided game," Lou Stoman was saying, speaking with the air of an expert. "Both teams have been wrecked by Selective Service, but Upstate has a little the best of it. I'm glad I have a chance to play this last game before going into the Navy."

"Makes it a little tough on the admirals," a Denville student called. "But they can stop the war and hold everything until you get there."

"Funny man!" Stoman commented. "It's my' idea that Upstate will win tomorrow by at least three touchdowns. I don't look for Denville to score at all. Sorry, but that's how it is."

"Oh, we've still got Joe Piper," somebody shouted.

"Piper? Oh, yes! He's a pretty good half, but not strong enough to carry the team. Edwards is laid up, and Piper has a second string end working with him."

"I'm the second string end," Hal said, thrusting his way through a group. "Maybe Upstate won't have it as easy as you think."

"Well, if it isn't old Fumblefist in person!" Stoman howled. "Understand you're slated for the Army, Fumblefist. That's a tough one for the generals."

"I'll manage to get along," Hal said. "So you don't think much of Joe Piper, huh?"

"Oh, I didn't say that," Stoman protested. "Piper's a good player. A little slow and cumbersome at times, but fair enough."

"Slow?" Hal roared. "He can run circles "around you. He can out dodge you. He thinks twice as fast as you. He can out punt you."

"Whoa!" Stoman begged. "If he's that good, maybe Upstate better pack up and go home. No sense in wearing the boys out trying to play."

Stoman laughed, winked at some of those nearest him, and pretended to be glancing at a magazine. Hal felt his temples throbbing. If he didn't get away from there, he was liable to take a smash at Lou Stoman, and that would ruin everything. It might be said he picked a fight deliberately in an attempt to injure Upstate's star player. Big Ed, who did not stand for brawling, would bench him if he had to play the game with ten men.

His face purple with wrath, Hal turned away deliberately and walked down the room toward the end of the fountain. Lucy gave him a swift glance. She had overheard everything as she kept busy mixing sodas and making malts. Her glance seemed to rebuke him for his outburst at Stoman.

The coeds were talking about the football dance. Bets on the game were being made quietly, for Pop Marks did not like wagering in his establishment. Students surged in and out, but the crowd was thinning as time for the evening meal approached.

Hal decided to wait a few minutes, thinking he might have a word with Lucy, and that possibly one of the team members would drop in and he could go to the training table with him for supper. He straddled a stool down toward the end of the fountain, glanced at a magazine he had picked off the rack.

The Upstate band went marching past, on its way to the campus to serenade the old president of Denville. Almost all those in the Soda Bar hurried out to the walk. It grew suddenly quiet in the place. Hal heard Stoman talking, and glanced up from the magazine to find him in conversation with Lucy, who was busily washing glasses at the end of the fountain.

"How about it, Beautiful?" Stoman was saying. "Going to the dance with me? Good neighbor policy, and all that. Binding Upstate and Denville closer together."

Lucy laughed. "Oh, I don't know," she said. "I may be busy here."

"If you can't leave early, I'll call for you whenever you say," Stoman replied.

Lucy hesitated a moment, glanced at Hal swiftly once.

"All right, Mr. Stoman," she said. "I'll be ready at nine."

"Call me Lou, Beautiful. Nine it is. Going to the game tomorrow?"

"Of course. We close for the game," Lucy said.

"Keep your eye on me, Beautiful. That puff of smoke you'll notice sweeping down the field with the rapidity of a streak of light—that'll be me."

"Fancy yourself, don't you?" Lucy asked.

"Mere statement of fact," Stoman assured her. "I'll be here for you at nine."

Stoman swung off his stool and hurried out to the street to join some of his pals. Hal got down and walked slowly along the counter and tossed a quarter down. He showed Lucy the magazine, indicating the quarter was in payment.

"So you're going to the football dance with Lou Stoman?" Hal asked.

"He asked me, Hal, and I said I'd go with him."

"I thought you'd go with me."

"You never asked me," she reminded him.

"Maybe not, but I thought you'd understand."

"Can it be that you take me too much for granted, Hal?" she asked. "A girl thinks a lot of little attentions sometimes."

"Well, gosh, I thought you knew. So you're going with him? Is he the best you can pick? That swelled-up windbag?"

"Hal! Are you jealous?"

"Of Lou Stoman?" Hal said. "Any girl who prefers him to me can have him. Hope you have a fine time."

He stalked out of the Soda Bar, thrust his way through the crowd on the walk, and started toward where the evening meal was waiting.

He was boiling mad!

He was still mad the following afternoon as he dressed for the game. But not boiling mad. His rage was the cold and determined variety Joe Piper had mentioned.

Big Ed Bannis was walking around talking, as he always did when the men dressed for a game, giving bits of advice and making last suggestions. When the entire squad was dressed, Big Ed called them to attention.

"In this game, anything may happen," Big Ed told them. "The breaks will decide the game, so watch for the breaks. Don't let Stoman get away and down the field. I know he isn't liked personally, but he's a smooth player. Piper!"

"Yes, sir?" Joe asked.

"You're in the pink. A lot depends on you today, with Edwards laid up. The team's behind you. Keep trying every minute you're in there."

"Yes, sir!"

"Out you go, now. Give me a win."

The team cheered the coach, who stood aside with the trainer and team doctor, then the trot out upon the field began. Joe Piper was at Hal Lorney's side.

"Don't be nervous, lad," Piper said, as cheers greeted the team's appearance. "It's just another game. We'll do our best. Watch for tricks."

Intensity was written in Hal's face. But it wasn't caused by nervousness.

It was the result of a determination to upset Lou Stoman somehow before the game was done.

Upstate kicked off. Stoman did the kicking and got away a fine punt. The breeze caught and swerved it, and the ball came down straight at Hal.

"Lorney, take it," the field captain shouted.

Hal set himself for the catch, hoping and praying that he would not fumble this one. His team mates were running to get into position, and Upstate players were charging at him.

"Fumblefist," the Upstate rooters began howling, to bother him. "Fumblefist!"

Hal tried to think of nothing but the ball. The wind swerved it slightly again, and Hal almost missed it. He did not take it easily. It struck his breast and bounced, but he got his hands on it again. But, before he could take more than one stride, he was nailed in his tracks.

"The wind fooled me," Hal muttered, as he got into the huddle.

"Think nothing of it," the team captain said. "They'll be watching for Piper to carry the ball, so we won't let him take it. Left half off tackle. Let's go, gents."

They trotted to the lineup, and Hal and Piper put on a great show of expecting to make the play. Lou Stoman started toward them when the ball was snapped. The left half made a couple of yards, and Stoman looked disgusted.

Denville tried a smash through guard and got another yard. Then, Piper got the ball for an end run. With Hal guarding and the others of the interference coming along, Piper ran almost straight across the field. It was impossible to cut in. Every point was guarded by the strung-out Upstate players. Piper swerved down the field a few feet from the sideline, and made a first down. The Denville side of the stadium rocked with cheers.

A trick play at left end carried the ball to the middle of the field with no gain. Joe Piper carried the ball again in a playoff tackle, and Stoman came through to nail him. The play netted only a yard. The substitute left half got another try. In his eagerness, he fumbled, and an Upstate player recovered. Upstate had the ball on Denville's forty-yard line.

Upstate took charge of the game like a bunch of boys out for a wild holiday. Stoman passed, and Upstate made a first down. A second pass sent them to Denville's twenty-yard line. A trick play sent Stoman over for a touchdown, with the first quarter only half gone. The Denville rooters groaned. But they had one bit of good fortune. The tricky wind carried the kick wide of the goal posts, and the score remained at six points. Denville chose to receive again.

Upstate's next kickoff was run back better, the ball carrier being down in Upstate territory. Piper made a first down after a long end run. A pass failed. And then ill fortune seemed to descend upon Denville. Every move was blocked. They had to kick. The kick was bad, and Upstate ran it back into Denville territory.

The second quarter opened with the ball in Upstate's hands on Denville's forty-yard line. Lou Stoman faked a pass and got away for a broken field run. Twisting, dodging, reversing the field, the Upstate star went over the goal line again for the second Upstate touchdown.

Upstate's rooters screeched their approval. Denville's were glum. But again the wind carried Stoman's try for goal wide of the mark. But the first half ended with Upstate having twelve points.

In the dressing room, the Denville players had little to say. But Big Ed Bannis said plenty.

"So they've got twelve points," he roared. "So maybe you think this isn't Denville's day. It always gives the crowd a thrill to win a game in the last half, and especially in the last quarter. Two touchdowns will tie them. Get a goal kick on just one of 'em, and you win."

Big Ed stood with arms akimbo and looked them over. They avoided his glance.

"You'll kick off," he said. "Put the ball down in the coffin corner, Piper. The wind will be with you. Then, tear into 'em. Run wild. Watch for the breaks. Try everything. With both teams shattered, smooth team work isn't possible for either. Take a good look at those Upstate guys. Maybe they're brown and slant-eyed, huh? Maybe they're Japs. You think so for the time being, anyhow, and go after 'em accordingly. Let's go!"

Piper kicked to the coffin corner, and Upstate was held on its twenty-yard line. Stoman passed, but the pass' was not completed. A line charge netted Upstate only a yard. Stoman tried an end run, and Hal smashed him to earth.

"Well, if it isn't Fumblefist," Stoman said, as they got up. "Overplaying yourself today, huh? I'll tell your girl about it when I'm dancing with her tonight."

A completed pass sent Upstate fifteen yards down the field, and an offside penalty on the next play set her back five. The Denville team was smashing at everything now, fighting the attempt of Upstate to start a march down the field. Upstate's center made a bad pass, there was a fumble, and Denville recovered the ball.

They were about in the middle of the field.

Joe Piper called for a pass. He spotted an eligible receiver far down the field at the last moment, and arched a speedy pass into the man's hands. The Upstate safety man charged and tackled, and failed, and Denville had a touchdown.

That made everybody feel better. With the wind in the right direction now, and quiet for a moment, Piper kicked the goal for the extra point.

"Another touchdown, and we've got 'em," Hal said.

"Providing they don't score again," Piper reminded him.

After the touchdown, the third quarter ended. The wind would not be in Denville's favor now. And Denville had to make the kickoff and put the ball into Upstate's hands.

The kick wasn't so good. As the two teams lined up, Hal saw that Lou Stoman was furious. He had been hoping to keep Denville scoreless and roll up a big score for Upstate himself. Stoman was playing for headlines today, and it began to look like he wouldn't get them.

The ball was snapped, and Stoman faded back to pass. Hal charged past the opposing end and went at him. Stoman had to get the pass away in a hurry, and it was incomplete.

"I'm seeing too much of you, Fumblefist," Stoman growled.

"Trying to scare somebody?" Hal growled in reply.

They battled until the middle of the last quarter, with Upstate managing to retain the ball, but with Stoman unable to get away for a broken field run. Many of his passes were going wrong, too. And Lou Stoman was growing ugly. Upstate was penalized for offside play, and once Stoman was warned against unnecessary roughness.

"We've got to get the ball," Joe Piper said to Hal. "They're on our thirty-five yard line. It's a long way home. They'll start playing for time, and that'll ruin everything."

"Stoman's too eager to make another touchdown," Hal said.

Upstate came out of the huddle with a snap. Signals were called. The pass was delayed slightly. There was some sort of trick reverse, but both Hal and Joe Piper saw that Stoman got the ball eventually and was going to try a sneak end run into the open and then a break down the field or a lateral.

Two more Denville players caught the play, too. The four charged at Stoman, smashed his interference and got to him. Piper made the tackle, then came the pile-up.

The referee's whistle shrilled and Hal lurched to his feet. The others got up, all except Joe Piper. He was twisting and writhing with pain. The whistle sounded again, and the doctor was motioned to the field.

Hal knelt beside Piper as the doctor came trotting with his little black bag.

"What happened, Joe?" Hal asked.

"Somebody—used a knee on me."

Hal got up as the doctor knelt quickly beside Piper. Hal saw Lou Stoman standing a few feet away, his eyes glinting.

"Tough for Denville," he heard Stoman say. "But anybody's liable to get hurt now and then. We had the game on ice, anyhow."

Hal looked straight at him, and Stoman sneered and turned away. Hal felt sure Stoman had hurt Piper deliberately, that he had been trying to do it for some time. Icy rage came to him. The little affair about Lucy and the dance had been enough. But now, since Stoman had deliberately hurt Joe Piper, Hal Lorney was speechless with fury.

He passed close to Stoman as the men milled around.

"Keep out of my way, rat," Hal muttered.

Piper was carried away with a cheer for him ringing across the field, and a substitute came into the game. Over on the sideline, Big Ed was striding back and forth shaking his fists. The referee ordered play resumed.

Upstate still had the ball on Denville's thirty-five yard line. Less than six minutes of playing time remained. To win, Denville had to get possession of the ball and make a touchdown. That would give them one point to the good, and another goal kick would make the margin two points. With a substitute in Piper's position, it looked hopeless.

Upstate tried an off-tackle play which gave them two yards. They huddled again, came to positions, and Hal guessed that Stoman was going to try a pass, try for another touchdown. The ball was snapped, and Stoman faded back to pass. Hal charged forward with the others. The opposing end delayed him a little. But the Denville right tackle got away, made a wild spring into the air, and intercepted the pass.

Hal was away and running by that time, some distance to the tackle's right. The tackle tried to run, but saw he was going to be pocketed.

"Hal!" he called.

Hal charged on, realizing that the tackle was going to throw a lateral. If he caught the ball and kept on, nobody but the Upstate safety man would be between him and the goal line. Here was a chance to wipe that nickname of Fumblefist off the slate.

He SAW the ball coming at him like a bullet. He did as Joe Piper had told him—concentrated on the ball. He forgot the charging enemy, the crowd, did not hear the yells that came from the tiers of seats. The ball thudded against him, and he clasped it, lurched aside an instant, then was away.

He heard the cheers now, the wild howls of the Denville rooters. Hal knew speedy Upstate men were behind him, and that his team-mates could give him little help. Also the safety man ahead was watching him, getting into position.

He ran as he never had before on the football field. Something gave him extra speed. The goal line seemed miles away. He heard feet pounding the earth behind him, and swerved and a tackler missed.

His heart was hammering, his breathing became painful. He saw the safety man as if through a red haze. The collision was coming in an instant, unless he could avoid it.

The safety man was rushing in, set to make a flying tackle. Hal stumbled, was off balance an instant, then gathered himself and went on. The stumble spoiled the safety man's timing. His fingers brushed Hal's leg, and Hal staggered slightly again. Then he was going on, and the safety man was sprawled on the ground behind him.

He heard a tempest of cheers, saw the goal line coming nearer. He stumbled again, and fell. But the touchdown had been scored.

Team-mates helped him to his feet, slapped his back with broad palms, shouted into his ears.

"Fumblefist!" the Denville rooters were howling. "Fumblefist!" But Hal smiled at the howls. They meant the nickname in a friendly spirit now.

The fullback kicked the goal. Denville was on the big end of a fourteen-to-twelve score.

"Only time left for the kickoff," the team captain told Hal. "Everybody a little careful, and we have got 'em."

The fullback put a good kick down in a corner, and the Denville players went down the field like a bunch nothing could stop, stopping the ball carrier at Upstate's thirty-yard line. Lou Stoman tried a wide end run. It gave Upstate four yards—and the gun was fired.

Crowds of rooters swarmed upon the field. Hal found himself boosted to shoulders and carried. Big Ed fought his way through the crowd and got to him.

"Good boy, Fumblefist," the coach shouted "You made your one game in the regular lineup count."

"How's Joe?" Hal called.

"He'll be all right. Just a bad bruise on the kneecap."

"I know who gave it to him," Hal said.

Then they were in the dressing room, preparing to shed their playing clothes and go to the showers. Joe Piper was stretched on a cot, the doctor still beside him. Hal hurried to him.

"You came through. Fumblefist," Joe Piper said. "Good lad!"

"Thanks, Joe."

"You got cold mad. That's what did it."

"I had things to make me mad," Hal said. "Stoman hurt you purposely, didn't he?"

"Oh, it's over now. Let's forget it."

"I'd rather do something about it," Hal declared. The others had moved aside, and Piper beckoned Hal closer.

"Don't look Lou Stoman up and smash him because of me, pal," Piper said. "It's not worth it. He'll have that sort of thing taken out of him when he gets to boot camp. They don't like dirty players in the Navy. The Navy will either make a proper man of him or do the smashing and save you the trouble."

"Maybe I'll smash him on my own account," Hal said.

"You mean because of Lucy?" Piper grinned. "I arranged that, Hal. Thought that if you got jealous you'd get mad enough to play good football, and maybe get an idea you'd better brace up and ask a fine girl the fatal question."

"How do you mean you arranged it?"

"I explained to Lucy, and told her to make you jealous by flirting with Lou Stoman, if you and Stoman happened to be in the Soda Bar at the same time. She only flirted with him a little, and he asked her to go to the dance with him because he knew it'd make you mad. But making you mad that way was the worst thing he could do. You won us a ball game."

Quietly Hal shook his head in disagreement. "It—well, it was luck," he said.

"Luck that the pass was intercepted just then, maybe. But it wasn't luck that you caught and held the ball, and got down the field faster than you ever did before in your life. It wasn't luck that you weren't a 'fumblefist' at the crucial moment, Hal."

Hal went to the showers, and dressed. The men were commencing to scatter. Training was broken. Such banned things as soft drinks and pie and cake were on the preferred list now.

Joe Piper was able to stand, and a car was waiting to take him to his frat house, the doctor ready to go along. There was a commotion and a lot of shouting outside. The door was hurled open, and a group appeared, Lou Stoman in their midst.

"Doctor still here?" somebody asked. "Stoman's got a couple of cuts and several bad bruises on his face. Better fix him up."

"What happened?" Big Ed asked.

"Oh, he spoke out of turn when he left his dressing room, and a Denville man smashed him down. Just a healthy fist fight, with Stoman on the short end. He can't take that face to the football dance tonight, though."

So it happened that Hal Lorney drifted into the Soda Bar that evening a few minutes before nine. Pop Marks was behind the counter.

"A choc malt," Hal ordered. "Nice and thick and foamy."

"Heard you covered yourself with glory today," Marks said, as he started to make the drink.

"Where's Lucy?" Hal asked.

"In the back room."

She emerged at that moment, looking mighty pretty in a dance frock. Hal got down from the stool and walked back to talk to her where others wouldn't overhear.

"I understand that Lou Stoman isn't able to keep his dates this evening," Hal said. "He can't take you to the dance. But I don't mind playing second fiddle, if you care to drag me along with you."

"Hal, you'll never be second fiddle to me," she said softly.

"And I've got something I want to talk to you about, after the dance. Something important."

"I'll be ready to listen, Hal," she said. "I—I've been ready to listen for some time."

The Adventure Of The Speckled Band
Arthur Conan Doyle

On glancing over my notes of the seventy odd cases in which I have during the last eight years studied the methods of my friend Sherlock Holmes, I find many tragic, some comic, a large number merely strange, but none commonplace; for, working as he did rather for the love of his art than for the acquirement of wealth, he refused to associate himself with any investigation which did not tend towards the unusual, and even the fantastic. Of all these varied cases, however, I cannot recall any which presented more singular features than that which was associated with the well-known Surrey family of the Roylotts of Stoke Moran. The events in question occurred in the early days of my association with Holmes, when we were sharing rooms as bachelors in Baker Street. It is possible that I might have placed them upon record before, but a promise of secrecy was made at the time, from which I have only been freed during the last month by the untimely death of the lady to whom the pledge was given. It is perhaps as well that the facts should now come to light, for I have reasons to know that there are widespread rumors as to the death of Dr. Grimesby Roylott which tend to make the matter even more terrible than the truth.

It was early in April in the year '83 that I woke one morning to find Sherlock Holmes standing, fully dressed, by the side of my bed. He was a late riser, as a rule, and as the clock on the mantelpiece showed me that it was only a quarter-past seven, I blinked up at him in some surprise, and perhaps just a little resentment, for I was myself regular in my habits.

"Very sorry to knock you up, Watson," said he, "but it's the common lot this morning. Mrs. Hudson has been knocked up, she retorted upon me, and I on you."

"What is it, then--a fire?"

"No; a client. It seems that a young lady has arrived in a considerable state of excitement, who insists upon seeing me. She is waiting now in the sitting-room. Now, when young ladies wander about the metropolis at this hour of the morning, and knock sleepy people up out of their beds, I presume that it is something very pressing which they have to communicate. Should it prove to be an interesting case, you would, I am sure, wish to follow it from the outset. I thought, at any rate, that I should call you and give you the chance."

"My dear fellow, I would not miss it for anything."

I had no keener pleasure than in following Holmes in his professional investigations, and in admiring the rapid deductions, as swift as intuitions, and yet always founded on a logical basis with which he unraveled the problems which were submitted to him. I rapidly threw on my clothes and was ready in a few minutes to accompany my friend down to the sitting-room. A lady dressed in black and heavily veiled, who had been sitting in the window, rose as we entered.

"Good-morning, madam," said Holmes cheerily. "My name is Sherlock Holmes. This is my intimate friend and associate, Dr. Watson, before whom you can speak as freely as before myself. Ha! I am glad to see that Mrs. Hudson has had the good sense to light the fire. Pray draw up to it, and I shall order you a cup of hot coffee, for I observe that you are shivering."

"It is not cold which makes me shiver," said the woman in a low voice, changing her seat as requested.

"What, then?"

"It is fear, Mr. Holmes. It is terror." She raised her veil as she spoke, and we could see that she was indeed in a pitiable state of agitation, her face all drawn and gray, with restless frightened eyes, like those of some hunted animal. Her features and figure were those of a woman of thirty, but her hair was shot with premature gray, and her expression was weary and haggard. Sherlock Holmes ran her over with one of his quick, all-comprehensive glances.

"You must not fear," said he soothingly, bending forward and patting her forearm. "We shall soon set matters right, I have no doubt. You have come in by train this morning, I see."
"You know me, then?"

"No, but I observe the second half of a return ticket in the palm of your left glove. You must have started early, and yet you had a good drive in a dog-cart, along heavy roads, before you reached the station."

The lady gave a violent start and stared in bewilderment at my companion.

"There is no mystery, my dear madam," said he, smiling. "The left arm of your jacket is spattered with mud in no less than seven places. The marks are perfectly fresh. There is no vehicle save a dog-cart which throws up mud in that way, and then only when you sit on the left-hand side of the driver."

"Whatever your reasons may be, you are perfectly correct," said she. "I started from home before six, reached Leatherhead at twenty past, and came in by the first train to Waterloo. Sir, I can stand this strain no longer; I shall go mad if it continues. I have no one to turn to--none, save only one, who cares for me, and he, poor fellow, can be of little aid. I have heard of you, Mr. Holmes; I have heard of you from Mrs. Farintosh, whom you helped in the hour of her sore need. It was from her that I had your address. Oh, sir, do you not think that you could help me, too, and at least throw a little light through the dense darkness which surrounds me? At present it is out of my power to reward you for your services, but in a month or six weeks I shall be married, with the control of my own income, and then at least you shall not find me ungrateful."

Holmes turned to his desk and, unlocking it, drew out a small case-book, which he consulted.

"Farintosh," said he. "Ah yes, I recall the case; it was concerned with an opal tiara. I think it was before your time, Watson. I can only say, madam, that I shall be happy to devote the same care to your case as I did to that of your friend. As to reward, my profession is its own reward; but you are at liberty to defray whatever expenses I may be put to, at the time which suits you best. And now I beg that you will lay before us everything that may help us in forming an opinion upon the matter."

"Alas!" replied our visitor, "the very horror of my situation lies in the fact that my fears are so vague, and my suspicions depend so entirely upon small points, which might seem trivial to another, that even he to whom of all others I have a right to look for help and advice looks upon all that I tell him about it as the fancies of a nervous woman. He does not say so, but I can read it from his soothing answers and averted eyes. But I have heard, Mr. Holmes, that you can see deeply into the manifold wickedness of the human heart. You may advise me how to walk amid the dangers which encompass me."

"I am all attention, madam."

"My name is Helen Stoner, and I am living with my stepfather, who is the last survivor of one of the oldest Saxon families in England, the Roylotts of Stoke Moran, on the western border of Surrey."

Holmes nodded his head. "The name is familiar to me," said he.

"The family was at one time among the richest in England, and the estates extended over the borders into Berkshire in the north, and Hampshire in the west. In the last century, however, four successive heirs were of a dissolute and wasteful disposition, and the family ruin was eventually completed by a gambler in the days of the Regency. Nothing was left save a few acres of ground, and the two-hundred-year-old house, which is itself crushed under a heavy mortgage. The last squire dragged out his existence there, living the horrible life of an aristocratic pauper; but his only son, my stepfather, seeing that he must adapt himself to the new conditions, obtained an advance from a relative, which enabled him to take a medical degree and went out to Calcutta, where, by his professional skill and his force of character, he established a large practice. In a fit of anger, however, caused by some robberies which had been perpetrated in the house, he beat his native butler to death and narrowly escaped a capital sentence. As it was, he suffered a long term of imprisonment and afterwards returned to England a morose and disappointed man.

"When Dr. Roylott was in India he married my mother, Mrs. Stoner, the young widow of Major-General Stoner, of the Bengal Artillery. My sister Julia and I were twins, and we were only two years old at the time of my mother's re-marriage. She had a considerable sum of money--not less than 1000 pounds a year--and this she bequeathed to Dr. Roylott entirely while we resided with him, with a provision that a certain annual sum should be allowed to each of us in the event of our marriage. Shortly after our return to England my mother died--she was killed eight years ago in a railway accident near Crewe. Dr. Roylott then abandoned his attempts to establish himself in practice in London and took us to live with him in the old ancestral house at Stoke Moran. The money which my mother had left was enough for all our wants, and there seemed to be no obstacle to our happiness.

"But a terrible change came over our stepfather about this time. Instead of making friends and exchanging visits with our neighbors, who had at first been overjoyed to see a Roylott of Stoke Moran back in the old family seat, he shut himself up in his house and seldom came out save to indulge in ferocious quarrels with whoever might cross his path. Violence of temper approaching to mania has been hereditary in the men of the family, and in my stepfather's case it had, I believe, been intensified by his long residence in the tropics. A series of disgraceful brawls took place, two of which ended in the police-court, until at last he became the terror of the village, and the folks would fly at his approach, for he is a man of immense strength, and absolutely uncontrollable in his anger.

"Last week he hurled the local blacksmith over a parapet into a stream, and it was only by paying over all the money which I could gather together that I was able to avert another public exposure. He had no friends at all save the wandering gypsies, and he would give these vagabonds leave to encamp upon the few acres of bramble-covered land which represent the family estate, and would accept in return the hospitality of their tents, wandering away with them sometimes for weeks on end. He has a passion also for Indian animals, which are sent over to him by a correspondent, and he has at this moment a cheetah and a baboon, which wander freely over his grounds and are feared by the villagers almost as much as their master.

"You can imagine from what I say that my poor sister Julia and I had no great pleasure in our lives. No servant would stay with us, and for a long time we did all the work of the house.

She was but thirty at the time of her death, and yet her hair had already begun to whiten, even as mine has."

"Your sister is dead, then?"

"She died just two years ago, and it is of her death that I wish to speak to you. You can understand that, living the life which I have described, we were little likely to see anyone of our own age and position. We had, however, an aunt, my mother's maiden sister, Miss Honoria Westphail, who lives near Harrow, and we were occasionally allowed to pay short visits at this lady's house. Julia went there at Christmas two years ago, and met there a half-pay major of marines, to whom she became engaged. My stepfather learned of the engagement when my sister returned and offered no objection to the marriage; but within a fortnight of the day which had been fixed for the wedding, the terrible event occurred which has deprived me of my only companion."

Sherlock Holmes had been leaning back in his chair with his eyes closed and his head sunk in a cushion, but he half opened his lids now and glanced across at his visitor.

"Pray be precise as to details," said he.

"It is easy for me to be so, for every event of that dreadful time is seared into my memory. The manor-house is, as I have already said, very old, and only one wing is now inhabited. The bedrooms in this wing are on the ground floor, the sitting-rooms being in the central block of the buildings. Of these bedrooms the first is Dr. Roylott's, the second my sister's, and the third my own. There is no communication between them, but they all open out into the same corridor. Do I make myself plain?"

"Perfectly so."

"The windows of the three rooms open out upon the lawn. That fatal night Dr. Roylott had gone to his room early, though we knew that he had not retired to rest, for my sister was troubled by the smell of the strong Indian cigars which it was his custom to smoke. She left her room, therefore, and came into mine, where she sat for some time, chatting about her approaching wedding. At eleven o'clock she rose to leave me, but she paused at the door and looked back.

"'Tell me, Helen,' said she, 'have you ever heard anyone whistle in the dead of the night?'

"'Never,' said I.

"'I suppose that you could not possibly whistle, yourself, in your sleep?'

"Certainly not. But why?"

"'Because during the last few nights I have always, about three in the morning, heard a low, clear whistle. I am a light sleeper, and it has awakened me. I cannot tell where it came from perhaps from the next room, perhaps from the lawn. I thought that I would just ask you whether you had heard it.'

"'No, I have not. It must be those wretched gypsies in the plantation.'

"'Very likely. And yet if it were on the lawn, I wonder that you did not hear it also.'

"'Ah, but I sleep more heavily than you.'

"'Well, it is of no great consequence, at any rate.' She smiled back at me, closed my door, and a few moments later I heard her key turn in the lock."

"Indeed," said Holmes. "Was it your custom always to lock yourselves in at night?"

"Always."

"And why?"

"I think that I mentioned to you that the doctor kept a cheetah and a baboon. We had no feeling of security unless our doors were locked."

"Quite so. Pray proceed with your statement."

"I could not sleep that night. A vague feeling of impending misfortune impressed me. My sister and I, you will recollect, were twins, and you know how subtle are the links which bind two souls which are so closely allied. It was a wild night. The wind was howling outside, and the rain was beating and splashing against the windows. Suddenly, amid all the hubbub of the gale, there burst forth the wild scream of a terrified woman. I knew that it was my sister's voice. I sprang from my bed, wrapped a shawl round me, and rushed into the corridor. As I opened my door I seemed to hear a low whistle, such as my sister described, and a few moments later a clanging sound, as if a mass of metal had fallen. As I ran down the passage, my sister's door was unlocked, and revolved slowly upon its hinges. I stared at it horror-stricken, not knowing what was about to issue from it. By the light of the corridor-lamp I saw my sister appear at the opening, her face blanched with terror, her hands groping for help, her whole figure swaying to and fro like that of a drunkard. I ran to her and threw my arms round her, but at that moment her knees seemed to give way and she fell to the ground. She writhed as one who is in terrible pain, and her limbs were dreadfully convulsed. At first I thought that she had not recognized me, but as I bent over her she suddenly shrieked out in a voice which I shall never forget, 'Oh, my God! Helen! It was the band! The speckled band!' There was something else which she would fain have said, and she stabbed with her finger into the air in the direction of the doctor's room, but a fresh convulsion seized her and choked her words. I rushed out, calling loudly for my stepfather, and I met him hastening from his room in his dressing-gown. When he reached my sister's side she was unconscious, and though he poured brandy down her throat and sent for medical aid from the village, all efforts were in vain, for she slowly sank and died without having recovered her consciousness. Such was the dreadful end of my beloved sister."

"One moment," said Holmes, "are you sure about this whistle and metallic sound? Could you swear to it?"

"That was what the county coroner asked me at the inquiry. It is my strong impression that I heard it, and yet, among the crash of the gale and the creaking of an old house, I may possibly have been deceived."

"Was your sister dressed?"

"No, she was in her night-dress. In her right hand was found the charred stump of a match, and in her left a match-box."

"Showing that she had struck a light and looked about her when the alarm took place. That is important. And what conclusions did the coroner come to?"

"He investigated the case with great care, for Dr. Roylott's conduct had long been notorious in the county, but he was unable to find any satisfactory cause of death. My evidence showed that the door had been fastened upon the inner side, and the windows were blocked by old-fashioned shutters with broad iron bars, which were secured every night. The walls were carefully sounded, and were shown to be quite solid all round, and the flooring was also thoroughly examined, with the same result. The chimney is wide, but is barred up by four large staples. It is certain, therefore, that my sister was quite alone when she met her end. Besides, there were no marks of any violence upon her."

"How about poison?"

"The doctors examined her for it, but without success."

"What do you think that this unfortunate lady died of, then?"

"It is my belief that she died of pure fear and nervous shock, though what it was that frightened her I cannot imagine."

"Were there gypsies in the plantation at the time?"

"Yes, there are nearly always some there."

"Ah, and what did you gather from this allusion to a band--a speckled band?"

"Sometimes I have thought that it was merely the wild talk of delirium, sometimes that it may have referred to some band of people, perhaps to these very gypsies in the plantation. I do not know whether the spotted handkerchiefs which so many of them wear over their heads might have suggested the strange adjective which she used."

Holmes shook his head like a man who is far from being satisfied.

"These are very deep waters," said he; "pray go on with your narrative."

"Two years have passed since then, and my life has been until lately lonelier than ever. A month ago, however, a dear friend, whom I have known for many years, has done me the honor to ask my hand in marriage. His name is Armitage--Percy Armitage--the second son of Mr. Armitage, of Crane Water, near Reading. My stepfather has offered no opposition to the match, and we are to be married in the course of the spring. Two days ago some repairs were started in the west wing of the building, and my bedroom wall has been pierced, so that I have had to move into the chamber in which my sister died, and to sleep in the very bed in which she slept. Imagine, then, my thrill of terror when last night, as I lay awake, thinking over her terrible fate, I suddenly heard in the silence of the night the low whistle which had been the herald of her own death. I sprang up and lit the lamp, but nothing was to be seen in the room. I was too shaken to go to bed again, however, so I dressed, and as soon as it was daylight I slipped down, got a dog-cart at the Crown Inn, which is opposite, and drove to Leatherhead, from whence I have come on this morning with the one object of seeing you and asking your advice."

"You have done wisely," said my friend. "But have you told me all?"

"Yes, all."

"Miss Roylott, you have not. You are screening your stepfather."

"Why, what do you mean?"

For answer Holmes pushed back the frill of black lace which fringed the hand that lay upon our visitor's knee. Five little livid spots, the marks of four fingers and a thumb, were printed upon the white wrist.

"You have been cruelly used," said Holmes.

The lady colored deeply and covered over her injured wrist. "He is a hard man," she said, "and perhaps he hardly knows his own strength."

There was a long silence, during which Holmes leaned his chin upon his hands and stared into the crackling fire.

"This is a very deep business," he said at last. "There are a thousand details which I should desire to know before I decide upon our course of action. Yet we have not a moment to lose. If we were to come to Stoke Moran to-day, would it be possible for us to see over these rooms without the knowledge of your stepfather?"

"As it happens, he spoke of coming into town to-day upon some most important business. It is probable that he will be away all day, and that there would be nothing to disturb you. We have a housekeeper now, but she is old and foolish, and I could easily get her out of the way."

"Excellent. You are not averse to this trip, Watson?"

"By no means."

"Then we shall both come. What are you going to do yourself?"

"I have one or two things which I would wish to do now that I am in town. But I shall return by the twelve o'clock train, so as to be there in time for your coming."

"And you may expect us early in the afternoon. I have myself some small business matters to attend to. Will you not wait and breakfast?"

"No, I must go. My heart is lightened already since I have confided my trouble to you. I shall look forward to seeing you again this afternoon." She dropped her thick black veil over her face and glided from the room.

"And what do you think of it all, Watson?" asked Sherlock Holmes, leaning back in his chair.

"It seems to me to be a most dark and sinister business."

"Dark enough and sinister enough."

"Yet if the lady is correct in saying that the flooring and walls are sound, and that the door, window, and chimney are impassable, then her sister must have been undoubtedly alone when she met her mysterious end."

"What becomes, then, of these nocturnal whistles, and what of the very peculiar words of the dying woman?"

"I cannot think."

"When you combine the ideas of whistles at night, the presence of a band of gypsies who are on intimate terms with this old doctor, the fact that we have every reason to believe that the doctor has an interest in preventing his stepdaughter's marriage, the dying allusion to a band, and, finally, the fact that Miss Helen Stoner heard a metallic clang, which might have been caused by one of those metal bars that secured the shutters falling back into its place, I think that there is good ground to think that the mystery may be cleared along those lines."

"But what, then, did the gypsies do?"

"I cannot imagine."

"I see many objections to any such theory."

"And so do I. It is precisely for that reason that we are going to Stoke Moran this day. I want to see whether the objections are fatal, or if they may be explained away. But what in the name of the devil!"

The exclamation had been drawn from my companion by the fact that our door had been suddenly dashed open, and that a huge man had framed himself in the aperture. His costume was a peculiar mixture of the professional and of the agricultural, having a black top-hat, a long frock-coat, and a pair of high gaiters, with a hunting-crop swinging in his hand. So tall was he that his hat actually brushed the cross bar of the doorway, and his breadth seemed to span it across from side to side. A large face, seared with a thousand wrinkles, burned yellow with the sun, and marked with every evil passion, was turned from one to the other of us, while his deep-set, bile-shot eyes, and his high, thin, fleshless nose, gave him somewhat the resemblance to a fierce old bird of prey.

"Which of you is Holmes?" asked this apparition.

"My name, sir; but you have the advantage of me," said my companion quietly.

"I am Dr. Grimesby Roylott, of Stoke Moran."

"Indeed, Doctor," said Holmes blandly. "Pray take a seat."

"I will do nothing of the kind. My stepdaughter has been here. I have traced her. What has she been saying to you?"

"It is a little cold for the time of the year," said Holmes.

"What has she been saying to you?" screamed the old man furiously.

"But I have heard that the crocuses promise well," continued my companion imperturbably.

"Ha! You put me off, do you?" said our new visitor, taking a step forward and shaking his hunting-crop. "I know you, you scoundrel! I have heard of you before. You are Holmes, the meddler."

My friend smiled.

"Holmes, the busybody!"

His smile broadened.

"Holmes, the Scotland Yard Jack-in-office!"

Holmes chuckled heartily. "Your conversation is most entertaining," said he. "When you go out close the door, for there is a decided draught."

"I will go when I have said my say. Don't you dare to meddle with my affairs. I know that Miss Stoner has been here. I traced her! I am a dangerous man to fall foul of! See here." He stepped swiftly forward, seized the poker, and bent it into a curve with his huge brown hands.

"See that you keep yourself out of my grip," he snarled, and hurling the twisted poker into the fireplace he strode out of the room.

"He seems a very amiable person," said Holmes, laughing. "I am not quite so bulky, but if he had remained I might have shown him that my grip was not much more feeble than his own." As he spoke he picked up the steel poker and, with a sudden effort, straightened it out again.

"Fancy his having the insolence to confound me with the official detective force! This incident gives zest to our investigation, however, and I only trust that our little friend will not suffer from her imprudence in allowing this brute to trace her. And now, Watson, we shall order breakfast, and afterwards I shall walk down to Doctors' Commons, where I hope to get some data which may help us in this matter."

It was nearly one o'clock when Sherlock Holmes returned from his excursion. He held in his hand a sheet of blue paper, scrawled over with notes and figures.

"I have seen the will of the deceased wife," said he. "To determine its exact meaning I have been obliged to work out the present prices of the investments with which it is concerned. The total income, which at the time of the wife's death was little short of 1100 pounds, is now, through the fall in agricultural prices, not more than 750 pounds. Each daughter can claim an income of 250 pounds, in case of marriage. It is evident, therefore, that if both girls had married, this beauty would have had a mere pittance, while even one of them would cripple him to a very serious extent. My morning's work has not been wasted, since it has proved that he has the very strongest motives for standing in the way of anything of the sort. And now, Watson, this is too serious for dawdling, especially as the old man is aware that we are interesting ourselves in his affairs; so if you are ready, we shall call a cab and drive to Waterloo. I should be very much obliged if you would slip your revolver into your pocket. An Eley's No. 2 is an excellent argument with gentlemen who can twist steel pokers into knots. That and a tooth-brush are, I think, all that we need."

At Waterloo we were fortunate in catching a train for Leatherhead, where we hired a trap at the station inn and drove for four or five miles through the lovely Surrey laries. It was a perfect day, with a bright sun and a few fleecy clouds in the heavens. The trees and wayside hedges were just throwing out their first green shoots, and the air was full of the pleasant smell of the moist earth. To me at least there was a strange contrast between the sweet promise of the spring and this sinister quest upon which we were engaged. My companion sat in the front of the trap, his arms folded, his hat pulled down over his eyes, and his chin sunk upon his breast, buried in the deepest thought. Suddenly, however, he started, tapped me on the shoulder, and pointed over the meadows

"Look there!" said he.

A heavily timbered park stretched up in a gentle slope, thickening into a grove at the highest point. From amid the branches there jutted out the gray gables and high roof-tree of a very old mansion.

"Stoke Moran?" said he.

"Yes, sir, that be the house of Dr. Grimesby Roylott," remarked the driver.

"There is some building going on there," said Holmes; "that is where we are going."

"There's the village," said the driver, pointing to a cluster of roofs some distance to the left; "but if you want to get to the house, you'll find it shorter to get over this stile, and so by the foot-path over the fields. There it is, where the lady is walking."

"And the lady, I fancy, is Miss Stoner," observed Holmes, shading his eyes. "Yes, I think we had better do as you suggest."

We got off, paid our fare, and the trap rattled back on its way to Leatherhead.

"I thought it as well," said Holmes as we climbed the stile, "that this fellow should think we had come here as architects, or on some definite business. It may stop his gossip. Good-afternoon, Miss Stoner. You see that we have been as good as our word."

Our client of the morning had hurried forward to meet us with a face which spoke her joy. "I have been waiting so eagerly for you," she cried, shaking hands with us warmly. "All has turned out splendidly. Dr. Roylott has gone to town, and it is unlikely that he will be back before evening."

"We have had the pleasure of making the doctor's acquaintance," said Holmes, and in a few words he sketched out what had occurred. Miss Stoner turned white to the lips as she listened.

"Good heavens!" she cried, "he has followed me, then."

"So it appears."

"He is so cunning that I never know when I am safe from him. What will he say when he returns?"

"He must guard himself, for he may find that there is someone more cunning than himself upon his track. You must lock yourself up from him to-night. If he is violent, we shall take you away to your aunt's at Harrow. Now, we must make the best use of our time, so kindly take us at once to the rooms which we are to examine."

The building was of gray, lichen-blotched stone, with a high central portion and two curving wings, like the claws of a crab, thrown out on each side. In one of these wings the windows were broken and blocked with wooden boards, while the roof was partly caved in, a picture of ruin. The central portion was in little better repair, but the right-hand block was comparatively modern, and the blinds in the windows, with the blue smoke curling up from the chimneys, showed that this was where the family resided. Some scaffolding had been erected against the end wall, and the stone-work had been broken into, but there were no signs of any workmen at the moment of our visit. Holmes walked slowly up and down the ill-trimmed lawn and examined with deep attention the outsides of the windows.

"This, I take it, belongs to the room in which you used to sleep, the center one to your sister's, and the one next to the main building to Dr. Roylott's chamber?"

"Exactly so. But I am now sleeping in the middle one."

"Pending the alterations, as I understand. By the way, there does not seem to be any very pressing need for repairs at that end wall."

"There were none. I believe that it was an excuse to move me from my room."

"Ah! that is suggestive. Now, on the other side of this narrow wing runs the corridor from which these three rooms open. There are windows in it, of course?"

"Yes, but very small ones. Too narrow for anyone to pass through."

"As you both locked your doors at night, your rooms were unapproachable from that side. Now, would you have the kindness to go into your room and bar your shutters?"

Miss Stoner did so, and Holmes, after a careful examination through the open window, endeavored in every way to force the shutter open, but without success. There was no slit through which a knife could be passed to raise the bar. Then with his lens he tested the hinges, but they were of solid iron, built firmly into the massive masonry. "Hum!" said he, scratching his chin in some perplexity, "my theory certainly presents some difficulties. No one could pass these shutters if they were bolted. Well, we shall see if the inside throws any light upon the matter."

A small side door led into the whitewashed corridor from which the three bedrooms opened. Holmes refused to examine the third chamber, so we passed at once to the second, that in which Miss Stoner was now sleeping, and in which her sister had met with her fate. It was a homely little room, with a low ceiling and a gaping fireplace, after the fashion of old country-houses. A brown chest of drawers stood in one corner, a narrow white-counterpaned bed in another, and a dressing-table on the left-hand side of the window. These articles, with two small wicker-work chairs, made up all the furniture in the room save for a square of Wilton carpet in the center. The boards round and the paneling of the walls were of brown, worm-eaten oak, so old and discolored that it may have dated from the original building of the house. Holmes drew one of the chairs into a corner and sat silent, while his eyes travelled round and round and up and down, taking in every detail of the apartment.

"Where does that bell communicate with?" he asked at last pointing to a thick belt-rope which hung down beside the bed, the tassel actually lying upon the pillow.

"It goes to the housekeeper's room."

"It looks newer than the other things?"

"Yes, it was only put there a couple of years ago."

"Your sister asked for it, I suppose?"

"No, I never heard of her using it. We used always to get what we wanted for ourselves."

"Indeed, it seemed unnecessary to put so nice a bell-pull there. You will excuse me for a few minutes while I satisfy myself as to this floor." He threw himself down upon his face with his lens in his hand and crawled swiftly backward and forward, examining minutely the cracks between the boards. Then he did the same with the wood-work with which the chamber was paneled. Finally he walked over to the bed and spent some time in staring at it and in running his eye up and down the wall. Finally he took the bell-rope in his hand and gave it a brisk tug.

"Why, it's a dummy," said he.

"Won't it ring?"

"No, it is not even attached to a wire. This is very interesting. You can see now that it is fastened to a hook just above where the little opening for the ventilator is."

"How very absurd! I never noticed that before."

"Very strange!" muttered Holmes, pulling at the rope. "There are one or two very singular points about this room. For example, what a fool a builder must be to open a ventilator into another room, when, with the same trouble, he might have communicated with the outside air!"

"That is also quite modern," said the lady.

"Done about the same time as the bell-rope?" remarked Holmes.

"Yes, there were several little changes carried out about that time."

"They seem to have been of a most interesting character--dummy bell-ropes, and ventilators which do not ventilate. With your permission, Miss Stoner, we shall now carry our researches into the inner apartment."

Dr. Grimesby Roylott's chamber was larger than that of his step-daughter, but was as plainly furnished. A camp-bed, a small wooden shelf full of books, mostly of a technical character an armchair beside the bed, a plain wooden chair against the wall, a round table, and a large iron safe were the principal things which met the eye. Holmes walked slowly round and examined each and all of them with the keenest interest.

"What's in here?" he asked, tapping the safe.

"My stepfather's business papers."

"Oh! you have seen inside, then?"

"Only once, some years ago. I remember that it was full of papers."

"There isn't a cat in it, for example?"

"No. What a strange idea!"

"Well, look at this!" He took up a small saucer of milk which stood on the top of it.

"No; we don't keep a cat. But there is a cheetah and a baboon."

"Ah, yes, of course! Well, a cheetah is just a big cat, and yet a saucer of milk does not go very far in satisfying its wants, I daresay. There is one point which I should wish to determine." He squatted down in front of the wooden chair and examined the seat of it with the greatest attention.

"Thank you. That is quite settled," said he, rising and putting his lens in his pocket. "Hello! Here is something interesting!"

The object which had caught his eye was a small dog lash hung on one corner of the bed. The lash, however, was curled upon itself and tied so as to make a loop of whipcord.

"What do you make of that, Watson?"

"It's a common enough lash. But I don't know why it should be tied."

"That is not quite so common, is it? Ah, me! It's a wicked world, and when a clever man turns his brains to crime it is the worst of all. I think that I have seen enough now, Miss Stoner, and with your permission we shall walk out upon the lawn."

I had never seen my friend's face so grim or his brow so dark as it was when we turned from the scene of this investigation. We had walked several times up and down the lawn, neither Miss Stoner nor myself liking to break in upon his thoughts before he roused himself from his reverie.

"It is very essential, Miss Stoner," said he, "that you should absolutely follow my advice in every respect."

"I shall most certainly do so."

"The matter is too serious for any hesitation. Your life may depend upon your compliance."

"I assure you that I am in your hands."

"In the first place, both my friend and I must spend the night in your room."

Both Miss Stoner and I gazed at him in astonishment.

"Yes, it must be so. Let me explain. I believe that that is the village inn over there?"

"Yes, that is the Crown."

"Very good. Your windows would be visible from there?"

"Certainly."

"You must confine yourself to your room, on pretense of a headache, when your stepfather comes back. Then when you hear him retire for the night, you must open the shutters of your window, undo the hasp, put your lamp there as a signal to us, and then withdraw quietly with everything which you are likely to want into the room which you used to occupy. I have no doubt that, in spite of the repairs, you could manage there for one night."

"Oh, yes, easily."

"The rest you will leave in our hands."

"But what will you do?"

"We shall spend the night in your room, and we shall investigate the cause of this noise which has disturbed you."

"I believe, Mr. Holmes, that you have already made up your mind," said Miss Stoner, laying her hand upon my companion's sleeve.

"Perhaps I have."

"Then, for pity's sake, tell me what was the cause of my sister's death."

"I should prefer to have clearer proofs before I speak."

"You can at least tell me whether my own thought is correct, and if she died from some sudden fright."

"No, I do not think so. I think that there was probably some more tangible cause. And now, Miss Stoner, we must leave you for if Dr. Roylott returned and saw us our journey would be in vain. Good-bye, and be brave, for if you will do what I have told you, you may rest assured that we shall soon drive away the dangers that threaten you."

Sherlock Holmes and I had no difficulty in engaging a bedroom and sitting-room at the Crown Inn. They were on the upper floor, and from our window we could command a view of the avenue gate, and of the inhabited wing of Stoke Moran Manor House. At dusk we saw Dr. Grimesby Roylott drive past, his huge form looming up beside the little figure of the lad who drove him. The boy had some slight difficulty in undoing the heavy iron gates, and we heard the hoarse roar of the doctor's voice and saw the fury with which he shook his clinched fists at him. The trap drove on, and a few minutes later we saw a sudden light spring up among the trees as the lamp was lit in one of the sitting-rooms.

"Do you know, Watson," said Holmes as we sat together in the gathering darkness, "I have really some scruples as to taking you to-night. There is a distinct element of danger."

"Can I be of assistance?"

"Your presence might be invaluable."

"Then I shall certainly come."

"It is very kind of you."

"You speak of danger. You have evidently seen more in these rooms than was visible to me."

"No, but I fancy that I may have deduced a little more. I imagine that you saw all that I did."

"I saw nothing remarkable save the bell-rope, and what purpose that could answer I confess is more than I can imagine."

"You saw the ventilator, too?"

"Yes, but I do not think that it is such a very unusual thing to have a small opening between two rooms. It was so small that a rat could hardly pass through."

"I knew that we should find a ventilator before ever we came to Stoke Moran."

"My dear Holmes!"

"Oh, yes, I did. You remember in her statement she said that her sister could smell Dr. Roylott's cigar. Now, of course that suggested at once that there must be a communication between the two rooms. It could only be a small one, or it would have been remarked upon at the coroner's inquiry. I deduced a ventilator."

"But what harm can there be in that?"

"Well, there is at least a curious coincidence of dates. A ventilator is made, a cord is hung, and a lady who sleeps in the bed dies. Does not that strike you?"

"I cannot as yet see any connection."

"Did you observe anything very peculiar about that bed?"

"No."

"It was clamped to the floor. Did you ever see a bed fastened like that before?"

"I cannot say that I have."

"The lady could not move her bed. It must always be in the same relative position to the ventilator and to the rope--or so we may call it, since it was clearly never meant for a bell-pull."

"Holmes," I cried, "I seem to see dimly what you are hinting at. We are only just in time to prevent some subtle and horrible crime."

"Subtle enough and horrible enough. When a doctor does go wrong he is the first of criminals. He has nerve and he has knowledge. Palmer and Pritchard were among the heads of their profession. This man strikes even deeper, but I think, Watson, that we shall be able to strike deeper still. But we shall have horrors enough before the night is over; for goodness' sake let us have a quiet pipe and turn our minds for a few hours to something more cheerful."

About nine o'clock the light among the trees was extinguished, and all was dark in the direction of the Manor House. Two hours passed slowly away, and then, suddenly, just at the stroke of eleven, a single bright light shone out right in front of us.

"That is our signal," said Holmes, springing to his feet; "it comes from the middle window."

As we passed out he exchanged a few words with the landlord, explaining that we were going on a late visit to an acquaintance, and that it was possible that we might spend the night there. A moment later we were out on the dark road, a chill wind blowing in our faces, and one yellow light twinkling in front of us through the gloom to guide us on our somber errand.

There was little difficulty in entering the grounds, for unrepaired breaches gaped in the old park wall. Making our way among the trees, we reached the lawn, crossed it, and were about to enter through the window when out from a clump of laurel bushes there darted what seemed to be a hideous and distorted child, who threw itself upon the grass with writhing limbs and then ran swiftly across the lawn into the darkness.

"My God!" I whispered; "did you see it?"

Holmes was for the moment as startled as I. His hand closed like a vise upon my wrist in his agitation. Then he broke into a low laugh and put his lips to my ear.

"It is a nice household," he murmured. "That is the baboon."

I had forgotten the strange pets which the doctor affected. There was a cheetah, too; perhaps we might find it upon our shoulders at any moment. I confess that I felt easier in my mind when, after following Holmes's example and slipping off my shoes, I found myself inside the bedroom. My companion noiselessly closed the shutters, moved the lamp onto the table, and cast his eyes round the room. All was as we had seen it in the daytime. Then creeping up to me and making a trumpet of his hand, he whispered into my ear again so gently that it was all that I could do to distinguish the words:

"The least sound would be fatal to our plans."

I nodded to show that I had heard.

"We must sit without light. He would see it through the ventilator."

I nodded again.

"Do not go asleep; your very life may depend upon it. Have your pistol ready in case we should need it. I will sit on the side of the bed, and you in that chair."

I took out my revolver and laid it on the corner of the table.

Holmes had brought up a long thin cane, and this he placed upon the bed beside him. By it he laid the box of matches and the stump of a candle. Then he turned down the lamp, and we were left in darkness.

How shall I ever forget that dreadful vigil? I could not hear a sound, not even the drawing of a breath, and yet I knew that my companion sat open-eyed, within a few feet of me, in the same state of nervous tension in which I was myself. The shutters cut off the least ray of light, and we waited in absolute darkness.

From outside came the occasional cry of a night-bird, and once at our very window a long drawn catlike whine, which told us that the cheetah was indeed at liberty. Far away we could hear the deep tones of the parish clock, which boomed out every quarter of an hour. How long they seemed, those quarters! Twelve struck, and one and two and three, and still we sat waiting silently for whatever might befall.

Suddenly there was the momentary gleam of a light up in the direction of the ventilator, which vanished immediately, but was succeeded by a strong smell of burning oil and heated metal. Someone in the next room had lit a dark-lantern. I heard a gentle sound of movement, and then all was silent once more, though the smell grew stronger. For half an hour I sat with straining ears. Then suddenly another sound became audible--a very gentle, soothing sound, like that of a small jet of steam escaping continually from a kettle. The instant that we heard it, Holmes sprang from the bed, struck a match, and lashed furiously with his cane at the bell-pull.

"You see it, Watson?" he yelled. "You see it?"

But I saw nothing. At the moment when Holmes struck the light I heard a low, clear whistle, but the sudden glare flashing into my weary eyes made it impossible for me to tell what it was at which my friend lashed so savagely. I could, however, see that his face was deadly pale and filled with horror and loathing. He had ceased to strike and was gazing up at the ventilator when suddenly there broke from the silence of the night the most horrible cry to which I have ever listened. It swelled up louder and louder, a hoarse yell of pain and fear and anger all mingled in the one dreadful shriek. They say that away down in the village, and even in the distant parsonage, that cry raised the sleepers from their beds. It struck cold to our hearts, and I stood gazing at Holmes, and he at me, until the last echoes of it had died away into the silence from which it rose.

"What can it mean?" I gasped.

"It means that it is all over," Holmes answered. "And perhaps, after all, it is for the best. Take your pistol, and we will enter Dr. Roylott's room."

With a grave face he lit the lamp and led the way down the corridor. Twice he struck at the chamber door without any reply from within. Then he turned the handle and entered, I at his heels, with the cocked pistol in my hand.

It was a singular sight which met our eyes. On the table stood a dark-lantern with the shutter half open, throwing a brilliant beam of light upon the iron safe, the door of which was ajar. Beside this table, on the wooden chair, sat Dr. Grimesby Roylott clad in a long gray dressing-gown, his bare ankles protruding beneath, and his feet thrust into red heelless Turkish slippers. Across his lap lay the short stock with the long lash which we had noticed during the day. His chin was cocked upward and his eyes were fixed in a dreadful, rigid stare at the corner of the ceiling. Round his brow he had a peculiar yellow band, with brownish speckles, which seemed to be bound tightly round his head. As we entered he made neither sound nor motion.

"The band! the speckled band!" whispered Holmes.

I took a step forward. In an instant his strange headgear began to move, and there reared itself from among his hair the squat diamond-shaped head and puffed neck of a loathsome serpent.

"It is a swamp adder!" cried Holmes; "the deadliest snake in India. He has died within ten seconds of being bitten. Violence does, in truth, recoil upon the violent, and the schemer falls into the pit which he digs for another. Let us thrust this creature back into its den, and we can then remove Miss Stoner to some place of shelter and let the county police know what has happened."

As he spoke he drew the dog-whip swiftly from the dead man's lap, and throwing the noose round the reptile's neck he drew it from its horrid perch and, carrying it at arm's length, threw it into the iron safe, which he closed upon it.

Such are the true facts of the death of Dr. Grimesby Roylott, of Stoke Moran. It is not necessary that I should prolong a narrative which has already run to too great a length by telling how we broke the sad news to the terrified girl, how we conveyed her by the morning train to the care of her good aunt at Harrow, of how the slow process of official inquiry came to the conclusion that the doctor met his fate while indiscreetly playing with a dangerous pet. The little which I had yet to learn of the case was told me by Sherlock Holmes as we travelled back next day.

"I had," said he, "come to an entirely erroneous conclusion which shows, my dear Watson, how dangerous it always is to reason from insufficient data. The presence of the gypsies, and the use of the word 'band,' which was used by the poor girl, no doubt to explain the appearance which she had caught a hurried glimpse of by the light of her match, were sufficient to put me upon an entirely wrong scent. I can only claim the merit that I instantly reconsidered my position when, however, it became clear to me that whatever danger threatened an occupant of the room could not come either from the window or the door. My attention was speedily drawn, as I have already remarked to you, to this ventilator, and to the bell-rope which hung down to the bed. The discovery that this was a dummy, and that the bed was clamped to the floor, instantly gave rise to the suspicion that the rope was there as a bridge for something passing through the hole and coming to the bed. The idea of a snake instantly occurred to me, and when I coupled it with my knowledge that the doctor was furnished with a supply of creatures from India, I felt that I was probably on the right track. The idea of using a form of poison which could not possibly be discovered by any chemical test was just such a one as would occur to a clever and ruthless man who had had an Eastern training. The rapidity with which such a poison would take effect would also, from his point of view, be an advantage. It would be a sharp-eyed coroner, indeed, who could distinguish the two little dark punctures which would show where the poison fangs had done their work. Then I thought of the whistle. Of course he must recall the snake before the morning light revealed it to the victim. He had trained it, probably by the use of the milk which we saw, to return to him when summoned. He would put it through this ventilator at the hour that he thought best, with the certainty that it would crawl down the rope and land on the bed. It might or might not bite the occupant, perhaps she might escape every night for a week, but sooner or later she must fall a victim.

"I had come to these conclusions before ever I had entered his room. An inspection of his chair showed me that he had been in the habit of standing on it, which of course would be necessary in order that he should reach the ventilator. The sight of the safe, the saucer of milk, and the loop of whipcord were enough to finally dispel any doubts which may have remained. The metallic clang heard by Miss Stoner was obviously caused by her stepfather hastily closing the door of his safe upon its terrible occupant. Having once made up my mind, you know the steps which I took in order to put the matter to the proof. I heard the creature hiss as I have no doubt that you did also, and I instantly lit the light and attacked it."

"With the result of driving it through the ventilator."

"And also with the result of causing it to turn upon its master at the other side. Some of the blows of my cane came home and roused its snakish temper, so that it flew upon the first person it saw. In this way I am no doubt indirectly responsible for Dr. Grimesby Roylott's death, and I cannot say that it is likely to weigh very heavily upon my conscience."

Undercover Kid
Grant Lane

Danny Garrett was sitting there in his room, listening to a new radio mystery show called *Midnight*, when he heard footsteps mounting the stairs. He could have told you right away who was coming up the stairs of his rooming house: Mike Ryan and Slug O'Donnel, his two headquarters' detective friends.

The kid, in his youthful and spectacular career as an associate of those headquarters men, had made quite a study of the sounds of people walking. It was only natural, because it was only until quite recently that he had been just another kid shining shoes on the sidewalks of New York. Now he was known as the Shoeshine Kid Detective.

He had often watched people's feet, their shoes, and especially the way they walked.

Take Mike Ryan, for instance, the way he was coming up the stairs. Plodding, stolid . . . *thump, thump, thump* . . . why, you could have pictured him as a detective without even *seeing* him.

Slug's footsteps were lighter and quicker. That was like Slug O'Donnel, who was a tall, thin guy as skinny as a straw. A quick, restless type.

Danny turned down the radio, waited until the footsteps had barely paused outside his door, then called, "Come in, you two."

Mike Ryan's big hulk was first through the opening doorway. A derby was pushed to the back of his head and he was chewing on a black cigar. He was puffing just a trifle, too.

"Hello, Danny," said Mike. "How's it?"

Danny said, "You're eating too much again, Mike, you're getting fat."

Behind Ryan, skinny Slug O'Donnel grinned and said, "You're not kidding'!" He frowned at Danny. "How'd you know it was us?"

"I could tell," Danny said. Ryan had parked himself on the edge of the bed, and Slug had slumped into the one arm chair, his long, thin body bending at angles like a folding clothes-dryer. The kid's bright blue eyes slid to the alarm clock on the dresser. It was after ten o'clock, and he wondered what brought his detective friends up here at this hour of the night.

"How come?" he asked.

"How come what?" said Slug.

"Dropping up here at this hour?"

"Oh." Ryan took the unlighted cigar out of his mouth, studied it, reached for a pad of matches. "Just thought we'd drop around, Danny."

Danny thought, any other night they'd be down at headquarters playing pinochle. There was something up, he could tell.

He said, "Don't look like two guys trying to be palsy-walsy. What's on your minds?"

"Well," murmured Slug O'Donnel, "we were wondering' about tomorrow night. You were going to that hockey game at the Garden, weren't you?"

The kid's face brightened. Every year one of his old customers—a banker downtown—gave him a ticket to this game, the lead game of the season, and Danny had been looking forward to it for weeks. "Sure!" he said quickly. "I've got a ticket—" He paused, his blue eyes clouding.

He knew from the expression on Mike Ryan's heavy Irish face that something was coming.

"You see, kid," started Ryan, "we've got a little job, a tough assignment, sort of. We need your help."

Slug added, "Yeah. It's got to be handled right away, too."

"What?" asked Danny.

"We're trying to locate a guy," said Mike Ryan.

Danny looked at them. He frowned. Then he said, "So do you have to work nights in order to find a person? Why did you ask me about tomorrow night? Nothing in the world is going to make me miss that hockey—"

"This guy we want is a murderer," interrupted Mike Ryan.

"More than that!" put in Slug. "A cop killer. Remember Tommy Shevlin from the D.A.'s office, kid?"

Danny nodded, his eyes clouding. Tommy Shevlin had once been a headquarters man. Recently he had transferred over to the D.A.'s office as a special investigator. He was a longstanding personal friend of Mike Ryan's.

Answering the question in Danny's eyes, Mike said grimly, "Tommy Shevlin was on a case, trailing a guy. Tommy found him. And then we found Tommy—murdered!"

Danny stood up. Though not yet quite fourteen, he was tall and wiry. He had red hair and there were some freckles on his lean face.

Tense, he asked, "And this murderer—you're trying to find him?"

"Exactly!" announced Ryan. "All we know about him is that he usually goes by the moniker of Les Drake. He's wanted on several charges. We have reason to believe he killed a guy even before Tommy Shevlin got to him, and got murdered also. We've got fingerprints, and so if we *do* find this fellow Drake we'll know whether we have the right man or not."

"But you've never seen him?" prodded the kid. "He's never been mugged?"

137

"Never," said Slug.

"Then how do you expect to pick him up?"

Mike Ryan put his big hands on his knees and leaned toward Danny. "That's where you come in, kid. You see, this guy Drake has a sister. We figured sooner or later Drake would try to get in touch with her. By watching the sister, we'd nab Drake."

"Sure," agreed Danny. "That should be a simple job. Certainly the New York police department has enough men to handle it—"

"The trouble is," said Slug, moving restlessly up and down the bedroom, "this sister, too, has disappeared!"

Danny sighed and looked hopelessly at his two friends. "Then you're right back where you started from. So why get me all upset about that hockey game? There's no reason why I still can't go—"

He paused, because Ryan was talking again, and what Ryan was saying brought the kid up alert.

". . . and so," Ryan was saying, "this sister of Drake's has a kid—a girl about your own age. Her name's Sally, and the mother has left her at this small town up the river a ways. The kid's going to school there in the village and boarding out at a small rooming house. We've got all the information and we even have arrangements for you to stay there too."

"In fact," said Slug cheerfully, "the woman who runs the place is expecting you tomorrow morning. We've told her your father is an army man, overseas, and that he's a war hero. She also thinks it's swell you're going to board at her place and—"

"Why?" said Danny quietly.

Slug stared at the kid. "Why?" he repeated. "Don't you see? Sooner or later this kid's mother will come to visit her. Or maybe she'll write. Your job is to get chummy with this girl Sally. Keep your eyes open. Watch for the letters sent by her mother. See where they come from. Once we locate the *mother*, the next step will be to shadow *her*. Eventually Les Drake will visit her, then—bingo—we got him!'"

"You leave from Grand Central at 9:30 tomorrow morning," Mike Ryan said.

Danny's red hair almost bristled. "So!" he exclaimed. "The two of you had it all fixed up before you even came up here to see me! You certainly take a lot for granted. Why can't *you* two guys go to that town and do your own shadowing of this girl Sally—"

"Because," said Slug quickly, "we'd be recognized as coppers in an instant. Imagine Mike, here, in a village of five hundred people, or so! He's got detective written all over him. We're figuring that Les Drake *himself* might come to that town, and if he ever spotted us . . ."

They kept talking. Danny argued with them. His heart had been set on seeing that hockey game the following night. Besides, why should he spy on some girl named Sally, who was probably a nice sweet kid—

He said, "I'm not going to do it."

Mike and his partner kept talking.

About eleven o'clock the following morning, Danny got off the local train at a small town up the Hudson River. It was a hamlet nestled in the foothills of the mountains near West Point. It was a quiet and friendly little place. The station agent went into explicit detail in telling the kid just how to get to Mrs. Thompson's place.

Twenty minutes later Mrs. Thompson herself was standing in the doorway of Danny's second-floor room and chattering like a magpie.

"My goodness!" she was saying. "Your father a major in Europe! It's proud I am to have you, Danny. On the phone, your uncle said—"

Danny was unpacking a suitcase. He looked at the short, stout woman. There was some flour on her arms and in the house he could smell pies baking. "My uncle?" he said.

"Yes—Mr. Ryan. He said I was to make arrangements about your going to school here and everything. You start tomorrow morning, and you'll be in the same class with Sally. My, she's such a lovely girl. Incidentally, she'll be home soon for lunch and you'll meet her . . ."

Mrs. Thompson kept talking, and Danny was thinking, *So Mike Ryan's my uncle now, huh? And they've even arranged it so that I'm to go to school here in the town. Nice guys!*

He didn't think he was going to like this job at all!

Not that the kid wasn't intensely interested in detective work. Since that eventful day when he had first met Mike Ryan and O'Donnel when he had been a shoeshine kid down near Centre Street headquarters, and had helped his two friends nab a crook, he had made a reputation for himself as the "kid detective."

Danny had an unusual ability for spotting clues and remembering people. He had an alert, agile mind and made a thorough study of police procedure. He even carried a special badge given to him by the police commissioner himself. In New York, he was quite famous.

But Ryan had assured him that his name would mean nothing up here in this small village. People up here were not interested in crooks and the goings-on of the New York police department. So they had arranged it that Danny use his own name. That way, he would feel more natural and would be less apt to make a slip.

But the kid still didn't like this idea of spying on some girl named Sally. From the buildup they'd been giving him about her, he guessed she was some homely-faced kid who was as fresh as they come!

Shortly after twelve noon, Mrs. Thompson called upstairs and told Danny that lunch was ready. He combed his hair, and went downstairs, and that's when he met this girl Sally.

He was trying to eat his lunch, and at the same time he was watching her covertly. She was a quiet, shy girl with clear gray eyes and a sweet face. There was something about her, and Danny guessed that maybe she was lonesome.

In a way, Danny was a romantic kid. There was a manner about this girl Sally Mitchell that affected him. He wondered if she was happy.

Later, after she had gone back to school, Danny hung around his room. Mrs. Thompson had said something about going down to the village to do some shopping. Danny was to make himself right at home, she called upstairs.

The afternoon mail came while Mrs. Thompson was out. Danny went downstairs and took the letters out of the tin mailbox outside the front door. He had heard the mailman's whistle blow, something you never heard in New York. There was a letter for Sally. It was in a woman's neat handwriting, and was from Rochester, New York. There was no return address however. There was no doubt at all that it was from the mother of the girl he must spy on.

Danny stared at it as he placed it with Mrs. Thompson's mail on the hall table. He remembered what Ryan and Slug had told him. They were cops, seeking a man who had killed a cop friend. They had no compunction at all when on a case like that.

They had suggested that Danny get one of Sally's letters while she was out, steam it open or something, and to find out all he could about her mother. Maybe learn her exact address and if anything was said in the letter about this man Les Drake.

And Danny kept staring at the letter, and finally he shook his head. She was a nice kid. He couldn't pry into one of her personal letters.

For two cents, right now, he'd call New York, reverse the charges, and get Ryan on the phone at headquarters and tell him the whole thing was off!

He went out and sat on the top steps of the front porch, chin cupped in his hands. He didn't like this kind of police work. Tangling with a real crook was different; he'd done that lots of times. But spying on a nice girl like Sally Mitchell . . .

The kid had never had a girl, but he thought now that if he ever *did* have a girlfriend, he'd like someone like Sally. That's why he felt the way he did about this . . .

He sat there thinking the thing over a long time, and before he knew it Sally was home from school.

"Hello," she said brightly as she came up the walk.

Danny spoke to her, smiling, and watched her as she went inside the house. He saw her look at the letters on the hall table, her face lighting up as she spied the topmost letter, the one postmarked Rochester. She ran up to her room with the letter in her hand.

It was from her mother, all right, Danny knew. And maybe inside that letter was some mention of her mother's brother—Les Drake—who had killed a cop friend of Ryan's. Ryan and Slug were *depending* upon him to find out!

He remembered Mike's explicit plans. Mike and Slug were going to drive up here from New York tomorrow night. They'd arranged to keep a rendezvous with Danny an hour after dark. He was to meet them just a half a block away, where this street intersected the through State route from New York. You could see the intersection from the porch, because Mrs. Thompson's house was the last one on the street.

Even as Danny glanced toward the corner, which Mike Ryan had so carefully mapped out, a car turned in from the highway and came slowly down the village street. Danny merely glanced at it. He was still thinking about Sally, upstairs. Perhaps she'd come down soon and maybe he could talk to her. Maybe she'd say something about the letter or her mother, and that way Danny could get her talking. She might even say something about this man Les Drake!

The car—a business coupe—that had passed a few moments ago came back down the street. One thing about it caught the kid's attention. The gas ration sticker—that and the New York State license number! There was a detail that bothered him . . .

Behind him, Sally came out on the porch and said, "Would you like to take a walk?"

"Sure," said Danny, forgetting all about the car.

They walked down-street, to the single block that was the shopping center of the village. It led downhill, and you could see the river, the mountains rising up all around the shoreline. Quite a few cars were parked along the curb, and people were shopping. There was a lunch room and a soda fountain two doors away.

Sally talked about school, and the teachers, and what it would like for Danny tomorrow. He watched her fine, oval face, her deep gray eyes. She had soft chestnut hair. She was a pretty girl, and he liked her a lot. He didn't remember a thing she said about the school which he was supposed to attend.

She had to buy some writing paper. Oddly, she never mentioned her mother, which was the one thing in which Danny was interested. Afterwards, he said, "Let's have a soda," and pointed the way to the ice cream store.

He was holding the door for her, as she went inside, when he noticed the car across the street and the tall, lean man who was climbing out of it. He was a dark-haired fellow who was wearing a dark fedora and dark topcoat. He headed into the lunchroom without glancing right or left.

Yet Danny had the feeling the man might have been following them in the car!

"Looking for someone?" asked Sally, who was waiting for him just inside the store.

"Huh . . . no," Danny said quickly, catching up with her and heading toward a booth.

He was curious about that car.

Afterwards, going out of the store, Sally took a letter from her purse and said, "Mind dropping this in the mailbox for me, Danny?" She nodded toward a mailbox on the corner.

Danny's back was toward her as he stepped toward the mailbox, and for an instant his eyes saw the address on the letter. The words were immediately written indelibly on his quick mind. *Mrs. G. K. Mitchell*—and the location was in Rochester!

Starting up the hill a moment later with Sally, the kid's gaze slid toward the nearby lunchroom. He saw the tall dark man still seated at the counter. He tried to get a glimpse of the man's face, but could not. Then he and Sally were beyond the lunchroom.

Ryan and Slug had said no photograph had ever been taken of this murderer—Les Drake. Thus there was no way of recognizing the man even if Danny *did* see him. How was Danny to *know* him?

One thing Danny could do. He could telephone Ryan in New York and tell him this address in Rochester. Then maybe he wouldn't have to spy on Sally anymore. Ryan and Slug could take over. This was one assignment that the kid didn't like at all.

He walked Sally home, and Mrs. Thompson was there, and so the kid had no chance to get downtown again in order to call New York. Mrs. Thompson kept right on talking, right through dinner even, and afterwards she suggested that the three of them take in the early show at the theater downtown. Mickey Rooney was playing.

Danny made excuses. He had some things to get ready for school tomorrow, he said. He was tired from his trip. Sally looked disappointed and it made him feel like a heel.

But after they had gone, Danny immediately put through a call to Mike Ryan. He caught him in his office at Centre Street headquarters. He told Ryan about the Rochester address, explaining how he felt certain it was the mother's address.

Ryan's voice boomed cheerfully over the phone. "Swell, kid! Swell! That must be it, all right. Who else would she be writing to? We'll get Rochester on it right away. We'll have them assign someone to pick up her mother and question her. Don't worry, we'll find out about this guy Drake!"

Then Mike added, "Slug and I will pick you up tomorrow night just as we said. You stick around, Danny, just in case you pick up something else. But I think this is all we need. We'll have a line on Les Drake before morning, I'll bet you."

A thought flashed through Danny's mind. "But what about Sally?" he asked quickly. "What if Les Drake comes to see *her*? A dangerous guy like that . . . why, there's no telling . . .'"

Mike cut in, "Don't worry about Sally. That's why her mother put her down there to go to school. The kid doesn't even *know* about Les Drake, and we've learned he doesn't know where she is either. It's the mother he'll try to see. We know he's up against it for money, and he'll come to her like he has before. We *know* these things, Danny."

"I hope so," the kid said doubtfully, and after Ryan had assured him they'd pick him up tomorrow night, he hung up.

A half hour later, while Danny was sitting upstairs in his room, he noticed a car roll past the house in the dark. Twice again a car passed, and he was positive it was the same one— because there was something too deliberate in the way the person drove by. On this isolated side street, not one other car went by in hours.

It bothered Danny. He thought of Sally downtown there with Mrs. Thompson. Part of their walk home would be along shadowed streets, and he kept thinking of that business coupe with the ration sticker and license plates from upstate. New York State had a system of license tags which designated what county a car was registered in. He had noticed this detail early this afternoon. Funny about that fellow in the car!

Danny slipped on his leather zipper jacket and went out. The air was cool and crisp, and he walked quickly down the side street. But he saw no sign of the car again.

He hung around downtown, watching for it, until Mrs. Thompson and Sally came out of the show. He saw no sign of the coupe or the tall man again.

On the way home, Sally said, "I thought you were tired. We guessed you had gone to bed."

"My goodness, yes," said Mrs. Thompson.

Danny told them, "It's still pretty early. I wasn't sleepy."

Neither was he sleepy later, after Mrs. Thompson and Sally had retired. Danny sat in the darkness of his room, at the window, watching out into the quiet night. He kept thinking that maybe Les Drake had not been able to locate Sally's mother, but maybe he knew where *Sally* was! He might come here, forcing her to tell where her mother was living. A guy like that, a murderer, and Sally such a swell girl . . .

He sat there until long past midnight, but he saw no sign of the car again. Finally, he went to bed.

The following morning Sally waited for him. She said gaily, "I'll walk you to school. You'll like it here."

Mrs. Thompson followed them to the door. "I won't be here for dinner tonight," she told them. "My sister Nettie has the sewing circle this evening, and I'm going down there for a bit. But I'll be home early. You'll find everything all feed in the ice box."

Danny thought it was nice being with Sally, walking to school with her and. all, but the school business itself bothered him.

In New York he did all his studying alone, at home. Between times he shined shoes or hung around headquarters with his two detective friends.

Somehow, he struggled through the tedious day. There was too much inaction to suit him. At three o'clock, he met Sally and suggested walking home with her.

She said, "Today's my special Red Cross class. I'll be here for an hour or so yet. But I'll see you at home, Danny."

He went home and hung around. He even took a stroll around the village to kill some time.

At six o'clock, Sally wasn't, home yet!

Danny even walked back to the school, and found all the doors locked. He had no idea where Sally might have gone, especially with Mrs. Thompson away for the evening. He didn't even know where Mrs. Thompson was!

He went back to the house, terribly upset, and kept watching for Sally to come home. It was starting to get dark, and the air was colder. Surely she wouldn't have just stayed out, with it cold and all like this!

Restless, he kept going up and downstairs to his room. Sally's room door was open. He glanced inside, at her shoes lined up in orderly fashion beneath the bed, at her dresses hanging up in neat, fashion in the closet, the door of which was partly open. She was a meticulous girl . .
.

Odd then, he thought, that the bureau drawers should be left open in helter-skelter fashion! He stepped across the room, saw instantly that, contents of the bureau had been rummaged through as though by someone seeking something in a hurry. It didn't seem like Sally at all, he decided worriedly.

Then his glance froze on the rug.

Apparently in getting ready for school that morning, Sally had spilled some powder. It had scattered in a fine, thin layer on the rug.

And now, distinctly visible in the thin layer of powder, was the imprint of a shoe. A large imprint, quite clearly defined.

A man's footprint!

Danny's blood ran cold. Someone had been here in the house, probably after Mrs. Thompson had left, and they had been right up here in Sally's room. And a person who had no right to be— because Mrs. Thompson, Danny knew, was a widow!

And why wasn't Sally home yet, and what had happened?

He hurried downstairs again, grabbing his leather jacket from the hall chair, and started toward the front door. *He had to find her!*

Then footsteps ran across the front porch and the door burst open into the hallway. Sally came in, her usually pretty face strained and frightened. She was panting with excitement.

She cried, "Danny . . . that man . . . he followed me!"

"What man, Sally?"

"After school . . . I was on my way home and it was getting rather late. There was nobody around just at the time and I saw him following me in the car. I was so scared!"

Danny took hold of her hands. They were cold, and she was trembling. He said, "What did you do?"

"I cut through that lane halfway home from school. I saw him driving around and around the block. I hid in that old barn on the Turner place—about half a mile from here—until it started to get dark and I was afraid to stay. Then . . . then I ran all the way home. I was really scared, Danny."

Danny kept holding her hands, and her excitement subsided a little. He asked directly, "Sally, do you know a man named Les Drake?"

She shook her head. "Why?"

"Never mind," he told her. He was thinking. It was Les Drake, all right, no doubt about it. The tall, dark man he had spotted in the business coupe yesterday. Les Drake had been right

145

here in this house sometime this afternoon and had searched through Sally's room looking for something.

Her mother's address, obviously. And he couldn't have found it, otherwise why had he followed Sally home from school. And Les Drake was a dangerous murderer!

If Ryan and Slug were only here . . .

Danny's glance went to the glass of the front hall door. It was dark outside now. Ryan had said they'd be here about a half-hour after dark, at the meeting place just down the street at the corner of the State road.

He looked at Sally and asked, "How's your nerve? I mean, will you stay here alone for a few minutes?"

Her deep gray eyes held on Danny's face. "W-why?"

"Two friends of mine are meeting me soon," he said. "They happen to be— detectives. Look, do this. Go up to your room and lock the door. Don't torn on the light. But if you hear *anyone* come up on the porch, or near the house, switch on your light. I'll be able to see it from the corner. I'll run right back."

"You're sure?" Sally asked worriedly.

"Sure! Now don't worry," He moved toward the front door. "Now lock this door after me when I go out."

A moment later he was moving through the dark shadows of the street. If Mike Ryan and Slug only arrived on schedule, if something didn't delay them, maybe they could help Danny locate this man in the coupe—

He had gone less than a hundred yards when his steps slowed, and he slid into the blacker shadows caused by one of the old elms lining the street.

Just ahead, near the end of the block, a car was parked. It was a coupe!

There was a stretch of woods on one side of the road, empty lots on the other. A desolate section. Danny was positive it was the tall, dark-haired man's car, the one he had seen several times now.

He waited. He wondered if the man was in the car.

Danny glanced over his shoulder, back at Mrs. Thompson's house, and his blood froze. The light was on in Sally's room. The man was *there*—at the house!

Danny leaped down the street. There was no thought of danger to himself now. He wasn't even thinking of Ryan and Slug O'Donnel. He was a kid who, when danger came, was not afraid— especially when it threatened a girl like Sally!

146

On a sudden thought, he drew up short and raced back to where the coupe was parked. He bent down near the license plate in the rear and noted the number. It was the same car all right.

An instant later he was streaking back toward the house. He saw the ladder placed below Sally's window!

He had just reached the front steps when the front door opened and the man came hurrying out. One of the tall man's arms clutched Sally's shoulders. His free hand was clamped over her mouth.

Danny yelled, "Hey!" and slammed toward the man.

The fellow released Sally and spun toward the kid. His fist lashed out and he uttered an oath of surprise. His blow missed the kid's jaw. Danny sank his hard fist into the man's midriff, and there was a grunt of surprise and pain.

The kid was quick. And hard and tough. Sally was crying as she cringed back near the porch rail.

The man tried to grapple with Danny Garrett, but the kid stayed clear, diving in for a quick punch, then sliding agilely clear again. He yelled to Sally, "Run! Get down the street. Get someone!"

The girl started to dodge past them. For an instant Danny's gaze swept toward her, to make certain that she was all right. It was the instant of time the tall man needed.

His fist crashed alongside Danny's jaw. The kid wasn't knocked out, but he staggered backwards. His foot tripped across the topmost step and he went tumbling downward. The back of his head crashed the bottom step and he rolled, dazed, onto the grass.

He tried to struggle to his feet, and his head reeled. He slumped down again . . .

How long it was before his thoughts cleared completely he wasn't sure. Seconds probably. Then he was on his feet and running. He heard the car starter turning over down the street. The starter kept grinding.

As he neared the car Danny saw a blurred form climb out and hurry to raise the hood. There was a soft, angry curse in the night.

Danny was six feet from the fellow when his foot scuffed some gravel in the roadway. The tall man whirled, saw the kid, muttered something and leaped in for the attack. His strong fingers caught the kid's jacket collar and started to twist.

Danny struggled. The leather coat was being twisted tightly around, his throat. A moment more and he would be strangled.

Danny fought wildly. But his strength was no match for the tall man's. The coat collar was gagging him. . . . His thoughts blurred hazily.

He remembered something like a brilliant light striking him in the face. It was a car . . . a car swinging in from the State road. The next moment brakes were squealing and the car was coming to a fast stop.

Danny heard Mike Ryan's voice boom from the car, "Say! What's going on?"

And then Danny got his breath long enough to cry out: "Mike! It's him! Les Drake!"

The rest was all pretty crazy and mixed up. The man released the kid and started a dive toward the nearby woods. Shots crashed out. He heard Mike Ryan calling out, and he vaguely remembered that Slug was there, too.

Also, a woman—a small, trim-looking woman had climbed out of Ryan's car. She stared at Danny, and you could see the resemblance to Sally in her fine features.

She was running toward Danny Garrett.

Danny swung and looked inside the car. Sally was there, all right. The man had bound her wrists with a cord and there was a gag which had been jammed hastily into her mouth. Danny remembered yanking the gag loose. His head was reeling and he was feeling funny.

He heard Sally cry out, "Mother!" and then that's the last thing he did remember.

Then he was in bed and big Mike Ryan was there, and Slug, and the girl's mother. And Mrs. Thompson fluttering around in the background saying, "My goodness! Who would have ever thought—"

Danny tried to sit up. Mike Ryan said cautiously. "Better take it easy, kid. You got an awful lump on the back of your head. It's nothing serious, luckily. All you need is a little rest. . . ."

Danny stared up at them. "That man," he asked, "was he—"

Ryan nodded. "Yes, he was Les Drake! Slug winged him. We've turned him over to the State troopers, temporarily. He'll be taken back to the city to stand trial for that cop's murder."

Ryan turned and looked at the small, nice-looking woman. "Sally's mother has positively identified him. It's Drake, all right."

Danny looked at her. She said, "He was not my real brother. He was a half-brother. He was never—any good." She came up to the bed and touched Danny's arm. "You're a brave young man!"

Ryan added, "We checked on that Rochester address, kid." He looked at the woman. "Rochester police learned that Drake had been trying to locate Mrs. Mitchell. She got away just before he found her, and went to the local police. Then Drake ducked town in a stolen car—the one you saw, kid."

Danny said, "I wondered about the car. It had upstate license plates and yet it carried only an A-card gas sticker. I wondered how anyone could drive so far on only an A-card."

Ryan nodded. "He had stolen gas ration books, too." He nodded to Mrs. Mitchell again. "Sally's mother came directly to New York in order to help us. She was afraid of this man Drake. Just recently she learned he was a killer. She got in this afternoon and we brought her up here with us."

Danny said suddenly, "Where's Sally?" And then, worried, "Is . . . is she all right?"

The woman smiled and touched Danny's arm again. "Thanks to you, Danny—yes! She's getting ready for bed. I'll call her."

And then they had all stepped outside a moment, and Sally came quietly into the room. She was wearing a blue bathrobe over her pajamas, and Danny thought she looked prettier than ever with her hair hanging loose down around her shoulders.

She sat down on the edge of the bed and asked, "How do you feel, Danny?"

He grinned. "I feel swell."

Big Mike Ryan stuck his head inside the room. "Hey, kid," he said, "we're sure lucky. If that guy's car hadn't stalled, he'd of got clean away!"

Danny motioned toward his jacket, which he saw hanging on a chair. "You'll find the rotor in my pocket. I removed it from the distributor. That way, you can't start a car. A truck driver showed me that trick."

Ryan smiled and said to Sally, "He's a smart boy. He really doesn't need to go to school."

Danny raised up quickly on an elbow and exclaimed, "Wait a minute! I think I'd like to go to school up here." He realized suddenly that Sally was holding his hand. He thought she was pretty swell.

Mike Ryan looked startled. He started to say, "You'd *like* to go to school . . ." Next he swung hurriedly toward the hallway. He appeared worried. "Hey, Slug!" he bellowed. "Come here a minute!"

Dr. Heidegger's Experiment
Nathaniel Hawthorne

That very singular man, old Dr. Heidegger, once invited four venerable friends to meet him in his study. There were three white-bearded gentlemen, Mr. Medbourne, Colonel Killigrew, and Mr. Gascoigne, and a withered gentlewoman, whose name was the Widow Wycherly. They were all melancholy old creatures, who had been unfortunate in life, and whose greatest misfortune it was that they were not long ago in their graves. Mr. Medbourne, in the vigor of his age, had been a prosperous merchant, but had lost his all by a frantic speculation, and was now little better than a mendicant. Colonel Killigrew had wasted his best years, and his health and substance, in the pursuit of sinful pleasures, which had given birth to a brood of pains, such as the gout, and divers other torments of soul and body. Mr. Gascoigne was a ruined politician, a man of evil fame, or at least had been so till time had buried him from the knowledge of the present generation, and made him obscure instead of infamous. As for the Widow Wycherly, tradition tells us that she was a great beauty in her day; but, for a long while past, she had lived in deep seclusion, on account of certain scandalous stories which had prejudiced the gentry of the town against her. It is a circumstance worth mentioning that each of these three old gentlemen, Mr. Medbourne, Colonel Killigrew, and Mr. Gascoigne, were early lovers of the Widow Wycherly, and had once been on the point of cutting each other's throats for her sake. And, before proceeding further, I will merely hint that Dr. Heidegger and all his foul guests were sometimes thought to be a little beside themselves,--as is not unfrequently the case with old people, when worried either by present troubles or woeful recollections.

"My dear old friends," said Dr. Heidegger, motioning them to be seated, "I am desirous of your assistance in one of those little experiments with which I amuse myself here in my study."

If all stories were true, Dr. Heidegger's study must have been a very curious place. It was a dim, old-fashioned chamber, festooned with cobwebs, and besprinkled with antique dust. Around the walls stood several oaken bookcases, the lower shelves of which were filled with rows of gigantic folios and black-letter quartos, and the upper with little parchment-covered duodecimos. Over the central bookcase was a bronze bust of Hippocrates, with which, according to some authorities, Dr. Heidegger was accustomed to hold consultations in all difficult cases of his practice. In the obscurest corner of the room stood a tall and narrow oaken closet, with its door ajar, within which doubtfully appeared a skeleton. Between two of the bookcases hung a looking-glass, presenting its high and dusty plate within a tarnished gilt frame. Among many wonderful stories related of this mirror, it was fabled that the spirits of all the doctor's deceased patients dwelt within its verge, and would stare him in the face whenever he looked thitherward. The opposite side of the chamber was ornamented with the full-length portrait of a young lady, arrayed in the faded magnificence of silk, satin, and brocade, and with a visage as faded as her dress. Above half a century ago, Dr. Heidegger had been on the point of marriage with this young lady; but, being affected with some slight disorder, she had swallowed one of her lover's prescriptions, and died on the bridal evening. The greatest curiosity of the study remains to be mentioned; it was a ponderous folio volume, bound in black leather, with massive silver clasps. There were no letters on the back, and nobody could tell the title of the book. But it was well known to be a book of magic; and once, when a chambermaid had lifted it, merely to brush away the dust, the skeleton had rattled in its closet, the picture of the young lady had stepped one foot upon the floor, and several ghastly faces had peeped forth from the mirror; while the brazen head of Hippocrates frowned, and said,--"Forbear!"

Such was Dr. Heidegger's study. On the summer afternoon of our tale a small round table, as black as ebony, stood in the center of the room, sustaining a cut-glass vase of beautiful form and elaborate workmanship. The sunshine came through the window, between the heavy festoons of two faded damask curtains, and fell directly across this vase; so that a mild splendor was reflected from it on the ashen visages of the five old people who sat around. Four champagne glasses were also on the table.

"My dear old friends," repeated Dr. Heidegger, "may I reckon on your aid in performing an exceedingly curious experiment?"

Now Dr. Heidegger was a very strange old gentleman, whose eccentricity had become the nucleus for a thousand fantastic stories. Some of these fables, to my shame be it spoken, might possibly be traced back to my own veracious self; and if any passages of the present tale should startle the reader's faith, I must be content to bear the stigma of a fiction monger.

When the doctor's four guests heard him talk of his proposed experiment, they anticipated nothing more wonderful than the murder of a mouse in an air pump, or the examination of a cobweb by the microscope, or some similar nonsense, with which he was constantly in the habit of pestering his intimates. But without waiting for a reply, Dr. Heidegger hobbled across the chamber, and returned with the same ponderous folio, bound in black leather, which common report affirmed to be a book of magic. Undoing the silver clasps, he opened the volume, and took from among its black-letter pages a rose, or what was once a rose, though now the green leaves and crimson petals had assumed one brownish hue, and the ancient flower seemed ready to crumble to dust in the doctor's hands.

"This rose," said Dr. Heidegger, with a sigh, "this same withered and crumbling flower, blossomed five and fifty years ago. It was given me by Sylvia Ward, whose portrait hangs yonder; and I meant to wear it in my bosom at our wedding. Five and fifty years it has been treasured between the leaves of this old volume. Now, would you deem it possible that this rose of half a century could ever bloom again?"

"Nonsense!" said the Widow Wycherly, with a peevish toss of her head. "You might as well ask whether an old woman's wrinkled face could ever bloom again."

"See!" answered Dr. Heidegger.

He uncovered the vase, and threw the faded rose into the water which it contained. At first, it lay lightly on the surface of the fluid, appearing to imbibe none of its moisture. Soon, however, a singular change began to be visible. The crushed and dried petals stirred, and assumed a deepening tinge of crimson, as if the flower were reviving from a deathlike slumber; the slender stalk and twigs of foliage became green; and there was the rose of half a century, looking as fresh as when Sylvia Ward had first given it to her lover. It was scarcely full blown; for some of its delicate red leaves curled modestly around its moist bosom, within which two or three dewdrops were sparkling.

"That is certainly a very pretty deception," said the doctor's friends; carelessly, however, for they had witnessed greater miracles at a conjurer's show; "pray how was it effected?"

"Did you never hear of the 'Fountain of Youth?'" asked Dr. Heidegger, "which Ponce De Leon, the Spanish adventurer, went in search of two or three centuries ago?"

"But did Ponce De Leon ever find it?" said the Widow Wycherly.

"No," answered Dr. Heidegger, "for he never sought it in the right place. The famous Fountain of Youth, if I am rightly informed, is situated in the southern part of the Floridian peninsula, not far from Lake Macaco. Its source is overshadowed by several gigantic magnolias, which, though numberless centuries old, have been kept as fresh as violets by the virtues of this wonderful water. An acquaintance of mine, knowing my curiosity in such matters, has sent me what you see in the vase."

"Ahem!" said Colonel Killigrew, who believed not a word of the doctor's story; "and what may be the effect of this fluid on the human frame?"

"You shall judge for yourself, my dear colonel," replied Dr. Heidegger; "and all of you, my respected friends, are welcome to so much of this admirable fluid as may restore to you the

152

bloom of youth. For my own part, having had much trouble in growing old, I am in no hurry to grow young again. With your permission, therefore, I will merely watch the progress of the experiment."

While he spoke, Dr. Heidegger had been filling the four champagne glasses with the water of the Fountain of Youth. It was apparently impregnated with an effervescent gas, for little bubbles were continually ascending from the depths of the glasses, and bursting in silvery spray at the surface. As the liquor diffused a pleasant perfume, the old people doubted not that it possessed cordial and comfortable properties; and though utter sceptics as to its juvenescent power, they were inclined to swallow it at once. But Dr. Heidegger besought them to stay a moment.

"Before you drink, my respectable old friends," said he, "it would be well that, with the experience of a lifetime to direct you, you should draw up a few general rules for your guidance, in passing a second time through the perils of youth. Think what a sin and shame it would be, if, with your peculiar advantages, you should not become patterns of virtue and wisdom to all the young people of the age!"

The doctor's four venerable friends made him no answer, except by a feeble and tremulous laugh; so very ridiculous was the idea that, knowing how closely repentance treads behind the steps of error, they should ever go astray again.

"Drink, then," said the doctor, bowing: "I rejoice that I have so well selected the subjects of my experiment."

With palsied hands, they raised the glasses to their lips. The liquor, if it really possessed such virtues as Dr. Heidegger imputed to it, could not have been bestowed on four human beings who needed it more woefully. They looked as if they had never known what youth or pleasure was, but had been the offspring of Nature's dotage, and always the gray, decrepit, sapless, miserable creatures, who now sat stooping round the doctor's table, without life enough in their souls or bodies to be animated even by the prospect of growing young again. They drank off the water, and replaced their glasses on the table.

Assuredly there was an almost immediate improvement in the aspect of the party, not unlike what might have been produced by a glass of generous wine, together with a sudden glow of cheerful sunshine brightening over all their visages at once. There was a healthful suffusion on their cheeks, instead of the ashen hue that had made them look so corpse-like. They gazed at one another, and fancied that some magic power had really begun to smooth away the deep and sad inscriptions which Father Time had been so long engraving on their brows. The Widow Wycherly adjusted her cap, for she felt almost like a woman again.

"Give us more of this wondrous water!" cried they, eagerly. "We are younger--but we are still too old! Quick--give us more!"

"Patience, patience!" quote Dr. Heidegger, who sat watching the experiment with philosophic coolness. "You have been a long time growing old. Surely, you might be content to grow young in half an hour! But the water is at your service."

Again he filled their glasses with the liquor of youth, enough of which still remained in the vase to turn half the old people in the city to the age of their own grandchildren. While the bubbles were yet sparkling on the brim, the doctor's four guests snatched their glasses from the table, and swallowed the contents at a single gulp. Was it delusion? Even while the draught was passing down their throats, it seemed to have wrought a change on their whole systems. Their eyes grew clear and bright; a dark shade deepened among their silvery locks, they sat around the table, three gentlemen of middle age, and a woman, hardly beyond her buxom prime.

"My dear widow, you are charming!" cried Colonel Killigrew, whose eyes had been fixed upon her face, while the shadows of age were flitting from it like darkness from the crimson daybreak.

The fair widow knew, of old, that Colonel Killigrew's compliments were not always measured by sober truth; so she started up and ran to the mirror, still dreading that the ugly visage of an old woman would meet her gaze. Meanwhile, the three gentlemen behaved in such a manner as proved that the water of the Fountain of Youth possessed some intoxicating qualities; unless, indeed, their exhilaration of spirits were merely a lightsome dizziness caused by the sudden removal of the weight of years. Mr. Gascoigne's mind seemed to run on political topics, but whether relating to the past, present, or future, could not easily be determined, since the same ideas and phrases have been in vogue these fifty years. Now he rattled forth full-throated sentences about patriotism, national glory, and the people's right; now he muttered some perilous stuff or other, in a sly and doubtful whisper, so cautiously that even his own conscience could scarcely catch the secret; and now, again, he spoke in measured accents, and a deeply deferential tone, as if a royal ear were listening to his well-turned periods. Colonel Killigrew all this time had been trolling forth a jolly bottle song, and ringing his glass in symphony with the chorus, while his eyes wandered toward the buxom figure of the Widow Wycherly. On the other side of the table, Mr. Medbourne was involved in a calculation of dollars and cents, with which was strangely intermingled a project for supplying the East Indies with ice, by harnessing a team of whales to the polar icebergs.

As for the Widow Wycherly, she stood before the mirror curtseying and simpering to her own image, and greeting it as the friend whom she loved better than all the world beside. She thrust her face close to the glass, to see whether some long-remembered wrinkle or crow's foot had indeed vanished. She examined whether the snow had so entirely melted from her hair that the venerable cap could be safely thrown aside. At last, turning briskly away, she came with a sort of dancing step to the table.

"My dear old doctor," cried she, "pray favor me with another glass!"

"Certainly, my dear madam, certainly!" replied the complaisant doctor; "see! I have already filled the glasses."

There, in fact, stood the four glasses, brimful of this wonderful water, the delicate spray of which, as it effervesced from the surface, resembled the tremulous glitter of diamonds. It was now so nearly sunset that the chamber had grown duskier than ever; but a mild and moonlike splendor gleamed from within the vase, and rested alike on the four guests and on the doctor's venerable figure. He sat in a high-backed, elaborately-carved, oaken arm-chair, with a gray dignity of aspect that might have well befitted that very Father Time, whose power had never been disputed, save by this fortunate company. Even while quaffing the third draught of the Fountain of Youth, they were almost awed by the expression of his mysterious visage.

But, the next moment, the exhilarating gush of young life shot through their veins. They were now in the happy prime of youth. Age, with its miserable train of cares and sorrows and diseases, was remembered only as the trouble of a dream, from which they had joyously awoke. The fresh gloss of the soul, so early lost, and without which the world's successive scenes had been but a gallery of faded pictures, again threw its enchantment over all their prospects. They felt like new-created beings in a new-created universe.

"We are young! We are young!" they cried exultingly.

Youth, like the extremity of age, had effaced the strongly-marked characteristics of middle life, and mutually assimilated them all. They were a group of merry youngsters, almost maddened with the exuberant frolicsomeness of their years. The most singular effect of their gayety was an impulse to mock the infirmity and decrepitude of which they had so lately been the victims. They laughed loudly at their old-fashioned attire, the wide-skirted coats and flapped waistcoats of the young men, and the ancient cap and gown of the blooming girl. One limped across the floor like a gouty grandfather; one set a pair of spectacles astride of his nose, and pretended to pore over the black-letter pages of the book of magic; a third seated himself in an arm-chair, and strove to imitate the venerable dignity of Dr. Heidegger. Then all shouted mirthfully, and leaped about the room. The Widow Wycherly--if so fresh a damsel could be called a widow--tripped up to the doctor's chair, with a mischievous merriment in her rosy face.

"Doctor, you dear old soul," cried she, "get up and dance with me!" And then the four young people laughed louder than ever, to think what a queer figure the poor old doctor would cut.

"Pray excuse me," answered the doctor quietly. "I am old and rheumatic, and my dancing days were over long ago. But either of these gay young gentlemen will be glad of so pretty a partner."

"Dance with me, Clara!" cried Colonel Killigrew

"No, no, I will be her partner!" shouted Mr. Gascoigne.

"She promised me her hand, fifty years ago!" exclaimed Mr. Medbourne.

They all gathered round her. One caught both her hands in his passionate grasp another threw his arm about her waist--the third buried his hand among the glossy curls that clustered beneath the widow's cap. Blushing, panting, struggling, chiding, laughing, her warm breath fanning each of their faces by turns, she strove to disengage herself, yet still remained in their triple embrace. Never was there a livelier picture of youthful rivalship, with bewitching beauty for the prize. Yet, by a strange deception, owing to the duskiness of the chamber, and the antique dresses which they still wore, the tall mirror is said to have reflected the figures of the three old, gray, withered grandsires, ridiculously contending for the skinny ugliness of a shriveled grandam.

But they were young: their burning passions proved them so. Inflamed to madness by the coquetry of the girl-widow, who neither granted nor quite withheld her favors, the three rivals began to interchange threatening glances. Still keeping hold of the fair prize, they grappled fiercely at one another's throats. As they struggled to and fro, the table was overturned, and the vase dashed into a thousand fragments. The precious Water of Youth flowed in a bright stream across the floor, moistening the wings of a butterfly, which, grown old in the decline of summer, had alighted there to die. The insect fluttered lightly through the chamber, and settled on the snowy head of Dr. Heidegger.

"Come, come, gentlemen!--come, Madam Wycherly," exclaimed the doctor, "I really must protest against this riot."

They stood still and shivered; for it seemed as if gray Time were calling them back from their sunny youth, far down into the chill and darksome vale of years. They looked at old Dr.

Heidegger, who sat in his carved arm-chair, holding the rose of half a century, which he had rescued from among the fragments of the shattered vase. At the motion of his hand, the four rioters resumed their seats; the more readily, because their violent exertions had wearied them, youthful though they were.

"My poor Sylvia's rose!" ejaculated Dr. Heidegger, holding it in the light of the sunset clouds; "it appears to be fading again."

And so it was. Even while the party were looking at it, the flower continued to shrivel up, till it became as dry and fragile as when the doctor had first thrown it into the vase. He shook off the few drops of moisture which clung to its petals.

"I love it as well thus as in its dewy freshness," observed he, pressing the withered rose to his withered lips. While he spoke, the butterfly fluttered down from the doctor's snowy head, and fell upon the floor.

His guests shivered again. A strange chillness, whether of the body or spirit they could not tell, was creeping gradually over them all. They gazed at one another, and fancied that each fleeting moment snatched away a charm, and left a deepening furrow where none had been before. Was it an illusion? Had the changes of a lifetime been crowded into so brief a space, and were they now four aged people, sitting with their old friend, Dr. Heidegger?

"Are we grown old again, so soon?" cried they, dolefully.

In truth they had. The Water of Youth possessed merely a virtue more transient than that of wine. The delirium which it created had effervesced away. Yes! they were old again. With a shuddering impulse, that showed her a woman still, the widow clasped her skinny hands before her face, and wished that the coffin lid were over it, since it could be no longer beautiful.

"Yes, friends, ye are old again," said Dr. Heidegger, "and lo! the Water of Youth is all lavished on the ground. Well--I bemoan it not; for if the fountain gushed at my very doorstep, I would not stoop to bathe my lips in it--no, though its delirium were for years instead of moments. Such is the lesson ye have taught me!"

But the doctor's four friends had taught no such lesson to themselves. They resolved forthwith to make a pilgrimage to Florida, and quaff at morning, noon, and night, from the Fountain of Youth.

The Machine That Won the War
Isaac Asimov

The celebration had a long way to go and even in the silent depths of Multivac's underground chambers, it hung in the air.

If nothing else, there was the mere fact of isolation and silence. For the first time in a decade, technicians were not scurrying about the vitals of the giant computer, the soft lights did not wink out their erratic patterns, the flow of information in and out had halted.

It would not be halted long, of course, for the needs of peace would be pressing. Yet now, for a day, perhaps for a week, even Multivac might celebrate the great time, and rest.

Lamar Swift took off the military cap he was wearing and looked down the long and empty main corridor of the enormous computer. He sat down rather wearily in one of the technician's swing-stools, and his uniform, in which he had never been comfortable, took on a heavy and wrinkled appearance.

He said, "I'll miss it all after a grisly fashion. It's hard to remember when we weren't at war with Deneb, and it seems against nature now to be at peace and to look at the stars without anxiety."

The two men with the Executive Director of the Solar Federation were both younger than Swift. Neither was as gray. Neither looked quite as tired.

John Henderson, thin-lipped and finding it hard to control the relief he felt in the midst of triumph, said, "They're destroyed! They're destroyed! It's what I keep saying to myself over and over and I still can't believe it. We all talked so much, over so many years, about the menace hanging over

Earth and all its worlds, over every human being, and all the time it was true, every word of it. And now we're alive and it's the Denebians who are shattered and destroyed. They'll be no menace now, ever again."

"Thanks to Multivac," said Swift, with a quiet glance at the imperturbable Jablonsky, who through all the war had been Chief Interpreter of science's oracle. "Right, Max?"

Jablonsky shrugged. Automatically, he reached for a cigarette and decided against it. He alone, of all the thousands who had lived in the tunnels within Multivac, had been allowed to smoke, but toward the end he had made definite efforts to avoid making use of the privilege.

He said, "Well, that's what they say." His broad thumb moved in the direction of his right shoulder, aiming upward.

"Jealous, Max?"

"Because they're shouting for Multivac? Because Multivac is the big hero of mankind in this war?" Jablonsky's craggy face took on an air of suitable contempt. "What's that to me? Let Multivac be the machine that won the war, if it pleases them."

Henderson looked at the other two out of the corners of his eyes. In this short interlude that the three had instinctively sought out in the one peaceful corner of a metropolis gone mad; in this entr'acte between the dangers of war and the difficulties of peace; when, for one moment, they might all find surcease; he was conscious only of his weight of guilt.

Suddenly, it was as though that weight were too great to be borne longer. It had to be thrown off, along with the war; now!

Henderson said, "Multivac had nothing to do with victory. It's just a machine."

"A big one," said Swift.

"Then just a big machine. No better than the data fed it." For a moment, he stopped, suddenly unnerved at what he was saying.

Jablonsky looked at him, his thick fingers once again fumbling for a cigarette and once again drawing back. "You should know. You supplied the data. Or is it just that you're taking the credit?"

'Wo," said Henderson, angrily. "There is no credit. What do you know of the data Multivac had to use; predigested from a hundred subsidiary computers here on Earth, on the Moon, on Mars, even on Titan. With Titan always delayed and always that feeling that its figures would introduce an unexpected bias."

"It would drive anyone mad," said Swift, with gentle sympathy.

Henderson shook his head. "It wasn't just that. I admit that eight years ago when I replaced Lepont as Chief Programmer, I was nervous. But there was an exhilaration about things in those days. The war was still long-range; an adventure without real danger. We hadn't reached the point where manned vessels had had to take over and where interstellar warps could swallow up a planet clean, if aimed correctly. But then, when the real difficulties began-"

Angrily-he could finally permit anger-he said, "You know nothing about it."

"Well," said Swift. "Tell us. The war is over. We've won."

"Yes." Henderson nodded his head. He had to remember that. Earth had won so all had been for the best. "Well, the data became meaningless."

"Meaningless? You mean that literally?" said Jablonsky.

"Literally. What would you expect? The trouble with you two was that you weren't out in the thick of it. You never left Multivac, Max, and you, Mr. Director, never left the Mansion except on state visits where you saw exactly what they wanted you to see."

"I was not as unaware of that," said Swift, "as you may have thought."

"Do you know," said Henderson, "to what extent data concerning our production capacity, our resource potential, our trained manpower-everything of importance to the war effort, in fact-had become unreliable and untrustworthy during the last half of the war? Group leaders, both civilian and military, were intent on projecting their own improved image, so to speak, so they obscured the bad and magnified the good. Whatever the machines might do, the men who programmed them and interpreted the results had their own skins to think of and competitors to stab. There was no way of stopping that. I tried, and failed."

"Of course," said Swift, in quiet consolation. "I can see that you would."

This time Jablonsky decided to light his cigarette. "Yet I presume you provided Multivac with data in your programming. You said nothing to us about unreliability."

"How could I tell you? And if I did, how could you afford to believe me?" demanded Henderson, savagely. "Our entire war effort was geared to Multivac. It was the one great weapon on our side, for the Denebians had nothing like it. What else kept up morale in the face of doom but the assurance that Multivac would always predict and circumvent any Denebian move, and would always direct and prevent the circumvention of our moves? Great Space, after our Spy-warp was blasted out of hyperspace we lacked any reliable Denebian data to feed Multivac and we didn't dare make that public."

"True enough," said Swift.

"Well, then," said Henderson, "if I told you the data was unreliable, what could you have done but replace me and refuse to believe me? I couldn't allow that."

"What did you do?" said Jablonsky.

"Since the war is won, I'D tell you what I did. I corrected the data."

"How?" asked Swift.

"Intuition, I presume. I juggled them till they looked right. At first, I hardly dared, I changed a bit here and there to correct what were obvious impossibilities. When the sky didn't collapse about us, I got braver. Toward the end, I scarcely cared. I just wrote out the necessary data as it was needed. I even had the Multivac Annex prepare data for me according to a private programming pattern I had devised for the purpose."

"Random figures?" said Jablonsky.

"Not at all. I introduced a number of necessary biases." Jablonsky smiled, quite unexpectedly, his dark eyes sparkling behind the crinkling of the lower lids. "Three times a report was brought me about unauthorized uses of the Annex, and I let it go each time. If it had mattered, I would have followed it up and spotted you, John, and found out what you were doing. But, of course, nothing about Multivac mattered in those days, so you got away with it."

"What do you mean, nothing mattered?" asked Henderson, suspiciously.

"Nothing did. I suppose if I had told you this at the time, it would have spared you your agony, but then if you had told me what you were doing, it would have spared me mine. What made you think Multivac was in working order, whatever the data you supplied it?"

"Not in working order?" said Swift.

"Not really. Not reliably. After all, where were my technicians in the last years of the war? I'll tell you, they were feeding computers on a thousand different space devices. They were gone! I had to make do with kids I couldn't trust and veterans who were out-of-date. Besides, do you think I could trust the solid-state components coming out of Cryogenics in the last years? Cryogenics wasn't any better placed as far as personnel was concerned than I was. To me, it didn't matter whether the data being supplied Multivac were reliable or not. The results weren't reliable. That much I knew."

"What did you do?" asked Henderson.

"I did what you did, John. I introduced the bugger factor. I adjusted matters in accordance with intuition-and that's how the machine won the war."

Swift leaned back in the chair and stretched his legs out before him. "Such revelations. It turns out then that the material handed me to guide me in my decision-making capacity was a man-made interpretation of man-made data. Isn't that right?"

"It looks so," said Jablonsky.

"Then I perceive I was correct in not placing too much reliance upon it," said Swift.

"You didn't?" Jablonsky, despite what he had just said, managed to look professionally insulted.

"I'm afraid I didn't. Multivac might seem to say, Strike here, not there; do this, not that; wait, don't act. But I could never be certain that what Multivac seemed to say, it really did say; or what it really said, it really meant. I could never be certain."

"But the final report was always plain enough, sir," said Jablonsky.

"To those who did not have to make the decision, perhaps. Not to me. The horror of the responsibility of such decisions was unbearable and not even Multivac was sufficient to remove the weight. But the point is I was justified in doubting and there is tremendous relief in that." Caught up in the conspiracy of mutual confession, Jablonsky put titles aside, "What was it you did then, Lamar? After all, you did make decisions. How?"

"Well, it's time to be getting back perhaps but-I'll tell you first. Why not? I did make use of a computer, Max, but an older one than Multivac, much older."

He groped in his own pocket for cigarettes, and brought out a package along with a scattering of small change; old-fashioned coins dating to the first years before the metal shortage had brought into being a credit system tied to a computer-complex.

Swift smiled rather sheepishly. "I still need these to make money seem substantial to me. An old man finds it hard to abandon the habits of youth." He put a cigarette between his lips and dropped the coins one by one back into his pocket.

He held the last coin between his fingers, staring absently at it. "Multivac is not the first computer, friends, nor the best-known, nor the one that can most efficiently lift the load of decision from the shoulders of the executive. A machine did win the war, John; at least a very simple computing device did; one that I used every time I had a particularly hard decision to make."

With a faint smile of reminiscence, he flipped the coin he held. It glinted in the air as it spun and came down in Swift's outstretched palm. His hand closed over it and brought it down on the back of his left hand. His right hand remained in place, hiding the coin.

"Heads or tails, gentlemen?" said Swift.

The Monkey's Paw
W.W. Jacobs

I

Without, the night was cold and wet, but in the small parlor of Laburnam Villa the blinds were drawn and the fire burned brightly. Father and son were at chess, the former, who possessed ideas about the game involving radical changes, putting his king into such sharp and unnecessary perils that it even provoked comment from the white-haired old lady knitting placidly by the fire.

"Hark at the wind," said Mr. White, who, having seen a fatal mistake after it was too late, was amiably desirous of preventing his son from seeing it.

"I'm listening," said the latter, grimly surveying the board as he stretched out his hand. "Check."

"I should hardly think that he'd come to-night," said his father, with his hand poised over the board.

"Mate," replied the son.

"That's the worst of living so far out," bawled Mr. White, with sudden and unlooked-for violence; "of all the beastly, slushy, out-of-the-way places to live in, this is the worst. Pathway's a bog, and the road's a torrent. I don't know what people are thinking about. I suppose because only two houses in the road are let, they think it doesn't matter."

"Never mind, dear," said his wife, soothingly; "perhaps you'll win the next one."

Mr. White looked up sharply, just in time to intercept a knowing glance between mother and son. The words died away on his lips, and he hid a guilty grin in his thin grey beard.

"There he is," said Herbert White, as the gate banged to loudly and heavy footsteps came toward the door.

The old man rose with hospitable haste, and opening the door, was heard condoling with the new arrival. The new arrival also condoled with himself, so that Mrs. White said, "Tut, tut!" and coughed gently as her husband entered the room, followed by a tall, burly man, beady of eye and rubicund of visage.

"Sergeant-Major Morris," he said, introducing him.

The sergeant-major shook hands, and taking the proffered seat by the fire, watched contentedly while his host got out whiskey and tumblers and stood a small copper kettle on the fire.

At the third glass his eyes got brighter, and he began to talk, the little family circle regarding with eager interest this visitor from distant parts, as he squared his broad shoulders in the chair and spoke of wild scenes and doughty deeds; of wars and plagues and strange peoples.

"Twenty-one years of it," said Mr. White, nodding at his wife and son. "When he went away he was a slip of a youth in the warehouse. Now look at him."

"He don't look to have taken much harm," said Mrs. White, politely.

"I'd like to go to India myself," said the old man, "just to look round a bit, you know."

"Better where you are," said the sergeant-major, shaking his head. He put down the empty glass, and sighing softly, shook it again.

"I should like to see those old temples and fakirs and jugglers," said the old man. "What was that you started telling me the other day about a monkey's paw or something, Morris?"

"Nothing," said the soldier, hastily. "Leastways nothing worth hearing."

"Monkey's paw?" said Mrs. White, curiously.

"Well, it's just a bit of what you might call magic, perhaps," said the sergeant-major, offhandedly.

His three listeners leaned forward eagerly. The visitor absent-mindedly put his empty glass to his lips and then set it down again. His host filled it for him.

"To look at," said the sergeant-major, fumbling in his pocket, "it's just an ordinary little paw, dried to a mummy."

He took something out of his pocket and proffered it. Mrs. White drew back with a grimace, but her son, taking it, examined it curiously.

"And what is there special about it?" inquired Mr. White as he took it from his son, and having examined it, placed it upon the table.

"It had a spell put on it by an old fakir," said the sergeant-major, "a very holy man. He wanted to show that fate ruled people's lives, and that those who interfered with it did so to their sorrow. He put a spell on it so that three separate men could each have three wishes from it."

His manner was so impressive that his hearers were conscious that their light laughter jarred somewhat.

"Well, why don't you have three, sir?" said Herbert White, cleverly.

The soldier regarded him in the way that middle age is wont to regard presumptuous youth. "I have," he said, quietly, and his blotchy face whitened.

"And did you really have the three wishes granted?" asked Mrs. White.

"I did," said the sergeant-major, and his glass tapped against his strong teeth.

"And has anybody else wished?" persisted the old lady.

"The first man had his three wishes. Yes," was the reply; "I don't know what the first two were, but the third was for death. That's how I got the paw."

His tones were so grave that a hush fell upon the group.

"If you've had your three wishes, it's no good to you now, then, Morris," said the old man at last. "What do you keep it for?"

The soldier shook his head. "Fancy, I suppose," he said, slowly. "I did have some idea of selling it, but I don't think I will. It has caused enough mischief already. Besides, people won't buy. They think it's a fairy tale; some of them, and those who do think anything of it want to try it first and pay me afterward."

"If you could have another three wishes," said the old man, eyeing him keenly, "would you have them?"

"I don't know," said the other. "I don't know."

He took the paw, and dangling it between his forefinger and thumb, suddenly threw it upon the fire. White, with a slight cry, stooped down and snatched it off.

"Better let it burn," said the soldier, solemnly.

"If you don't want it, Morris," said the other, "give it to me."

"I won't," said his friend, doggedly. "I threw it on the fire. If you keep it, don't blame me for what happens. Pitch it on the fire again like a sensible man."

The other shook his head and examined his new possession closely. "How do you do it?" he inquired.

"Hold it up in your right hand and wish aloud," said the sergeant-major, "but I warn you of the consequences."

"Sounds like the Arabian Nights," said Mrs. White, as she rose and began to set the supper. "Don't you think you might wish for four pairs of hands for me?"

Her husband drew the talisman from pocket, and then all three burst into laughter as the sergeant-major, with a look of alarm on his face, caught him by the arm.

"If you must wish," he said, gruffly, "wish for something sensible."

Mr. White dropped it back in his pocket, and placing chairs, motioned his friend to the table. In the business of supper the talisman was partly forgotten, and afterward the three sat listening in an enthralled fashion to a second instalment of the soldier's adventures in India.

"If the tale about the monkey's paw is not more truthful than those he has been telling us," said Herbert, as the door closed behind their guest, just in time for him to catch the last train, "we shan't make much out of it."

"Did you give him anything for it, father?" inquired Mrs. White, regarding her husband closely.

"A trifle," said he, coloring slightly. "He didn't want it, but I made him take it. And he pressed me again to throw it away."

"Likely," said Herbert, with pretended horror. "Why, we're going to be rich, and famous and happy. Wish to be an emperor, father, to begin with; then you can't be henpecked."

He darted round the table, pursued by the maligned Mrs. White armed with an antimacassar.

Mr. White took the paw from his pocket and eyed it dubiously. "I don't know what to wish for, and that's a fact," he said, slowly. "It seems to me I've got all I want."

"If you only cleared the house, you'd be quite happy, wouldn't you?" said Herbert, with his hand on his shoulder. "Well, wish for two hundred pounds, then; that'll just do it."

His father, smiling shamefacedly at his own credulity, held up the talisman, as his son, with a solemn face, somewhat marred by a wink at his mother, sat down at the piano and struck a few impressive chords.

"I wish for two hundred pounds," said the old man distinctly.

A fine crash from the piano greeted the words, interrupted by a shuddering cry from the old man. His wife and son ran toward him.

"It moved," he cried, with a glance of disgust at the object as it lay on the floor.

"As I wished, it twisted in my hand like a snake."

"Well, I don't see the money," said his son as he picked it up and placed it on the table, "and I bet I never shall."

"It must have been your fancy, father," said his wife, regarding him anxiously.

He shook his head. "Never mind, though; there's no harm done, but it gave me a shock all the same."

They sat down by the fire again while the two men finished their pipes. Outside, the wind was higher than ever, and the old man started nervously at the sound of a door banging upstairs. A silence unusual and depressing settled upon all three, which lasted until the old couple rose to retire for the night.

"I expect you'll find the cash tied up in a big bag in the middle of your bed," said Herbert, as he bade them good-night, "and something horrible squatting up on top of the wardrobe watching you as you pocket your ill-gotten gains."

He sat alone in the darkness, gazing at the dying fire, and seeing faces in it. The last face was so horrible and so simian that he gazed at it in amazement. It got so vivid that, with a little uneasy laugh, he felt on the table for a glass containing a little water to throw over it. His hand grasped the monkey's paw, and with a little shiver he wiped his hand on his coat and went up to bed.

II.

In the brightness of the wintry sun next morning as it streamed over the breakfast table he laughed at his fears. There was an air of prosaic wholesomeness about the room which it had lacked on the previous night, and the dirty, shriveled little paw was pitched on the sideboard with a carelessness which betokened no great belief in its virtues.

"I suppose all old soldiers are the same," said Mrs. White. "The idea of our listening to such nonsense! How could wishes be granted in these days? And if they could, how could two hundred pounds hurt you, father?"

"Might drop on his head from the sky," said the frivolous Herbert.

"Morris said the things happened so naturally," said his father, "that you might if you so wished attribute it to coincidence."

"Well, don't break into the money before I come back," said Herbert as he rose from the table. "I'm afraid it'll turn you into a mean, avaricious man, and we shall have to disown you."

His mother laughed, and following him to the door, watched him down the road; and returning to the breakfast table, was very happy at the expense of her husband's credulity. All of which did not prevent her from scurrying to the door at the postman's knock, nor prevent her from referring somewhat shortly to retired sergeant-majors of bibulous habits when she found that the post brought a tailor's bill.

"Herbert will have some more of his funny remarks, I expect, when he comes home," she said, as they sat at dinner.

"I dare say," said Mr. White, pouring himself out some beer; "but for all that, the thing moved in my hand; that I'll swear to."

"You thought it did," said the old lady soothingly.

"I say it did," replied the other. "There was no thought about it; I had just—— What's the matter?"

His wife made no reply. She was watching the mysterious movements of a man outside, who, peering in an undecided fashion at the house, appeared to be trying to make up his mind to enter. In mental connection with the two hundred pounds, she noticed that the stranger was well dressed, and wore a silk hat of glossy newness. Three times he paused at the gate, and then walked on again. The fourth time he stood with his hand upon it, and then with sudden resolution flung it open and walked up the path. Mrs. White at the same moment placed her hands behind her, and hurriedly unfastening the strings of her apron, put that useful article of apparel beneath the cushion of her chair.

She brought the stranger, who seemed ill at ease, into the room. He gazed at her furtively, and listened in a preoccupied fashion as the old lady apologized for the appearance of the room, and her husband's coat, a garment which he usually reserved for the garden. She then waited as patiently as her sex would permit, for him to broach his business, but he was at first strangely silent.

"I—was asked to call," he said at last, and stooped and picked a piece of cotton from his trousers. "I come from 'Maw and Meggins.'"

The old lady started. "Is anything the matter?" she asked, breathlessly. "Has anything happened to Herbert? What is it? What is it?"

Her husband interposed. "There, there, mother," he said, hastily. "Sit down, and don't jump to conclusions. You've not brought bad news, I'm sure, sir;" and he eyed the other wistfully.

"I'm sorry—" began the visitor.

"Is he hurt?" demanded the mother, wildly.

The visitor bowed in assent. "Badly hurt," he said, quietly, "but he is not in any pain."

"Oh, thank God!" said the old woman, clasping her hands. "Thank God for that! Thank "

She broke off suddenly as the sinister meaning of the assurance dawned upon her and she saw the awful confirmation of her fears in the other's averted face. She caught her breath, and turning to her slower-witted husband, laid her trembling old hand upon his. There was a long silence.

"He was caught in the machinery," said the visitor at length in a low voice.

"Caught in the machinery," repeated Mr. White, in a dazed fashion, "yes."

He sat staring blankly out at the window, and taking his wife's hand between his own, pressed it as he had been wont to do in their old courting-days nearly forty years before.

"He was the only one left to us," he said, turning gently to the visitor. "It is hard."

The other coughed, and rising, walked slowly to the window. "The firm wished me to convey their sincere sympathy with you in your great loss," he said, without looking round. "I beg that you will understand I am only their servant and merely obeying orders."

There was no reply; the old woman's face was white, her eyes staring, and her breath inaudible; on the husband's face was a look such as his friend the sergeant might have carried into his first action.

"I was to say that 'Maw and Meggins' disclaim all responsibility," continued the other. "They admit no liability at all, but in consideration of your son's services, they wish to present you with a certain sum as compensation."

Mr. White dropped his wife's hand, and rising to his feet, gazed with a look of horror at his visitor. His dry lips shaped the words, "How much?"

"Two hundred pounds," was the answer.

Unconscious of his wife's shriek, the old man smiled faintly, put out his hands like a sightless man, and dropped, a senseless heap, to the floor.

III.

In the huge new cemetery, some two miles distant, the old people buried their dead, and came back to a house steeped in shadow and silence. It was all over so quickly that at first they could hardly realize it, and remained in a state of expectation as though of something else to happen —something else which was to lighten this load, too heavy for old hearts to bear.

But the days passed, and expectation gave place to resignation—the hopeless resignation of the old, sometimes miscalled, apathy. Sometimes they hardly exchanged a word, for now they had nothing to talk about, and their days were long to weariness.

It was about a week after that the old man, waking suddenly in the night, stretched out his hand and found himself alone. The room was in darkness, and the sound of subdued weeping came from the window. He raised himself in bed and listened.

"Come back," he said, tenderly. "You will be cold."

"It is colder for my son," said the old woman, and wept afresh.

The sound of her sobs died away on his ears. The bed was warm, and his eyes heavy with sleep. He dozed fitfully, and then slept until a sudden wild cry from his wife awoke him with a start.

"The paw!" she cried wildly. "The monkey's paw!"

He started up in alarm. "Where? Where is it? What's the matter?"

She came stumbling across the room toward him. "I want it," she said, quietly. "You've not destroyed it?"

"It's in the parlor, on the bracket," he replied, marveling. "Why?"

She cried and laughed together, and bending over, kissed his cheek.

"I only just thought of it," she said, hysterically. "Why didn't I think of it before? Why didn't you think of it?"

"Think of what?" he questioned.

"The other two wishes," she replied, rapidly. "We've only had one."

"Was not that enough?" he demanded, fiercely.

"No," she cried, triumphantly; "we'll have one more. Go down and get it quickly, and wish our boy alive again."

The man sat up in bed and flung the bedclothes from his quaking limbs. "Good God, you are mad!" he cried, aghast.

"Get it," she panted; "get it quickly, and wish—Oh, my boy, my boy!"

Her husband struck a match and lit the candle. "Get back to bed," he said, unsteadily. "You don't know what you are saying."

"We had the first wish granted," said the old woman, feverishly; "why not the second?"

"A coincidence," stammered the old man.

"Go and get it and wish," cried his wife, quivering with excitement.

The old man turned and regarded her, and his voice shook. "He has been dead ten days, and besides he—I would not tell you else, but—I could only recognize him by his clothing. If he was too terrible for you to see then, how now?"

"Bring him back," cried the old woman, and dragged him toward the door. "Do you think I fear the child I have nursed?"

He went down in the darkness, and felt his way to the parlor, and then to the mantelpiece. The talisman was in its place, and a horrible fear that the unspoken wish might bring his mutilated son before him ere he could escape from the room seized upon him, and he caught his breath as he found that he had lost the direction of the door. His brow cold with sweat, he felt his way round the table, and groped along the wall until he found himself in the small passage with the unwholesome thing in his hand.

Even his wife's face seemed changed as he entered the room. It was white and expectant, and to his fears seemed to have an unnatural look upon it. He was afraid of her.

"Wish!" she cried, in a strong voice.

"It is foolish and wicked," he faltered.

"Wish!" repeated his wife.

He raised his hand. "I wish my son alive again."

The talisman fell to the floor, and he regarded it fearfully. Then he sank trembling into a chair as the old woman, with burning eyes, walked to the window and raised the blind.

He sat until he was chilled with the cold, glancing occasionally at the figure of the old woman peering through the window. The candle-end, which had burned below the rim of the china candlestick, was throwing pulsating shadows on the ceiling and walls, until, with a flicker larger than the rest, it expired. The old man, with an unspeakable sense of relief at the failure of the talisman, crept back to his bed, and a minute or two afterward the old woman came silently and apathetically beside him.

Neither spoke, but lay silently listening to the ticking of the clock. A stair creaked, and a squeaky mouse scurried noisily through the wall. The darkness was oppressive, and after lying for some time screwing up his courage, he took the box of matches, and striking one, went downstairs for a candle.

At the foot of the stairs the match went out, and he paused to strike another; and at the same moment a knock, so quiet and stealthy as to be scarcely audible, sounded on the front door.

The matches fell from his hand and spilled in the passage. He stood motionless, his breath suspended until the knock was repeated. Then he turned and fled swiftly back to his room, and closed the door behind him. A third knock sounded through the house.

"What's that?" cried the old woman, starting up.

"A rat," said the old man in shaking tones—"a rat. It passed me on the stairs."

His wife sat up in bed listening. A loud knock resounded through the house.

"It's Herbert!" she screamed. "It's Herbert!"

She ran to the door, but her husband was before her, and catching her by the arm, held her tightly.

"What are you going to do?" he whispered hoarsely.

"It's my boy; it's Herbert!" she cried, struggling mechanically. "I forgot it was two miles away. What are you holding me for? Let go. I must open the door."

"For God's sake don't let it in," cried the old man, trembling.

"You're afraid of your own son," she cried, struggling. "Let me go. I'm coming, Herbert; I'm coming."

There was another knock, and another. The old woman with a sudden wrench broke free and ran from the room. Her husband followed to the landing, and called after her appealingly as she hurried downstairs. He heard the chain rattle back and the bottom bolt drawn slowly and stiffly from the socket. Then the old woman's voice, strained and panting.

"The bolt," she cried, loudly. "Come down. I can't reach it."

But her husband was on his hands and knees groping wildly on the floor in search of the paw. If he could only find it before the thing outside got in. A perfect fusillade of knocks reverberated through the house, and he heard the scraping of a chair as his wife put it down in the passage against the door. He heard the creaking of the bolt as it came slowly back, and at the same moment he found the monkey's paw, and frantically breathed his third and last wish.

The knocking ceased suddenly, although the echoes of it were still in the house. He heard the chair drawn back, and the door opened. A cold wind rushed up the staircase, and a long loud wail of disappointment and misery from his wife gave him courage to run down to her side, and then to the gate beyond. The street lamp flickering opposite shone on a quiet and deserted road.

The Night the Ghost Got In
James Thurber

The ghost that got into our house on the night of November 17, 1915, raised such a hullabaloo of misunderstanding that I am sorry I didn't just let it keep on walking, and go to bed. Its advent caused my mother to throw a shoe through a window of the house next door and ended up with my grandfather shooting a gun. I am sorry, therefore, as I have said, that I ever paid any attention to the footsteps.

They began about a quarter past one o'clock in the morning, a rhythmic, quick-cadenced walking around the dining room table. My mother was asleep in one room upstairs; my brother Herman in another; and grandfather was in the attic. I had just stepped out of the bathtub and was busily rubbing myself with a towel when I heard the steps. They were the steps of a man walking rapidly around the dining room table downstairs. The light from the bathroom shone down the back steps, which dropped directly into the dining room. The steps kept going round and round the table; at regular intervals a board creaked, when it was trod upon. I supposed at first that it was my father or my brother Roy, who had gone to Indianapolis but were expected home at any time. I suspected next that it was a burglar. It did not enter my mind until later that it was a ghost.

After the walking had gone on for perhaps three minutes, I tiptoed to Herman's room. "Psst!" I hissed in the dark, shaking him. "There's something downstairs!" I said. Instantly the steps began again, circled the dining room table like a man running, and started up the stairs toward us, heavily, two at a time. The light still shone palely down the stairs; we saw nothing coming; we only heard the steps. Herman rushed to his room and slammed the door. I slammed shut the door at the stairs top and held my knee against it. After a long minute, I slowly opened it again. There was nothing there. There was no sound. None of us ever heard the ghost again.

The slamming of the doors had awoken mother; she peered out of her room. "What on earth are you boys doing?" she demanded. "What was all that running around downstairs?" said mother. So she had heard the steps, too! We just looked at her. "Burglars!" she shouted intuitively. I tried to quiet her by starting lightly downstairs.

"Come on, Herman," I said.

"I'll stay with mother," he said. "She's all excited."

I stepped back onto the landing.

Don't either of you go a step," said mother. "We'll call the police." Since the phone was downstairs, I didn't see how we were going to call the police-nor did I want the police-but mother made one of her quick decisions. She flung up a window of her bedroom which faced the bedroom windows of the house of a neighbor, picked up a shoe, and whammed it through a pane of glass across the narrow space occupied by a retired engraver named Bodwell and his wife.

It was now about two o'clock of a moonless night; clouds hung black and low. Bodwell was at the window in a minute, shouting, frothing a little, shaking his fist. "We'll sell the house and go back to Peoria," we could hear Mrs. Bodwell saying. It was some time before mother "got through" to Bodwell. "Burglars!" she shouted. "Burglars in the house!" Herman and I hadn't dared to tell her that it was not burglars but ghosts, for she was even more afraid of ghosts than of burglars. Bodwell at first thought that she meant that there were burglars in his house, but finally he quieted down and called the police for us over an extension phone by his bed. After he had disappeared from the window, mother made as if to throw another shoe, not because there was further need of it but, as she later explained, because the thrill of heaving a shoe through a window glass had enormously taken her fancy. I prevented her.

The police were on hand in a commendably short time. "Open up!" cried a hoarse voice. "We're men from Headquarters!" I wanted to go down and let them in, since there they were, but mother wouldn't hear of it. "You haven't a stitch on," she pointed out. "You'd catch your death." I wound the towel around me again. Finally the cops put their shoulders to our big heavy front door with its thick beveled glass and broke it in: I could hear a rending of wood and a splash of glass on the floor of the hall. Their lights played all over the living room and crisscrossed nervously in the dining room, stabbed into hallways, shot up the front stairs and finally up the back. They caught me standing in my towel at the top. A heavy policeman bounded up the steps. "Who are you?" he demanded. "I live here," I said. "Well whattsa matta, ya hot?" he asked. It was, as a matter of fact, cold; I went to my room and pulled on some trousers. On my way out, a cop stuck a gun into my ribs. "Whatta you doin' here?" he demanded. "I live here," I said.

The officer in charge reported to mother. "No sign of nobody, lady," he said. "Musta got away-whatt'd he look like?" "There were two or three of them," mother said, "whooping and carrying on and slamming doors. "Funny," said the cop. "All ya windows and doors was locked on the inside tight as a tick."

"No sign o' nothing," said the cop who had first spoken to mother. "This guy," he explained to the others, jerking a thumb at me, "was nekked. The lady seems historical." They all nodded, but said nothing; just looked at me. In the small silence we all heard a creaking in the attic. Grandfather was turning over in bed. "What's 'at?" snapped a policeman. Five or six cops sprang for the attic door before I could intervene or explain. I realized that it would be bad if they burst in on grandfather unannounced, or even announced. He was going through a phase in which he believed that General Meade's men, under steady hammering by Stonewall Jackson, were beginning to retreat and even desert.

When I got to the attic, things were pretty confused. Grandfather had evidently jumped to the conclusion that the police were deserters from Meade's army, trying to hide away in his attic. He bounded out of bed wearing a long flannel nightgown over long woolen underwear, a nightcap, and a leather jacket around his chest. The cops must have realized at once that the indignant, white-haired old man belonged in the house, but they had no chance to say so. "Back, ye cowardly dogs!" roared grandfather. "Back t' the lines, ye lily-livered cattle!" With that, he fetched an officer a flat-handed smack alongside his head that sent him sprawling. The others beat a retreat, but not fast enough; grandfather grabbed an officer's gun from its holster and let fly. The report seemed to crack the rafters; smoke filled the attic. Somehow, we all finally got downstairs again and locked the door against the old gentleman. He fired once or twice more in the darkness and then went back to bed. "That was grandfather," I explained to one officer, out of breath. "He thinks you're deserters." "I'll say he does," said the officer.

The cops were reluctant to leave without getting their hands on somebody besides grandfather; the night had been distinctly a defeat for them. Furthermore, they obviously didn't like the "layout"; something looked-and I can see their viewpoint- phony.

"What was the matter with those policemen?" mother asked, after they had gone. "Grandfather shot at them," I said. "What for?" she demanded. I told her they were deserters. "Of all things!" said mother. "They were such nice-looking young men."

Grandfather was fresh as a daisy and full of jokes at breakfast next morning. We thought at first he had forgotten all about what had happened, but he hadn't. Over his third cup of coffee, he glared at Herman and me. "What was the idée of all them cops tarryhootin' round the house last night?" he demanded. He had us there.

The Snow Image: A Childish Miracle
Nathaniel Hawthorne

One afternoon of a cold winter's day, when the sun shone forth with chilly brightness, after a long storm, two children asked leave of their mother to run out and play in the new-fallen snow. The elder child was a little girl, whom, because she was of a tender and modest disposition, and was thought to be very beautiful, her parents, and other people who were familiar with her, used to call Violet. But her brother was known by the style and title of Peony, on account of the ruddiness of his broad and round little phiz, which made everybody think of sunshine and great scarlet flowers. The father of these two children, a certain Mr. Lindsey, it is important to say, was an excellent but exceedingly matter-of-fact sort of man, a dealer in hardware, and was sturdily accustomed to take what is called the common-sense view of all matters that came under his consideration. With a heart about as tender as other people's, he had a head as hard and impenetrable, and therefore, perhaps, as empty, as one of the iron pots which it was a part of his business to sell. The mother's character, on the other hand, had a strain of poetry in it, a trait of unworldly beauty,--a delicate and dewy flower, as it were, that had survived out of her imaginative youth, and still kept itself alive amid the dusty realities of matrimony and motherhood.

So, Violet and Peony, as I began with saying, besought their mother to let them run out and play in the new snow; for, though it had looked so dreary and dismal, drifting downward out of the gray sky, it had a very cheerful aspect, now that the sun was shining on it. The children dwelt in a city, and had no wider play-place than a little garden before the house, divided by a white fence from the street, and with a pear-tree and two or three plum-trees overshadowing it, and some rose-bushes just in front of the parlor-windows. The trees and shrubs, however, were now leafless, and their twigs were enveloped in the light snow, which thus made a kind of wintry foliage, with here and there a pendent icicle for the fruit.

"Yes, Violet,--yes, my little Peony," said their kind mother, "you may go out and play in the new snow."

Accordingly, the good lady bundled up her darlings in woolen jackets and wadded sacks, and put comforters round their necks, and a pair of striped gaiters on each little pair of legs, and worsted mittens on their hands, and gave them a kiss apiece, by way of a spell to keep away Jack Frost. Forth sallied the two children, with a hop-skip-and-jump, that carried them at once into the very heart of a huge snow-drift, whence Violet emerged like a snow-bunting, while little Peony floundered out with his round face in full bloom. Then what a merry time had they! To look at them, frolicking in the wintry garden, you would have thought that the dark and pitiless storm had been sent for no other purpose but to provide a new plaything for Violet and Peony; and that they themselves had been created, as the snow-birds were, to take delight only in the tempest, and in the white mantle which it spread over the earth.

At last, when they had frosted one another all over with handfuls of snow, Violet, after laughing heartily at little Peony's figure, was struck with a new idea.

"You look exactly like a snow-image, Peony," said she, "if your cheeks were not so red. And that puts me in mind! Let us make an image out of snow,--an image of a little girl,--and it shall be our sister, and shall run about and play with us all winter long. Won't it be nice?"

"Oh yes!" cried Peony, as plainly as he could speak, for he was but a little boy. "That will be nice! And mamma shall see it!"

"Yes," answered Violet; "mamma shall see the new little girl. But she must not make her come into the warm parlor; for, you know, our little snow-sister will not love the warmth."

And forthwith the children began this great business of making a snow-image that should run about; while their mother, who was sitting at the window and overheard some of their talk, could not help smiling at the gravity with which they set about it. They really seemed to imagine that there would be no difficulty whatever in creating a live little girl out of the snow. And, to say the truth, if miracles are ever to be wrought, it will be by putting our hands to the work in precisely such a simple and undoubting frame of mind as that in which Violet and Peony now undertook to perform one, without so much as knowing that it was a miracle. So thought the mother; and thought, likewise, that the new snow, just fallen from heaven, would be excellent material to make new beings of, if it were not so very cold. She gazed at the children a moment longer, delighting to watch their little figures,--the girl, tall for her age, graceful and agile, and so delicately colored that she looked like a cheerful thought more than a physical reality; while Peony expanded in breadth rather than height, and rolled along on his short and sturdy legs as substantial as an elephant, though not quite so big. Then the mother resumed her work. What it was I forget; but she was either trimming a silken bonnet for Violet, or darning a pair of stockings for little Peony's short legs. Again, however, and again, and yet other against, she could not help turning her head to the window to see how the children got on with their snow-image.

Indeed, it was an exceedingly pleasant sight, those bright little souls at their task! Moreover, it was really wonderful to observe how knowingly and skillfully they managed the matter. Violet assumed the chief direction, and told Peony what to do, while, with her own delicate fingers, she shaped out all the nicer parts of the snow-figure. It seemed, in fact, not so much to be made by the children, as to grow up under their hands, while they were playing and prattling about it. Their mother was quite surprised at this; and the longer she looked, the more and more surprised she grew.

"What remarkable children mine are!" thought she, smiling with a mother's pride; and, smiling at herself, too, for being so proud of them. "What other children could have made anything so like a little girl's figure out of snow at the first trial? Well; but now I must finish Peony's new frock, for his grandfather is coming to-morrow, and I want the little fellow to look handsome."

So she took up the frock, and was soon as busily at work again with her needle as the two children with their snow-image. But still, as the needle travelled hither and thither through the seams of the dress, the mother made her toil light and happy by listening to the airy voices of Violet and Peony. They kept talking to one another all the time, their tongues being quite as active as their feet and hands. Except at intervals, she could not distinctly hear what was said, but had merely a sweet impression that they were in a most loving mood, and were enjoying themselves highly, and that the business of making the snow-image went prosperously on. Now and then, however, when Violet and Peony happened to raise their voices, the words were as audible as if they had been spoken in the very parlor where the mother sat. Oh how delightfully those words echoed in her heart, even though they meant nothing so very wise or wonderful, after all!

But you must know a mother listens with her heart much more than with her ears; and thus she is often delighted with the trills of celestial music, when other people can hear nothing of the kind.

"Peony, Peony!" cried Violet to her brother, who had gone to another part of the garden, "bring me some of that fresh snow, Peony, from the very farthest corner, where we have not been trampling. I want it to shape our little snow-sister's bosom with. You know that part must be quite pure, just as it came out of the sky!"

"Here it is, Violet!" answered Peony, in his bluff tone,--but a very sweet tone, too,--as he came floundering through the half-trodden drifts. "Here is the snow for her little bosom. O Violet, how beau-ti-ful she begins to look!"

"Yes," said Violet, thoughtfully and quietly; "our snow-sister does look very lovely. I did not quite know, Peony, that we could make such a sweet little girl as this."

The mother, as she listened, thought how fit and delightful an incident it would be, if fairies, or still better, if angel-children were to come from paradise, and play invisibly with her own

177

darlings, and help them to make their snow-image, giving it the features of celestial babyhood! Violet and Peony would not be aware of their immortal playmates,--only they would see that the image grew very beautiful while they worked at it, and would think that they themselves had done it all.

"My little girl and boy deserve such playmates, if mortal children ever did!" said the mother to herself; and then she smiled again at her own motherly pride.

Nevertheless, the idea seized upon her imagination; and, ever and anon, she took a glimpse out of the window, half dreaming that she might see the golden-haired children of paradise sporting with her own golden-haired Violet and bright-cheeked Peony.

Now, for a few moments, there was a busy and earnest, but indistinct hum of the two children's voices, as Violet and Peony wrought together with one happy consent. Violet still seemed to be the guiding spirit, while Peony acted rather as a laborer, and brought her the snow from far and near. And yet the little urchin evidently had a proper understanding of the matter, too!

"Peony, Peony!" cried Violet; for her brother was again at the other side of the garden. "Bring me those light wreaths of snow that have rested on the lower branches of the pear-tree. You can clamber on the snowdrift, Peony, and reach them easily. I must have them to make some ringlets for our snow-sister's head!"

"Here they are, Violet!" answered the little boy. "Take care you do not break them. Well done! Well done! How pretty!"

"Does she not look sweetly?" said Violet, with a very satisfied tone; "and now we must have some little shining bits of ice, to make the brightness of her eyes. She is not finished yet. Mamma will see how very beautiful she is; but papa will say, 'Tush! nonsense!--come in out of the cold!'"

"Let us call mamma to look out," said Peony; and then he shouted lustily, "Mamma! mamma!! mamma!!! Look out, and see what a nice 'little girl we are making!"

The mother put down her work for an instant, and looked out of the window. But it so happened that the sun--for this was one of the shortest days of the whole year--had sunken so nearly to the edge of the world that his setting shine came obliquely into the lady's eyes. So she was dazzled, you must understand, and could not very distinctly observe what was in the garden. Still, however, through all that bright, blinding dazzle of the sun and the new snow, she beheld a small white figure in the garden, that seemed to have a wonderful deal of human likeness about it. And she saw Violet and Peony,--indeed, she looked more at them than at the image,--she saw the two children still at work; Peony bringing fresh snow, and Violet applying it to the figure as scientifically as a sculptor adds clay to his model. Indistinctly as she discerned the snow-child, the mother thought to herself that never before was there a snow-figure so cunningly made, nor ever such a dear little girl and boy to make it.

"They do everything better than other children," said she, very complacently. "No wonder they make better snow-images!"

She sat down again to her work, and made as much haste with it as possible; because twilight would soon come, and Peony's frock was not yet finished, and grandfather was expected, by railroad, pretty early in the morning. Faster and faster, therefore, went her flying fingers. The children, likewise, kept busily at work in the garden, and still the mother listened, whenever she could catch a word. She was amused to observe how their little imaginations had got mixed up with what they were doing, and carried away by it. They seemed positively to think that the snow-child would run about and play with them.

"What a nice playmate she will be for us, all winter long!" said Violet. "I hope papa will not be afraid of her giving us a cold! Sha'n't you love her dearly, Peony?"

"Oh yes!" cried Peony. "And I will hug her, and she shall sit down close by me and drink some of my warm milk!"

"Oh no, Peony!" answered Violet, with grave wisdom. "That will not do at all. Warm milk will not be wholesome for our little snow-sister. Little snow people, like her, eat nothing but icicles. No, no, Peony; we must not give her anything warm to drink!"

There was a minute or two of silence; for Peony, whose short legs were never weary, had gone on a pilgrimage again to the other side of the garden. All of a sudden, Violet cried out, loudly and joyfully,--"Look here, Peony! Come quickly! A light has been shining on her cheek out of that rose-colored cloud! and the color does not go away! Is not that beautiful!"

"Yes; it is beau-ti-ful," answered Peony, pronouncing the three syllables with deliberate accuracy. "O Violet, only look at her hair! It is all like gold!"

"Oh certainly," said Violet, with tranquility, as if it were very much a matter of course. "That color, you know, comes from the golden clouds, that we see up there in the sky. She is almost finished now. But her lips must be made very red,--redder than her cheeks. Perhaps, Peony, it will make them red if we both kiss them!"

Accordingly, the mother heard two smart little smacks, as if both her children were kissing the snow-image on its frozen mouth. But, as this did not seem to make the lips quite red enough, Violet next proposed that the snow-child should be invited to kiss Peony's scarlet cheek.

"Come, 'little snow-sister, kiss me!" cried Peony.

"There! she has kissed you," added Violet, "and now her lips are very red. And she blushed a little, too!"

"Oh, what a cold kiss!" cried Peony.

Just then, there came a breeze of the pure west-wind, sweeping through the garden and rattling the parlor-windows. It sounded so wintry cold, that the mother was about to tap on the window-pane with her thimbled finger, to summon the two children in, when they both cried out to her with one voice. The tone was not a tone of surprise, although they were evidently a good deal excited; it appeared rather as if they were very much rejoiced at some event that had now happened, but which they had been looking for, and had reckoned upon all along.

"Mamma! mamma! We have finished our little snow-sister, and she is running about the garden with us!"

"What imaginative little beings my children are!" thought the mother, putting the last few stitches into Peony's frock. "And it is strange, too that they make me almost as much a child as they themselves are! I can hardly help believing, now, that the snow-image has really come to life!"

"Dear mamma!" cried Violet, "pray look out and see what a sweet playmate we have!"

The mother, being thus entreated, could no longer delay to look forth from the window. The sun was now gone out of the sky, leaving, however, a rich inheritance of his brightness among those purple and golden clouds which make the sunsets of winter so magnificent. But there was not the slightest gleam or dazzle, either on the window or on the snow; so that the good lady could look all over the garden, and see everything and everybody in it. And what do you think she saw there? Violet and Peony, of course, her own two darling children. Ah, but whom or what did she see besides? Why, if you will believe me, there was a small figure of a girl, dressed all in white, with rose-tinged cheeks and ringlets of golden hue, playing about the garden with the two children! A stranger though she was, the child seemed to be on as familiar terms with Violet and Peony, and they with her, as if all the three had been playmates during the whole of their little lives. The mother thought to herself that it must certainly be the daughter of one of the neighbors, and that, seeing Violet and Peony in the garden, the child had run across the street to play with them. So this kind lady went to the door, intending to invite the little runaway into her comfortable parlor; for, now that the sunshine was withdrawn, the atmosphere, out of doors, was already growing very cold.

But, after opening the house-door, she stood an instant on the threshold, hesitating whether she ought to ask the child to come in, or whether she should even speak to her. Indeed, she almost doubted whether it were a real child after all, or only a light wreath of the new-fallen snow, blown hither and thither about the garden by the intensely cold west-wind. There was certainly something very singular in the aspect of the little stranger. Among all the children of the neighborhood, the lady could remember no such face, with its pure white, and delicate rose-color, and the golden ringlets tossing about the forehead and cheeks. And as for her dress, which was entirely of white, and fluttering in the breeze, it was such as no reasonable woman would put upon a little girl, when sending her out to play, in the depth of winter. It made this kind and careful mother shiver only to look at those small feet, with nothing in the world on them, except a very thin pair of white slippers. Nevertheless, airily as she was clad, the child seemed to feel not the slightest inconvenience from the cold, but danced so lightly over the snow that the tips of her toes left hardly a print in its surface; while Violet could but just keep pace with her, and Peony's short legs compelled him to lag behind.

Once, in the course of their play, the strange child placed herself between Violet and Peony, and taking a hand of each, skipped merrily forward, and they along with her. Almost immediately, however, Peony pulled away his little fist, and began to rub it as if the fingers were tingling with cold; while Violet also released herself, though with less abruptness, gravely remarking that it was better not to take hold of hands. The white-robed damsel said not a word, but danced about, just as merrily as before. If Violet and Peony did not choose to play with her, she could make just as good a playmate of the brisk and cold west-wind, which kept blowing her all about the garden, and took such liberties with her, that they seemed to have been friends for a long time. All this while, the mother stood on the threshold, wondering how a little girl could look so much like a flying snow-drift, or how a snow-drift could look so very like a little girl.
She called Violet, and whispered to her.

"Violet my darling, what is this child's name?" asked she. "Does she live near us?"

"Why, dearest mamma," answered Violet, laughing to think that her mother did not comprehend so very plain an affair, "this is our little snow-sister whom we have just been making!"

"Yes, dear mamma," cried Peony, running to his mother, and looking up simply into her face. "This is our snow-image! Is it not a nice 'little child?'"

At this instant a flock of snow-birds came flitting through the air. As was very natural, they avoided Violet and Peony. But--and this looked strange--they flew at once to the white-robed child, fluttered eagerly about her head, alighted on her shoulders, and seemed to claim her as an old acquaintance. She, on her part, was evidently as glad to see these little birds, old Winter's grandchildren, as they were to see her, and welcomed them by holding out both her hands. Hereupon, they each and all tried to alight on her two palms and ten small fingers and thumbs, crowding one another off, with an immense fluttering of their tiny wings. One dear little bird nestled tenderly in her bosom; another put its bill to her lips. They were as joyous, all the while, and seemed as much in their element, as you may have seen them when sporting with a snow-storm.

Violet and Peony stood laughing at this pretty sight; for they enjoyed the merry time which their new playmate was having with these small-winged visitors, almost as much as if they themselves took part in it.

"Violet," said her mother, greatly perplexed, "tell me the truth, without any jest. Who is this little girl?"

"My darling mamma," answered Violet, looking seriously into her mother's face, and apparently surprised that she should need any further explanation, "I have told you truly who she is. It is our little snow-image, which Peony and I have been making. Peony will tell you so, as well as I."

"Yes, mamma," asseverated Peony, with much gravity in his crimson little phiz; "this is 'little snow-child. Is not she a nice one? But, mamma, her hand is, oh, so very cold!"

While mamma still hesitated what to think and what to do, the street-gate was thrown open, and the father of Violet and Peony appeared, wrapped in a pilot-cloth sack, with a fur cap drawn down over his ears, and the thickest of gloves upon his hands. Mr. Lindsey was a middle-aged man, with a weary and yet a happy look in his wind-flushed and frost-pinched face, as if he had been busy all the day long, and was glad to get back to his quiet home. His eyes brightened at the sight of his wife and children, although he could not help uttering a word or two of surprise, at finding the whole family in the open air, on so bleak a day, and after sunset too. He soon perceived the little white stranger sporting to and fro in the garden, like a dancing snow-wreath, and the flock of snow-birds fluttering about her head.

"Pray, what little girl may that be?" inquired this very sensible man. "Surely her mother must be crazy to let her go out in such bitter weather as it has been to-day, with only that flimsy white gown and those thin slippers!"

"My dear husband," said his wife, "I know no more about the little thing than you do. Some neighbor's child, I suppose. Our Violet and Peony," she added, laughing at herself for repeating so absurd a story, "insist that she is nothing but a snow-image, which they have been busy about in the garden, almost all the afternoon."

As she said this, the mother glanced her eyes toward the spot where the children's snow-image had been made. What was her surprise, on perceiving that there was not the slightest trace of so much labor!--no image at all!--no piled up heap of snow!--nothing whatever, save the prints of little footsteps around a vacant space!

"This is very strange!" said she.

"What is strange, dear mother?" asked Violet. "Dear father, do not you see how it is? This is our snow-image, which Peony and I have made, because we wanted another playmate. Did not we, Peony?"

"Yes, papa," said crimson Peony. "This be our 'little snow-sister. Is she not beau-ti-ful? But she gave me such a cold kiss!"

"Poh, nonsense, children!" cried their good, honest father, who, as we have already intimated, had an exceedingly common-sensible way of looking at matters. "Do not tell me of making live figures out of snow. Come, wife; this little stranger must not stay out in the bleak air a moment longer. We will bring her into the parlor; and you shall give her a supper of warm bread and milk, and make her as comfortable as you can. Meanwhile, I will inquire among the neighbors; or, if necessary, send the city-crier about the streets, to give notice of a lost child."

So saying, this honest and very kind-hearted man was going toward the little white damsel, with the best intentions in the world. But Violet and Peony, each seizing their father by the hand, earnestly besought him not to make her come in.

"Dear father," cried Violet, putting herself before him, "it is true what I have been telling you! This is our little snow-girl, and she cannot live any longer than while she breathes the cold west-wind. Do not make her come into the hot room!"

"Yes, father," shouted Peony, stamping his little foot, so mightily was he in earnest, "this be nothing but our 'little snow-child! She will not love the hot fire!"

"Nonsense, children, nonsense, nonsense!" cried the father, half vexed, half laughing at what he considered their foolish obstinacy. "Run into the house, this moment! It is too late to play any longer, now. I must take care of this little girl immediately, or she will catch her death-a-cold!"

"Husband! dear husband!" said his wife, in a low voice,--for she had been looking narrowly at the snow-child, and was more perplexed than ever,--"there is something very singular in all this. You will think me foolish,--but--but--may it not be that some invisible angel has been attracted by the simplicity and good faith with which our children set about their undertaking? May he not have spent an hour of his immortality in playing with those dear little souls? and so the result is what we call a miracle. No, no! Do not laugh at me; I see what a foolish thought it is!"

"My dear wife," replied the husband, laughing heartily, "you are as much a child as Violet and Peony."

And in one sense so she was, for all through life she had kept her heart full of childlike simplicity and faith, which was as pure and clear as crystal; and, looking at all matters through this transparent medium, she sometimes saw truths so profound that other people laughed at them as nonsense and absurdity.

But now kind Mr. Lindsey had entered the garden, breaking away from his two children, who still sent their shrill voices after him, beseeching him to let the snow-child stay and enjoy herself in the cold west-wind. As he approached, the snow-birds took to flight. The little white damsel, also, fled backward, shaking her head, as if to say, "Pray, do not touch me!" and roguishly, as it appeared, leading him through the deepest of the snow. Once, the good man stumbled, and floundered down upon his face, so that, gathering himself up again, with the snow sticking to his rough pilot-cloth sack, he looked as white and wintry as a snow-image of the largest size. Some of the neighbors, meanwhile, seeing him from their windows, wondered what could possess poor Mr. Lindsey to be running about his garden in pursuit of a snow-drift, which the west-wind was driving hither and thither! At length, after a vast deal of trouble, he chased the little stranger into a corner, where she could not possibly escape him. His wife had been looking on, and, it being nearly twilight, was wonder-struck to observe how the snow-child gleamed and sparkled, and how she seemed to shed a glow all round about her; and when driven into the corner, she positively glistened like a star! It was a frosty kind of brightness, too, like that of an icicle in the moonlight. The wife thought it strange that good Mr. Lindsey should see nothing remarkable in the snow-child's appearance.

"Come, you odd little thing!" cried the honest man, seizing her by the hand, "I have caught you at last, and will make you comfortable in spite of yourself. We will put a nice warm pair of worsted stockings on your frozen little feet, and you shall have a good thick shawl to wrap yourself in. Your poor white nose, I am afraid, is actually frost-bitten. But we will make it all right. Come along in."

And so, with a most benevolent smile on his sagacious visage, all purple as it was with the cold, this very well-meaning gentleman took the snow-child by the hand and led her towards the house. She followed him, droopingly and reluctant; for all the glow and sparkle was gone out of her figure; and whereas just before she had resembled a bright, frosty, star-gemmed evening, with a crimson gleam on the cold horizon, she now looked as dull and languid as a thaw. As kind Mr. Lindsey led her up the steps of the door, Violet and Peony looked into his face,--their eyes full of tears, which froze before they could run down their cheeks,--and again entreated him not to bring their snow-image into the house.

"Not bring her in!" exclaimed the kind-hearted man. "Why, you are crazy, my little Violet!-- quite crazy, my small Peony! She is so cold, already, that her hand has almost frozen mine, in spite of my thick gloves. Would you have her freeze to death?"

His wife, as he came up the steps, had been taking another long, earnest, almost awe-stricken gaze at the little white stranger. She hardly knew whether it was a dream or no; but she could not help fancying that she saw the delicate print of Violet's fingers on the child's neck. It looked just as if, while Violet was shaping out the image, she had given it a gentle pat with her hand, and had neglected to smooth the impression quite away.

"After all, husband," said the mother, recurring to her idea that the angels would be as much delighted to play with Violet and Peony as she herself was,--"after all, she does look strangely like a snow-image! I do believe she is made of snow!"

A puff of the west-wind blew against the snow-child, and again she sparkled like a star.

"Snow!" repeated good Mr. Lindsey, drawing the reluctant guest over his hospitable threshold. "No wonder she looks like snow. She is half frozen, poor little thing! But a good fire will put everything to rights!"

Without further talk, and always with the same best intentions, this highly benevolent and common-sensible individual led the little white damsel--drooping, drooping, drooping, more and more out of the frosty air, and into his comfortable parlor. A Heidenberg stove, filled to the brim with intensely burning anthracite, was sending a bright gleam through the isinglass of its iron door, and causing the vase of water on its top to fume and bubble with excitement. A warm, sultry smell was diffused throughout the room. A thermometer on the wall farthest from the stove stood at eighty degrees. The parlor was hung with red curtains, and covered with a red carpet, and looked just as warm as it felt. The difference betwixt the atmosphere here and the cold, wintry twilight out of doors, was like stepping at once from Nova Zembla to the hottest part of India, or from the North Pole into an oven. Oh, this was a fine place for the little white stranger!

The common-sensible man placed the snow-child on the hearth-rug, right in front of the hissing and fuming stove.

"Now she will be comfortable!" cried Mr. Lindsey, rubbing his hands and looking about him, with the pleasantest smile you ever saw. "Make yourself at home, my child."

Sad, sad and drooping, looked the little white maiden, as she stood on the hearth-rug, with the hot blast of the stove striking through her like a pestilence. Once, she threw a glance wistfully toward the windows, and caught a glimpse, through its red curtains, of the snow-covered roofs, and the stars glimmering frostily, and all the delicious intensity of the cold night. The bleak wind rattled the window-panes, as if it were summoning her to come forth. But there stood the snow-child, drooping, before the hot stove!

But the common-sensible man saw nothing amiss.

"Come wife," said he, "let her have a pair of thick stockings and a woolen shawl or blanket directly; and tell Dora to give her some warm supper as soon as the milk boils. You, Violet and Peony, amuse your little friend. She is out of spirits, you see, at finding herself in a strange place. For my part, I will go around among the neighbors, and find out where she belongs."

The mother, meanwhile, had gone in search of the shawl and stockings; for her own view of the matter, however subtle and delicate, had given way, as it always did, to the stubborn materialism of her husband. Without heeding the remonstrances of his two children, who still kept murmuring that their little snow-sister did not love the warmth, good Mr. Lindsey took his departure, shutting the parlor-door carefully behind him. Turning up the collar of his sack over his ears, he emerged from the house, and had barely reached the street-gate, when he was recalled by the screams of Violet and Peony, and the rapping of a thimbled finger against the parlor window.

"Husband! husband!" cried his wife, showing her horror-stricken face through the window-panes. "There is no need of going for the child's parents!"

"We told you so, father!" screamed Violet and Peony, as he re-entered the parlor. "You would bring her in; and now our poor--dear-beau-ti-ful little snow-sister is thawed!"

And their own sweet little faces were already dissolved in tears; so that their father, seeing what strange things occasionally happen in this every-day world, felt not a little anxious lest his children might be going to thaw too! In the utmost perplexity, he demanded an explanation of his wife. She could only reply, that, being summoned to the parlor by the cries of Violet and Peony, she found no trace of the little white maiden, unless it were the remains of a heap of snow, which, while she was gazing at it, melted quite away upon the hearth-rug.

"And there you see all that is left of it!" added she, pointing to a pool of water in front of the stove.

"Yes, father," said Violet looking reproachfully at him, through her tears, "there is all that is left of our dear little snow-sister!"

"Naughty father!" cried Peony, stamping his foot, and--I shudder to say--shaking his little fist at the common-sensible man. "We told you how it would be! What for did you bring her in?"

And the Heidenberg stove, through the isinglass of its door, seemed to glare at good Mr. Lindsey, like a red-eyed demon, triumphing in the mischief which it had done!

This, you will observe, was one of those rare cases, which yet will occasionally happen, where common-sense finds itself at fault. The remarkable story of the snow-image, though to that sagacious class of people to whom good Mr. Lindsey belongs it may seem but a childish affair, is, nevertheless, capable of being moralized in various methods, greatly for their edification. One of its lessons, for instance, might be, that it behooves men, and especially men of benevolence, to consider well what they are about, and, before acting on their philanthropic purposes, to be quite sure that they comprehend the nature and all the relations of the business in hand. What has been established as an element of good to one being may prove absolute mischief to another; even as the warmth of the parlor was proper enough for children of flesh and blood, like Violet and Peony,--though by no means very wholesome, even for them,--but involved nothing short of annihilation to the unfortunate snow-image.

But, after all, there is no teaching anything to wise men of good Mr. Lindsey's stamp. They know everything,--oh, to be sure!--everything that has been, and everything that is, and everything that, by any future possibility, can be. And, should some phenomenon of nature or providence transcend their system, they will not recognize it, even if it come to pass under their very noses.

"Wife," said Mr. Lindsey, after a fit of silence, "see what a quantity of snow the children have brought in on their feet! It has made quite a puddle here before the stove. Pray tell Dora to bring some towels and mop it up!"

Only A Sucker Bites
J. C. Stanley

There were small weeds growing around the entrance, and a school of horned minnows swam up, peered inside into the murky darkness and swam past. I didn't care. I was full of years and besides, I wasn't hungry. Far ahead, through the iridescent gleam of the water, I saw the stump, and smiled to myself. For I knew who lurked behind its twisted branches.

A small shadow came by and I moved quickly. The minnow tasted good. Yet I had swallowed him without any consciousness of desire. It was just that he had ventured too close. I was busy, concentrating on that patch of gloom ahead out there near the center of the lake.

Then I saw them! There were eight or nine of them, fat, juicy sunfish, swimming close to each other, the leader a bit ahead of the rest. I swam closer to the mouth of the cave. It happened with the quickness of death.

He was a streak of light, a lance of speckled fire eating into their midst. Silvery streaks parted the water as the small fish tried desperately to escape Tenhag. But only five got away. Tenhag had had his breakfast.

I came all the way to the lip of the cave.

Tenhag was a killer. The worst kind, the kind who killed for the sheer joy of killing. It was impossible that anyone could be that hungry. His ravening mouth seemed never to have its fill of food. Nor did he fight and kill the natural things which were food for him. Whatever came across his path was legitimate prey; yes, even the females of our tribe. That was why they had outlawed him. Yet I had to admire those very qualities which the rest hated.

I swam close to him and saw him move to one side, the long muscles contracting in sudden tension, as he waited to see what large shadow was crossing his path. He saw me and waited.

I had to admit the size of him; I was smaller by half a foot, not so lean. But I was older, wiser, nor did my jaws bear the scars of the hooks, nor my flanks and belly the scars of teeth. His had both. He followed, a head behind me.

"Where do you go?" he asked.

"To the wild celery weed," I said. "It is warm there, and soon the sun will be up. I know of a nest of ducklings . . ."

There was no need to say more. Food was the only thing on his mind. But there were other things on my mind. Age was with me, and the remembrance of things past. They stirred in me as I thought of the plump, Jerra, the one who swam by the side of Arget, the king.

We lurked, the two of us, in the wild celery weed. The sun came up. I felt the waters warm and saw the clearness grow above. It would not be long before the little furry food swam out . . .

Once more he swam beside me. And this time, even he was full. I headed back to the cave. "Why is it," he asked, "that *you* come to me. I am an outlaw."

"And what is an outlaw?" I asked. "Once I was king. Now Arget is king . . . You know the law of the tribe. I was king and did not fight for my kingship. So now I live my years out in peace. But I do not like Arget . . ."

He lay deeper, into the slime at the bottom. Yet though he said nothing, I knew my words had stirred him. He also hated Arget.

"But you can go back," he said. "Even though Arget is king. I have seen him swim beside you . . ."

I did not answer. The wheel I had started in revolving would not stop now until it had completed its circle.

When we awoke, the sun was high. Its light filtered down to where we lay. I stirred and the movement woke Tenhag. He seemed barely to move yet in an instant he was at the mouth of the cave. I saw his head swivel in search. I joined him.

Wordlessly, he started out. His long, lean length cleaved the water and broke a path for me. He headed upstream, to where the perch collected in the afternoon, close to the logs near the inlet. But we had overslept. There were those others who came to search for food. We saw the wild swirl of waters before we reached the spot. Our cousins had beaten us to the perch. And though they were many to our two, they fled before us.

Tenhag raged in the water. He turned this way and that, his speckled body flashing silver streaks of light, as he twisted about, searching for even a single morsel. But there was not even one. They had fled.

I saw the long length of boat before Tenhag did. Calling a warning, I went for deep water. Nor did I turn to see if he followed. It wasn't till I was down in the weeds at the bottom that I turned to see where Tenhag was. What I saw made me shoot back up again. Whether he had snapped at the red covered thing in anger or because he was hungry, I didn't know. But he had and it wasn't another fish he had taken.

I swam beside him, as he headed for the shore, and I saw the length of line in his mouth. He had taken the bait clean and deep. Whoever had hooked him had hooked him good. But they had never had such as Tenhag on their line. He was no walleye, or pickerel. He was a northern, and we are made of fighting stock.

The line trailed deep as Tenhag zoomed with terrific speed for shallow water. All the instincts which a hundred fights had given him were aroused. Suddenly, and with a movement that was like light, he turned his full length, and went straight down. But not for long. Whoever was at the end of the line was also a fighter. Tenhag was pulled up sharp.

And now he went straight up. Not to stop at the water's edge, but to continue straight up in a wild leap. I saw his tail go out of the water, so high did he go. And when he came down it was straight down.

He went past me, whirled, and suddenly stopped moving. I wondered if he had gone crazy. And so must have the man above. But Tenhag must have weighed better than thirty pounds. And when the fisherman started to drag that dead weight up, it was more than a job. Tenhag let him drag him on until he had almost breasted the water again. And Tenhag made his move. It was the last thing the fisherman had thought, that a fish would come straight for the boat. For a bare instant the line went slack. And in that instant Tenhag whirled again and went in the opposite direction, with all the speed at his command. That did it. The line parted with a singing sound. And Tenhag was free. But only from the man.

For now there was another enemy to face, and more than one. We had come too close to Arget's domain. And two of his clan had been attracted by the commotion of the fight and had swam close to see what it was about. The sight of Tenhag, the line still trailing from his jaws was too much for them. He was their sworn enemy, and wounded or otherwise, was fair game for them. They attacked instantly.

It should have been over in an instant. Tenhag still had the cruel hook in his jaw. He was at a great disadvantage. Yet he turned to give battle.

The first of his attackers, a giant of a warrior, was even larger than Tenhag, but younger, with less fighting experience. He came straight at him, and at the last second shot to one side to come in from there. But he had come faster than his companion. And had arrived first. It was the only mistake he made. But it was also the last. Tenhag waited until the gaping jaws were spread only a foot from him before he moved. Then it was to face the other. The great teeth closed along the side of the attacker's head and ripped along the jaw, taking away one eye and the part of the neck. And Tenhag whirled on the second.

The second was older, wiser, and a better fighter. He moved in a slow circle around Tenhag, watching and waiting the chance to bore in. He wasn't going to make the same mistake the first made. The two circled for a very short time. Tenhag was the first to attack. Straight in, then down and from the bottom up. But the other wasn't to be taken in so easily. As swift as Tenhag, he whirled and ripped downward, their teeth clashing as they met. And again the circling and watching. Once the other made a feint to bore in and Tenhag tensed to meet the charge. But it was only a feint. And once again it was Tenhag who came forward.

This time he came in from the side. But just as he reached the other, he stopped, started downward. And the other whirled again to meet the new thrust. Only now Tenhag stopped, stood almost straight up on his tail and came from above, trying to get the other at the joint of the neck.

It was a mistake on Tenhag's part. Either the fight with the man had taken more from him than he thought, or he had lost some of the speed necessary, but he was a little too slow.

At any rate, the other managed to get out of the way, and as Tenhag went by, the other came in from above.

It was then I moved. I was old and slow, but the other's back was to me. He never knew what hit him. My teeth were still long and sharp. I needed only the first slash. He fell to the bottom, with slow, jerky movements.   We had to get out. There were others beside these two, I knew. We did not travel in schools as the lesser fish, but we were still where enemies lay thick about us. And this time when I turned tail and sped away, Tenhag followed swiftly.

We were in luck. Halfway to where I had found a hiding place, way down deep in the slime of the deepest part of the lake, we came across a pair of bluegills. And we ate them.

Tenhag could not be still. He swam back and forth agitatedly, as though he were in torment.

"Someday," he said, and stopped.

"Yes . . .?"

"I will meet Arget," Tenhag said. "I will meet him on my terms. May it be soon." My friend had desires on the kingship. Good! That suited me also. But there were one or two things first.

"And how will you know?" I asked.

He couldn't answer. I had the answer, though.

"You," I said, "are an outlaw. But I am free to come and go as I please. I will go back to the tribe. Who knows but that someday I will find the place where Arget can be found?"

I watched him swim away and knew that I had sowed the seeds deeply enough.

It was as though I had never left. Arget swam close, rubbed his side against mine, and swam away to where Jerra moved among the tall weeds. The others lay quiet or moved in search of food. I found a deep place and watched.

A pair of young ones made play. They swam swiftly about in simulated combat. The older fish paid small attention to them. They knew it was but in preparation for their later years. A pike lives but to eat or fight.

But though there were many there, it is only when we go out into the waters away from our feeding grounds that we travel alone, none came near. I was an outcast, to be tolerated only. For I had run from combat.

I found a warm place and sank into it. I was asleep but for my eyes. They never left off watching Arget and the plump, Jerra. She was the finest female I had ever seen. A something stirred in me, a something which had not been stirred in a long time. I wanted her. But first Arget had to be taken care of.

The days went by slowly. Nothing much marred the serenity. We ate, slept and ate. Once there was a fight between Arget and another who rose to challenge him. We gathered around and watched. The one who fought was barely old enough to consider himself a fighter. It did not take Arget long. A half-dozen lunges, a few slashes of the sharp teeth, and it was over.

And the days went by.

But though I was as the rest, I was not like them. For they did not know the passing of time. I did. What I had to do had to be done before mating time. Already the days of heat were drawing to a close. The sun no longer warmed the water as it did before.

We each had our favorite feeding spot. Arget's was near a clump of weeds almost in the center of the lake. It was here the bass came to feed on smaller fish. Arget was fond of bass.

One day I swam away, nor did anyone notice my passing. I had a rendezvous to make. Tenhag was there as if he had been waiting my coming. I swam in and rested. The huge length of his body went to and fro past me. At last I spoke:

"I have found many things."

"What is it that you have found?" he asked.

"Where our brothers feed . . . where they fight

. . . and who goes where and with whom," I said.

"It is good to know," Tenhag said.

"Aye," I said. "For instance, in the bulrushes where the water is deepest near the shore, they go two by two, as though in fear. But Arget is the bravest. The bass lie close near the weeds and rocks by the bottom. He goes there alone."

"It is good to know," Tenhag said.

"Aye," I said. "Before the first streak of light comes to make shadows in the water, Arget finds his hunger appeased there . . ."

I waited a while and continued:

"He is a mighty eater. And he eats his fill. One cannot fight well on a full belly . . ."

"Full or otherwise . . ." Tenhag said.

But I broke in:

"The rest will never know how much he had eaten. They will only know that you are king, and that you fought him alone, for I will be among them."

"I do not like it," Tenhag said.

"Like it or not," I said. "You will never live to fight him alone except this way. You are an outlaw and cannot challenge."

"I will fight them all, one by one," Tenhag said.

"You will have time for that later," I said. "First, Arget."

He had to agree.

The seeds I had sown were starting to ripen. Jerra would soon be mine.

"There is only one thing," Tenhag stopped me as I started back.

"Yes?"

"Where the bass feed deepest is where our brothers travel most," he said. "For in order to go to the east shore they must go across the center of the lake."

I had forgotten.

I thought quickly. There had to be a way out. But where? I knew their habits. It was true what Tenhag said. What was to be done? And the solution came; find them other feeding grounds. It wasn't as hard as it sounded. The lake was twenty or so miles across. I thought back in my memory. Where, in the long days gone by had I found food? Because we fed until there was no more, feeding grounds did not last too long. Soon, the smaller ones became frightened off, or learned to be more wary.

Once, in the years ago, I had found a school of horn-headed minnows in where we most disliked to go, shallow water. I kept the secret to myself. But I was younger then, more voracious, and soon they had made for other waters. Perhaps . . .?

But I was in luck. They had come back.

The tribe had grown more irritable. The younger fish had grown. Soon they would seek mates, would have fights which were more than just the play of their youth. One of them

193

snapped at me as I passed. I gave it a wider berth and continued to where some of the oldsters lay.

"It is good to be old," I said to one. "When one is young, food is gulped quickly, as though there isn't going to be enough. Now we can pick and choose. Even go afield in search of delicacies. Like the horned minnow."

"The horned minnow?" he said. "I haven't seen one of those in a while."

I told him where he could find them. Another heard and swam close. I told him also. I knew the rest would hear of it soon. And once more I left.

I did not go far. The depths are full of places where one could stay and hide . . . and watch.

Early the next morning, a while before the sun came up, they swam out toward the feeding grounds. I watched them skirt the edge of the lake away from where Arget had his favorite feeding. I did not wait to see the last of them off. I had never swam so fast, not since I had run from Arget.

But Tenhag was not in his hole. I had forgotten that he was always hungry. The lake was large. It could take me a whole day to find him. It would have to wait. I had waited a long time. Another day would make little difference.

This time I made sure I'd find him. I came as it turned dark. But he wasn't there. I waited all the night, but he didn't return. Early the next morning I started out in search of him. One by one I visited the places where food was to be found. I missed only the minnow feeding grounds.

I found him. But it was a sore and wounded Tenhag that I found. He had had a fight with another. Inwardly, I raged at him. He had set my plans back, if not made them impossible. He needed rest. To fight Arget he would have to be in the best of condition.

"I could not help it," he said. "There was this school of bass. I plunged in, and from the other side came another. We met and fought. I won but he was a good opponent."

That was fine, I thought. He was a good opponent.

"But Arget," I said. "We haven't much time."

"Tomorrow," he said. "I will meet him."

"Not the way you are," I said. "Tomorrow, *we* meet him."

"How do you mean?" he asked.

"You are in no condition to meet him, wounded as you are. He will make minnow bait of you."

It was the wrong note. I realized it the instant I said it, and almost at the same time made amends: ". . . And that, Tenhag, will do you no good. Everyone knows you are the bravest pike in the lake. But even the bravest pike must use his head when the odds are against him."

"You mean we will both go to meet him?" Tenhag asked.

I thought I had made it clear. But I answered, "Yes," anyway.

"Very well. But I do not want you to interfere unless he is in much better condition than I," Tenhag said.

I agreed.

We were just in time. Another moment and we would have missed him. He swam away from the weed-grown hiding place of the bass, a long, lean, muscular length of destruction.

He was swimming lazily, but at sight of the two of us, a change came over him. He knew without being challenged that this was a great moment in his life. Tenhag hated him; Arget was the cause of his being made an outlaw, and when he saw the two of us, he knew we had come for the one purpose of killing him. But fear was not in him.

"A challenge, Arget!" Tenhag cried. "For the kingship."

"I do not fight outlaws," Arget said.

"But I fight kings," Tenhag said, and made his first dive.

I swam quickly away from them, and moved back and forth, watching them and waiting for the moment which I knew had to come, the moment Arget would come too close to me.

It didn't seem possible that Tenhag stood any chance. Arget was in the prime of his life, and though his body bore many honorable scars of combat, he at least was fresh. Tenhag was not.

Arget, wise fighter, waited for Tenhag. He wanted to see the method of the other's attack. But it was impossible to gauge correctly, either the caliber or method of a fighter like Tenhag. Firstly, Tenhag had always bought life dearly, and improvised as he fought; secondly and last, Tenhag was not like any other opponent. He never gave up, though he was wounded unto death.

Tenhag dove in a frontal attack. Arget let him come in and did not move away. He wanted the first slash of his teeth to be the last. But Tenhag also wanted the same thing. Their teeth met and their jaws almost locked; if they had the fight would have been over for the both of them that instant. But somehow they managed to disengage their mouths. Blood was scored by both.

They circled warily for a while, and again it was Tenhag who attacked. He started as though he were going to continue the circle, then came in from the side. Arget almost bent double and slashed at the other as he went by, but in turn felt Tenhag's razor-sharp teeth also. It was only flesh wounds they both inflicted.

The next blow was given by Arget.

He came in from below, and as Tenhag turned to meet him, Arget sinuously moved his huge head back along the length of Tenhag's body and slashed at the tail fin. Had he caught it properly, Tenhag would have been an easy prey. The tail fin is our method of maneuver.

Another fighter would have sent it out of harm's way. Not Tenhag. It was as though he felt what Arget desired of him. For instead, he slapped powerfully at the gaping jaws and knocked Arget sideways. It was as though he knew that Arget had wanted him to turn the fin away. Because if he had, Arget would simply have continued the dive and caught it.

Tenhag gave the other no chance to recover. He was instantly on Arget, his jaws wide-open, ready to slash or envelope. And Arget used discretion. It was then I saw where Tenhag, unless he made quick work, would lose out. Arget was much the swifter swimmer.

Arget made for the weeds and rocks. It seemed as if a thousand smaller fish hid there. They erupted from the weed-grown grotto, as if the devil of all fishes were after them.

Tenhag followed, and I after the two.

But Arget made a mistake in choosing the grotto, though he knew it well. For Tenhag had lived for a long time in such surroundings, and could play hide and seek as well, if not better, than the other.

I could not follow the play of their fight too well. The weeds grew thick, and the rocks would hide their swiftly moving bodies now and then. Once I saw them, they seemed joined, so close were they pressed, and they were tearing at each other in wild frenzy. But I also saw in that instant, that they were not inflicting the kinds of wounds from which they would die. It was as if they only wanted to tear each other to bits. Then they were gone from view again.

Quite suddenly, they came out of the grotto, Arget in the lead. The other was almost on his tail. And I saw that Tenhag had done much better than Arget. Blood came from a dozen wounds on the king's body.

Either Arget had grown tired during combat or he had eaten too much or his wounds were beginning to slow him down, but he was not so swift. On the other hand, Tenhag seemed to have gained speed. He was only half a length behind the other.

And in a hundred feet, he caught Arget. Though he didn't catch him as he wished, from behind. Arget turned at the last second and the battle was on again. Arget fought with desperation born of despair.

Once more they met head on. Arget gave up his power tactics. He used the method of slash and get away. And for the first time, it began to pay. For now Tenhag became tired. It seemed as if he couldn't quite manage to get away fast enough to escape. Arget's teeth left more and more scars. Yet as often as they met in the tough hide of Tenhag, they somehow always just missed a vital spot. And now Tenhag was running from the other.

It was not a straight run. He swam first straightaway, then from side to side, and again doubled on his self. And always, half a length behind, Arget trailed, desperately trying for the death bite.

It was only when they entered the grotto again, that I *knew* Tenhag's intention. He had led Arget to believe that he was wounded so badly he was only trying to escape. And Arget had fallen for the ruse. Tenhag had done his best work in the grotto. Now he was back among the weeds and rocks.

I was a few seconds behind them.

Now the fight raged with increasing terribleness. Tenhag was done with subterfuge. It was as if he realized that it was to be now or never. He attacked, and as many times as he was repulsed, he came back until by the sheer power and will of him, Arget was brought to bay, helpless.

I saw the lean sides, blood-covered, of the king, heave, as moved back and forth in rhythmic movement, his large eye watching every move of Tenhag.

Now Tenhag took care. It was going to be a single last lunge and . . . death!

Yet Arget was not done. He had his last reserves to call on, though they were limited. For as Tenhag swept in, Arget swam backward into an opening behind him. Tenhag did not care. He followed. I did not want to miss a single second of the battle, and moved slowly behind them.

Once more they were together and now there was no room for maneuvering. The grotto was at its narrowest. In fact it was almost too tight a squeeze for Tenhag. He could only come straight forward. But Arget was half a length smaller, and the difference almost proved Tenhag's undoing. Though Arget was wounded badly, he had a last strength to call on.

Three times Arget whirled and dove in and each time Tenhag could not fend off the great teeth. The last time Arget struck it was at a vulnerable point, the juncture of the throat to the head. Another inch and the fight would have ended. Tenhag barely escaped, though Arget tore a great piece of flesh out. And this time it was Tenhag who used discretion. He backed out of the grotto.

The instant he came out he whirled and came toward open water. Arget could do nothing else but follow. I could have touched Tenhag as he came by me. As it was, the desperation in his eyes was plain to be seen. It was time for my move. For Arget followed the other in a straight line.

197

It was time, but I didn't move.

For as I turned with them I saw something for which I had not taken into account. The savagery of the fight had attracted not alone the curious of our world, the pan fish and minnows, but also the larger ones, Arget's tribe. All around us they swam idly, their eyes intent on the battle.

A single move toward Arget would have meant my death.

It was up to Tenhag now. He had to prevail over the king. But it looked like he was through. Arget was on him. They were side by side, and Tenhag turned his head inward, trying for a last slashing bite. But it was an old trick, well-known to Arget, who simply moved his own head, and came in and up. It should have been the end.

And it was, for Arget.

He had come in and around, his head twisting to get under Tenhag so that he could get the soft underside of the throat. Arget's jaws were wide. And as he twisted his head, the trailing line which Tenhag had ripped from the fisherman's pole, twined itself in some manner around Arget's jaw. He yanked savagely at it, trying to free himself. But all he succeeded in doing was bring the other's teeth closer. Tenhag made one last snap, and in the proper place. Blood spouted from Arget's throat, and he began the last twisting roll toward the bottom of the lake.

Tenhag was now king!

Outcast though he was, it was still the rule of the tribe. He had fought the king in fair combat and won. Slowly, the rest joined him as he swam for the tribal grounds. And beside him, Jerra, plumper than ever, more desirable, swam beside him. I moved alongside, rubbed sides with Tenhag, and said:

"One favor, king. The female Jerra."

But I had forgotten that Tenhag had been without a female for a long time. And Jerra was the loveliest of them all. He flicked me contemptuously with his tail. It was Arget all over again. I had gained nothing!

I swam away, my blood boiling. A dace-headed minnow floated by and I snapped savagely at it.

It eluded me at the first snap but I tried again and caught it.

It wasn't till the hook sank deep into my jaw that I knew the minnow wasn't alive. . . .

THE END

POETRY

POETRY

Daffodils
William Wordsworth

I wander'd lonely as a cloud

That floats on high o'er vales and hills,
When all at once I saw a crowd,
    A host, of golden daffodils;
Beside the lake, beneath the trees,
Fluttering and dancing in the breeze.

Continuous as the stars that shine

    And twinkle on the Milky Way,
They stretch'd in never-ending line
    Along the margin of a bay:
Ten thousand saw I at a glance,
Tossing their heads in sprightly dance.

The waves beside them danced; but they

    Out-did the sparkling waves in glee:
A poet could not but be gay,
    In such a jocund company:
I gazed -- and gazed -- but little thought
What wealth the show to me had brought:

For oft, when on my couch I lie

    In vacant or in pensive mood,
They flash upon that inward eye
    Which is the bliss of solitude;
And then my heart with pleasure fills,
    And dances with the daffodils.

A Red, Red Rose
Robert Burns

O my Luve's like a red, red rose
That's newly sprung in June;
O my Luve's like the melodie
That's sweetly play'd in tune.

As fair art thou, my bonnie lass,
So deep in luve am I:
And I will luve thee still, my dear,
Till a' the seas gang dry:

Till a' the seas gang dry, my dear,
And the rocks melt wi' the sun:
I will luve thee still, my dear,
While the sands o' life shall run.

And fare thee well, my only Luve
And fare thee well, a while!
And I will come again, my Luve,
Tho' it were ten thousand mile.

Have You Got A Brook In Your Little Heart
Emily Dickinson

Have you got a brook in your little heart,
Where bashful flowers blow,
And blushing birds go down to drink,
And shadows tremble so?

And nobody knows, so still it flows,
That any brook is there;
And yet your little draught of life
Is daily drunken there.

Then look out for the little brook in March,
When the rivers overflow,
And the snows come hurrying from the hills,
And the bridges often go.

And later, in August it may be,
When the meadows parching lie,
Beware, lest this little brook of life
Some burning noon go dry!

Come Down, O Maid
Alfred Tennyson

Come down, O maid, from yonder mountain height:
What pleasure lives in height (the shepherd sang),
In height and cold, the splendour of the hills?
But cease to move so near the Heavens, and cease
To glide a sunbeam by the blasted Pine,
To sit a star upon the sparkling spire;
And come, for Love is of the valley, come,
For Love is of the valley, come thou down
And find him; by the happy threshold, he,
Or hand in hand with Plenty in the maize,
Or red with spirted purple of the vats,
Or foxlike in the vine; nor cares to walk
With Death and Morning on the silver horns,
Nor wilt thou snare him in the white ravine,
Nor find him dropt upon the firths of ice,
That huddling slant in furrow-cloven falls
To roll the torrent out of dusky doors:
But follow; let the torrent dance thee down
To find him in the valley; let the wild
Lean-headed Eagles yelp alone, and leave
The monstrous ledges there to slope, and spill
Their thousand wreaths of dangling water-smoke,
That like a broken purpose waste in air:
So waste not thou; but come; for all the vales
Await thee; azure pillars of the hearth
Arise to thee; the children call, and I
Thy shepherd pipe, and sweet is every sound,
Sweeter thy voice, but every sound is sweet;
Myriads of rivulets hurrying thro' the lawn,
The moan of doves in immemorial elms,
And murmuring of innumerable bees.

The Voice Of The Lobster
Lewis Carroll

"Tis the voice of the Lobster: I heard him declare
'You have baked me too brown, I must sugar my hair.'
As a duck with its eyelids, so he with his nose
Trims his belt and his buttons, and turns out his toes.
When the sands are all dry, he is gay as a lark,
And will talk in contemptuous tones of the Shark:
But, when the tide rises and sharks are around,
His voice has a timid and tremulous sound.'

Im Nobody! Who Are You?
Emily Dickinson
I'm nobody! Who are you?
Are you nobody, too?
Then there's a pair of us -- don't tell!
They'd advertise -- you know!

How dreary to be somebody!
How public like a frog
To tell one's name the livelong day
To an admiring bog!

Casey at the Bat
Ernest Lawrence Thayer

The Outlook wasn't brilliant for the Mudville nine that day:
The score stood four to two, with but one inning more to play.
And then when Cooney died at first, and Barrows did the same,
A sickly silence fell upon the patrons of the game.

A straggling few got up to go in deep despair. The rest
Clung to that hope which springs eternal in the human breast;
They thought, if only Casey could get but a whack at that -
We'd put up even money, now, with Casey at the bat.

But Flynn preceded Casey, as did also Jimmy Blake,
And the former was a lulu and the latter was a cake;
So upon that stricken multitude grim melancholy sat,
For there seemed but little chance of Casey's getting to the bat.

But Flynn let drive a single, to the wonderment of all,
And Blake, the much despis-ed, tore the cover off the ball;
And when the dust had lifted, and the men saw what had occurred,
There was Jimmy safe at second and Flynn a-hugging third.

Then from 5,000 throats and more there rose a lusty yell;
It rumbled through the valley, it rattled in the dell;
It knocked upon the mountain and recoiled upon the flat,
For Casey, mighty Casey, was advancing to the bat.

There was ease in Casey's manner as he stepped into his place;
There was pride in Casey's bearing and a smile on Casey's face.
And when, responding to the cheers, he lightly doffed his hat,
No stranger in the crowd could doubt 'twas Casey at the bat.

Ten thousand eyes were on him as he rubbed his hands with dirt;
Five thousand tongues applauded when he wiped them on his shirt.
Then while the writhing pitcher ground the ball into his hip,
Defiance gleamed in Casey's eye, a sneer curled Casey's lip.

And now the leather-covered sphere came hurtling through the air,
And Casey stood a-watching it in haughty grandeur there.
Close by the sturdy batsman the ball unheeded sped-
"That ain't my style," said Casey. "Strike one," the umpire said.

From the benches, black with people, there went up a muffled roar,
Like the beating of the storm-waves on a stern and distant shore.
"Kill him! Kill the umpire!" shouted someone on the stand;
And its likely they'd a-killed him had not Casey raised his hand.

With a smile of Christian charity great Casey's visage shone;
He stilled the rising tumult; he bade the game go on;
He signaled to the pitcher, and once more the spheroid flew;
But Casey still ignored it, and the umpire said, "Strike two."

"Fraud!" cried the maddened thousands, and echo answered fraud;
But one scornful look from Casey and the audience was awed.
They saw his face grow stern and cold, they saw his muscles strain,
And they knew that Casey wouldn't let that ball go by again.

The sneer is gone from Casey's lip, his teeth are clenched in hate;
He pounds with cruel violence his bat upon the plate.
And now the pitcher holds the ball, and now he lets it go,
And now the air is shattered by the force of Casey's blow.

Oh, somewhere in this favored land the sun is shining bright;
The band is playing somewhere, and somewhere hearts are light,
And somewhere men are laughing, and somewhere children shout;
But there is no joy in Mudville - mighty Casey has struck out.

It Couldn't Be Done
Edgar Albert Guest

Somebody said that it couldn't be done,
But, he with a chuckle replied
That "maybe it couldn't," but he would be one
Who wouldn't say so till he'd tried.
So he buckled right in with the trace of a grin
On his face. If he worried he hid it.
He started to sing as he tackled the thing
That couldn't be done, and he did it.

Somebody scoffed: "Oh, you'll never do that;
At least no one has done it";
But he took off his coat and he took off his hat,
And the first thing we knew he'd begun it.
With a lift of his chin and a bit of a grin,
Without any doubting or quiddit,
He started to sing as he tackled the thing
That couldn't be done, and he did it.

There are thousands to tell you it cannot be done,
There are thousands to prophesy failure;
There are thousands to point out to you one by one,
The dangers that wait to assail you.
But just buckle it in with a bit of a grin,
Just take off your coat and go to it;
Just start to sing as you tackle the thing
That "couldn't be done," and you'll do it.

If
Rudyard Kipling

If you can keep your head when all about you
Are losing theirs and blaming it on you;
If you can trust yourself when all men doubt you,
But make allowance for their doubting too:
If you can wait and not be tired by waiting,
Or, being lied about, don't deal in lies,
Or being hated don't give way to hating,
And yet don't look too good, nor talk too wise;

If you can dream---and not make dreams your master;
If you can think---and not make thoughts your aim,
If you can meet with Triumph and Disaster
And treat those two impostors just the same:.
If you can bear to hear the truth you've spoken
Twisted by knaves to make a trap for fools,
Or watch the things you gave your life to, broken,
And stoop and build'em up with worn-out tools;

If you can make one heap of all your winnings
And risk it on one turn of pitch-and-toss,
And lose, and start again at your beginnings,
And never breathe a word about your loss:
If you can force your heart and nerve and sinew
To serve your turn long after they are gone,
And so hold on when there is nothing in you
Except the Will which says to them: "Hold on!"

If you can talk with crowds and keep your virtue,
Or walk with Kings---nor lose the common touch,
If neither foes nor loving friends can hurt you,
If all men count with you, but none too much:
If you can fill the unforgiving minute
With sixty seconds' worth of distance run,
Yours is the Earth and everything that's in it,
And---which is more---you'll be a Man, my son!

When I Have Fears That I May Cease To Be
John Keats

WHEN I have fears that I may cease to be
Before my pen has glean'd my teeming brain,
Before high piled books, in charact'ry,
Hold like rich garners the full-ripen'd grain;
When I behold, upon the night's starr'd face,
Huge cloudy symbols of a high romance,
And think that I may never live to trace
Their shadows, with the magic hand of chance;
And when I feel, fair creature of an hour!
That I shall never look upon thee more,
Never have relish in the faery power
Of unreflecting love!—then on the shore
Of the wide world I stand alone, and think
Till Love and Fame to nothingness do sink.

The Windmill
Henry Wadsworth Longfellow

Behold! a giant am I!
Aloft here in my tower,
With my granite jaws I devour
The maize, and the wheat, and the rye,
And grind them into flour.

I look down over the farms;
In the fields of grain I see
The harvest that is to be,
And I fling to the air my arms,
For I know it is all for me.

I hear the sound of flails
Far off, from the threshing-floors
In barns, with their open doors,
And the wind, the wind in my sails,
Louder and louder roars.

I stand here in my place,
With my foot on the rock below,
And whichever way it may blow
I meet it face to face,
As a brave man meets his foe.

And while we wrestle and strive
My master, the miller, stands
And feeds me with his hands;
For he knows who makes him thrive,
Who makes him lord of lands.

On Sundays I take my rest;
Church-going bells begin
Their low, melodious din;
I cross my arms on my breast,
And all is peace within.

The Charge Of The Light Brigade
Alfred, Lord Tennyson

Half a league, half a league,
Half a league onward,
All in the valley of Death
Rode the six hundred.
"Forward, the Light Brigade!
"Charge for the guns!" he said:
Into the valley of Death
Rode the six hundred.

"Forward, the Light Brigade!"
Was there a man dismay'd?
Not tho' the soldier knew
Someone had blunder'd:
Theirs not to make reply,
Theirs not to reason why,
Theirs but to do and die:
Into the valley of Death
Rode the six hundred.

Cannon to right of them,
Cannon to left of them,
Cannon in front of them
Volley'd and thunder'd;
Storm'd at with shot and shell,
Boldly they rode and well,
Into the jaws of Death,
Into the mouth of Hell
Rode the six hundred.

Flash'd all their sabres bare,
Flash'd as they turn'd in air,
Sabring the gunners there,
Charging an army, while
All the world wonder'd:
Plunged in the battery-smoke
Right thro' the line they broke;
Cossack and Russian
Reel'd from the sabre stroke
Shatter'd and sunder'd.
Then they rode back, but not
Not the six hundred.
Cannon to right of them,
Cannon to left of them,
Cannon behind them
Volley'd and thunder'd;
Storm'd at with shot and shell,
While horse and hero fell,
They that had fought so well
Came thro' the jaws of Death
Back from the mouth of Hell,
All that was left of them,
Left of six hundred.
When can their glory fade?
O the wild charge they made!
All the world wondered.
Honor the charge they made,
Honor the Light Brigade,
Noble six hundred.

The Highwayman
Alfred Noyes

Part One

The wind was a torrent of darkness among the gusty trees,
The moon was a ghostly galleon tossed upon cloudy seas,
The road was a ribbon of moonlight over the purple moor,
And the highwayman came riding—
Riding—riding—
The highwayman came riding, up to the old inn-door.

He'd a French cocked-hat on his forehead, a bunch of lace at his chin,
A coat of the claret velvet, and breeches of brown doe-skin;
They fitted with never a wrinkle: his boots were up to the thigh!
And he rode with a jewelled twinkle,
His pistol butts a-twinkle,
His rapier hilt a-twinkle, under the jewelled sky.

Over the cobbles he clattered and clashed in the dark inn-yard,
And he tapped with his whip on the shutters, but all was locked and barred;
He whistled a tune to the window, and who should be waiting there
But the landlord's black-eyed daughter,
Bess, the landlord's daughter,
Plaiting a dark red love-knot into her long black hair.

And dark in the dark old inn-yard a stable-wicket creaked
Where Tim the ostler listened; his face was white and peaked;
His eyes were hollows of madness, his hair like mouldy hay,
But he loved the landlord's daughter,
The landlord's red-lipped daughter,
Dumb as a dog he listened, and he heard the robber say—

'One kiss, my bonny sweetheart, I'm after a prize to-night,
But I shall be back with the yellow gold before the morning light;
Yet, if they press me sharply, and harry me through the day,
Then look for me by moonlight,
Watch for me by moonlight,
I'll come to thee by moonlight, though hell should bar the way.'

He rose upright in the stirrups; he scarce could reach her hand,
But she loosened her hair i' the casement! His face burnt like a brand
As the black cascade of perfume came tumbling over his breast;
And he kissed its waves in the moonlight,
(Oh, sweet, black waves in the moonlight!)
Then he tugged at his rein in the moonliglt, and galloped away to the West.

214

Part Two

He did not come in the dawning; he did not come at noon;
And out o' the tawny sunset, before the rise o' the moon,
When the road was a gypsy's ribbon, looping the purple moor,
A red-coat troop came marching—
Marching—marching—
King George's men came matching, up to the old inn-door.

They said no word to the landlord, they drank his ale instead,
But they gagged his daughter and bound her to the foot of her narrow bed;
Two of them knelt at her casement, with muskets at their side!
There was death at every window;
And hell at one dark window;
For Bess could see, through her casement, the road that he would ride.

They had tied her up to attention, with many a sniggering jest;
They had bound a musket beside her, with the barrel beneath her breast!
'Now, keep good watch!' and they kissed her.
She heard the dead man say—
Look for me by moonlight;
Watch for me by moonlight;
I'll come to thee by moonlight, though hell should bar the way!

She twisted her hands behind her; but all the knots held good!
She writhed her hands till her fingers were wet with sweat or blood!
They stretched and strained in the darkness, and the hours crawled by like years,
Till, now, on the stroke of midnight,
Cold, on the stroke of midnight,
The tip of one finger touched it! The trigger at least was hers!

The tip of one finger touched it; she strove no more for the rest!
Up, she stood up to attention, with the barrel beneath her breast,
She would not risk their hearing; she would not strive again;
For the road lay bare in the moonlight;
Blank and bare in the moonlight;
And the blood of her veins in the moonlight throbbed to her love's retrain .

Tlot-tlot; tlot-tlot! Had they heard it? The horse-hoofs ringing clear;
Tlot-tlot, tlot-tlot, in the distance? Were they deaf that they did not hear?
Down the ribbon of moonlight, over the brow of the hill,
The highwayman came riding,
Riding, riding!
The red-coats looked to their priming! She stood up, straight and still!

Tlot-tlot, in the frosty silence! Tlot-tlot, in the echoing night!
Nearer he came and nearer! Her face was like a light!
Her eyes grew wide for a moment; she drew one last deep breath,
Then her finger moved in the moonlight,
Her musket shattered the moonlight,
Shattered her breast in the moonlight and warned him—with her death.

He turned; he spurred to the West; he did not know who stood
Bowed, with her head o'er the musket, drenched with her own red blood!
Not till the dawn he heard it, his face grew grey to hear
How Bess, the landlord's daughter,
The landlord's black-eyed daughter,
Had watched for her love in the moonlight, and died in the darkness there.

Back, he spurred like a madman, shrieking a curse to the sky,
With the white road smoking behind him and his rapier brandished high!
Blood-red were his spurs i' the golden noon; wine-red was his velvet coat,
When they shot him down on the highway,
Down like a dog on the highway,
And he lay in his blood on the highway, with the bunch of lace at his throat.

And still of a winter's night, they say, when the wind is in the trees,
When the moon is a ghostly galleon tossed upon cloudy seas,
When the road is a ribbon of moonlight over the purple moor,
A highwayman comes riding—
Riding—riding—
A highwayman comes riding, up to the old inn-door.

Over the cobbles he clatters and clangs in the dark inn-yard;
He taps with his whip on the shutters, but all is locked and barred;
He whistles a tune to the window, and who should be waiting there
But the landlord's black-eyed daughter,
Bess, the landlord's daughter,
Plaiting a dark red love-knot into her long black hair.

Paul Revere's Ride
Henry Wadsworth Longfellow

Listen my children and you shall hear
Of the midnight ride of Paul Revere,
On the eighteenth of April, in Seventy-five;
Hardly a man is now alive
Who remembers that famous day and year.

He said to his friend, "If the British march
By land or sea from the town to-night,
Hang a lantern aloft in the belfry arch
Of the North Church tower as a signal light,–
One if by land, and two if by sea;
And I on the opposite shore will be,
Ready to ride and spread the alarm
Through every Middlesex village and farm,
For the country folk to be up and to arm."

Then he said "Good-night!" and with muffled oar
Silently rowed to the Charlestown shore,
Just as the moon rose over the bay,
Where swinging wide at her moorings lay
The Somerset, British man-of-war;
A phantom ship, with each mast and spar
Across the moon like a prison bar,
And a huge black hulk, that was magnified
By its own reflection in the tide.

Meanwhile, his friend through alley and street
Wanders and watches, with eager ears,
Till in the silence around him he hears
The muster of men at the barrack door,
The sound of arms, and the tramp of feet,
And the measured tread of the grenadiers,
Marching down to their boats on the shore.

Then he climbed the tower of the Old North Church,
By the wooden stairs, with stealthy tread,

To the belfry chamber overhead,
And startled the pigeons from their perch
On the sombre rafters, that round him made
Masses and moving shapes of shade,–
By the trembling ladder, steep and tall,
To the highest window in the wall,
Where he paused to listen and look down
A moment on the roofs of the town
And the moonlight flowing over all.

Beneath, in the churchyard, lay the dead,
In their night encampment on the hill,
Wrapped in silence so deep and still
That he could hear, like a sentinel's tread,
The watchful night-wind, as it went
Creeping along from tent to tent,
And seeming to whisper, "All is well!"
A moment only he feels the spell
Of the place and the hour, and the secret dread
Of the lonely belfry and the dead;
For suddenly all his thoughts are bent
On a shadowy something far away,
Where the river widens to meet the bay,–
A line of black that bends and floats
On the rising tide like a bridge of boats.

Meanwhile, impatient to mount and ride,
Booted and spurred, with a heavy stride
On the opposite shore walked Paul Revere.
Now he patted his horse's side,
Now he gazed at the landscape far and near,
Then, impetuous, stamped the earth,
And turned and tightened his saddle girth;
But mostly he watched with eager search
The belfry tower of the Old North Church,
As it rose above the graves on the hill,
Lonely and spectral and sombre and still.

And lo! as he looks, on the belfry's height
A glimmer, and then a gleam of light!
He springs to the saddle, the bridle he turns,
But lingers and gazes, till full on his sight
A second lamp in the belfry burns.

A hurry of hoofs in a village street,
A shape in the moonlight, a bulk in the dark,
And beneath, from the pebbles, in passing, a spark
Struck out by a steed flying fearless and fleet;
That was all! And yet, through the gloom and the light,
The fate of a nation was riding that night;
And the spark struck out by that steed, in his flight,
Kindled the land into flame with its heat.
He has left the village and mounted the steep,
And beneath him, tranquil and broad and deep,
Is the Mystic, meeting the ocean tides;
And under the alders that skirt its edge,
Now soft on the sand, now loud on the ledge,
Is heard the tramp of his steed as he rides.

It was twelve by the village clock
When he crossed the bridge into Medford town.
He heard the crowing of the cock,
And the barking of the farmer's dog,
And felt the damp of the river fog,
That rises after the sun goes down.

It was one by the village clock,
When he galloped into Lexington.
He saw the gilded weathercock
Swim in the moonlight as he passed,
And the meeting-house windows, black and bare,
Gaze at him with a spectral glare,
As if they already stood aghast
At the bloody work they would look upon.

It was two by the village clock,
When he came to the bridge in Concord town.

He heard the bleating of the flock,
And the twitter of birds among the trees,
And felt the breath of the morning breeze
Blowing over the meadow brown.
And one was safe and asleep in his bed
Who at the bridge would be first to fall,
Who that day would be lying dead,
Pierced by a British musket ball.

You know the rest. In the books you have read
How the British Regulars fired and fled,—
How the farmers gave them ball for ball,
From behind each fence and farmyard wall,
Chasing the redcoats down the lane,
Then crossing the fields to emerge again
Under the trees at the turn of the road,
And only pausing to fire and load.

So through the night rode Paul Revere;
And so through the night went his cry of alarm
To every Middlesex village and farm,—
A cry of defiance, and not of fear,
A voice in the darkness, a knock at the door,
And a word that shall echo for evermore!
For, borne on the night-wind of the Past,
Through all our history, to the last,
In the hour of darkness and peril and need,
The people will waken and listen to hear
The hurrying hoof-beats of that steed,
And the midnight message of Paul Revere.

Ode to the West Wind
Percy Shelley

I

O wild West Wind, thou breath of Autumn's being,
Thou, from whose unseen presence the leaves dead
Are driven, like ghosts from an enchanter fleeing,

Yellow, and black, and pale, and hectic red,
Pestilence-stricken multitudes: O thou,
Who chariotest to their dark wintry bed

The wingéd seeds, where they lie cold and low,
Each like a corpse within its grave, until
Thine azure sister of the Spring shall blow

Her clarion o'er the dreaming earth, and fill
(Driving sweet buds like flocks to feed in air)
With living hues and odours plain and hill:

Wild Spirit, which art moving everywhere;
Destroyer and preserver; hear, oh, hear!

II

Thou on whose stream, 'mid the steep sky's commotion,
Loose clouds like earth's decaying leaves are shed,
Shook from the tangled boughs of Heaven and Ocean,

Angels of rain and lightning: there are spread
On the blue surface of thine aery surge,
Like the bright hair uplifted from the head

Of some fierce Maenad, even from the dim verge
Of the horizon to the zenith's height,
The locks of the approaching storm. Thou dirge

Of the dying year, to which this closing night
Will be the dome of a vast sepulchre,
Vaulted with all thy congregated might

Of vapors, from whose solid atmosphere
Black rain, and fire, and hail will burst: oh, hear!

III

Thou who didst waken from his summer dreams
The blue Mediterranean, where he lay,
Lulled by the coil of his crystalline streams,

Beside a pumice isle in Baiae's bay,
And saw in sleep old palaces and towers
Quivering within the wave's intenser day,

All overgrown with azure moss and flowers
So sweet, the sense faints picturing them! Thou
For whose path the Atlantic's level powers

Cleave themselves into chasms, while far below
The sea-blooms and the oozy woods which wear
The sapless foliage of the ocean, know

Thy voice, and suddenly grow gray with fear,
And tremble and despoil themselves: oh, hear!

IV

If I were a dead leaf thou mightest bear;
If I were a swift cloud to fly with thee;
A wave to pant beneath thy power, and share

The impulse of thy strength, only less free
Than thou, O uncontrollable! If even
I were as in my boyhood, and could be

The comrade of thy wanderings over Heaven,
As then, when to outstrip thy skiey speed
Scarce seemed a vision; I would ne'er have striven

As thus with thee in prayer in my sore need.
Oh, lift me as a wave, a leaf, a cloud!
I fall upon the thorns of life! I bleed!

A heavy weight of hours has chained and bowed
One too like thee: tameless, and swift, and proud.

V

Make me thy lyre, even as the forest is:
What if my leaves are falling like its own!
The tumult of thy mighty harmonies

Will take from both a deep, autumnal tone,
Sweet though in sadness. Be thou, Spirit fierce,
My spirit! Be thou me, impetuous one!

Drive my dead thoughts over the universe
Like withered leaves to quicken a new birth!
And, by the incantation of this verse,

Scatter, as from an unextinguished hearth
Ashes and sparks, my words among mankind!
Be through my lips to unawakened earth

The trumpet of a prophecy! O Wind,
If Winter comes, can Spring be far behind?

O Captain! My Captain!
Walt Whitman

O Captain! my Captain! our fearful trip is done;
The ship has weather'd every rack, the prize we sought is won
The port is near, the bells I hear, the people all exulting,
While follow eyes the steady keel, the vessel grim and daring:
But O heart! heart! heart!
O the bleeding drops of red,
Where on the deck my Captain lies,
Fallen cold and dead.

O Captain! my Captain! rise up and hear the bells;
Rise up—for you the flag is flung—for you the bugle trills;
For you bouquets and ribbon'd wreaths—for you the shores a-crowding;
For you they call, the swaying mass, their eager faces turning;
Here Captain! dear father!
This arm beneath your head;
It is some dream that on the deck,
You've fallen cold and dead.

My Captain does not answer, his lips are pale and still;
My father does not feel my arm, he has no pulse nor will;
The ship is anchor'd safe and sound, its voyage closed and done;
From fearful trip, the victor ship, comes in with object won;
Exult, O shores, and ring, O bells!
But I, with mournful tread,
Walk the deck my Captain lies,
Fallen cold and dead.

He Never Smiled Again
Felicia Dorothea Hemans

The bark that held the prince went down,
The sweeping waves rolled on;
And what was England's glorious crown
To him that wept a son?
He lived, for life may long be borne
Ere sorrow breaks its chain:
Why comes not death to those who mourn?
He never smiled again.

There stood proud forms before his throne,
The stately and the brave;
But who could fill the place of one,—
That one beneath the wave?
Before him passed the young and fair,
In pleasure's reckless train;
But seas dashed o'er his son's bright hair—
He never smiled again.

He sat where festal bowls went round;
He heard the minstrel sing;
He saw the tourney's victor crowned
Amid the knightly ring.

A murmur of the restless deep
Was bent with every strain,
A voice of winds that would not sleep—
He never smiled again.

Hearts, in that time, closed o'er the trace
Of vows once fondly poured,
And strangers took the kinsman's place
At many a joyous board;

The Witch Of Atlas
Percy Bysshe Shelley
XVI.

And odours in a kind of aviary
Of ever-blooming Eden-trees she kept,
Clipped in a floating net, a love-sick Fairy
Had woven from dew-beams while the moon yet slept;
As bats at the wired window of a dairy.
They beat their vans; and each was an adept,
When loosed and missioned, making wings of winds,
To stir sweet thoughts or sad, in destined minds.

XVII.

And liquors clear and sweet, whose healthful might
Could medicine the sick soul to happy sleep,
And change eternal death into a night
Of glorious dreams -- or if eyes needs must weep,
Could make their tears all wonder and delight,
She in her crystal vials did closely keep:
If men could drink of those clear vials, 'tis said
The living were not envied of the dead.

XVIII.

Her cave was stored with scrolls of strange device,
The works of some Saturnian Archimage,
Which taught the expiations at whose price
Men from the Gods might win that happy age
Too lightly lost, redeeming native vice;
And which might quench the Earth-consuming rage
Of gold and blood -- till men should live and move
Harmonious as the sacred stars above;

XIX.

And how all things that seem untameable,
Not to be checked and not to be confined,
Obey the spells of Wisdom's wizard skill;
Time, earth, and fire -- the ocean and the wind,
And all their shapes -- and man's imperial will;
And other scrolls whose writings did unbind
The inmost lore of Love -- let the profane
Tremble to ask what secrets they contain.

XX.

And wondrous works of substances unknown,
To which the enchantment of her father's power
Had changed those ragged blocks of savage stone,
Were heaped in the recesses of her bower;
Carved lamps and chalices, and vials which shone
In their own golden beams -- each like a flower,
Out of whose depth a fire-fly shakes his light
Under a cypress in a starless night.

XXI.

At first she lived alone in this wild home,
And her own thoughts were each a minister,
Clothing themselves, or with the ocean foam,
Or with the wind, or with the speed of fire,
To work whatever purposes might come
Into her mind; such power her mighty Sire
Had girt them with, whether to fly or run,
Through all the regions which he shines upon.

XXII.

The Ocean-nymphs and Hamadryades,
Oreads and Naiads, with long weedy locks,
Offered to do her bidding through the seas,
Under the earth, and in the hollow rocks,
And far beneath the matted roots of trees,
And in the gnarlèd heart of stubborn oaks,
So they might live for ever in the light
Of her sweet presence -- each a satellite.

XXIII.

"This may not be," the wizard maid replied;
"The fountains where the Naiades bedew
Their shining hair, at length are drained and dried;
The solid oaks forget their strength, and strew
Their latest leaf upon the mountains wide;
The boundless ocean like a drop of dew
Will be consumed -- the stubborn centre must
Be scattered, like a cloud of summer dust.

Ode On A Grecian Urn
John Keats

Thou still unravish'd bride of quietness,
Thou foster-child of silence and slow time,
Sylvan historian, who canst thus express
A flowery tale more sweetly than our rhyme:
What leaf-fring'd legend haunts about thy shape
Of deities or mortals, or of both,
In Tempe or the dales of Arcady?
What men or gods are these? What maidens loth?
What mad pursuit? What struggle to escape?
What pipes and timbrels? What wild ecstasy?

Heard melodies are sweet, but those unheard
Are sweeter; therefore, ye soft pipes, play on;
Not to the sensual ear, but, more endear'd,
Pipe to the spirit ditties of no tone:
Fair youth, beneath the trees, thou canst not leave
Thy song, nor ever can those trees be bare;
Bold Lover, never, never canst thou kiss,
Though winning near the goal yet, do not grieve;
She cannot fade, though thou hast not thy bliss,
For ever wilt thou love, and she be fair!

Ah, happy, happy boughs! that cannot shed
Your leaves, nor ever bid the Spring adieu;
And, happy melodist, unwearied,
For ever piping songs for ever new;
More happy love! more happy, happy love!
For ever warm and still to be enjoy'd,
For ever panting, and for ever young;
All breathing human passion far above,
That leaves a heart high-sorrowful and cloy'd,
A burning forehead, and a parching tongue.

227

Who are these coming to the sacrifice?
To what green altar, O mysterious priest,
Lead'st thou that heifer lowing at the skies,
And all her silken flanks with garlands drest?
What little town by river or sea shore,
Or mountain-built with peaceful citadel,
Is emptied of this folk, this pious morn?
And, little town, thy streets for evermore
Will silent be; and not a soul to tell
Why thou art desolate, can e'er return.

O Attic shape! Fair attitude! with brede
Of marble men and maidens overwrought,
With forest branches and the trodden weed;
Thou, silent form, dost tease us out of thought
As doth eternity: Cold Pastoral!
When old age shall this generation waste,
Thou shalt remain, in midst of other woe
Than ours, a friend to man, to whom thou say'st,
"Beauty is truth, truth beauty,—that is all
Ye know on earth, and all ye need to know."

FOLKLORE

The Monkey And The Crocodile

PART I

A monkey lived in a great tree on a river bank.

In the river there were many Crocodiles. A Crocodile watched the Monkeys for a long time, and one day she said to her son: "My son, get one of those Monkeys for me. I want the heart of a Monkey to eat."

"How am I to catch a Monkey?" asked the little Crocodile. "I do not travel on land, and the Monkey does not go into the water."

"Put your wits to work, and you'll find a way," said the mother.

And the little Crocodile thought and thought.

At last he said to himself: "I know what I'll do. I'll get that Monkey that lives in a big tree on the river bank. He wishes to go across the river to the island where the fruit is so ripe."

So the Crocodile swam to the tree where the Monkey lived. But he was a stupid Crocodile.

"Oh, Monkey," he called, "come with me over to the island where the fruit is so ripe."

"How can I go with you?" asked the Monkey. "I do not swim."

"No--but I do. I will take you over on my back," said the Crocodile.

The Monkey was greedy, and wanted the ripe fruit, so he jumped down on the Crocodile's back.

"Off we go!" said the Crocodile.

"This is a fine ride you are giving me!" said the Monkey.

"Do you think so? Well, how do you like this?" asked the Crocodile, diving.

"Oh, don't!" cried the Monkey, as he went under the water. He was afraid to let go, and he did not know what to do under the water.

When the Crocodile came up, the Monkey sputtered and choked. "Why did you take me under water, Crocodile?" he asked.

"I am going to kill you by keeping you under water," answered the Crocodile. "My mother wants Monkey-heart to eat, and I'm going to take yours to her."

"I wish you had told me you wanted my heart," said the Monkey, "then I might have brought it with me."

"How strange!" said the stupid Crocodile. "Do you mean to say that you left your heart back there in the tree?"

231

"That is what I mean," said the Monkey. "If you want my heart, we must go back to the tree and get it. But we are so near the island where the ripe fruit is, please take me there first."

"No, Monkey," said the Crocodile, "I'll take you straight back to your tree. Never mind the ripe fruit. Get your heart and bring it to me at once. Then we'll see about going to the island."

"Very well," said the Monkey.

But no sooner had he jumped onto the bank of the river than--whisk! up he ran into the tree.

From the topmost branches he called down to the Crocodile in the water below:

"My heart is way up here! If you want it, come for it, come for it!"

PART II

The monkey soon moved away from that tree. He wanted to get away from the Crocodile, so that he might live in peace.

But the Crocodile found him, far down the river, living in another tree.

In the middle of the river was an island covered with fruit-trees.

Half-way between the bank of the river and the island, a large rock rose out of the water. The Monkey could jump to the rock, and then to the island. The Crocodile watched the Monkey crossing from the bank of the river to the rock, and then to the island.

He thought to himself, "The Monkey will stay on the island all day, and I'll catch him on his way home at night."

The Monkey had a fine feast, while the Crocodile swam about, watching him all day.

Toward night the Crocodile crawled out of the water and lay on the rock, perfectly still.

When it grew dark among the trees, the Monkey started for home. He ran down to the river bank, and there he stopped.

"What is the matter with the rock?" the Monkey thought to himself. "I never saw it so high before. The Crocodile is lying on it!"

But he went to the edge of the water and called: "Hello, Rock!"

No answer.

Then he called again: "Hello, Rock!"

Three times the Monkey called, and then he said: "Why is it, Friend Rock, that you do not answer me to-night?"

"Oh," said the stupid Crocodile to himself, "the rock answers the Monkey at night. I'll have to answer for the rock this time."

So he answered: "Yes, Monkey! What is it?"

The Monkey laughed, and said: "Oh, it's you, Crocodile, is it?"

"Yes," said the Crocodile. "I am waiting here for you. I am going to eat you."

"You have caught me in a trap this time," said the Monkey. "There is no other way for me to go home. Open your mouth wide so I can jump right into it."

Now the Monkey well knew that when Crocodiles open their mouths wide, they shut their eyes.

While the Crocodile lay on the rock with his mouth wide open and his eyes shut, the Monkey jumped.

But not into his mouth! Oh, no! He landed on the top of the Crocodile's head, and then sprang quickly to the bank. Up he whisked into his tree.

When the Crocodile saw the trick the Monkey had played on him, he said: "Monkey, you have great cunning. You know no fear. I'll let you alone after this."

"Thank you, Crocodile, but I shall be on the watch for you just the same," said the Monkey.

The Bad Kangaroo
Arnold Lobel

There was a small Kangaroo who was bad in school. He put thumbtacks on the teacher's chair. He threw spitball across the classroom. He set off firecrackers in the lavatory and spread glue on the doorknobs.

"Your behavior is impossible!" said the school principal. "I am going to see your parents. I will tell them what a problem you are!"

The principal went to visit Mr. and Mrs. Kangaroo. He sat down in a living-room chair. "Ouch! cried the principal. "There is a thumbtack in this chair!"

"Yes, I know," said Mr. Kangaroo. "I enjoy putting thumbtacks in chairs."

A spitball hit the principal on his nose. "Forgive me," said Mrs. Kangaroo, "but I can never resist throwing those things."

There was a loud booming sound in the bathroom. "Keep calm," said Mr. Kangaroo to the principal. "The firecrackers that we keep in the medicine chest have just exploded. We love the noise."

The principal rushed for the front door. In an instant he was stuck to the doorknob. "Pull hard," said Mrs. Kangaroo. "There are little globs of glue on all of our doorknobs."

The principal pulled himself free. He dashed out of the house and ran off down the street. "Such a nice person," said Mr. Kangaroo. "I wonder why he left so quickly."

"No doubt he had another appointment," said Mrs. Kangaroo. "Never mind, supper is ready."

Mr. and Mrs. Kangaroo and their son enjoyed their evening meal. After the dessert, they all threw spitballs at each other across the dining-room table.

A child's conduct will reflect the ways of his parents.

The Twilight Of The Gods

Although Loke was bound, and could do no more harm, Balder could not come back; and so Asgard was no longer the heaven it used to be. The gods were there, but the sunshine and the summer had somehow lost their glory, and were thenceforth pale and faint. At last there came a winter such as neither man nor god had ever seen before. The days were short and dark, blinding storms followed fast upon each other and left mountains of snow behind, fierce winds swept the sky and troubled the sea, and the bitter air froze the very hearts of men into sullen despair. The deepest rivers were fast bound, the fiercest animals died in their lairs, there was no warmth in the sun, and even the icy brightness of the stars was dimmed by drifting snow. The whole earth was buried in a winter so bitter that the gods shivered in Asgard.

The long nights and the short, dark days followed fast upon each other, and as the time drew near when summer would come again men's hearts grew light with hope once more. Each day they looked into the sullen skies, through which clouds of snow were whirling, and said to each other, "To-morrow the summer will come;" but when the morrow came no summer came with it. And all through the months that in other days had been beautiful with flowers the snow fell steadily, and the cold winds blew fiercely, while eyes grew sad and hearts heavy with waiting for a summer that did not come. And it never came again; for this was the terrible Fimbul-winter, long foretold, from which even the gods could not escape. In Jotunheim there was joy among the frost-giants as they shouted to each other through the howling storms, "The Fimbul-winter has come at last." At first men shuddered as they whispered, "Can it be the Fimbul-winter?" But when they knew it beyond all doubting a blind despair filled them, and they were reckless alike of good or evil. Over the whole earth war followed fast upon war, and everywhere there were wrangling and fighting and murder. It hardly snowed fast enough to cover the blood-stains. Mothers forgot to love their little children, and brothers struck each other down as if they were the bitterest enemies.

Three years passed without one breath of the warm south wind or the blossoming of a single flower, and three other years darker and colder succeeded them. A savage joy filled the hearts of the frost-giants, and they shook their clenched hands at Asgard as if they had mastered the gods at last. On the earth there was nothing but silence and despair, and among the gods only patient waiting for the end. One day, as the sun rose dim and cold, a deep howl echoed through the sky, and a great wolf sprang up from the underworld and leaped vainly after it. All day long, through the frosty air, that terrible cry was heard, and all day the giant wolf ran close behind, slowly gaining in the chase. At last, as the sun went down over the snow-covered mountains, the wolf, with a mighty spring, reached and devoured it. The glow upon the hills went out in blackness; it was the last sunset. Faint and colorless the moon rose, and another howl filled the heavens as a second wolf sprang upon her track, ran swiftly behind, and devoured her also. Then came an awful darkness over all as, one by one, the stars fell from heaven, and blackness and whirling snow wrapped all things in their folds. The end had come; the last great battle was to be fought; Ragnarok, the Twilight of the Gods, was at hand.

Suddenly a strange sound broke in upon the darkness and was heard throughout all the worlds; on a lofty height the eagle Egder struck his prophetic harp. The earth shook, mountains crumbled, rocks were rent, and all fetters were broken. Loke shook off his chains and rushed out of his cavern, his heart hot with hate and burning with revenge, the terrible Fenris-wolf broke loose, and out of the deep sea the Midgard-serpent drew his long folds toward the land, lashing the water into foam as he passed. From every quarter the enemies of the gods gathered for the last great battle on the plain of Vigrid, which was a hundred miles wide on each side. Thither came the Fenris-wolf, his hungry jaws stretched so far apart that they reached from earth to heaven; the Midgard-serpent, with fiery eyes and pouring out floods of venom; the awful host of Hel with Loke at their head; the grim ranks of the frost-giants marching behind Hrym; and, last of all, the glittering fire-giants of Muspelheim, the fire-world, with Surt at the front.

The long line of enemies already stretched across the plain when Heimdal, standing on the rainbow bridge, blew the Gjallar-horn to call the gods. No sooner had Odin heard the terrible call to arms than he mounted and rode swiftly to Mimer's fountain, that he might know how to lead the gods into battle. When he came, the Norns sat veiled beneath the tree, silent and idle, for their work was done, and Ygdrasil began to quiver as if its very roots had been loosened. What Odin said to Mimer no one will ever know. He had no sooner finished speaking than Heimdal blew a second blast, and out of Asgard the gods rode forth to the last great battle, the golden helmet and shining armor of Odin leading the way. There was a momentary hush as the two armies confronted each other, and then the awful fight began. Shouts of rage rose from the frost-giants, and the armor of the fire-giants fairly broke into blaze as they rushed forward. The Fenris-wolf howled wildly, the hosts of Hel grew dark and horrible with rage, and the Midgard-serpent coiled its scaly length to strike. But before a blow had been struck the shining forms of the gods were seen advancing, and their battle-cry rang strong and clear across the field. Odin and Thor started side by side, but were soon separated. Odin sprang upon the wolf, and after a terrible struggle was devoured. Thor singled out his old enemy, the Midgard-serpent, and in a furious combat slew him; but as the monster died it drew its folds together with a mighty effort and poured upon Thor such a deadly flood of venom that he fell back nine paces, sank down and died. Frey encountered Surt, and because he had not the sword he had given long before to Skirner, could not defend himself, and he too was slain. The dog Garm rushed upon Tyr, the sword-god, and both were killed, Tyr missing the arm which he lost when the Fenris-wolf was bound.

And now the battle was at its height, and over the whole field gods, monsters, and giants were fighting with the energy of despair. Heimdal and Loke met, struggled, and fell together, and Vidar rushed upon the wolf which had devoured Odin, and tore him limb from limb. Then Surt strode into the middle of the armies, and in an awful pause flung a flaming firebrand among the worlds. There was a breathless hush, a sudden rush of air, a deadly heat, and the whole universe burst into blaze. A roaring flame filled all space and devoured all worlds, Ygdrasil fell in ashes, the earth sank beneath the sea. No sun, no moon, no stars, no earth, no Asgard, no Hel, no Jotunheim; gods, giants, monsters, and men all dead! Nothing remained but a vast abyss filled with the moaning seas, and brooded over by a pale, colorless light. Ragnarok, the end of all things, the Twilight of the Gods, had come.

The Magic Apples

It is not very amusing to be a king. Father Odin often grew tired of sitting all day long upon his golden throne in Valhalla above the heavens. He wearied of welcoming the new heroes whom the Valkyries brought him from wars upon the earth, and of watching the old heroes fight their daily deathless battles. He wearied of his wise ravens, and the constant gossip which they brought him from the four corners of the world; and he longed to escape from everyone who knew him to some place where he could pass for a mere stranger, instead of the great king of the Æsir, the mightiest being in the whole universe, of whom everyone was afraid.

Sometimes he longed so much that he could not bear it. Then—he would run away. He disguised himself as a tall old man, with white hair and a long, gray beard. Around his shoulders he threw a huge blue cloak, that covered him from top to toe, and over his face he pulled a big slouch hat, to hide his eyes. For his eyes Odin could not change—no magician has ever learned how to do that. One was empty; he had given the eye to the giant Mimer in exchange for wisdom.

Usually Odin loved to go upon these wanderings alone; for an adventure is a double adventure when one meets it single-handed. It was a fine game for Odin to see how near he could come to danger without feeling the grip of its teeth. But sometimes, when he wanted company, he would whisper to his two brothers, Hœnir and red Loki. They three would creep out of the palace by the back way; and, with a finger on the lip to Heimdal, the watchman, would silently steal over the rainbow bridge which led from Asgard into the places of men and dwarfs and giants.

Wonderful adventures they had, these three, with Loki to help make things happen. Loki was a sly, mischievous fellow, full of his pranks and his capers, not always kindly ones. But he was clever, as well as malicious; and when he had pushed folk into trouble, he could often help them out again, as safe as ever. He could be the jolliest of companions when he chose, and Odin liked his merriment and his witty talk.

One day Loki did something which was no mere jest nor easily forgiven, for it brought all Asgard into danger. And after that Father Odin and his children thought twice before inviting Loki to join them in any journey or undertaking. This which I am about to tell was the first really wicked deed of which Loki was found guilty, though I am sure his red beard had dabbled in secret wrongs before.

One night the three high gods, Odin, Hœnir, and Loki, stole away from Asgard in search of adventure. Over mountains and deserts, great rivers and stony places, they wandered until they grew very hungry. But there was no food to be found—not even a berry or a nut.

Oh, how footsore and tired they were! And oh, how faint! The worst of it ever is that—as you must often have noticed—the heavier one's feet grow, the lighter and more hollow becomes one's stomach; which seems a strange thing, when you think of it. If only one's feet became as light as the rest of one feels, folk could fairly fly with hunger. Alas! This is not so.

The three Æsir drooped and drooped, and seemed on the point of starving, when they came to the edge of a valley. Here, looking down, they saw a herd of oxen feeding on the grass.

"Hola!" shouted Loki. "Behold our supper!" Going down into the valley, they caught and killed one of the oxen, and, building a great bonfire, hung up the meat to roast. Then the three sat around the fire and smacked their lips, waiting for the meat to cook. They waited for a long time.

"Surely, it is done now," said Loki, at last; and he took the meat from the fire. Strange to say, however, it was raw as ere the fire was lighted. What could it mean? Never before had meat required so long a time to roast. They made the fire brighter and re-hung the beef for a thorough basting, cooking it even longer than they had done at first. When again they came to carve the meat, they found it still uneatable. Then, indeed, they looked at one another in surprise.

"What can this mean?" cried Loki, with round eyes.

"There is some trick!" whispered Hœnir, looking around as if he expected to see a fairy or a witch meddling with the food.

"We must find out what this mystery betokens," said Odin thoughtfully. Just then there was a strange sound in the oak-tree under which they had built their fire.

"What is that?" Loki shouted, springing to his feet. They looked up into the tree, and far above in the branches, near the top, they spied an enormous eagle, who was staring down at them, and making a queer sound, as if he were laughing.

"Ho-ho!" croaked the eagle. "I know why your meat will not cook. It is all my doing, masters."

The three Æsir stared in surprise. Then Odin said sternly: "Who are you, Master Eagle? And what do you mean by those rude words?"

"Give me my share of the ox, and you shall see," rasped the eagle, in his harsh voice. "Give me my share, and you will find that your meat will cook as fast as you please."

Now the three on the ground were nearly famished. So, although it seemed very strange o be arguing with an eagle, they cried, as if in one voice: "Come down, then, and take your share." They thought that, being a mere bird, he would want but a small piece.

The eagle flapped down from the top of the tree. Dear me! What a mighty bird he was! Eight feet across the wings was the smallest measure, and his claws were as long and strong as ice-hooks. He fanned the air like a whirlwind as he flew down to perch beside the bonfire. Then in his beak and claws he seized a leg and both shoulders of the ox, and started to fly away.

"Hold, thief!" roared Loki angrily, when he saw how much the eagle was taking. "That is not your share; you are no lion, but you are taking the lion's share of our feast. Begone, Scarecrow, and leave the meat as you found it!" Thereat, seizing a pole, he struck at the eagle with all his might.

Then a strange thing happened. As the great bird flapped upward with his prey, giving a scream of malicious laughter, the pole which Loki still held stuck fast to the eagle's back, and Loki was unable to let go of the other end.

"Help, help!" he shouted to Odin and to Hœnir, as he felt himself lifted off his feet. But they could not help him. "Help, help!" he screamed, as the eagle flew with him, now high, now low, through brush and bog and briar, over treetops and the peaks of mountains. On and on they went, until Loki thought his arm would be pulled out, like a weed torn up by the roots. The eagle would not listen to his cries nor pause in his flight, until Loki was almost dead with pain and fatigue.

"Hark you, Loki," screamed the eagle, going a little more slowly; "no one can help you except me. You are bewitched, and you cannot pull away from this pole, nor loose the pole from me, until I choose. But if you will promise what I ask, you shall go free."

Then Loki groaned: "O eagle, only let me go, and tell me who you really are, and I will promise whatever you wish."

The eagle answered: "I am the giant Thiasse, the enemy of the Æsir. But you ought to love me, Loki, for you yourself married a giantess."

Loki moaned: "Oh, yes! I dearly love all my wife's family, great Thiasse. Tell me what you want of me?"

"I want this," quoth Thiasse gruffly. "I am growing old, and I want the apples which Idun keeps in her golden casket, to make me young again. You must get them for me."

Now these apples were the fruit of a magic tree, and were more beautiful to look at and more delicious to taste than any fruit that ever grew. The best thing about them was that whoever tasted one, be he ever so old, grew young and strong again. The apples belonged to a beautiful lady named Idun, who kept them in a golden casket. Every morning the Æsir came to her to be refreshed and made over by a bite of her precious fruit. That is why in Asgard no one ever waxed old or ugly. Even Father Odin, Hœnir, and Loki, the three travelers who had seen the very beginning of everything, when the world was made, were still sturdy and young. And so long as Idun kept her apples safe, the faces of the family who sat about the table of Valhalla would be rosy and fair like the faces of children.

"O friend giant!" cried Loki. "You know not what you ask! The apples are the most precious treasure of Asgard, and Idun keeps watch over them as if they were dearer to her than life itself. I never could steal them from her, Thiasse; for at her call all Asgard would rush to the rescue, and trouble would buzz about my ears like a hive of bees let loose."

"Then you must steal Idun herself, apples and all. For the apples I must have, and you have promised, Loki, to do my bidding."

Loki sniffed and thought, thought and sniffed again. Already his mischievous heart was planning how he might steal Idun away. He could hardly help laughing to think how angry the Æsir would be when they found their beauty-medicine gone forever. But he hoped that, when he had done this trick for Thiasse, now and then the giant would let him have a nibble of the magic apples; so that Loki himself would remain young long after the other Æsir were grown old and feeble. This thought suited Loki's malicious nature well.

"I think I can manage it for you, Thiasse," he said craftily. "In a week I promise to bring Idun and her apples to you. But you must not forget the great risk which I am running, nor that I am your relative by marriage. I may have a favor to ask in return, Thiasse."

Then the eagle gently dropped Loki from his claws. Falling on a soft bed of moss, Loki jumped up and ran back to his traveling companions, who were glad and surprised to see him again. They had feared that the eagle was carrying him away to feed his young eaglets in some far-off nest. Ah, you may be sure that Loki did not tell them who the eagle really was, nor confess the wicked promise which he had made about Idun and her apples.

After that the three went back to Asgard, for they had had adventure enough for one day.

The days flew by, and the time came when Loki must fulfill his promise to Thiasse. So one morning he strolled out into the meadow where Idun loved to roam among the flowers. There he found her, sitting by a tiny spring, and holding her precious casket of apples on her lap. She was combing her long golden hair, which fell from under a wreath of spring flowers, and she was very beautiful. Her green robe was embroidered with buds and blossoms of silk in many colors, and she wore a golden girdle about her waist. She smiled as Loki came, and tossed him a posy, saying: "Good-morrow, red Loki. Have you come for a bite of my apples? I see a wrinkle over each of your eyes which I can smooth away."

"Nay, fair lady," answered Loki politely, "I have just nibbled of another apple, which I found this morning. Verily, I think it is sweeter and more magical than yours."

Idun was hurt and surprised.

"That cannot be, Loki," she cried. "There are no apples anywhere like mine. Where found you this fine fruit?" and she wrinkled up her little nose scornfully.

"Oho! I will not tell anyone the place," chuckled Loki, "except that it is not far, in a little wood. There is a gnarled old apple-tree, and on its branches grow the most beautiful red-cheeked apples you ever saw. But you could never find it."

"I should like to see these apples, Loki, if only to prove how far less good they are than mine. Will you bring me some?"

"That I will not," said Loki teasingly. "Oh, no! I have my own magic apples now, and folk will be coming to me for help instead of to you."

Idun began to coax him, as he had guessed that she would: "Please, please, Loki, show me the place!"

At first he would not, for he was a sly fellow, and knew how to lead her on. At last, he pretended to yield.

"Well, then, because I love you, Idun, better than all the rest, I will show you the place, if you will come with me. But it must be a secret—no one must ever know."

All girls like secrets.

"Yes—Yes!" cried Idun eagerly. "Let us steal away now, while no one is looking."

This was just what Loki hoped for.

"Bring your own apples," he said, "that we may compare them with mine. But I know mine are better."

"I know mine are the best in all the world," returned Idun, pouting. "I will bring them, to show you the difference."

Off they started together, she with the golden casket under her arm; and Loki chuckled wickedly as they went. He led her for some distance, further than she had ever strayed before, and at last she grew frightened.

"Where are you taking me, Loki?" she cried. "You said it was not far. I see no little wood, no old apple-tree."

"It is just beyond, just a little step beyond," he answered. So on they went. But that little step took them beyond the boundary of Asgard—just a little step beyond, into the space where the giants lurked and waited for mischief.

Then there was a rustling of wings, and *whirr-rr-rr!* Down came Thiasse in his eagle dress. Before Idun suspected what was happening, he fastened his claws into her girdle and flapped away with her, magic apples and all, to his palace in Jotunheim, the Land of Giants.

Loki stole back to Asgard, thinking that he was quite safe, and that no one would discover his villainy. At first Idun was not missed. But after a little the gods began to feel signs of age, and went for their usual bite of her apples. Then they found that she had disappeared, and a great terror fell upon them. Where had she gone? Suppose she should not come back!

The hours and days went by, and still she did not return. Their fright became almost a panic. Their hair began to turn gray, and their limbs grew stiff and gouty so that they hobbled down Asgard streets. Even Freia, the loveliest, was afraid to look in her mirror, and Balder the beautiful grew pale and haggard. The happy land of Asgard was like a garden over which a burning wind had blown,—all the flower-faces were faded and withered, and springtime was turned into yellow fall.

If Idun and her apples were not quickly found, the gods seemed likely to shrivel and blow away like autumn leaves. They held a council to inquire into the matter, endeavoring to learn who had seen Idun last, and whither she had gone. It turned out that one morning Heimdal had seen her strolling out of Asgard with Loki, and no one had seen her since. Then the gods understood; Loki was the last person who had been with her—this must be one of Loki's tricks. They were filled with anger. They seized and bound Loki and brought him before the council. They threatened him with torture and with death unless he should tell the truth. And Loki was so frightened that finally he confessed what he had done.

Then indeed there was horror in Asgard. Idun stolen away by a wicked giant! Idun and her apples lost, and Asgard growing older every minute! What was to be done? Big Thor seized Loki and threw him up in the air again and again, so that his heels touched first the moon and then the sea; you can still see the marks upon the moon's white face. "If you do not bring Idun back from the land of your wicked wife, you shall have worse than this!" he roared. "Go and bring her *now.*"

"How can I do that?" asked Loki, trembling.

"That is for you to find," growled Thor. "Bring her you must. Go!"

Loki thought for a moment. Then he said:—"I will bring her back if Freia will loan me her falcon dress. The giant dresses as an eagle. I, too, must guise me as a bird, or we cannot outwit him."

Then Freia hemmed and hawed. She did not wish to loan her feather dress, for it was very precious. But all the Æsir begged; and finally she consented.

It was a beautiful great dress of brown feathers and gray, and in it Freia loved to skim like a falcon among the clouds and stars. Loki put it on, and when he had done so he looked exactly like a great brown hawk. Only his bright black eyes remained the same, glancing here and there, so that they lost sight of nothing.

With a whirr of his wings Loki flew off to the north, across mountains and valleys and the great river Ifing, which lay between Asgard and Giant Land. And at last he came to the palace of Thiasse the giant.

It happened, fortunately, that Thiasse had gone fishing in the sea, and Idun was left alone, weeping and broken-hearted. Presently she heard a little tap on her window, and, looking up, she saw a great brown bird perching on the ledge. He was so big that Idun was frightened and gave a scream. But the bird nodded pleasantly and croaked: "Don't be afraid, Idun. I am a friend. I am Loki, come to set you free."

"Loki! Loki is no friend of mine. He brought me here," she sobbed. "I don't believe you came to save me."

"That is indeed why I am here," he replied, "and a dangerous business it is, if Thiasse should come back before we start for home."

"How will you get me out?" asked Idun doubtfully. "The door is locked, and the window is barred."

"I will change you into a nut," said he, "and carry you in my claws."

"What of the casket of apples?" queried Idun. "Can you carry that also?"

Then Loki laughed long and loudly.

"What welcome to Asgard do you think I should receive without the apples?" he cried. "Yes, we must take them, indeed."

Idun came to the window, and Loki, who was a skillful magician, turned her into a nut and took her in one claw, while in the other he seized the casket of apples. Then off he whirred out of the palace grounds and away toward Asgard's safety.

In a little while Thiasse returned home, and when he found Idun and her apples gone, there was a hubbub, you may be sure! However, he lost little time by smashing mountains and breaking trees in his giant rage; that fit was soon over. He put on his eagle plumage and started in pursuit of the falcon.

Now an eagle is bigger and stronger than any other bird, and usually in a long race he can beat even the swift hawk who has an hour's start. Presently Loki heard behind him the shrill scream of a giant eagle, and his heart turned sick. But he had crossed the great river, and already was in sight of Asgard. The aged Æsir were gathered on the rainbow bridge watching eagerly for Loki's return; and when they spied the falcon with the nut and the casket in his talons, they knew who it was. A great cheer went up, but it was hushed in a moment, for they saw the eagle close after the falcon; and they guessed that this must be the giant Thiasse, the stealer of Idun.

Then there was a great shouting of commands, and a rushing to and fro. All the gods, even Father Odin and his two wise ravens, were busy gathering chips into great heaps on the walls of Asgard. As soon as Loki, with his precious burden, had fluttered weakly over the wall, dropping to the ground beyond, the gods lighted the heaps of chips which they had piled, and soon there was a wall of fire, over which the eagle must fly. He was going too fast to stop. The flames roared and crackled, but Thiasse flew straight into them, with a scream of fear and rage. His feathers caught fire and burned, so that he could no longer fly, but fell headlong to the ground inside the walls. Then Thor, the thunder-lord, and Týr, the mighty war-king, fell upon him and slew him, so that he could never trouble the Æsir anymore.

There was great rejoicing in Asgard that night, for Loki changed Idun again to a fair lady; whereupon she gave each of the eager gods a bite of her life-giving fruit, so that they grew young and happy once more, as if all these horrors had never happened.

Not one of them, however, forgot the evil part which Loki had played in these doings. They hid the memory, like a buried seed, deep in their hearts. Thenceforward the word of Loki and the honor of his name were poor coin in Asgard; which is no wonder.

The Drawing Of The Sword

In the olden days in Britain it came to pass that Uther the king died, and none but Merlin, the wise man and magician of the realm, knew that he left a son Arthur, who had been delivered to Merlin at his birth to be trained in all things by him. So for a long time the realm stood in great peril, for every lord that was mighty made himself stronger, and many strove to be king.

Then Merlin went to the Archbishop of Canterbury and counseled him to send for all the lords of the realm, and all the gentlemen of arms, be they earls or barons or knights, to come to London at Christmas time, and there God would show by a sign who was to be rightly king over all England. So the archbishop summoned them all. And many of them made clean their lives, that they might be more acceptable to God.

At Christmas time all the lords and earls and barons and knights came together from every side unto London to await the sign which should show who should be king. And behold, when they came out from their morning devotions, there in the churchyard they saw standing a great stone. It was of the same breadth and height on every side, and its appearance was like marble. And in the midst of it was an anvil of steel a foot high, and therein stood a fair sword, naked without sheath or guard, and about it were written letters of gold which said thus: "Whoso pulleth this sword out from this stone is rightwise king born of all England."

Then the people marveled, and all the lords went to gaze upon the stone and the sword. When they read the reading, some tried to pull the sword. One by one the lords and gentlemen of arms, such as would have been king, essayed to pull it. But none might stir the sword, nor even move it.

"He is not here," said the archbishop, "that shall achieve the sword. But doubt not God will make him known. Now this is my counsel, that we choose ten knights, men of good fame, who shall guard this sword. And upon New Year's Day let the barons make a joust and tournament in which every knight of the realm who will shall play. Perchance at that tourney it shall be made known who shall win the sword." And so it was done as the archbishop said.

Upon New Year's Day the barons rode to the field, and among them were Sir Hector, Sir Kay his son, and young Arthur, whom Merlin had caused to be brought up by Sir Hector as his own son. As they rode, Sir Kay found that he had no sword with him, for he had left it behind at his father's lodging, and he prayed young Arthur to ride back for it.

"I will well," said Arthur, and he rode swiftly back; but when he came to the house it was closed, so that he could not by any means make his way in, for the lady and all the servants were gone to see the jousting.

Then was Arthur angry and said to himself, "Nevertheless, my brother Kay shall not be without a sword this day. I will ride to the churchyard and take the sword that I saw there sticking in a stone."

He rode with all speed to the churchyard, and alighted there and tied his horse to the stile. When he came to the stone he found no knights there, for they were at the jousting. So he grasped the sword by the handles, and lightly and fiercely pulled it out of the stone, and took his horse and rode till he came to Sir Kay, and delivered to him the sword.

When Sir Kay saw the blade that Arthur had brought him, he knew well that it was the sword of the stone. Straightway he rode to his father, Sir Hector, and said, "Sir, lo, here is the sword of the stone; wherefore I must be king of this land."

But Sir Hector said to him, "Swear to me by thy knightly honor how thou camest by this sword."

"Sir," said Kay, "by my brother Arthur, for he brought it to me."

"How gat ye this sword?" said Sir Hector to Arthur.

"Sir, I will tell you. When I came home for my brother's sword, I found no one at home to deliver it to me. Yet, thought I, my brother Sir Kay should not be swordless. So I went in all haste and pulled out of the stone in the churchyard this blade which I had seen sticking there as I passed in the way."

"Found ye any knights about this sword?" said Sir Hector.

"None," said Arthur.

"Now," said Sir Hector, "I understand ye must be king of this land."

"Wherefore I?" asked Arthur, "and for what cause?"

"Because God will have it so; for there should never man have drawn out this sword but he that should rightwise be king of this land."

He led Arthur and Sir Kay to the churchyard, and Arthur read the words that were written there, which in his haste to get the sword he had not seen.

"Now," quoth Sir Hector, "let me see whether you can put the sword there as it was and pull it out again."

"That is no mastery," replied Arthur, and he put it into the stone and drew it out again.

"Once more put it in," commanded Sir Hector, and this time he himself essayed to pull it out, but he could neither move nor stir it.

"Do thou try," he said to Sir Kay. And anon Kay pulled at the sword with all his might, but it would not be moved.

"Now shalt thou essay," said Sir Hector to Arthur.

"I will well," said Arthur, and drew it out easily. That was the third time Arthur had drawn it forth.

Therewithal Sir Hector kneeled down before Arthur, and so likewise did Sir Kay.

"Alas!" quoth Arthur, "mine own dear father and brother, why kneel ye to me?"

"Nay, nay, my lord Arthur," returned Sir Hector, "it is not so. I was never your father, nor of your blood, but I wot well ye are of an higher blood than ever I thought ye were."

Then Sir Hector told him all, how Merlin had brought Arthur to him at his birth, and how he had nourished and trained him by Merlin's commandment.

Arthur was sore grieved when he understood that Sir Hector was not his father.

"Sir," said Hector, "will ye be to me a good and gracious lord when ye are king?"

"Else were I to blame," said Arthur, "for ye are the man in all the world I am most beholden to, and to my good lady and mother your wife, that hath fostered me and kept me as well and as tenderly as her own. And if ever it be God's will that I be king, as ye say, ye shall desire of me what I may do, and I shall not fail you. God forbid I should fail you while you and I live."

Therewithal they went all three unto the archbishop and told him how the sword was achieved and by whom. On Twelfth Day all the barons came to the churchyard, and he who wished essayed to take the sword. But there before them all there was none that could draw it save Arthur. Wherefore many lords were angry and said that it was a great shame unto them all and unto the realm to be governed by a boy, and he of no high blood. So it fell out that the crowning of a king was put off till Candlemas, when all the barons should meet there again. (But ten knights were ordained to watch the sword by day and by night. They set a pavilion over the stone, and five always watched.)

At Candlemas many more great lords came thither to win the sword, but none might prevail. And as Arthur did at Christmas, so he did at Candlemas, and pulled out the sword easily. Again the barons were sore aggrieved, and yet again they delayed. As Arthur did at Candlemas, so did he once more at Easter. And still they would not crown him king. Then the archbishop of Canterbury and many of the best knights were full of indignation, and they made a guard of the most worthy knights, those whom King Uther had loved best and trusted most in his day, and all these, with many others, were always about Arthur day and night until the feast of Pentecost.

At the feast of Pentecost all manner of men essayed once more to pull out the sword, but still none might prevail but Arthur. He pulled it out before all the lords and common people who were there, wherefore all the people cried out, "We will have Arthur for our king; we will have no more delay, for we all see that it is God's will that he shall be our king, and he that holdeth out against him, him will we slay."

Thereupon they all kneeled down, both rich and poor, and cried Arthur mercy because they had delayed so long. And Arthur forgave them, and took the sword between his hands and offered it up on the altar where the archbishop was. So was he made knight by the best man that was there.

Anon, when Arthur had been made a knight, was the coronation made, and there did he swear to his lords and his people to be a true king, and to stand for justice from henceforth all the days of his life.

How Robin Hood Came To Live In The Green Wood

Very many years ago there ruled over England a king, who was called Richard Cœur de Lion. Cœur de Lion is French and means lion-hearted. It seems strange that an English king should have a French name. But more than a hundred years before this king reigned, a French duke named William came to England, defeated the English in a great battle, and declared himself king of all that southern part of Britain called England.

He brought with him a great many Frenchmen, or Normans, as they were called from the name of the part of France over which this duke ruled. These Normans were all poor though they were very proud and haughty. They came with Duke William to help him fight because he promised to give them money and lands as a reward. Now Duke William had not a great deal of money nor many lands of his own. So when he had beaten the English, or Saxons, as they were called in those days, he stole lands and houses, money and cattle from the Saxon nobles and gave them to the Normans. The Saxon nobles themselves had very often become the servants of these proud Normans. Thus it came about that two races lived in England, each speaking their own language, and each hating the other.

This state of things lasted for a very long time. Even when Richard became king, more than a hundred years after the coming of Duke William, there was still a great deal of hatred between the two races.

Richard Cœur de Lion, as his name tells you, was a brave and noble man. He loved danger; he loved brave men and noble deeds. He hated all mean and cruel acts, and the cowards who did them. He was ever ready to help the weak against the strong, and had he stayed in England after he became king he might have done much good. He might have taught the proud Norman nobles that true nobility rests in being kind and gentle to those less strong and less fortunate than ourselves, and not in fierceness and cruelty.

Yet Richard himself was neither meek nor gentle. He was indeed very fierce and terrible in battle. He loved to fight with people who were stronger or better armed than himself. He would have been ashamed to hurt the weak and feeble.

But Richard did not stay in England. Far, far over the seas there is a country called Palestine. There our Lord was born, lived, and died. Christian people in all ages must think tenderly and gratefully of that far-off country. But at this time it had fallen into the hands of the heathen. It seemed to Christian people in those days that it would be a terrible sin to allow wicked heathen to live in the Holy Land. So they gathered together great armies of brave men from every country in the world and sent them to try to win it back. Many brave deeds were done, many terrible battles fought, but still the heathen kept possession.

Then brave King Richard of England said he too would fight for the city of our Lord. So he gathered together as much money as he could find, and as many brave men as would follow him, and set out for the Holy Land. Before he went away he called two bishops who he thought were good and wise men, and said to them: "Take care of England while I am gone. Rule my people wisely and well, and I will reward you when I return." The bishops promised to do as he asked. Then he said farewell and sailed away.

Now King Richard had a brother who was called Prince John. Prince John was quite different from King Richard in every way. He was not at all a nice man. He was jealous of Richard because he was king, and angry because he himself had not been chosen to rule while Richard was in Palestine. As soon as his brother had gone, John went to the bishops and said, "You must let me rule while the king is away." And the bishops allowed him to do so. Deep down in his wicked heart John meant to make himself king altogether, and never let Richard come back any more.

A sad time now began for the Saxons. John tried to please the haughty Normans because they were great and powerful, and he hoped they would help to make him king. He thought the best way to please them was to give them land and money. So as he had none of his own (he was indeed called John Lackland) he took it from the Saxons and gave it to the Normans. Thus many of the Saxons once more became homeless beggars, and lived a wild life in the forests, which covered a great part of England at this time.

Now among the few Saxon nobles who still remained, and who had not been robbed of their lands and money, there was one called Robert, Earl of Huntingdon. He had one son also named Robert, but people called him Robin. He was a favorite with everyone. Tall, strong, handsome, and full of fun, he kept his father's house bright with songs and laughter. He was brave and fearless too, and there was no better archer in all the countryside. And with it all he was gentle and tender, never hurting the weak nor scorning the poor.

But Robert of Huntingdon had a bitter enemy. One day this enemy came with many soldiers behind him, determined to kill the earl and take all his goods and lands. There was a fierce and terrible fight, but in the end Robert and all his men were killed. His house was burned to the ground and all his money stolen. Only Robin was saved, because he was such a splendid archer that no soldier would go near him, either to kill him or take him prisoner. He fought bravely till the last, but when he saw that his father was dead and his home in flames, he had no heart to fight any longer. So taking his bow and arrows, he fled to the great forest of Sherwood.

Very fast he had to run, for Prince John's men were close behind him. Soon he reached the edge of the forest, but he did not stop there. On and on he went, plunging deeper and deeper under the shadow of the trees. At last he threw himself down beneath a great oak, burying his face in the cool, green grass.

His heart felt hot and bitter. He was full of rage and fierce thoughts of revenge. Cruel men in one day had robbed him of everything. His father, his home, servants, cattle, land, money, his name even, all were gone. He was bruised, hungry, and weary. Yet as he lay pressing his face against the cool, green grass, and clutching the soft, damp moss with his hands, it was not sorrow or pain he felt, but only a bitter longing for revenge.

The great, solemn trees waved gently overhead in the summer breeze, the setting sun sent shafts of golden light into the cool, blue shadows, birds sang their evening songs, deer rustled softly through the underwood, and bright-eyed squirrels leaped noiselessly from branch to branch. Everywhere there was calm and peace except in poor Robin's angry heart.

Robin loved the forest. He loved the sights and scents, and the sounds and deep silences of it. He felt as if it were a tender mother who opened her wide arms to him. Soon it comforted him, and at last the tears came hot and fast, and sobs shook him as he lay on the grass. The bitterness and anger had all melted out of his heart; only sorrow was left.

In the dim evening light Robin knelt bareheaded on the green grass to say his prayers. Then, still bareheaded, he stood up and swore an oath. This was the oath:—

"I swear to honor God and the King,

To help the weak and fight the strong,

To take from the rich and give to the poor,

Then he lay down on the grass under the trees with his good long bow beside him, and fell fast asleep.

And this is how Robin Hood first came to live in the Green Wood and have all his wonderful adventures.

Davy Crockett's Boast

When Davy Crockett went to Congress in 1827 he already had a considerable reputation as a remarkable hunter. Washington politicians deliberately puffed and exploited this reputation until Crockett had become a half-comic superhero.

I 'm that same David Crockett, fresh from the backwoods, half horse, half alligator, a little touched with the snapping-turtle; can wade the Mississippi, leap the Ohio, ride upon a streak of lightning, and slip without a scratch down a honey locust; can whip my weight in wildcats - and if any gentleman pleases, for a ten dollar bill, he may throw in a panther- hug a bear too close for comfort, and eat any man opposed to Jackson.

I had taken old Betsy, said he, and straggled off to the banks of the Mississippi River; and meeting with no game, I didn't like it a bit. I felt mighty wolfish about the head and ears, and thought I would spile if I wasn't kivured up in salt, for I hadn't had a fight in anyway 10 days; and I cum acrost a fellow floatin downstream, settin in the stern of his boat fast asleep.

Said I, "Hello, stranger! If you don't take keer your boat will run away with you" and he looked up and said he, "I don't value you." He looked up at me slantendicler, and I looked down upon him slantendicler; and he took out a chaw of turbaccur and held it up, and said he, "I don't value you that."

Said I, "Cum ashore, I can whip you"- I've been trying to git a fight all the mornin' and the varmint flapped his wings and crowed like a chicken. I ris up, shook my mane, and neighed like a horse. He run his boat plump head foremost ashore. I stood still waitin for him and sot my triggurs, that is, took off my shurt, and tied my galluses tight around my waist- and at it we went.

He was a right smart coon, but hardly a bait for such a fellur as me. I put it to him mighty droll. In 10 minutes he yelled enough, and swore I was a ripstavur.

Said I, "Ain't I the yaller flower of the forest! And I am all brimstone but the head and ears, and that's aquafortis."

Said he, "Stranger, you are a beauty: and if I know'd your name, I'd vote for you next election." Said I, "I'm that same David Crockett. You know what I'm made of. I've got the closest shootin rifle, the best 'coon dog, the biggest flask, and the ruffest racking horse in the district. I can kill more lickur, fool more varmints, and cool out more men than any man you can find in all Kentucky."

Said he, "'Good mornin, stranger- I'm satisfied." Said I, "Good mornin, sir; I feel much better since our meetin" but after I got away a piece I said, "Hello, friend, don't forget that vote.'"

The Man In The Middle

As it first reached me, the story had its setting in a subway local plodding toward Fort Hamilton Parkway at an hour long past one in the morning. The girl, a stenographer who lived out that way with her folks, had been to a theatre and supper party in Manhattan. One of the men at the supper had made what it would be effusive to call a half-hearted offer to see her home, but she had rewarded that heroic gesture by an amiable refusal. Accustomed to pushing competently about in the crowds downtown, the thought of an untimely jaunt into darkest Brooklyn seemed dreary but not alarming.

Her first disquiet came shortly after she got into the almost deserted train at the first stop beyond Myrtle A venue three forbidding ruffians. The man in the middle seemed so drunk that his companions were practically carrying him, and his insouciant legs had the curious detachment of a scarecrow's. Our heroine was eyeing these wastrels with distaste when she realized that the man in the middle had fixed one bleary eye upon her, and, nervously following the direction of his gaze, she saw that there on her wrist, defiantly visible, was her bracelet watch with its chain of diamonds. She hastily drew her sleeve down over it, made a slight pretense of looking up and down the car, and then, out of the corner of her eye, reconnoitered. It was true. Slouched down between his friends, he was looking at her, and out of the corners of their eyes, as furtive and as wary as herself, his companions were looking at her too.

Her heart sank. Two more stops and she would be at her own station. Suppose they followed her? Suppose there was no one on the echoing platform at that chilly hour, and no one in the change booth? In her imagination she was already trying to make her legs walk up the stairway to the street, sick with the knowledge that the monstrous three were following silently at her heels. Her knees turned to water. Panic possessed her. She had an impulse to tear her foolish watch from her wrist and pitch it across the aisle. She glanced up and down the car. By this time its only other occupants were a benign, bespectacled old gentleman and his wife, a serene white-haired couple who would not be much help if she should absurdly scream out to them that the mute threesome across the car were plotting assault and robbery, when, as some remnant of her reason told her, they were probably doing nothing of the kind. Besides, the old couple were getting up to leave at the next station. They were passing her on their way to the door. She had a numbing sense that all law and order was then and there taking its departure when, without looking at her and without moving his lips, the old gentleman said something.

"Follow us off this train."

It took her a second to realize that this was meant for her. In another, she found herself on the station platform, the door closing behind them. In still another, the train grunted, pulled itself together and lurched off into the tunnel, carrying the dreadful three with it. She wanted to laugh hysterically at her own relief. Now the old gentleman was speaking to her.

"My dear," he said," I apologize for issuing orders to you, but there was no time for ceremony. Did you notice those men who sat across from you?"

It seemed she had.

"Well," he went on, "I didn't like to leave you in the train with them. I am a doctor, my dear, and I could not help noticing an odd thing about that little group. Did you observe anything peculiar about that man in the middle?"

"He was very drunk," the girl said.

The doctor shook his head.

"Perhaps he had been," he admitted, "but not when they carried him into the train. When they carried him into the train, the man in the middle was dead."

Aladdin and the Wonderful Lamp

Once there lived a poor widow and her son, Aladdin. One day, Aladdin's uncle, Mustafa, came to visit them. He said, "Sister, why don't you let Aladdin come and work for me?" They agreed and Mustafa took Aladdin along with him. They walked in the desert and came to a cave. The cave was full of riches and treasures but Mustafa was afraid to go inside. He wanted Aladdin to go in and get him the treasures instead. "Go inside," commanded Mustafa, "and find me the jewels. You will also find a lamp. Bring it to me."

Aladdin went inside and found more riches than he could ever imagine. He found a beautiful ring and wore it on his finger. He also collected as many gems as he could, but before he could come out of the cave, Mustafa said, "Quick! Just hand me all, the jewels and the lamp!" Aladdin refused. Angry at the refusal, his cruel uncle blocked the entrance of the cave and left.

Aladdin sat in the dark and cried. Then he saw the old lamp and decided to light it. While cleaning it, he rubbed the lamp and out came a genie! "Master, I shall grant you three wishes," he said. Aladdin said, "Take me home!" In seconds, Aladdin was with his mother, counting the gems he had brought from the cave. Aladdin also brought the ring along with him and when he rubbed it, out came another genie! "Master, I shall grant you three wishes!" said the genie. "Make us rich and happy!" said Aladdin. And Aladdin and his mother lived happily.

One day, Aladdin saw the sultan's daughter and fell in love with her. He went to the palace with gems and asked for her hand in marriage. The king agreed to this. After marriage, Aladdin showered the princess with all the riches and gave her a huge palace to live in. When the sultan died, Aladdin ruled the kingdom. He was just and kind hearted and everybody was happy under his rule.

Meanwhile, Mustafa came to know how Aladdin found the magic lamp and became rich. He wanted to take the lamp back. So, one day, when Aladdin was away, Mustafa came to the palace dressed as a trader. He cried out, "Get new lamps for old ones! New lamps for old!" Hearing this, the princess took out the magic lamp and gave it to him. She did not know that the old lamp was indeed magical. She bought a shiny new lamp instead. Mustafa gladly took the lamp and went away. He then commanded the genie, "Send Aladdin's entire palace into the deserts in Africa!" And saying this, Mustafa, along with the princess in the palace, were sent to Africa. Aladdin, on coming back, found his wife and house missing. He searched for the palace for three long days. Finally, he rubbed his magic ring and asked the genie, "Please take me to my princess!" The genie agreed. When he met his wife, Aladdin and the princess decided to trick Mustafa.

One night, the princess said to Mustafa, "I don't think Aladdin will ever find me here! I might as well live as your slave for I am certain he is dead now!" Mustafa was very happy and ordered for a feast. During the feast, the princess got Mustafa drunk and he fell into a deep sleep.

In the meantime, the princess took the magic lamp to Aladdin. Together, they asked the genie of the lamp to take the entire palace back to Aladdin's kingdom. The genie then killed Mustafa and Aladdin and the princess lived happily ever after.

The Road To Fortune

One fine morning two young men were strolling together through the fields, when they perceived, at a great distance, a very high hill, on the top of which stood a beautiful castle, which sparkled so brightly in the sunshine that the youths were quite delighted, and could not help gazing at it.

"Let us go to it," said one of the lads.

"It is easy to say, 'Let us go,' but how can we walk so far?" retorted the other, who was a lazy fellow.

"You may do it easily," replied a clear voice behind them.

On looking around to see whence these words came, they perceived a beautiful fairy standing on a large ball, which rolled along with her upon it in the direction of the castle.

"It is no very difficult task for her, at all events. Look, she can get forward without moving a limb," said the lazy one, throwing himself down on the grass.

The other, however, was not so easily satisfied; for, without stopping to reflect, he started off after the fairy as fast as he could run, and catching hold of the skirts of her robe cried, "Who art thou?"

"I am Fortune," answered the fairy, "and yonder is my castle; follow me there! If thou reachest it before midnight, I will receive thee as a friend; but remember, should thou arrive one moment later, my door will be closed against thee."

With these words the fairy drew her robe from the hand of the young man, and went off so quickly upon her ball that she was soon out of sight.

The youth immediately ran back to his companion and told him all that had happened, adding: "I intend taking the fairy's advice. Will you accompany me?"

"Are you mad?" inquired the other; "for my part, if I had a good horse I should not mind the journey, but as for walking all that way, I certainly shall not attempt it."

"Farewell then," answered his comrade, who started off at a brisk pace in the direction of the castle.

The lazy one, however, reasoned thus to himself: "Exert yourself as much as you please, my worthy friend. Good fortune often comes while we are dozing; perhaps it may be my case to-day." And without more ado he stretched himself on the grass and fell fast asleep; not, however, before he had cast a longing glance at the beautiful castle on the hill. After sleeping some time he felt as though there were a warm wind blowing on his ear, and when he had stretched his slothful limbs and rubbed his sleepy eyes, he perceived a beautiful milk-white horse, ready saddled, standing beside him, shaking his mane and neighing lustily in the clear morning air.

"Ah, did I not say as much?" cried the youth. "Oh, if people would but trust to Fate! Come here, you fine creature! We must be good friends." So saying, he threw himself into the saddle, and the steed galloped off with him as swift as the wind. Thus mounted, our lazy friend very soon overtook his industrious companion, and hailing him as he passed cried: "Show respect to my horse's heels!" The other, however, continued on at a steady pace, without paying much heed to his satire.

About midday, on arriving at the summit of a beautiful hill, the horse suddenly stopped. "Quite right," cried his rider; "I find you are a very sagacious creature—;'soft and fairly' is a good proverb; the castle is now not very far off, but my appetite is a great deal nearer." So dismounting, he sought out a shady slope, and having laid down in the moss with his feet against the stump of a tree, he began to take some refreshment—;for happily he had a good supply of bread and sausage in his pocket, and a pleasant drink in his flask. As soon as the youth had satisfied his appetite, he began to feel rather drowsy, and, as is usual with indolent people, he gave full vent to the inclination, stretched himself on the moss, and fell into a sound sleep. Never had man a more pleasant sleep, nor accompanied with more delightful dreams. He imagined that he was already in the castle, reposing on silken cushions; and that all that he desired came to him immediately upon his beckoning with his little finger. After thus enjoying himself for some time, it seemed as though a firework went off with a great explosion; this was followed by strains of soft music, which went to the tune of a song he had often heard, every verse of which terminated with these words:

Healthful limbs and spirits gay,

Bear the traveler on his way."

This continued some time, when he awoke with the song still ringing in his ears, then rubbing his eyes, he perceived that the setting sun was fast sinking behind the castle, and heard the voice of his companion singing from the valley before him the very words he had heard in his dream.

"What a time I have slept!" cried the lazy fellow. "It is high time that I was getting on my way. Come here, my steed! Where are you?" But no steed was to be found; the only creature that he could see, after looking all around, was an old gray donkey, grazing on the top of a hill at some distance. He shouted and whistled with all his might, but the horse was gone quite out of hearing, and the old donkey did not seem to pay the least attention. So, after exerting his lungs to no purpose, the lazy fellow was obliged to go and try to make friends with the gray old beast, which allowed itself to be quietly mounted, and then trudged slowly on with him.

But our youth found this kind of traveling very different from the previous stage, for then he not only proceeded at a much quicker pace, but had a more comfortable seat, which was by no means an unimportant consideration with him. In the course of a short time it began to grow dark, and heavy clouds overspread the sky; already he could perceive that the castle was being lighted up, and now he began to be very frightened and anxious to get forward. The donkey, however, did not seem in any way to partake of his feelings, but continued on at even a slower pace than before. At length it became quite dark, and the donkey, after going slower and slower, came to a dead stand in the midst of a thick wood. All his entreaties were of no use, nor were threats and kicks of more avail; the donkey would not move. At last the rider became so exasperated that he struck it with his fist; but this did not much improve our lazy friend's condition, for the obstinate brute instantly flung up its hind legs, and by that process released itself of its burden, which fell heavily on the ground. It required much less violence than our youth experienced in his fall to prove to him that he was not lying on a satin couch, for his legs and arms were dreadfully bruised. He remained some time in this miserable plight, but the bright and inviting appearance of the lights in the castle at length attracted his attention.

"Ah!" thought he, "what beautiful beds must there be in that fine building!"

This thought alone aroused for a moment his sluggish energies, and he managed to get on his feet. "Perhaps," thought he, "the gray old donkey may by this time have got into a better temper." So he searched about for him in every direction; but after knocking his head against the trees here, tearing his face with the thorns there, and stumbling over roots and stones for a full quarter of an hour without finding it, he gave up the search as hopeless. It was high time, however, that he made some effort to get out of this dismal wood, which every now and then resounded with dreary howls, sounding very much as though they proceeded from the throats of hungry wolves. At last, when quite bewildered with fear, he suddenly stumbled against something soft and slimy; he knew by the touch that it was not the donkey, but fancying it to be in the form of a saddle, he was about to bestride it at once; yet shuddered at the thought. He was still hesitating when the castle clock struck, and he counted eleven. Recollecting that it was drawing near to the eventful time and that he had no other hope, he threw himself on what appeared to be the saddle. He found his seat tolerably easy, as it was very soft, and at his back was something to lean against; another great advantage was that the creature on which he was mounted seemed to be very surefooted; there was, however, one great objection to it, and that was the creeping pace at which it moved, for it went along much slower than even the obstinate donkey.

Proceeding thus for some time, he got so near to the [300] castle that he could count the windows, and in this occupation he was engaged when suddenly the moon shone out from between the clouds, and, oh, horror! what did he behold. The creature on which he sat was neither a horse nor a donkey, but an enormous snail, quite as large as a calf, and its house which it carried upon its back had served him to lean against! Now he could well understand why he had come at such a creeping pace. He turned as cold as death, and his hair stood on end with fright! But there was now no time for fear, for the castle clock had already made the woods resound with the first stroke of the midnight hour, just as his steed crawled out from the wood. Then how great was the young man's astonishment when he beheld the castle of Fortune in all its grandeur! Hitherto he had sat quietly on the snail, without hastening it, or in any way interfering with its pace; at the sight of the castle, however, he dashed both his heels into its sides, and attempted to urge it on. To this treatment the snail was quite unaccustomed, and instantly it drew its head into its shell and left the youth sprawling on the ground. The castle clock rang out the second stroke. Had the lazy fellow but mustered up resolution and trusted to his feet even then, he might have reached the castle in time. But no, there he stood crying bitterly and screaming out: "A beast! a beast! of whatever kind it may be, to carry me to yon castle."

The inmates of the building had already begun to extinguish the lights, and the moon being hidden by the clouds, he was again in total darkness. As the clock struck the third time he heard something moving near him, and, as well as he could make out in the dark, it seemed like a saddled horse: "Ah, that is my long-lost steed," cried he, "that Heaven has kindly sent to me at the needful moment!" As quickly as his lazy limbs would enable him, he leaped on the back of the creature. There was now only a little elevation to be surmounted, and he could easily see his companion standing at the open door of the castle waving his cap and beckoning him on. The clock chimed out the fourth [301] stroke when the creature whereon he sat began to move slowly; then went the fifth and sixth strokes, and it began to advance a little at a very awkward pace; at the seventh, the creature began to move, first sideways and then went backward! To his great horror and surprise the rider found that he could not throw himself off, though he struggled with all his might. By a passing ray of the moon, he discovered that the new steed on which he was riding was a horrid monster with ten legs, and from either side there extended a large claw with which it held him fast by the arms. The youth screamed loudly for help, but all to no purpose; the animal still kept receding farther and farther from the castle, while the eventful moment approached nearer and nearer, until the twelfth stroke proclaimed the midnight hour. A flitting ray of the moon displayed the castle once more to his view in all its splendor. But in the same moment the youth heard the door shut, and the rattling noise of chains and bolts. The entrance to the castle of Fortune was closed against him forever! The moon now shone again in full luster and discovered the horrid monster, that still kept carrying him away, to be nothing more nor less than an enormous crab. Where he went to on this uncommon steed I cannot tell; for the fact is, nobody ever troubled themselves further about the lazy fellow.

The Fisherman And His Wife

A fisherman and his wife lived in a hut close by the sea. They were very poor. The man used to go out in his boat all day to catch fish; and he would fish, and fish, and fish. Some days he caught all that he and his wife could eat; some days he caught more, and then they had fish to sell; and some days he caught none at all.

One day as he sat in his boat, with his fishing rod in his hand, and gazed at the sea, he felt his line pulled. He drew it up, and there was a fine large fish fast on the hook.

"Please put me back! please put me back!" said the fish.

"Why so?" said the fisherman.

"I am not a real fish," said the fish. "I may look like one, but I am a prince that has been bewitched. Please put me back and let me go."

"Of course I'll put you back," said the man. "I don't want to eat a fish that can talk. I would rather have no dinner at all."

Then he took the fish off the hook and threw it back into the sea. There was a long streak of blood in the water behind it as it sank out of sight. The fisherman gazed into the sea awhile, and then went home in his boat.

"Did you catch any fish to-day?" said his wife.

"Only one," he said. "I caught a fine large one, but it said that it was a prince, and so I threw it back into the sea."

"Did you ask it for anything?" said the woman.

"No," said the man. "What would I ask of a fish?"

"You might have asked it for a nice little cottage," she said. "It is hard to have to live all our lives in a wretched hut like this."

"Ask a fish for a cottage?" said he. "Do you think it would give us one?"

"Certainly," said she. "Have you never heard the song?

> 'Ask anything of a talking fish,
>
> And he will give you what you wish'

Now get into your boat and go and call him; say that we want a neat little cottage with three rooms, and a vine climbing over the door."

The man did not like to go back at all; but his wife kept talking and talking till at last he got into his boat and rowed away.

When he came to the place where he had caught the fish, the sea was green and dark, and not bright and clear as it had been before. He stood up in his boat and sang:—

> Once a prince, but now a fish,
>
> Come and listen to my wish.
>
> Come! for my wife, Nancy Bell,
>
> Wishes what I fear to tell."

All at once the fish stuck his head up out of the water and said, "Well, what is it you want?"

"I don't want anything," said the man. "But my wife wants a neat cottage with three rooms, and a vine climbing up over the door."

"Go home," said the fish. "She shall have it."

The man turned his boat and rowed back home; and there was his wife sitting on a bench in front of a neat little cottage. She took him by the hand and said, "Come in, come in. See how much better this is than the dirty hut which we had." They went in and looked at the pretty sitting room and the cozy bedroom, and the kitchen with everything in it that anybody could want. And outside was a yard with chickens and ducks running about, and a little garden full of good things to eat.

"Isn't this nice?" said the wife.

"Yes," said the man, "and we will live here and be happy all our lives."

"We'll think about it," said his wife.

All went very well for three or four weeks. Then the woman began to find fault with things. The house was too small for her, and so were the yard and the garden.

"How I should like to be a fine lady, and live in a great stone castle," she said.

"This cottage is good enough for me," said the man.

"It may be good enough for you," said she, "but it is not good enough for me. Go back to the fish and tell him to give us a great stone castle with high walls and towers."

"I don't like to go," said he. "The fish gave us the cottage, and he might not like it if we asked him for something else."

"He won't care," said the wife. "Go and ask him at once. I cannot bear to live in this little house another day. Go!"

The man got into his boat and rowed slowly away. When he came to the place where he had caught the fish, he stood up and sang:—

Once A Prince, But Now A Fish,
Come and listen to wife's wish.
Come! for my dear Nancy Bell
Wishes what I fear to tell."

"Well, what does she want now?" asked the fish.

"I like the cottage best," said the man; "but she wants to live in a great stone castle."

"A great stone castle it is," said the fish. "Go home. She is standing at the door, waiting for you."

So the fisherman turned his boat and rowed back home; and there, close by the sea, was a great stone castle; and a very fine lady who looked like his wife was standing at the door.

She took him by the hand, and they went in; and there was a broad hall with a marble floor; and upstairs and down, there were fine rooms with tables and chairs all covered with gold; and crowds of servants stood around ready to wait upon them; and the big table in the dining hall was loaded with food and drink such as they had never heard of before. After dinner the man and woman walked out to see their stables, and fine gardens, and the great park where were deer and hares and everything anybody could want.

"Isn't this grand?" said the wife.

"Yes," said the man, "and we will live and be happy all our lives."

"We'll think about it," said his wife.

All went well till the next morning. The wife woke up first and looked out of the window at the fine country which lay around the castle.

"Husband, get up!" she said. "Get up, and look out of the window. I wish I was the king of all this land."

"Why so?" said her husband. "I think we are well enough off as we are. I don't want to be king."

"Well, but *I* want to be king," said the wife. "Go back to the fish and tell him so."

The fisherman did not like to go. "It is not right! It is not right!" he said.

But his wife said, "Go at once!"

So he got into his boat and rowed away. When he came to the place where he had caught the fish, he stood up and sang:—

Once a prince, but now a fish,
Come and listen to wife's wish.
Come! for lady Nancy Bell

Wishes what I fear to tell."

"Well, what does she want now?" said the fish.

"I am ashamed to tell you," said the man; "but she wants to be king."

"Go home," said the fish; "she has her wish."

The fisherman turned his boat and rowed back home. When he got to the shore he saw that the castle was much larger than before; and there were sentinels at the gates, and crowds of soldiers were marching back and forth, and there was a great noise of drums and trumpets. Inside of the castle everything was of silver and gold; and in the great hall was his wife sitting on a throne of ivory and pearls. She had a crown of gold on her head, and many fine ladies and gentlemen stood around her.

"Isn't this glorious?" said she.

"Yes," said the man. "Now we have nothing else to wish for."

"I don't know about that," said his wife.

"But you will be satisfied now, won't you, wife?" he said.

"No, indeed, I will not," she said.

That night she lay in bed, thinking and thinking, and wishing that there was something else she could have. The fisherman slept well and soundly, for he had done a good deal of work that day, rowing his boat back and forth. But his wife turned from one side to the other the whole night through and did not sleep a wink. At last the sun began to rise, and when she saw the red light come in at her window, she thought: "Ha! How I should like to be the master of the sun!"

Then she shook her husband and said, "Get up! Get up! Go out to the fish and tell him that I want to be the master of the sun."

The fisherman was so frightened that he fell out of the bed. Then he rubbed his eyes and said: "What did you say, wife?"

"I want to be the master of the sun," she said. "I want to make it rise when I choose, and set when I choose, and stand still when I choose."

"Oh, wife," said the man, all in a tremble, "do you want to be a god?"

"That's just what I want to be," she said. "Go out to the fish and tell him so."

"You'd better let well enough alone," said the man. "You are king now; let us be contented!"

This made the woman very angry. She pushed him with her foot, and screamed: "I will not be contented! I will not be contented! Go, and do as I bid you!"

So the man hurried away to his boat. He tried to row out to his fishing place, but a great storm came up, and the waves were so high that he could not see which way to go. The sky was black as ink, and the thunder rolled, and the lightning flashed, and the winds blew terribly. So he shouted as loud as he could:—

> "Once a prince, but now a fish,
> Come and listen to wife's wish.
> Come! for king Nancy Bell
> Wishes what I fear to tell."

"Well, what does she want now?" said the fish.

"She wants—she wants to be the master of the sun," said the man, in a whisper.

"She wants to be a god, does she?" said the fish.

"Ah, yes! That is what she wants to be," said the man.

"Go home, then," said the fish. "You will find her in the poor little dirty hut by the sea." And there the fisherman and his wife are living to this day.

The Poor Rich Man, And The Rich Poor Man
Luke xvi: 1 to 31, to xviii: 1 to 34; Matthew xix: 13 to 30; xx: 17 to 19; Mark x: 13 to 34.

Another parable that Jesus gave was that of "The Rich Man and Lazarus." He said,

"There was a rich man; and he was dressed in garments of purple and fine linen, living every day in splendor. And at the gate leading to his house was laid a beggar named Lazarus, covered with sores, and seeking for his food the crumbs that fell from the rich man's table. Even the dogs of the street came and licked his sores.

"After a time the beggar died, and his soul was carried by the angels into Abraham's bosom. The rich man also died, and his body was buried. And in the world of the dead he lifted up his eyes, being in misery; and far away he saw Abraham, and Lazarus resting in his bosom. And he cried out and said, 'Father Abraham, have mercy on me, and send Lazarus, that he may dip the tip of his finger in water and cool my tongue, for I am suffering in this flame!'

"But Abraham said, 'Son, remember that you had your good things in your lifetime, and that Lazarus had his evil things; but now here he is comforted and you are in sufferings. And besides all this, between us and you there is a great gulf fixed, so that no one may cross over from us to you, and none can come from your place to us.'

"And he said, 'I pray, O father Abraham, if Lazarus cannot come to me, command that he be sent to my father's house, for I have five brothers, and let him speak to them, so that they will not come to this place of torment.'

"But Abraham said, 'They have Moses and the prophets; let them hear them!'

"And he said, 'O father Abraham, if one should go to them from the dead, they will turn to God.'

"And Abraham said, 'If they will not hear Moses and the prophets, they will not believe, even though one should rise from the dead!' "

And this was true, for as the people would not listen to the words of Moses and the prophets about Christ, they would not believe, even after Jesus himself arose from the dead. There was another parable of Jesus, called "The Unjust Steward."

"A certain rich man had a steward, a man who took the care of all his possessions. He heard that his steward was wasting his property; and he sent for him, and said, 'What is this that I hear about you? You shall soon give up your place, and be my steward no longer.'

"Then the steward said to himself, 'In a few days I shall lose my place; and what shall I do? I cannot work in the fields, and I am ashamed to go begging from door to door. But I have thought of a plan that will give me friends, so that when I am put out of my place, some people will take me into their houses, because of what I have done for them.'

"And this was his plan. He sent for the men who were in debt to his master, and said to the first one, 'How much do you owe to my master?'

"The man said, 'I owe him a thousand gallons of oil.'

"Then said the steward, 'You need only pay five hundred gallons.' Then to another he said, 'How much do you owe?'

"The man answered, 'I owe fifteen hundred bushels of wheat.' And the steward said to him, 'You need pay only twelve hundred bushels.'

"When his master heard of this which his steward had done, he said, 'That is a sharp, shrewd man, who takes care of himself.' "

And Jesus said, "Be as earnest and as thoughtful for the eternal life as men are for this present life."

Jesus did not approve the actions of this unjust steward, but he told his disciples to learn some good lessons even from his wrong deeds.

Jesus spoke another parable to show that people should pray always, and not be discouraged. It was the parable of "The Unjust Judge and the Widow." Jesus said:

"There was in a city a judge who did not fear God, nor seek to do right; nor did he care for man. And there was a poor widow in that city who had suffered wrong. She came to him over and over again, crying out, 'Do justice for me against my enemy who has done me wrong!'

"And for a time the judge, because he did not care for the right, would do nothing. But as the widow kept on crying, at last he said to himself, 'Even though I do not fear God nor care for man, yet because this widow troubles me and will not be still, I will give her justice, or else she will wear me out by her continual crying.'

And the Lord said, "Hear what this unjust judge says! And will not a just God do right for his own who cry to him by day and night, even though he may seem to wait long? I tell you that he will answer their prayer, and will answer it soon!"

And Jesus spoke another parable to some who thought that they were righteous and holy, and set others at naught. This was the parable of "The Pharisee and the Publican."

"Two men went up into the Temple to pray, the one a Pharisee, the other a publican. The Pharisee stood and prayed thus with himself, 'God, I thank thee that I am not as other men are. I do not rob, I do not deal unjustly. I am free from wickedness. I am not even like this publican. I fast twice in each week. I give to God one-tenth of all that I have.' But the publican standing afar off, would not lift up so much as his eyes unto heaven, but beat his breast, saying, 'God be merciful to me, a sinner!'

"I say unto you," said Jesus, "this man went down to his house having his sins forgiven rather than the other. For every one that lifted up himself shall be brought low; and he that is humble shall be lifted up."

And at this time the mothers brought to Jesus their little children, that he might lay his hands on them and bless them. The disciples were not pleased at this, and told them to take their children away. But Jesus called them to him, and said, "Suffer the little children to come unto me, and forbid them not, for of such is the kingdom of God. Whoever shall not receive the kingdom of God as a little child, he shall not enter into it." And he put his hands on them and blessed them. And a certain young man, a ruler, came running to Jesus, and said, "Good Master, what shall I do that I may have everlasting life?"

"Why do you call me good?" said Jesus. "No one is good except one, that is God. You know the commandments; keep them."

"What commandments?" asked the young man.

"Do not kill; do not commit adultery; do not steal; do not bear false witness; honor thy father and mother."

The young man said, "All these I have kept from my youth up. What do I need more than these?"

"One thing more you need to do," said Jesus. "Go sell all that you have, and give to the poor, and you shall have treasure in heaven. Then come and follow me."

But when he heard this he turned and went away very sad, for he was very rich. And when Jesus saw this, he said, "How hard it is for those that are rich to enter into the kingdom of God! It is easier for a camel to go through the eye of a needle than for a rich man to enter into the kingdom of God."

At this the disciples were filled with wonder. They said, "If that be so, then who can be saved?"

And Jesus said, "The things that are impossible with men are possible with God."

And Peter said, "Lord, we have left our homes and all that we have, and have followed thee."

And Jesus answered him, "Verily, I say to you, there is no man who has left house, or wife, or brothers, or parents, or children, for the sake of the kingdom of God, who shall not have given to him many more times in this life, and in the world to come life everlasting."

Then Jesus again told his twelve disciples of what was soon to come to pass, even in a few weeks. He said, "We are going up to Jerusalem, and there all the things written by the prophets about the Son of man shall come true. He shall be made a prisoner, and shall be mocked, and treated shamefully, and shall be spit upon, and beaten, and shall be killed; and then the third day he shall rise again."

But they could not understand these things, and they did not believe that their Master was to die.

The Visit Of The Wise Men

Then the child grew and grew, as other little children grow; and for a good while nothing happened except just the ordinary things. But one day, there came to the door some very extraordinary visitors.

Nobody knows how old the child was when they came. Indeed, St. Luke, who was much interested in the beautiful stories of our Lord's childhood, knew nothing about them. So far as he had learned, Joseph and Mary went back to Nazareth after the presentation in the temple, carrying the child with them. But St. Matthew had heard about the Wise Men. One would think, to read the story in St. Matthew's Gospel, that our Lord was as much as two years old when the Wise Men came. In that case, it was at Bethlehem that he learned to walk and to talk, and began to say his prayers, and to learn by heart some of the holy words of the Bible.

Meanwhile, away in the east, nobody knows where, men were watching the sky. They lived out of doors in those countries much more than we do, and the clouds and the stars were of great interest to them. Every night they looked to see the constellations rise and set; and when a comet blazed across the heavens, they were filled with wonder. They did not know that the stars were other worlds. They thought that they were shining jewels set in the blue roof of the sky. They imagined that they formed mysterious sentences, which one might read did he but know that celestial language, and thus learn the story of the earth, both past and future. Especially, they connected the great stars with the great kings; and one of their number, a magician named Balaam, had one day, in a vision, cried, "I see a star and a king!" meaning a king of the Jews.

These men were called Wise Men. They were very well acquainted with the sky, and knew the stars by name. And one night as they gazed, according to their custom, at the lights overhead, behold, there was a new star which none of them had seen before. There it shone, brighter than any of the others, low down in the western sky. And the men said, "There is the star, and in that direction, towards the west, is the land of the Jews. There is a king born! Let us go and see him."

So they started on their long journey. Some say that they were as great as they were wise; that they were kings; that there were three of them,—an old man named Caspar, and a middle-aged man named Melchior, and a young man named Balthaser; that they rode on camels and had a train of servants with them. Indeed, we may imagine whatever we please; for nobody knows anything about it.

On they came, then, over the hard wild ways which lead from the east to the west, till at last they reached Jerusalem; and there they stopped to ask their way. "Where is he," they said, "that is born King of the Jews? for we have seen his star in the east, and are come to worship him." But the people knew of only one king of the Jews, and his name was Herod; and he had been born so long ago that even now he was approaching the end of his bad life. That was not the king for whom they were looking. No: there was a new king, a little child. So they went about asking people in the streets, and the news spread,—the news of the appearance of these strange visitors and of the strange question which they asked. People said one to another, "Have you seen those three dark-faced pilgrims out of the far east? Have you heard what they are saying?" And men began to be afraid. They said, "Now there will be war. The two kings will fight for the crown."

Presently, King Herod heard what was happening in the city, and he too was troubled. The thought came into his heart that this new king might perhaps be the King of Glory. He knew that the people were waiting for a king, and that promises of his coming were written in the Bible. Herod was not a reader of the Bible, and he had no idea that the King of Glory was to come from heaven. All that he had in his mind was a vague knowledge that a great king was expected, and a clear conviction that when the king came there would be no more use for Herod; and he immediately determined that he would find the new king, if he could, and kill him in his cradle.

So he called the ministers together, and when they came he said, "Where is it that that king, of whom the Bible speaks, will be born, when he comes?" And the ministers looked into the Bible, and there it was, written down in black and white long, long before, that the King of Glory should be born in Bethlehem "And thou Bethlehem, in the land of Juda, art not the least among the princes of Juda; for out of thee shall come a Governor, that shall rule my people Israel."

Then Herod called the Wise Men privately, and they came to meet him in his palace, and he asked them many questions. He seemed particularly anxious to find out just how long ago it was when the star appeared. And the Wise Men, who were better acquainted with stars than they were with kings, answered him in all simplicity. And the king said, "You are to go to Bethlehem. Go, and search diligently for the young child; and when ye have found him, bring me word again, that I may come and worship him also." That is what he said,—the bad king, who meant to kill him.

Away they went, then, out of the king's palace, and made their way towards Bethlehem. And as they went, behold, they saw the strange star, shining again in the night sky, as they had seen it in their own land. And they rejoiced with exceeding great joy. The star seemed to go before them, leading them, and at last to stand still over the little village. And under the star was a house; and in the house, the King!

The house did not look much like a palace. Joseph was a carpenter, having nothing to live on but his daily wages. He could afford only the humblest lodgings. Neither did the child look much like a king. There he stood leaning against his mother's knee, looking at the strange visitors with great eyes of wonder, and probably more interested in the Wise Men's camels than he was in the Wise Men themselves. But the Wise Men kneeled before him and worshiped him. And when they had opened their treasures,— the queer-looking boxes and bundles which they had brought with them,—they presented unto him gifts, gold, and frankincense, and myrrh.

These gifts were of no use to the child. Frankincense and myrrh are kinds of fragrant gum which are found on trees and shrubs in the East, somewhat like the sticky substance which we find on pines. They were used to make incense. (Frankincense means simply pure incense.) That is, when put on burning coals they made a thick smoke with a sweet smell. Such was the incense which Zacharias was placing on the golden altar when he saw the angel. Thus frankincense and myrrh were used in the worship of God. Accordingly, the Wise Men's gifts were meant only to express the thoughts of their hearts. As they knelt before the child and spread them out at his feet, they said by these symbols what we say in the Te Deum when we sing, "Thou art the King of Glory, O Christ." And since the Wise Men were not Jews but Gentiles, Joseph and Mary may well have recited one to another, after they went, the great words of the Old Testament, "The Gentiles shall come to thy light, and kings to the brightness of thy rising. . . . They shall bring gold and incense; and they shall show forth the praises of the Lord."

That night, before the next day dawned, the Wise Men had a dream; and, in the same night, Joseph had a dream also. In the Wise Men's dream God told them about Herod, and warned them not to return to him, but to go back to their own country another way. In Joseph's dream, the angel of the Lord appeared and said, "Arise, and take the young child and his mother, and flee into Egypt, and be thou there until I bring thee word: for Herod will seek the young child to destroy him." So the Wise Men rose up, and, avoiding Jerusalem, went to their homes far in the east. And Joseph also waked and aroused Mary, and they made a hasty preparation for a long journey, and before it was light were a good distance on the road which led from Bethlehem toward the south.

And when the day came, Herod, too, opened his eyes, and he remembered the Wise Men and their errand. "This morning," he said to himself, "I shall know about the King." But the morning passed, and the afternoon also, and no word came from the Wise Men, and at last Herod saw that he would hear nothing more from them, and he was very angry. But he knew that Bethlehem was the place where the King should be born; and he knew, according to the time which he had diligently inquired of the Wise Men, that the King could not be more than two years old; so he sent men who killed all the little children in that village, all who were under two. And there was lamentation and weeping and great mourning in Bethlehem among the poor mothers and fathers. But meanwhile the King was on his way, all safe and sound, to Egypt.

Why The Sea Is Salt

Once upon a time, long, long ago, there were two brothers, the one rich and the other poor. When Christmas Eve came, the poor one had not a bite in the house, either of meat or bread; so he went to his brother, and begged him, in God's name, to give him something for Christmas Day. It was by no means the first time that the brother had been forced to give something to him, and he was not better pleased at being asked now than he generally was.

"If you will do what I ask you, you shall have a whole ham," said he. The poor one immediately thanked him, and promised this.

"Well, here is the ham, and now you must go straight to Dead Man's Hall," said the rich brother, throwing the ham to him.

"Well, I will do what I have promised," said the other, and he took the ham and set off. He went on and on for the livelong day, and at nightfall he came to a place where there was a bright light.

"I have no doubt this is the place," thought the man with the ham.

An old man with a long white beard was standing in the outhouse, chopping Yule logs.

"Good-evening," said the man with the ham.

"Good-evening to you. Where are you going at this late hour?" said the man.

"I am going to Dead Man's Hall, if only I am on the right track," answered the poor man.

"Oh! Yes, you are right enough, for it is here," said the old man. "When you get inside they will all want to buy your ham, for they don't get much meat to eat there; but you must not sell it unless you can get the hand-mill which stands behind the door for it. When you come out again I will teach you how to stop the hand-mill, which is useful for almost everything."

So the man with the ham thanked the other for his good advice, and rapped at the door.

When he got in, everything happened just as the old man had said it would: all the people, great and small, came round him like ants on an ant-hill, and each tried to outbid the other for the ham.

"By rights my old woman and I ought to have it for our Christmas dinner, but, since you have set your hearts upon it, I must just give it up to you," said the man. "But, if I sell it, I will have the hand-mill which is standing there behind the door."

At first they would not hear to this, and haggled and bargained with the man, but he stuck to what he had said, and the people were forced to give him the hand-mill. When the man came out again into the yard, he asked the old wood-cutter how he was to stop the hand-mill, and

276

when he had learned that, he thanked him and set off home with all the speed he could, but did not get there until after the clock had struck twelve on Christmas Eve.

"Where in the world have you been?" said the old woman. "Here I have sat waiting hour after hour, and have not even two sticks to lay across each other under the Christmas porridge-pot."

"Oh! I could not come before; I had something of importance to see about, and a long way to go, too; but now you shall just see!" said the man, and then he set the hand-mill on the table, and bade it first grind light, then a table-cloth, and then meat, and beer, and everything else that was good for a Christmas Eve's supper; and the mill ground all that he ordered. "Bless me!" said the old woman as one thing after another appeared; and she wanted to know where her husband had got the mill from, but he would not tell her that.

"Never mind where I got it; you can see that it is a good one, and the water that turns it will never freeze," said the man. So he ground meat and drink, and all kinds of good things, to last all Christmas-tide, and on the third day he invited all his friends to come to a feast.

Now when the rich brother saw all that there was at the banquet and in the house, he was both vexed and angry, for he grudged everything his brother had. "On Christmas Eve he was so poor that he came to me and begged for a trifle, for God's sake, and now he gives a feast as if he were both a count and a king!" thought he. "But, for heaven's sake, tell me where you got your riches from," said he to his brother.

"From behind the door," said he who owned the mill, for he did not choose to satisfy his brother on that point; but later in the evening, when he had taken a drop too much, he could not refrain from telling how he had come by the hand-mill. "There you see what has brought me all my wealth!" said he, and brought out the mill, and made it grind first one thing and then another. When the brother saw that, he insisted on having the mill, and after a great deal of persuasion got it; but he had to give three hundred dollars for it, and the poor brother was to keep it till the haymaking was over, for he thought: "If I keep it as long as that, I can make it grind meat and drink that will last many a long year." During that time you may imagine that the mill did not grow rusty, and when hay-harvest came the rich brother got it, but the other had taken good care not to teach him how to stop it. It was evening when the rich man got the mill home, and in the morning he bade the old woman go out and spread the hay after the mowers, and he would attend to the house himself that day, he said.

So, when dinner-time drew near, he set the mill on the kitchen-table, and said: "Grind herrings and milk pottage, and do it both quickly and well."

So the mill began to grind herrings and milk pottage, and first all the dishes and tubs were filled, and then it came out all over the kitchen-floor. The man twisted and turned it, and did all he could to make the mill stop, but, howsoever he turned it and screwed it, the mill went on grinding, and in a short time the pottage rose so high that the man was like to be drowned. So he threw open the parlor door, but it was not long before the mill had ground the parlor full too, and it was with difficulty and danger that the man could go through the stream of pottage and get hold of the door-latch. When he got the door open, he did not stay long in the room, but ran out, and the herrings and pottage came after him, and it streamed out over both farm and field. Now the old woman, who was out spreading the hay, began to think dinner was long in coming, and said to the women and the mowers: "Though the master does not call us home, we may as well go. It may be that he finds he is not good at making pottage and I should do well to help him." So they began to straggle homeward, but when they had got a little way up the hill they met the herrings and pottage and bread, all pouring forth and winding about one over the other, and the man himself in front of the flood. "Would to heaven that each of you had a hundred stomachs!   Take care that you are not drowned in the pottage!" he cried as he went by them as if Mischief were at his heels, down to where his brother dwelt. Then he begged him, for God's sake, to take the mill back again, and that in an instant, for, said he: "If it grind one hour more the whole district will be destroyed by herrings and pottage." But the brother would not take it until the other paid him three hundred dollars, and that he was obliged to do. Now the poor brother had both the money and the mill again. So it was not long before he had a farmhouse much finer than that in which his brother lived, but the mill ground him so much money that he covered it with plates of gold; and the farmhouse lay close by the sea-shore, so it shone and glittered far out to sea. Everyone who sailed by there now had to be put in to visit the rich man in the gold farmhouse, and everyone wanted to see the wonderful mill, for the report of it spread far and wide, and there was no one who had not heard tell of it.

After a long, long time came also a skipper who wished to see the mill. He asked if it could make salt. "Yes, it could make salt," said he who owned it, and when the skipper heard that, he wished with all his might and main to have the mill, let it cost what it might, for, he thought, if he had it, he would get off having to sail far away over the perilous sea for freights of salt. At first the man would not hear of parting with it, but the skipper begged and prayed, and at last the man sold it to him, and got many, many thousand dollars for it. When the skipper had got the mill on his back he did not stay there long, for he was so afraid that the man would change his mind, and he had no time to ask how he was to stop it grinding, but got on board his ship as fast as he could.

When he had gone a little way out to sea he took the mill on deck. "Grind salt, and grind both quickly and well," said the skipper. So the mill began to grind salt, till it spouted out like water, and when the skipper had got the ship filled he wanted to stop the mill, but whichever way he turned it, and how much whatsoever he tried, it went on grinding, and the heap of salt grew higher and higher, until at last the ship sank. There lies the mill at the bottom of the sea, and still, day by day, it grinds on; and that is why the sea is salt.

Why The Chipmunk's Back Is Striped

What a splendid lodge it was, and how grand War Eagle looked leaning against his back-rest in the firelight! From the tripod that supported the back-rest were suspended his weapons and his medicine-bundle, each showing the wonderful skill of the maker. The quiver that held the arrows was combined with a case for the bow, and colored quills of the porcupine had been deftly used to make it a thing of beauty. All about the lodge hung the strangely painted linings, and the firelight added richness to both color and design. War Eagle's hair was white, for he had known many snows; but his eyes were keen and bright as a boy's, as he gazed in pride at his grandchildren across the lodge-fire. He was wise, and had been in many battles, for his was a warlike tribe. He knew all about the world and the people in it. He was deeply religious, and every Indian child loved him for his goodness and brave deeds.

About the fire were Little Buffalo Calf, a boy of eleven years; Eyes-in-the-Water, his sister, a girl of nine; Fine Bow, a cousin of these, aged ten, and Bluebird, his sister, who was but eight years old.

Not a sound did the children make while the old warrior filled his great pipe, and only the snapping of the lodge-fire broke the stillness. Solemnly War Eagle lit the tobacco that had been mixed with the dried inner bark of the red willow, and for several minutes smoked in silence, while the children's eyes grew large with expectancy. Finally he spoke:

"Napa, Old-man, is very old indeed. He made this world, and all that is on it. He came out of the south, and travelled toward the north, making the birds and animals as he passed. He made the perfumes for the winds to carry about, and he even made the war-paint for the people to use. He was a busy worker, but a great liar and thief, as I shall show you after I have told you more about him. It was Old-man who taught the beaver all his cunning. It was Old-man who told the bear to go to sleep when the snow grew deep in winter, and it was he who made the curlew's bill so long and crooked, although it was not that way at first. Old-man used to live on this world with the animals and birds. There was no other man or woman then, and he was chief over all the animal-people and the bird-people. He could speak the language of the robin, knew the words of the bear, and understood the sign-talk of the beaver, too. He lived with the wolves, for they are the great hunters. Even to-day we make the same sign for a smart man as we make for the wolf; so you see he taught them much while he lived with them. Old-man made a great many mistakes in making things, as I shall show you after a while; yet he worked until he had everything good. But he often made great mischief and taught many wicked things. These I shall tell you about some day. Everybody was afraid of Old-man and his tricks and lies -- even the animal-people, before he made men and women. He used to visit the lodges of our people and make trouble long ago, but he got so wicked that Manitou grew angry at him, and one day in the month of roses, he built a lodge for Old-man and told him that he must stay in it forever. Of course he had to do that, and nobody knows where the lodge was built, nor in what country, but that is why we never see him as our grandfathers did, long, long ago.

"What I shall tell you now happened when the world was young. It was a fine summer day, and Old-man was travelling in the forest. He was going north and straight as an arrow -- looking at nothing, hearing nothing. No one knows what he was after, to this day. The birds and forest-people spoke politely to him as he passed but he answered none of them. The Pine-squirrel, who is always trying to find out other people's business, asked him where he was going, but Old-man wouldn't tell him. The woodpecker hammered on a dead tree to make him look that way, but he wouldn't. The Elk-people and the Deer-people saw him pass, and all said that he must be up to some mischief or he would stop and talk a while. The pine-trees murmured, and the bushes whispered their greeting, but he kept his eyes straight ahead and went on travelling.

"The sun was low when Old-man heard a groan" (here War Eagle groaned to show the children how it sounded), "and turning about he saw a warrior lying bruised and bleeding near a spring of cold water. Old-man knelt beside the man and asked: 'Is there war in this country? '

"'Yes,' answered the man. "This whole day long we have fought to kill a Person, but we have all been killed, I am afraid."

"'That is strange,' said Old-man; 'how can one Person kill so many men? Who is this Person, tell me his name!' but the man didn't answer -- he was dead. When Old-man saw that life had left the wounded man, he drank from the spring, and went on toward the north, but before long he heard a noise as of men fighting, and he stopped to look and listen. Finally he saw the bushes bend and sway near a creek that flowed through the forest. He crawled toward the spot, and peering through the brush saw a great Person near a pile of dead men, with his back against a pine-tree. The Person was full of arrows, and he was pulling them from his ugly body. Calmly the Person broke the shafts of the arrows, tossed them aside, and stopped the blood flow with a brush of his hairy hand. His head was large and fierce-looking, and his eyes were small and wicked. His great body was larger than that of a buffalo-bull and covered with scars of many battles.

"Old-man went to the creek, and with his buffalo-horn cup brought some water to the Person, asking as he approached:

"'Who are you, Person? Tell me, so I can make you a fine present, for you are great in war.'

"'I am Bad Sickness,' replied the Person. "Tribes I have met remember me and always will, for their bravest warriors are afraid when I make war upon them. I come in the night or I visit their camps in daylight. It is always the same; they are frightened and I kill them easily.""

"Ho!' said Old-man, 'tell me how to make Bad Sickness, for I often go to war myself.' He lied; for he was never in a battle in his life. The Person shook his ugly head and then Old-man said:

"'If you will tell me how to make Bad Sickness I will make you small and handsome. When you are big, as you now are, it is very hard to make a living; but when you are small, little food will make you fat. Your living will be easy because I will make your food grow everywhere.'

"Good,' said the Person, 'I will do it; you must kill the fawns of the deer and the calves of the elk when they first begin to live. When you have killed enough of them you must make a robe of their skins. Whenever you wear that robe and sing -- "now you sicken, now you sicken," the sickness will come -- that is all there is to it. '

"Good,' said Old-man, 'now lie down to sleep and I will do as I promised.'

"The Person went to sleep and Old-man breathed upon him until he grew so tiny that he laughed to see how small he had made him. Then he took out his paint sack and striped the Person's back with black and yellow. It looked bright and handsome and he waked the Person, who was now a tiny animal with a bushy tail to make him pretty.

"Now,' said Old-man, 'you are the Chipmunk, and must always wear those striped clothes. All of your children and their children, must wear them, too.'

"After the Chipmunk had looked at himself, and thanked Old-man for his new clothes, he wanted to know how he could make his living, and Old-man told him what to eat, and said he must cache the pine-nuts when the leaves turned yellow, so he would not have to work in the winter time.

"You are a cousin to the Pine-squirrel,' said Old-man, 'and you will hunt and hide as he does. You will be spry and your living will be easy to make if you do as I have told you.'

"He taught the Chipmunk his language and his signs, showed him where to live, and then left him, going on toward the north again. He kept looking for the cow-elk and doe-deer, and it was not long before he had killed enough of their young to make the robe as the Person told him, for they were plentiful before the white man came to live on the world. He found a shady place near a creek, and there made the robe that would make Bad Sickness whenever he sang the queer song, but the robe was plain, and brown in color. He didn't like the looks of it. Suddenly he thought how nice the back of the Chipmunk looked after he had striped it with his paints. He got out his old paint sack and with the same colors made the robe look very much like the clothes of the Chipmunk. He was proud of the work, and liked the new robe better; but being lazy, he wanted to save himself work, so he sent the South-wind to tell all the doe-deer and the cow-elk to come to him. They came as soon as they received the message, for they were afraid of Old-man and always tried to please him. When they had all reached the place where Old-man was he said to them:

"Do you see this robe?'

"Yes, we see it,' they replied.

"Well, I have made it from the skins of your children, and then painted it to look like the Chipmunk's back, for I like the looks of that Person's clothes. I shall need many more of these robes during my life; and every time I make one, I don't want to have to spend my time painting it; so from now on and forever your children shall be born in spotted clothes. I want it to be that way to save me work. On all the fawns there must be spots of white like this (here he pointed to the spots on Bad Sickness's robe) and on all of the elk-calves the spots shall not be so white and shall be in rows and look rather yellow.' Again he showed them his robe, that they might see just what he wanted.

"Remember,' he said, 'after this I don't want to see any of your children running about wearing plain clothing, because that would mean more painting for me. Now go away, and remember what I have said, lest I make you sick. '

"The cow-elk and the doe-deer were glad to know that their children's clothes would be beautiful, and they went away to their little ones who were hidden in the tall grass, where the wolves and mountain-lions would have a hard time finding them; for you know that in the tracks of the fawn there is no scent, and the wolf cannot trail him when he is alone. That is the way Manitou takes care of the weak, and all of the forest-people know about it, too.

"Now you know why the Chipmunk's back is striped, and why the fawn and elk-calf wear their pretty clothes.

"I hear the owls, and it is time for all young men who will someday be great warriors to go to bed, and for all young women to seek rest, lest beauty go away forever. Ho!"

283

Sleepy John

Once there was a lad named John, and he used to go to sleep always and everywhere. One day he came to an inn where some farmers were feeding their horses. So he crept into the cart, lay down on the straw, and went to sleep. When the farmers had driven some distance, they noticed John asleep in the cart. They thought: "What are we to do with him? We have a beer cask here. We'll put him in it and leave him in the forest." So they shut him in the cask, and off they drove.

John went on sleeping in the cask for a long time. Suddenly he woke up and found himself in the cask, but he did not know how he had got into it, neither did he know where he was. There was something running to and fro near the cask, so he looked through the bunghole and saw a great number of wolves gathered under the rocks. They had flocked round, attracted by the human smell. One of the wolves pushed his tail through the hole, and Sleepy John began to think that the hour of his death was approaching. But he wound the wolf's tail round his hand. The wolf was terrified, and, dragging the cask after him, he ran after the rest of the wolves, who set off in all directions. Their terror grew greater and greater as the cask bumped after them. At last the cask struck against a rock and was smashed. John let go the wolf, who took himself off as fast as he could.

Now John found himself in a wild mountain region. He began walking about among the mountains and he met a hermit. The hermit said to him: "You may stay here with me. I shall die in three days. Bury me then, and I will pay you well for it."

So John stayed with him, and, when the third day came, the hermit, who was about to die, gave him a stick, saying: "In what-ever direction you point this stick, you will find yourself there." Then he gave him a knapsack, saying: "Anything you want you will find in this knapsack." Then he gave him a cap, saying: "As soon as you put this cap on, nobody will be able to see you."

Then the hermit died, and John buried him.

John gathered his things together, pointed the stick, and said: "Let me be instantly in the town where the king lives." He found himself there on the instant, and he was told that the queen would every night wear out a dozen pairs of shoes, yet nobody was able to follow her track. The lords were all flocking to offer to follow the queen's traces, and John went too. He went into the palace and had himself announced to the king. When he came before the king, he said that he would like to trace the queen. The king asked him: "Who are you?"

He answered "Sleepy John."

The king said: "And how are you going to trace her, when you are sleeping all the time? If you fail to trace her you will lose your head."

John answered that he would try to trace her all the same.

When the evening was come the queen went to bed in one room and John went to bed in the next room, through which the queen had to pass. He did not go to sleep, but when the queen was going by he pretended to be in a deep slumber. So the queen lit a candle and scorched the soles of his feet to make sure that he was asleep. But John did not stir, and so she was certain that he was asleep. Then she took her twelve pairs of new shoes and off she went.

John got up, put his cap on, and pointed with his stick and said: "Let me be where the queen is."

Now, when the queen came to a certain rock, the earth opened before her and two dragons came to meet her. They took her on their backs and carried her as far as the lead forest. Then John said: "Let me be where the queen is," and instantly he was in the lead forest. So he broke off a twig for a proof and put it in his knapsack. But when he broke off the twig it gave out a shrill sound as if a bell were ringing. The queen was frightened, but she rode on again. John pointed with his stick and said: "Let me be where the queen is," and instantly he was in the tin forest. He broke off a twig again and put it in his knapsack, and it rang again. The queen turned pale, but she rode on again. John pointed with his stick again and said: "Let me be where the queen is," and instantly he was in the silver forest. He broke off a twig again and put it into his knapsack. As he broke it, it gave out a ringing sound and the queen fainted. The dragons hastened on again till they came to a green meadow.

A crowd of devils came to meet them here, and they revived the queen. Then they had a feast. Sleepy John was there too. The cook was not at home that day, so John sat down in his place, and, as he had his cap on, nobody could see him. They put aside a part of the food for the cook, but John ate it all. They were all surprised to see all the food they put aside disappearing. They could not make out what was happening, but they did not care very much. And when the banquet was at an end the devils began to dance with the queen, and they kept on dancing till the queen had worn out all her shoes. When her shoes were worn out, those two dragons took her on their backs again and brought her to the place where the earth had opened before her. John said: "Let me be where the queen is." By this time she was walking on the earth again, and he followed her. When they came near the palace he went ahead of the queen and went to bed; and, as the queen was going in, she saw him sleeping, and so she went to her own room and lay down and slept.

In the morning the lords gathered together and the king asked whether any of them had tracked the queen. But none of them could say "Yes."

So he summoned Sleepy John before him. John said:

"Gracious Lord King, I did indeed track her, and I know that she used up those twelve pairs of shoes on the green meadows in Hell."

The queen stood forth at once, and John took from his knapsack the leaden twig and said: "The queen was carried by two dragons towards Hell, and she came to the leaden forest; there I broke off this twig and the queen was frightened."

The king said: "That's no good. You might have made the twig yourself."

So John produced the tin twig from his knapsack and said: "After that the queen drove through the tin forest, and there I broke off this twig. That time the queen grew pale."

The king said: "You might have made even this twig."

So John produced the silver twig and said: "Afterwards the queen drove through the silver forest, and when I broke off this twig she fainted, and so she was till the devils brought her to life again."

The queen, seeing that all was known, cried out: "Let the earth swallow me!" and she was swallowed by the earth.

Sleepy John got the half of the kingdom, and, when the king died, the other half too.

Hacon Grizzlebeard

Once on a time there was a princess who was so proud and pert that no suitor was good enough for her. She made game of them all, and sent them about their business, one after the other; but though she was so proud, still new suitors kept on coming to the palace, for she was a beauty, the wicked hussey! So one day there came a prince to woo her, and his name was Hacon Grizzlebeard; but the first night he was there, the princess bade the king's fool cut off the ears of one of the prince's horses, and slit the jaws of the other up to the ears. When the prince went out to drive next day the princess stood in the porch and looked at him.

"Well!" she cried, "I never saw the like of this in all my life; the keen north wind that blows here has taken the ears off one of your horses, and the other has stood by and gaped at what was going on till his jaws have split right up to his ears."

And with that she burst out into a roar of laughter, ran in, slammed to the door, and let him drive off.

So he drove home; but as he went, he thought to himself that he would pay her off one day. After a bit, he put on a great beard of moss, threw a great fur cloak over his clothes, and dressed himself up just like any beggar. He went to a goldsmith and bought a golden spinning wheel, and sat down with it under the princess' window, and began to file away at his spinning wheel, and to turn it this way and that, for it wasn't quite in order, and besides, it wanted a stand.

So when the princess rose up in the morning, she came to the window and threw it up, and called out to the beggar if he would sell his golden spinning wheel?

"No; it isn't for sale," said Hacon Grizzlebeard; but if I may have leave to sleep outside your bed-room door tonight, I'll give it you."

Well, the princess thought it a good bargain; there could be no danger in letting him sleep outside her door.

So she got the wheel, and at night Hacon Grizzlebeard lay down outside her bedroom. But as the night wore on he began to freeze.

"Hutetutetutetu! It is so cold; do let me in," he cried.

"You've lost your wits outright, I think," said the princess.

"Oh, hutetutetutetu! It is so bitter cold, pray do let me in," said Hacon Grizzlebeard again.

"Hush, hush! Hold your tongue!" said the princess; "if my father were to know that there was a man in the house, I should be in a fine scrape."

"Oh, hutetutetutetu! I'm almost frozen to death; only let me come inside and lie on the floor," said Hacon Grizzlebeard.

There was no help for it. She had to let him in, and when he was, he lay on the ground and slept like a top.

Sometime after, Hacon came again with the stand to the spinning wheel, and sat down under the princess' window and began to file at it, for it was not quite fit for use. When she heard him filing, she threw up the window and began to talk to him, and to ask what he had there.

"Oh! Only the stand to that spinning wheel which your royal highness bought; for I thought, as you had the wheel, you might like to have the stand too."

"What do you want for it?" asked the princess; but it was not for sale any more than the wheel, but she might have them if she would give him leave to sleep on the floor of her bedroom next night.

Well, she gave him leave, only he was to be sure to lie still, and not to shiver and call out "hutetu," or any such stuff. Hacon Grizzlebeard promised fair enough, but as the night wore on he began to shiver and shake, and to ask whether he might not come nearer, and lie on the floor alongside the princess' bed.

There was no help for it; she had to give him leave, lest the king should hear the noise he made. So Hacon Grizzlebeard lay alongside the princess' bed, and slept like a top.

It was a long while before Hacon Grizzlebeard came again; but when he came he had with him a golden wool-winder, and he sat down and began to file away at it under the princess' window. Then came the old story over again. When the princess heard what was going on, she came to the window and asked him how he did, and whether he would sell the golden wool-winder?

"It is not to be had for money; but if you'll give me leave to sleep tonight in your bed-room, with my head on your bedstead, you shall have it for nothing," said Hacon Grizzlebeard. "Well, she would give him leave, if he only gave his word to be quiet and make no noise. So he said he would do his best to be still; but as the night wore on he began to shiver and shake, so that his teeth chattered again.

"Hutetutetutetu! It is so bitter cold! Oh, do let me get into bed and warm myself a little," said Hacon Grizzlebeard.

"Get into bed!" said the princess; "why, you must have lost your wits."

"Hutetutetutetu!" said Hacon. "Do let me get into bed. Hutetutetutetu."

"Hush, hush, be still for God's sake," said the princess; "if father knows there is a man in here, I shall be in a sad plight. I'm sure he'll kill me on the spot."

"Hutetutetutetu! Let me get into bed," said Hacon Grizzlebeard, who kept on shivering so that the whole room shook. Well, there was no help for it; she had to let him get into bed, where he slept both sound and soft; but a little while after the princess had a child, at which the king grew so wild with rage, that he was near making an end of both mother and babe.

Just after this happened, came Hacon Grizzlebeard tramping that way once more, as if by chance, and took his seat down in the kitchen, like any other beggar.

So when the princess came out and saw him, she cried, "Ah, God have mercy on me, for the ill-luck you have brought on me; father is ready to burst with rage; now let me follow you to your home."

"Oh! I'll be bound you're too well bred to follow me," said Hacon, "for I have a log hut to live in; and how I shall ever get food for you?"

"It's all the same to me how you get it, or whether you get it at all," she said; "only let me be with you, for if I stay here any longer, my father will be sure to take my life."

So she got leave to be with the beggar, as she called him, and they walked a long, long way, though she was but a poor hand at tramping. When she passed out of her father's land into another, she asked whose it was.

"Oh, this is Hacon Grizzlebeard's, if you must know," said he.

"Indeed!" said the princess; "I might have married him if I chose, and then I should not have had to walk about like a beggar's wife."

So, whenever they came to grand castles, and woods, and parks, and she asked whose they were, the beggar's answer was still the same: "Oh, they are Hacon Grizzlebeard's." And the princess was in a sad way that she had not chosen the man who had such broad lands. Last of all they came to a palace, where he said he was known, and where he thought he could get her work, so that they might have something to live on; so he built up a cabin by the wood-side for them to dwell in; and every day he went to the king's palace, as he said, to hew wood and draw water for the cook, and when he came back he brought a few scraps of meat; but they did not go very far.

One day, when he came home from the palace, he said,

"Tomorrow I will stay at home and look after the baby, but you must get ready to go to the palace, do you hear? For the prince said you were to come and try your hand at baking."

"I bake!" said the princess; "I can't bake, for I never did such a thing in my life."

"Well, you must go," said Hacon, "since the prince has said it. If you can't bake, you can learn; you have only got to look how the rest bake; and mind, when you leave, you must steal me some bread."

"I can't steal," said the princess.

"You can learn that too," said Hacon; you know we live on short commons. But take care that the prince doesn't see you, for he has eyes at the back of his head."

So when she was well on her way, Hacon ran by a short cut and reached the palace long before her, and threw off his rags and beard, and put on his princely robes.

The princess took her turn in the bakehouse, and did as Hacon bade her, for she stole bread till her pockets were crammed full. So when she was about to go home at even, the prince said:

"We don't know much of this old wife of Hacon Grizzlebeard's; I think we'd best see if she has taken anything away with her."

So he thrust his hand into all her pockets, and felt her all over, and when he found the bread, he was in a great rage, and led them all a sad life. She began to weep and bewail, and said:

"The beggar made me do it, and I couldn't help it."

"Well," said the prince at last, "it ought to have gone hard with you; but all the same, for the sake of the beggar you shall be forgiven this once."

When she was well on her way, he threw off his robes, put on his skin cloak, and his false beard, and reached the cabin before her. When she came home, he was busy nursing the baby.

"Well, you have made me do what it went against my heart to do. This is the first time I ever stole, and this shall be the last;" and with that she told him how it had gone with her, and what the prince had said.

A few days after Hacon Grizzlebeard came home at even and said:

"Tomorrow I must stay at home and mind the babe, for they are going to kill a pig at the palace, and you must help to make the sausages."

"I make sausages!" said the princess; "I can't do any such thing. I have eaten sausages often enough; but as to making them, I never made one in my life."

Well, there was no help for it; the prince had said it, and go she must. As for not knowing how, she was only to do what the others did, and at the same time Hacon bade her steal some sausages for him.

"Nay, but I can't steal them," she said; "you know how it went last time."

"Well, you can learn to steal; who knows but you may have better luck next time?" said Hacon Grizzlebeard.

When she was well on her way, Hacon ran by a short cut, reached the palace long before her, threw off his skin cloak and false beard, and stood in the kitchen with his royal robes before she came in. So the princess stood by when the pig was killed, and made sausages with the rest, and did as Hacon bade her, and stuffed her pockets full of sausages. But when she was about to go home at even, the prince said:

"This beggar's wife was long-fingered last time; we may as well just see if she hasn't carried anything off."

So he began to thrust his hands into her pockets, and when he found the sausages he was in a great rage again, and made a great to do, threatening to send for the constable and put her into the cage.

"Oh, God bless your royal highness; do let me off! The beggar made me do it," she said, and wept bitterly.

"Well," said Hacon, "you ought to smart for it; but for the beggar's sake you shall be forgiven."

When she was gone, he changed his clothes again, ran by the short cut, and when she reached the cabin, there he was before her. Then she told him the whole story, and swore, through thick and thin, it should be the last time he got her to do such a thing.

Now, it fell out a little time after, when the man came back from the palace, he said:

"Our prince is going to be married, but the bride is sick, so the tailor can't measure her for her wedding gown. And the prince's will is, that you should go up to the palace and be measured instead of the bride; for he says you are just the same height and shape. But after you have been measured, mind you don't go away; you can stand about, you know, and when the tailor cuts out the gown, you can snap up the largest pieces, and bring them home for a waistcoat for me."

"Nay, but I can't steal," she said; "besides, you know how it went last time."

"You can learn then," said Hacon, "and you may have better luck, perhaps."

She thought it bad, but still she went and did as she was told. She stood by while the tailor was cutting out the gown, and she swept down all the biggest scraps, and stuffed them into her pockets; and when she was going away, the prince said:

"We may as well see if this old girl has not been long-fingered this time too."

So he began to feel and search her pockets, and when he found the pieces he was in a rage, and began to stamp and scold at a great rate, while she wept and said:

"Ah, pray forgive me; the beggar bade me do it, and I couldn't help it."

"Well, you ought to smart for it," said Hacon; "but for the beggar's sake it shall be forgiven you."

So it went now just as it had gone before, and when she got back to the cabin, the beggar was there before her.

"Oh, Heaven help me," she said; "you will be the death of me at last by making me nothing but what is wicked. The prince was in such a towering rage that he threatened me both with the constable and cage."

Sometime after, Hacon came home to the cabin at even and said:

"Now, the prince's will is, that you should go up to the palace and stand for the bride, old lass! For the bride is still sick, and keeps her bed; but he won't put off the wedding; and he says, you are so like her, that no one could tell one from the other; so tomorrow you must get ready to go to the palace."

"I think you've lost your wits, both the prince and you," said she. "Do you think I look fit to stand in the bride's place? Look at me! Can any beggar's trull look worse than I?"

"Well, the prince said you were to go, and so go you must," said Hacon Grizzlebeard.

There was no help for it, go she must; and when, she reached the palace, they dressed her out so finely that no princess ever looked so smart.

The bridal train went to church, where she stood for the bride, and when they came back, there was dancing and merriment in the palace. But just as she was in the midst of dancing with the prince, she saw a gleam of light through the window, and lo! the cabin by the wood-side was all one bright flame.

"Oh, the beggar and the babe and the cabin," she screamed out, and was just going to swoon away.

"Here is the beggar and there is the babe, and so let the cabin burn away," said Hacon Grizzlebeard.

Then she knew him again, and after that the mirth and merriment began in right earnest; but since that I have never heard tell anything more about them.

NONFICTION

Indians Capture Daniel Boone
Peter Huber

In the spring of 1775 Daniel Boone led a group of settlers from North Carolina into the frontier in Kentucky, where they established a fortified village. In honor of their leader the settlers named their village Boonesborough. It was one of the first American settlements of any size in Kentucky.

The invasion of Kentucky by American settlers disturbed the Shawnee Indians. Although the Shawnees lived most of the year north of the Ohio River in what is now the state of Ohio, they regarded Kentucky as their private hunting ground and could foresee its ruination if increasing numbers of American settlers moved there.

The Shawnees refused to relinquish their ancestral lands without a struggle. Under the aggressive leadership of one of their chiefs, Blackfish, they planned to drive the settlers out of Boonesborough and back to North Carolina, whence they had come.

In the spring of 1777 Blackfish Jed an army of two hundred Shawnee warriors across the Ohio River and into Kentucky, where they intended to raid Boonesborough.

When the Indians arrived at Boonesborough they quickly discovered that, although they greatly outnumbered the settlers, they could not take the well-nigh impregnable fort. Blackfish and his men inflicted only a few casualties on the besieged settlers.

Nevertheless, by shooting at any settler who dared to venture outside the stockade which surrounded Boonesborough, Blackfish was able to confine the settlers to their fort throughout the summer. Consequently, the settlers were unable to plant and cultivate their cornfields which lay outside the stockade. As the settlers 'supply of corn from the crop of the previous year dwindled, it could not be replenished. By the time Blackfish and his warriors returned to their homes in Ohio in early fall, the settlers had run out of corn and were then forced to obtain almost all their food by hunting.

Normally, they preserved large amounts of meat by salting it. By midwinter, however, the settlers at Boonesborough had used up all their salt. Their only source of food now was game which had to be hunted daily in order to have fresh, unspoiled meat.

In this extremity, Daniel Boone and twenty-seven other men left Boonesborough in January in search of salt. The settlers, carrying heavy iron kettles, headed for salt springs located fifty miles north of Boonesborough. There they established a camp where they spent day after day boiling the brine from the springs in their iron kettles, until only the salty sediment remained.

The salt makers were not worried about Indian raids because they believed the Shawnees did not wage war in winter.

In early February, Boone left the salt makers' camp to go on a solitary scouting and hunting trip. He killed a buffalo, butchered it, and packed three to four hundred pounds of meat on his horse. As he was returning to the salt makers' camp, leading his heavily laden horse along a creek, he heard a faint sound behind him; looking back, he saw several Shawnee Indians on his trail.

In hopes that he could mount his horse and get away, he tried to unburden his horse by unfastening the meat he had strapped to the horse's back. He found that the straps had frozen to the meat. Abandoning his horse he ran away on foot from his pursuers. After running a half-mile, Boone, who was in his mid-forties, looked back and saw that his young stalkers were gaining on him. Bullets hit the ground on either side of him, spraying snow and another bullet shattered the powder horn that hung by his side. Boone hid behind a tree and leaned his rifle against it in token of surrender. The Indians shouting and laughing, came up to him.

The young braves, who had captured him, took Boone to the encampment of their chief, Blackfish, which was only three miles from where the braves had overtaken Boone. At the Indians' camp the warriors were impressed by Boone, whom they regarded as the chief of the Americans. In good American fashion they crowded around their prestigious captive, shook his hand, and exclaimed, "Howdy-do!"

Boone was ushered into the presence of the Shawnee chief, Blackfish. Blackfish, who was about the same age as Boone, was a small and wiry man who had the air of one accustomed to being obeyed.

Blackfish communicated with Boone through an interpreter, a black man named Pompey. The Shawnees had captured Pompey when he had been a slave boy in Virginia and had raised him as a Shawnee. Through Pompey, Blackfish told Boone that he was seeking vengeance for the murder of a fellow Shawnee chief by settlers in eastern Ohio. The chief had been on a peacemaking mission to the Ohio settlers when they had treacherously turned on him and killed him.

To avenge the death of his fellow chief, Blackfish intended to kill all of Boone's men at the salt springs. Then, Blackfish told Boone, he would advance on Boonesborough and, in a surprise attack, annihilate all the adult male settlers there. Generally, Indians did not kill women and children.

Since Blackfish had one hundred twenty men, and there were only twenty-seven settlers at the salt springs, Boone knew that there was no hope for the salt makers. Boone thought the settlers at Boonesborough were also doomed. With no survivors at the salt springs, there would be no one to warn the settlers at Boonesborough of the approach of the Indians.

To avoid this calamity, Boone tried to convince Blackfish that it would be unwise of him to kill the salt makers. Boone reminded Blackfish that he would be overburdened by having to feed the women and children he would take captive at Boonesborough. He pointed out to Blackfish that he could be relieved of this burden if he would spare the lives of the salt makers, who would assume the responsibility of feeding the captive women and children, many of whom were blood relatives of the salt makers. Boone told Blackfish that by killing the salt makers he would be losing the value of their labor. If the salt makers would be enslaved instead of killed, they could feed their women and children by hunting.

Boone assured Blackfish that he could persuade all the salt makers to surrender to Blackfish, thus preventing casualties within the Shawnee ranks. Blackfish could win a bloodless victory.

Blackfish was persuaded by Boone's logic.

On the day after his capture, Boone accompanied Blackfish and his men to the salt springs. When the salt makers saw themselves surrounded by Indians they seized their weapons, but Boone called to his men to lay down their arms. If they resisted, Boone shouted, they would most certainly be wiped out. Grudgingly, some of them cursing Boone as a traitor, the salt makers dropped their weapons.

Although Blackfish had agreed to spare the salt makers, some of his braves now cried out for blood, to avenge the murder of the Shawnee chief in eastern Ohio. The Indians debated for several hours whether the salt makers should live or die. Blackfish allowed Boone to have the last word in the debate. Boone addressed the Indians in English which was translated into the Shawnee language by Pompey. Boone reviewed the logical arguments he had previously presented to Blackfish. Then a vote was taken by the one hundred twenty Indians. Fifty-nine favored putting the salt makers to death~ sixty-one were for sparing them.

Immediately after the vote, Blackfish, Boone, the Shawnee warriors, and the captive salt makers started on a hundred mile journey to Chillicothe, a Shawnee town in Ohio. There was very little food to be had along the way. Some of the Indians ate their dogs, but the American captives preferred to go hungry. Boone showed them how to get some nourishment from the bark of trees. On February 18, 1778, ten days after they had left Kentucky, the little army of Shawnees and their captives arrived in Chillicothe, a town of several hundred log cabins and huts covered with buffalo hides.

The inhabitants had never seen their warriors return with so many captives. To celebrate the event the salt makers were forced to run the gauntlet and join in wild dances. The captives muttered to each other their resentment toward Boone for getting them into this intolerable situation. They expected to be enslaved by the Indians.

There was, however, another possible fate for the salt makers, besides slavery. The Shawnees, like other Indians, added new members to their nation by adopting captives with admirable traits or useful abilities. Families which had lost sons in battle were especially interested in adopting captives to take the places of sons they had lost.

News of Blackfish • s arrival in Chillicothe with the twenty-seven salt makers in tow quickly became known in neighboring Shawnee villages. Within a few days the streets of Chillicothe were filled with bereaved Indian parents who were looking for replacements for their departed sons.

As the leader of the Kentuckians, Boone was highly valued as a potential adopted son. Chief Blackfish, himself, wanted to adopt Boone.

There was only one blemish in Boone's record that might disqualify him as Blackfish's adopted son. That flaw was a suspicion that Boone killed Blackfish's son during a skirmish a few years previously. When questioned by the Indians, Boone admitted he might have fired the bullet which killed Blackfish's son. Many shots had been fired on both sides, including Boone's shot. It was impossible to tell whose shot had killed the young warrior, Boone said. "Many things happen in war," he said, "which are best forgotten."

For a tense moment Boone's questioners were silent. Then an Indian sitting next to him smiled and slapped Boone on the shoulder. "Brave man! All right!" said the Indian. "When we in war you kill me, I kill you. All right!'"

Blackfish decided that Boone was an acceptable adopted son. Boone believed that his adoption "must have been to replace that slain son."

Boone was conducted to a river where matrons submersed and scrubbed him. Then they plucked his hair leaving only a tuft on the top of his head as a scalp lock, which they decorated with ribbons and feathers. Finally, at the council house, amid much smoking and feasting, he was formally adopted as Blackfish's son. He was given an Indian name, "Sheltowee," which meant "Big Turtle" in the Shawnee language, a compliment to Boone s muscular build.

Boone, elevated to the rank of a chief's son, seemed to enjoy his life as an adopted Shawnee. One of the salt makers, who detested his life among the Shawnees, said that he could not understand "how Boone could be whistling and contented among the dirty Indians."

Boone and his adoptive father, Blackfish, shared a mutual respect for each other. Boone once referred to Blackfish as "one of Nature's noblemen."

While he lived in Chillicothe, Boone tried to create the impression that he had no desire to escape. When he had a chance to get away he never took advantage of the opportunity. Gradually he won the trust of his captors, who ceased to worry about his absconding.

Boone had lived among the Indians four months when he learned in June, 1778, that Blackfish was planning to attack Boonesborough. Boone decided that he must warn the settlers of their danger.

While Blackfish was away hunting with his warriors, Boone mounted a horse and headed for Kentucky. In order to put as much distance as possible between himself and his pursuers he ran the horse at top speed until it was exhausted. After dismounting, he ran as long as he was able. He then hid his trail by walking in streams, treading on rocks, and walking along logs. When he came to the Ohio River he crossed it by holding on to a floating log. He arrive d at Boonesborough on June 20. He had covered one hundred sixty miles in four days.

When Boone arrived at Boonesborough the settlers there did not recognize him at first; with his scalp lock he looked like an Indian. When they did recognize him they did not welcome him warmly. Some of the salt makers had escaped from Chillicothe and had returned to Boonesborough. They had not forgiven Boone for forcing them to surrender to Blackfish at the salt springs. They disapproved of his close tie to Blackfish. Some of the salt makers viewed Boone as a traitor who had sold them out to Blackfish.

When, however, Boone told the settlers that Blackfish was planning to lead a large army of warriors against Boonesborough, the salt makers quickly forgot their distrust of him and joined him in preparing to defend the little fort Boone sent a message by courier to the state authorities in Virginia of which Kentucky was then a county. He informed the Virginians of Blackfish's coming attack on Boonesborough and asked them to send help as soon as possible.

Blackfish's army of four hundred warriors arrived at Boonesborough two and a half months after Boone's return from Chillicothe. The Shawnees surrounded the small fortress, which was defended by sixty men. A flag of truce appeared, carried by Pompey, Blackfish's spokesman. Blackfish demanded the immediate surrender of Boonesborough.

Then a plaintive cry was heard: "Sheltowee, Sheltowee," Boone's Shawnee name. It was Blackfish, calling out to his adopted son. Pompey said that Blackfish wanted to see his son. Boone shouted back that he would meet Blackfish sixty yards from the gate of the stockade, within the range of the riflemen manning the fort. Boone walked out of the fort. Blackfish came to meet him, hand extended. "Howdy, my son."

'Howdy, Father."

They sat together on a blanket while Indian boys fanned them with leafy branches. The settlers watched this parley incredulously.

"My son, what made you run away from me?" Blackfish asked, tears running down his cheeks.

"Because I wanted to see my wife and children," said Boone.

"Well if you'd asked me, I'd have let you come."

Blackfish asked whether Boone would be willing to surrender if the settlers' safety was guaranteed. Boone said that he was not empowered to make that decision. All the settlers would have to be consulted.

Boone returned to the stockade. In a discussion among the settlers one of them said that he would shoot anyone who voted for surrender. The vote was unanimous for fighting, but the settlers delayed giving their answer to Blackfish. Expecting reinforcements from Virginia, Boone and the settlers wanted, if possible, to delay fighting until help arrived.

For his part, Blackfish postponed giving the settlers an ultimatum. Neither side appeared eager to begin hostilities.

After a silence of several hours, Pompey appeared again before the fort. Blackfish, said Pompey, wanted to see Boone's squaws. Blackfish and his men had heard much about Boone's pretty daughter, Jemima, who was married to one of the settlers, and wanted to see her. To humor his foe and delay the outbreak of hostilities, Boone complied with the request. Accompanied by riflemen and several other women, Jemima appeared in the open gate. From a hundred feet away Blackfish, Pompey, and a group of warriors stood looking on.

"Let down your hair," Pompey called out.

Removing their combs, the women let their hair fall over their shoulders.

Then the Indians departed, nodding with pleasure to each other.

Later, Blackfish asked Boone whether the settlers had decided to surrender. When Boone told Blackfish that all the settlers had voted to defend the fort, the Shawnee chief expressed disappointment. Then Blackfish made a surprise move. He said that he would call off the siege if the settlers would draw up a treaty with the Shawnees. Under the treaty, land north of the Ohio River would belong to the Shawnees; land south of the Ohio would belong to the settlers.

Blackfish's offer sounded generous to Boone; Blackfish was relinquishing the Shawnees' claim to Kentucky as their private hunting preserve. The settlers accepted Blackfish's offer.

On Wednesday, September 9, 1778, two days after the arrival of Blackfish's army, the women of Boonesborough prepared a great feast to celebrate the new accord with the Indians. The gate to the stockade was flung open. Blackfish and his warriors were invited to partake of the feast within the walls of the stockade. Indians and settlers mingled. Neither Boone nor Blackfish, however, quite trusted the other; just in case something would go wrong, sharpshooters on both sides were posted in locations that gave them a good view of the festivities.

To seal their agreement Blackfish advanced toward Boone with his arms extended for a friendly hug. Other Shawnees followed Blackfish's example and approached settlers in a similar amicable fashion. One of the settlers' nervous sharpshooters, however, misinterpreted the Indians' actions as being hostile rather than friendly and pulled the trigger of his loaded musket. In an instant, a scene of brotherly love was transformed into a deadly struggle.

Somehow, the settlers managed to drive the Indians out of the fort. As soon as the last Indian was outside, the gates were slammed shut.

The battle for the fort continued night and day. At night the Indians tossed flaming torches onto the roofs of the cabins, attempting to set the fort afire. Women and children, using long poles, succeeded in shoving the burning brands outside the fort.

For eleven days the settlers held out against the continued siege by the Indians. Then, on September 20, reinforcements from Virginia came to the rescue of Boonesborough. Blackfish and his army quietly departed and went home to Ohio.

No longer threatened by Blackfish, the salt makers resumed their feud with their leader, Boone. They accused him of treason for having forced them to surrender to Blackish at the salt springs. Boone was tried in a court martial, which completely exonerated him of the charges brought against him. It also recommended his promotion from captain to major in the local militia.

A year later Daniel Boone led a migration of a hundred families from Virginia into Kentucky.

In that same year Blackfish was wounded while defending Chillicothe against a raid by Ohio settlers. After his wound became infected, Blackfish died. Daniel Boone lived on till 1820, when he died in Missouri at age eighty-six.

Whitney And Howe

Eli Whitney

Few men have done more for the welfare of mankind than did Eli Whitney. He did not discover a new land, nor did he explore the untrodden wilderness or win a great battle. He invented a machine which revolutionized the cotton industry.

Eli Whitney was a native of Massachusetts. At nineteen he made up his mind to go to college. As his father did not see fit to send him, he earned the necessary money himself. Partly by teaching and partly by odd jobs at carpentry, he gathered enough to pay his way through Yale University. In 1792 he was graduated.

Soon after, Whitney secured a position as tutor in a Georgia family. But when he reached the South, he found the place filled. So he decided to study law. On the trip south he had become acquainted with Mrs. Greene, the widow of General Nathanael Greene, of Revolutionary fame. Hearing of his disappointment, Mrs. Greene now cordially invited him to make her plantation his home while he was studying law.

Whitney did many little things for his hostess to show that he appreciated her kindness. He made toys for the children and an embroidery frame for Mrs. Greene, which was an immense improvement over the awkward old-fashioned one she had been using. In fact, he had what has long been known as "Yankee ingenuity."

One day Mrs. Greene had as guests a number of plantation owners. They were speaking about the raising of cotton, and of how the value of the crop would be vastly increased if only someone could invent a machine that would strip the seeds from the cotton fiber. Mrs. Greene advised the men to lay the problem before her young friend, Eli Whitney. They explained the matter to him; but as he had not even seen the cotton fiber and its seeds, he was afraid he could do nothing. However, he said he would try.

At the time Whitney went to Georgia, cotton seeds were picked from the fiber by hand. It used to take a Negro a whole day to clean a single pound of cotton, and it took many slaves several months to clean an entire crop. Because of this vast amount of labor, the planters could not raise cotton at a profit. But if only someone could invent a cotton cleaner, the profits on cotton would be immense. This then was Whitney's problem.

All winter long he tinkered. By the spring of 1793 he had succeeded in contriving a machine with which one man could clean one thousand pounds of cotton in one day.

302

The machine consisted of two cylinders. On one were rows of teeth, which pulled the cotton through a grating too fine for the seeds to pass through. The other cylinder was covered with little brushes, which, as they met the teeth, brushed the cotton from them into a place prepared to catch it. And all this was done without in any way harming the seeds for the many uses they could be put to.

Whitney called the machine a cotton gin, "gin" being a contraction of the word "engine." He let only Mrs. Greene and a few others see his model. Yet, before long, nearly everyone in the South was talking about his wonderful invention; and, careful as he was, his shop was broken into, and his model was stolen. Before he could make another and get it patented there were several cotton gins in operation. All were copied from his stolen model, and it was years before Whitney received justice in connection with his great invention.

Immediately after the invention of the cotton gin the planters began to increase the size of their cotton fields, and every year more and more cotton was raised. In 1784 America exported three thousand pounds. In 1803, ten years after the cotton gin came into use, forty million pounds were exported.

Since Whitney's time, the increase in production has lowered the price of cotton goods from a dollar and fifty cents a yard to as low as five cents a yard, thus enabling the very poorest to buy cotton cloth.

And all this is due to Eli Whitney's cotton gin, and has been brought about in a little over a century. The cotton gin has helped not only the Southern cotton growers, but also the manufacturers of both North and South. It has done much to improve our foreign trade, and so has helped the commerce of the country at large. Improvements have been made upon the original cotton gin, but the Americans of the twentieth century owe as much to Eli Whitney's invention as did those of a hundred years ago.

Elias Howe

In colonial days making clothes was no easy matter. There are many, many stitches in even one simple garment. And when you think how many garments are necessary for one child, you can imagine how busy the mother of a large family must have been, when each stitch had to be done by hand.

There were traveling tailors, it is true, who would come and stay with a family and make the coats and trousers, and there were traveling cobblers, who made the shoes.

But every family could not afford to pay these helpers, and even those who could, had to make many other things besides coats and trousers and shoes. So, day after day and evening after evening saw the women of the family busily sewing, sewing, sewing, one stitch at a time, and all done by hand.

One mother whose evenings were spent in this way was Mrs. Elias Howe. Her husband was a poor young man. They lived in Boston and Mr. Howe worked in a Boston shop where machines were made for spinning and weaving. The old way of spinning and weaving was very slow, but by the use of these machines much time and labor were saved.

Mr. Howe was not very strong and his day's work tired him out. At night, fairly exhausted, he would lie down and rest. And as he rested, his eyes watched his wife's patient fingers sending her needle in and out, in and out. He knew she was tired, too, for she had three little children to care for all day as well as her house work to do. Still, she could not rest in the evening. She must sew every night to keep the children in clothes and add to her husband's small earnings. It seemed a pity. Wasn't there some easier way to do the same thing?

Several men had tried to make a sewing machine but none had succeeded. Surely, it was possible to make such a machine and Elias Howe decided to try. At the shop he gave every spare minute to his plans. His first machine had a needle pointed at both ends with an eye in the middle. For more than a year he tried to make this succeed. Next, he used two threads, making the stitch by means of a shuttle. This time he used a curved needle. And, this time, he had a machine which would actually sew.

By now Howe had given up his place in the shop and was poorer than ever. Fortunately, he was able to interest a Mr. Fisher in his machine, and Mr. Fisher took Howe and his family to board and furnished him the money to make a better machine than his rough model. In return for all this Mr. Fisher was to be half owner of the patent when it was secured.

By the spring of 1845, the new machine was made and, in 1846, was patented. Can you believe that such an invention was feared rather than received with joy? Tailors admitted that it might be useful, but they would have nothing to do with it. They and others who made their living by sewing thought it would ruin their trade. They talked against it and said it would throw many people out of work.

Mr. Fisher grew discouraged and withdrew from his agreement. Howe took his family to his father's home. And, now, came harder times than ever for the inventor and those dependent on him. He even went to England and tried to make something out of his invention over there. But, when he reached New York again, months later, he had less than a dollar in his pockets.

What was worse, while he was away, others had made copies of his machine and sold them. Sure of his patent, however, Howe began suits against these people and finally, after years of poverty and struggle, his rights were fully established and all manufacturers of the machine were forced to pay him a royalty.

Gradually, the usefulness of the sewing machine overcame the opposition to it, and it became a necessity. In 1863 Elias Howe's royalties were said to be $4,000 a day.

Of course, many improvements on Howe's machine were later made by others. In these he was much interested, and doubtless remembering his own hard times, he gladly helped their makers with advice, or money, or both. In his triumph, he was the soul of generosity to those working to follow where he had led.

Great Plague Strikes Europe
Erica Hershey

In 1346 Europeans heard news of a disaster in Asia, a plague that had depopulated India. Whole cities were rumored to be deserted, their streets littered with corpses.

In 1347 the plague spread through Persia and Syria to Egypt. That fall it struck southern Italy and Spain.

Europeans had no name for the disease; they simply called it "the Great Plague." The first symptom was a fever. Later symptoms included black swellings and blotches which oozed blood and pus. People who caught the plague usually died within three days of noticing the first symptoms in themselves.

In 1348 and 1349 the disease spread north from the Mediterranean through Europe. No accurate tally of the death toll was kept, but the Great Plague was certainly the worst disaster in European history. "Half the world died," was a popular estimate.

Physicians had no idea how to fight the plague. The medical faculty of the University of Paris reported that no earthly medicine could stop the disease, which had been caused by an astrological event, a conjunction of three planets in one constellation.

Some people hoped that they could maintain their health by staying drunk. According to Giovanni Boccaccio of Florence, "Many people believed that getting drunk, singing, celebrating, satisfying every appetite, laughing, and making a joke of everything that happened was the best medicine. So they roamed from tavern to tavern all day and night, drinking to excess." Others took the opposite tack, shutting themselves up in their houses and trying to live moderately to maintain their health. But neither excess nor moderation could protect people from the plague.

The disease spread very rapidly. Italian peasants believed that the contagion could be spread by eye contact, that a healthy man would fall sick if he met the hopeless gaze of a sick plague victim.

In terror of infection, healthy people often refused to nurse their sick relatives. According to Boccaccio, "The plague struck such fear into the hearts of men and women that brother abandoned brother, uncle abandoned nephew, sister, left brother, and very often wife abandoned husband. Even worse, almost unbelievable, fathers and mothers refused to care for their sick children, as if they belonged to somebody else."

To escape from plague-stricken cities, many people fled to the countryside. On the roads they met peasants fleeing from plague-stricken rural hamlets.

No place was safe. The contagion spread even through uninhabited forests. In one remote monastery, which was completely isolated from the rest of society, every monk died.

Animals, as well as humans, caught the plague. In some districts of England all the sheep died, leaving every pasture dotted with corpses. Throughout Europe hogs, horses, and dogs died with their masters.

Fearing that the end of the world was nigh, many Europeans flocked to join a new religious sect called the Flagellants, which was organized in 1348 to fight the plague by spiritual means. The Flagellants believed that the plague, like Noah's flood, had been sent by God to punish humanity for its sins. They believed that God was especially annoyed by wealth and corruption in the Catholic Church.

The new sect was violently anticlerical. No ordained priest was permitted to watch the rituals of the Flagellants, in which members of the sect whipped themselves, or took turns whipping each other under the direction of lay ministers called Masters. By this sacrifice, reenacting the scourging of Christ, The Flagellants hoped to persuade an angry Deity to spare the world. They sang hymns while they beat themselves bloody with leather whips tipped with iron spikes.

The Flagellants won adherents throughout Europe, becoming especially popular in Germany and Switzerland. During the summer of 1348, hundreds of groups of Flagellants went marching from town to town to stop the plague. On the march, Flagellants were not allowed to bathe, shave, change their clothes, or sleep in a bed, without special permission from their lay Master.

Priests, nobles, and city officials feared the Flagellants as potential troublemakers, but the common people usually greeted the marchers with enthusiasm. Seeking charms to protect them from the plague, many people dipped rags into the blood dripping from the self-inflicted wounds of the Flagellants. These rags were preserved like holy relics.

In every town, the Masters of the Flagellants preached sermons attacking corruption in the church. They also preached hatred of the Jews, inciting mobs to attack local ghettos.

With a strange illogic, the Flagellants believed that the plague was simultaneously an act of God and also, a satanic plot by Jewish conspirators. They claimed that the plague was spread by a poison, which had been brewed by a secret committee of rabbis in Toledo, Spain. This poison had been distributed to Jewish secret agents throughout Europe, who carried the deadly stuff in "narrow stitched leather bags." By dumping the poison into wells and streams, Jews were planning to kill all the Christians in Europe the Flagellants said.

To protect the Jews from this dangerous slander, Pope Clement VI issued a Bull in 1348 proclaiming that the Jews were innocent of the charge of well-poisoning. The Pope noted that "by a mysterious decree of God" the plague was killing Jews as well as Christians. He declared that Christians who blamed the pestilence on the Jews had been "seduced by that liar, the Devil," and he urged the Catholic clergy to protect the Jews from the Flagellants.

In Florence and many other cities of the Italian peninsula, the Pope's authority saved the local Jews from massacre. Further north, in France. Switzerland, Germany, and the Low Countries, the Flagellants carried out a campaign of genocide against the Jews.

When Flagellants organized a mob to attack the Jews in Cologne, priests and city officials ordered the rioters to disperse. Instead, the mob attacked and dispersed the officials. The rioters then rampaged through the ghetto, murdering every Jew they could catch.

Similar massacres were recorded in at least three hundred and fifty cities and towns. In Basel two hundred Jews were burned to death in a special house built for that purpose. In Strasbourg two thousand Jews were taken to the burial ground, where all who refused baptism were burned at the stake. In Mainz the local Jews gathered weapons and tried to defend themselves, but they were defeated in a street battle. Six thousand Jews then retreated to their ghetto and set fire to it, choosing suicide over execution or conversion.

After killing a majority of the Jews in what is now Germany, the Flagellants began directly attacking the Catholic Church. They invaded churches, looted altars, and assaulted priests, sometimes stoning them to death. The Flagellant Masters began administering the sacraments to their followers, hearing confessions and granting absolution.

The Flagellants lost their following when their campaign failed to stop the plague. The Flagellants had acquired no immunity from the disease; they died like everyone else.

As the plague receded in October of 1349, Pope Clement VI denounced the Flagellants as heretics. Since most plague survivors now viewed the Flagellants as false prophets of salvation, they were easily suppressed. The King of France outlawed flagellation, and authorities throughout Europe began arresting and hanging the Masters of the sect.

By the time the Great Plague ended in 1350, the Flagellants had disbanded. According to one contemporary chronicler, they "vanished as suddenly as they had come, like night phantoms or mocking ghosts."

The plague returned to attack Europe at intervals during the ensuing centuries. These later epidemics were less deadly than the Great Plague had been, perhaps because survivors of the Great Plague had passed resistant genes to their descendants.

Plague, sometimes called "bubonic plague" or the Black Death, is caused by a bacillus. It is mainly a disease of rodents. Flea bites spread the disease from rats and squirrels to human beings and domestic animals. Plague can also spread from one person to another, like a cold.

Today plague can usually be cured with antibiotics.

Alexander The Great

Alexander The Great, Son of Philip of Macedon and Olympias, daughter of Neoptolemus of Epirus, was born at Pella, 356 B.C. His mind was formed chiefly by Aristotle, who instructed him in every branch of human learning, especially in the art of government. Alexander was sixteen years of age when his father marched against Byzantium, and left the government in his hands during his absence. Two years afterward, he displayed singular courage at the battle of Charonea (338 B.C.), where he overthrew the Sacred Band of the Thebans. "My son," said Philip, as he embraced him after the conflict, "seek for thyself another kingdom, for that which I leave is too small for thee." The father and son quarreled, however, when the former divorced Olympias. Alexander took part with his mother, and fled to Epirus, to escape his father's vengeance; but receiving his pardon soon afterward, he returned, and accompanied him in an expedition against the Triballi, when he saved his life on the field. Philip, being appointed generalissimo of the Greeks, was preparing for a war with Persia, when he was assassinated (336 B.C.), and Alexander, not yet twenty years of age, ascended the throne.

After punishing his father's murderers, he marched on Corinth, and in a general assembly of the Greeks he caused himself to be appointed to the command of the forces against Persia. On his return to Macedon, he found the Illyrians and Triballi up in arms, whereupon he forced his way through Thrace, and was everywhere victorious. But now the Thebans had been induced, by a report of his death, to take up arms, and the Athenians, stimulated by the eloquence of Demosthenes, were preparing to join them. To prevent this coalition, Alexander rapidly marched against Thebes, which, refusing to surrender, was conquered and razed to the ground. Six thousand of the inhabitants were slain, and 30,000 sold into slavery; the house and descendants of the poet Pindar alone being spared. This severity struck terror into all Greece. The Athenians were treated with more leniency.

Alexander, having appointed Antipater his deputy in Europe, now prepared to prosecute the war with Persia. He crossed the Hellespont in the spring of 334 B.C., with 30,000 foot and 5,000 horse, attacked the Persian satraps at the River Granicus, and gained a complete victory, overthrowing the son-in-law of their king Darius with his own lance. As a result of the battle, most of the cities of Asia Minor at once opened their gates to the conqueror.

Alexander restored democracy in all the Greek cities; and as he passed through Gordium, cut the Gordian-knot, which none should loose but the ruler of Asia. During a dangerous illness at Tarsus, brought on by bathing in the Cydnus, he received a letter insinuating that Philip, his physician, had been bribed by Darius toy poison him. Alexander handed the letter to Philip, and at the same time swallowed the draught which the latter had prepared. As soon as he recovered, he advanced toward the defiles of Cilicia, in which Darius had stationed himself with an army of 600,000 men.

He arrived in November, 333 B.C., in the neighborhood of Issus, where, on the narrow plain between the mountains and the sea, the unwieldy masses of the Persians were thrown into confusion by the charge of the Macedonians, and fled in terror. On the left wing, 30,000 Greek mercenaries held out longer, but they, too, were at length compelled to yield. All the treasures as well as the family of Darius fell into the hands of the conqueror, who treated them with the greatest magnanimity. Overtures for peace, made by Darius on the basis of surrendering to Alexander all Asia west of the Euphrates, were rejected.

Alexander now turned toward Syria and Phœnicia. He occupied Damascus, where he found princely treasures, and secured to himself all the cities along the shores of the Mediterranean. Tyre, confident in its strong position, resisted him, but was conquered and destroyed, after seven months of incredible exertion (332 B.C.). Thence he marched victoriously through Palestine, where all the cities submitted to him except Gaza; it shared the same fate as Tyre. Egypt, weary of the Persian yoke, welcomed him as a deliverer; and in order to strengthen his dominion here, he restored all the old customs and religious institutions of the country, and founded Alexandria in the beginning of 331 B.C. Thence he marched through the Libyan Desert, in order to consult the oracle of Ammon, whose priest saluted him as a son of Zeus; and he returned with the conviction that he was indeed a god.

He then again set out to meet Darius; in October, 331 B.C., a great battle was fought on the plain stretching eastward to Arbela. Notwithstanding the immense superiority of his adversary, who had collected a new army of more than a million men, Alexander was not for a moment doubtful of victory. Heading the cavalry himself, he rushed on the Persians, and put them to flight; then hastened to the assistance of his left wing, which, in the meanwhile, had been sorely pressed. He was anxious to make Darius a prisoner, but Darius escaped on horseback, leaving his baggage and all his treasures a prey to the conqueror. Babylon and Susa, the treasure-houses of the East, opened their gates to Alexander, who next marched toward Persepolis, the capital of Persia, which he entered in triumph.

The marvelous successes of Alexander now began to dazzle his judgment and to inflame his passions. He became a slave to debauchery, and his caprices were as cruel as they were ungrateful. In a fit of drunkenness, and at the instigation of Thais, an Athenian courtesan, he set fire to Persepolis, the wonder of the world, and reduced it to a heap of ashes then, ashamed of the deed, he set out with his cavalry in pursuit of Darius. Learning that Bessus, the Bactrian satrap, held him a prisoner, he hastened his march, in the hope of saving him, but he found him mortally wounded (330 B.C.). He mourned over his fallen enemy, and caused him to be buried with all the customary honors, while he hunted down Bessus, who himself aspired to the throne, chasing him over the Oxus to Sogdiana (Bokhara).

Having discovered a conspiracy in which the son of Parmenio was implicated, he put both father and son to death, though Parmenio himself was innocent of any knowledge of the affair. This cruel injustice excited universal displeasure. In 329 he penetrated to the farthest known limits of Northern Asia, and overthrew the Scythians on the banks of the Jaxartes. In the following year he subdued the whole of Sogdiana, and married Roxana, whom he had taken prisoner. She was the daughter of Oxyartes, one of the enemy's captains, and was said to be the fairest of all the virgins of Asia. The murder of his foster-brother, Clitus, in a drunken brawl, was followed, in 327 B.C., by the discovery of a fresh conspiracy, in which Callisthenes, a nephew of Aristotle, was falsely implicated. For challenging Alexander's divinity, he was cruelly tortured and hanged.

In 327 B.C., proceeding to the conquest of India, hitherto known only by name, Alexander crossed the Indus near to the modern Attock, and pursued his way under the guidance of a native prince to the Hydaspes (Jhelum). He there was opposed by Porus, another native prince, whom he overthrew after a bloody contest, and there he lost his charger Bucephalus; thence he marched as lord of the country, through the Punjab, establishing Greek colonies. He then wished to advance to the Ganges, but the general murmuring of his troops obliged him, at the Hyphasis (modern Sutlej), to commence his retreat. On regaining the Hydaspes, he built a fleet, and sent one division of his army in it down the river, while the other followed along the banks, fighting its way through successive Indian armies. At length, having reached the ocean, he ordered Nearchus, the commander of the fleet, to sail thence to the Persian Gulf, while he himself struck inland with one division of his army, in order to return home through Gedrosia (Beluchistan). During this march his forces suffered fearfully from want of food and water. Of all the troops which had set out with Alexander, little more than a fourth part arrived with him in Persia (325 B.C.).

At Susa he married Stateira, the daughter of Darius, and he bestowed presents on those Macedonians (some ten thousand in number) who had married Persian women, his design being to unite the two nations. He also distributed liberal rewards among his soldiers. Soon afterward he was deprived, by death, of his favorite Hephestion. His grief was unbounded, and he interred the dead man with kingly honors. As he was returning from Ecbatana to Babylon, it is said that the Magi foretold that the latter city would prove fatal to him; but he despised their warnings. On the way, he was met by ambassadors from all parts of the world—Libya, Italy, Carthage, Greece, the Scythians, Celts, and Iberians.

At Babylon he was busy with gigantic plans for the future, both of conquest and civilization, when he was suddenly taken ill after a banquet, and died eleven days later, 323 B.C., in the thirty-second year of his age, and the thirteenth of his reign. His body was deposited in a golden coffin at Alexandria, by Ptolemaus, and divine honors were paid to him, not only in Egypt, but in other countries. He had appointed no heir to his immense dominions; but to the question of his friends, "Who should inherit them?" he replied, "The most worthy." After many disturbances, his generals recognized as Kings the weak-minded Aridæus—a son of Philip by Philinna, the dancer—and Alexander's posthumous son by Roxana, Alexander Ægus, while they shared the provinces among themselves, assuming the title of satraps. Perdiccas, to whom Alexander had, on his death-bed, delivered his ring, became guardian of the kings during their minority. The empire of Alexander soon broke up, and his dominions were divided among his generals.

Alexander was more than a conqueror. He diffused the language and civilization of Greece wherever victory led him, and planted Greek kingdoms in Asia, which continued to exist for some centuries. At the very time of his death, he was engaged in devising plans for the drainage of the unhealthy marshes around Babylon, and a better irrigation of the extensive plains. It is even supposed that the fever which he caught there, rather than his famous drinking-bout, was the real cause of his death. To Alexander, the ancient world owed a vast increase of its knowledge in geography, natural history, etc. He taught Europeans the road to India, and gave them the first glimpses of that magnificence and splendor which has dazzled and captivated their imagination for more than two thousand years.

SS *Sultana*

Sultana was a Mississippi River side-wheel steamboat that exploded on April 27, 1865 in the greatest maritime disaster in United States history. An estimated 1,800 of her 2,427 passengers died when three of the boat's four boilers exploded and she burned to the waterline and sank near Memphis. This disaster has long since, past and present, been overshadowed in the press by other recent events. John Wilkes Booth, President Lincoln's assassin, was killed the day before.

The wooden steamboat was constructed in 1863 by the John Litherbury Boatyard in Cincinnati, and intended for the lower Mississippi cotton trade. Registering 1,719 tons, the steamer normally carried a crew of 85. For two years, she ran a regular route between St. Louis and New Orleans, frequently commissioned to carry troops.

The Tragedy

Under the command of Captain J. C. Mason of St. Louis, *Sultana* left New Orleans on April 21, 1865, with 75 to 100 cabin passengers, deck passengers, and numerous head of livestock bound for market in St. Louis. At Vicksburg, she stopped for a series of hasty repairs to the boilers and to take on more passengers. Rather than have a bad boiler replaced, a small patch repair was made to reinforce a leaking area. A section of bulged boiler plate was removed, and a patch of lesser thickness than the parent plate was riveted in its place. This repair took about one day, whereas a complete replacement of the boiler would have taken about three days. During her time in port, men tried to muscle, bribe, and threaten their way on board, until the boat was bursting at the seams with soldiers. More than 2,000 men crowded aboard.

Most of the new passengers were Union soldiers, chiefly from Ohio and just released from Confederate prison camps such as Cahawba and Andersonville. The U.S. government had contracted with *Sultana* to transport these former prisoners of war back to their homes. With a legal capacity of only 376, she was severely overcrowded. Many of the passengers had been weakened by their incarceration and associated illnesses. Passengers were packed into every available space, and the overflow was so severe that the decks were completely packed.

The cause of the explosion was too much pressure and low water in the boiler. There was reason to believe allowable working steam pressure was exceeded in an attempt to overcome the spring river current. The boiler (or boilers) gave way when the steamer was 7 to 9 miles (11 to 14 km) north of Memphis at 2:00 am. The enormous explosion flung some of the passengers on deck into the water, and destroyed a large section of the boat. The forward part of the upper decks collapsed into the exposed furnace boxes which soon caught fire and soon turned the remaining superstructure into an inferno, the glare of which was visible as far away as Memphis.

The first boat on the scene was the southbound steamer *Bostonia II*, coming downriver on her maiden voyage, which arrived at about 3:00 am, an hour after the explosion, and overtook the burning wreck to rescue scores of survivors. The hulk of the *Sultana* drifted about six miles to the west bank of the river, and sank at around dawn near Mound City and present-day Marion, Arkansas. Other vessels joined the rescue, including the steamers *Silver Spray*, *Jenny Lind*, and *Pocohontas*, and the Navy tin clad *Essex* and the side-wheel gunboat USS *Tyler*, manned by volunteers. The ship's regular crew had been discharged days before.

Passengers who survived the initial explosion had to risk their lives in the icy spring runoff of the Mississippi or burn with the boat. Many died of drowning or hypothermia. Some survivors were plucked from the tops of semi-submerged trees along the Arkansas shore. Bodies of victims continued to be found downriver for months, some as far as Vicksburg. Many bodies were never recovered. *Sultana*'s officers, including Captain Mason, were among those who perished.

About 700 survivors, many with horrible burns, were transported to hospitals in Memphis. Up to 200 of them died later from burns or exposure. Newspaper accounts indicate that the people of Memphis had sympathy for the victims despite the fact that they had recently been enemies. The Chicago Opera Troupe staged a benefit, the crew of *Essex* raised $1,000, and the mayor took in three survivors.

Monuments and historical markers to *Sultana* and her victims have been erected at Memphis; Muncie, Indiana; Marion; Vicksburg; Cincinnati; Knoxville; Hillsdale, Michigan; and Mansfield, Ohio.

Casualties

The exact death toll is unknown. Estimates range from 1,300 to 1,900, higher than the Titanic disaster on the North Atlantic 47 years later. The official count by the United States Customs Service was 1,800. Of the total casualties, Ohio lost the most of any state, with 791 dead. Indiana lost 491 persons, with Kentucky suffering 194 dead. It is estimated that of the Ohio casualties, over fifty were Cincinnatians. Final estimates of survivors were between 700 and 800. Many of the dead were interred at the Memphis National Cemetery.

Cause

The official cause of the *Sultana* disaster was determined to be mismanagement of water levels in the boiler, exacerbated by the fact that the vessel was severely overcrowded and top heavy. As the steamboat made her way north following the twists and turns of the river, she listed severely to one side then the other. Her four boilers were interconnected and mounted side-by-side, so that if the boat tipped sideways, water would tend to run out of the highest boiler. With the fires still going against the empty boiler, this created hot spots. When the boat tipped the other way, water rushing back into the empty boiler would hit the hot spots and flash instantly to steam, creating a sudden surge in pressure. This effect of careening could have been minimized by maintaining high water levels in the boilers. The official inquiry found that the boat's boilers exploded due to the combined effects of careening, low water level, and a faulty repair to a leaky boiler made a few days earlier.

In 1888, a St. Louis resident named William Streetor claimed that his former business partner, Robert Louden, made a death bed confession of having sabotaged *Sultana* by a coal torpedo. Louden, a former Confederate agent and saboteur who operated in and around St. Louis, had the opportunity and motive to attack it and may have had access to the means. (Thomas Edgeworth Courtenay, the inventor of the coal torpedo, was a former resident of St. Louis and was involved in similar acts of sabotage against Union shipping interests.) Supporting Louden's claim are eyewitness reports that a piece of artillery shell was observed in the wreckage. Louden's claim is controversial, however, and most scholars support the official explanation. The location of the explosion, from the top rear of the boilers, far away from the fireboxes, tends to indicate that Louden's claim of sabotage was pure bravado.

The episode of *History Detectives*, which aired on July 2, 2014, reviewed the known evidence and then focused on the question of why the steamboat was allowed to be crowded to several times its normal capacity before departure. The report blamed a Quartermaster named Reuben Hatch, an individual with a long history of corruption and incompetence, who was able to keep his job due to political connections: Among others, he was a close relative of Illinois politician Ozias M. Hatch. Reuben Hatch had authorized the large crowd of soldiers, garnering a ten-dollar fee for every soldier boarded on the steamboat. President Abraham Lincoln, Secretary of War Edwin Stanton and General of the Army Ulysses S. Grant were also implicated, as they wrote letters whitewashing Reuben Hatch's incredible and lengthy record of criminality and irresponsibility in his duties as an Army quartermaster. The letters reside in the National Archives in Washington DC. Hatch refused three separate subpoenas to appear before Congress and give testimony before dying in 1871, having escaped justice due to his numerous highly placed patrons--including two Republican presidents.

The Destruction Of Pompeii

In the days of the Emperor Titus a catastrophe, among the most awful in ancient history, occurred under the still smoking mountain of Vesuvius. For suddenly, without note or warning, two entire cities—Pompeii and Herculaneum—were wiped from the face of the earth. They were buried alive, and the people perished as they were pursuing their daily work and pleasure, by the eruption of the volcano in their midst. "Day was turned into night and light into darkness: an inexpressible quantity of dust and ashes was poured out, deluging land, sea, air, and burying two entire cities, while the people were sitting in the theatre." So writes an old historian.

Pompeii was an old town near the sea-coast of southern Italy, in a beautiful region under the shadow of Mount Vesuvius. It had been a Greek colony in the old days, when the Greeks occupied most of this part. But at this time—79 A.D.—it had been a Roman colony for some twenty-four years, and was a favorite resort of the Romans. It was a miniature Rome, with its tiny palaces, its forum, its theatre, its circus; a miniature Rome, too, in its luxury, its indolence, its very corruption. Crowded in the glassy bay outside were ships of commerce, and gilded galleys for the pleasure of the rich citizens, while the tall masts of the Roman fleet under the command of Pliny could be seen afar off.

It was the 23rd of November, and the afternoon was wearing on, when from the top of Vesuvius rose a lofty column of black smoke which, after rising high into the air, spread itself out into a cloud in the shape of a giant pine-tree. As the afternoon advanced the cloud increased in size and density, while the mountain cast up ashes and red-hot stones.

Panic-stricken, the inhabitants fled from the city, knowing not which way to turn. By this time the earth was trembling beneath them, and shock after shock of earthquake rent the ground. Darkness now came on, and all through that long black night the terror-stricken people must have made their way towards the seashore and along the coast. The account of these days has come to us, vivid in detail, from the pen of Pliny, who was an eyewitness of the whole thing, and whose uncle, commanding the Roman fleet at the time, died, suffocated by the vapor and flames from the burning mountain.

"Though it was now morning," says Pliny, who was with his mother some fourteen miles from the doomed city of Pompeii, "the light was exceedingly faint and languid. The buildings all around us tottered, and there was a great risk of our being overwhelmed. Then at last we decided on leaving the town. The mass of the inhabitants followed us, terror-stricken, pressing on us and pushing us forwards with their crowded ranks. When we got beyond the buildings we stopped in the midst of a most dangerous and dreadful scene. The sea seemed to roll back upon itself as if driven from its banks by the quaking of the earth, while a black and dreadful cloud, broken by zig-zags of flame, darted out a long train of fire like flashes of lightning, only much larger. The ashes now began to fall upon us. I turned my head and observed behind us a thick smoke, which came rolling after us like a torrent.

"Meanwhile the cloud descended and covered land and sea with a black darkness.

"Save yourself, begged Pliny's mother, thinking this was the end. "I am old and content to die, provided I am not the cause of your death too."

"I will only be saved with you,' answered young Pliny, taking her hand and urging her onwards."

Another shower of ashes and a dense mist now closed them in, and soon night came on. They could hear the shrieks of the women, the children crying for help, and the shouts of the men through the darkness. Ashes and fire still rained down upon them, until at last the dreary night was over. Day dawned; the sun shone faintly through the murky atmosphere, showing the whole country lying under a thick coating of white ashes, as under deep snow.

Though a great number of people escaped, some two thousand were buried by the ashes that completely covered the whole town. For the next fifteen hundred years the buried cities lay wrapped in sleep, their very existence forgotten, their site undiscovered.

Then, in the sixteenth century, a great Italian engineer built an aqueduct right through the ruins of Pompeii. But it was not till two hundred years later that any real discovery took place. Then, by royal orders, men began to dig out the buried ruins of the old towns of Pompeii and Herculaneum. From that day to this digging has gone on at intervals, until now we know just what the old town was like. We can walk over the old streets along which the Romans walked before ever this terrible catastrophe came upon them.

Here, to-day, may be seen the old buildings, houses and villas with paintings on the walls. They are as fresh as if done but yesterday: here are their pavements of mosaic, their baths, their shops, their temples, and the eight gates by which the old city is entered.

The streets are very narrow, and it is clear that only one chariot could pass at a time. Still may be seen the marks of the chariot-wheels, crossing and recrossing each other in the few broad streets, but worn into ruts in the narrow ones.

But perhaps most startling of all the strange things to be seen in this old city of the dead past are the very old Romans themselves. Overtaken suddenly in the midst of life, they were covered with the burning ashes, which hardened on them, encasing the human figure and preserving it through the long ages.

So we see them, lying in the museum which stands at the entrance to the town. Mostly they lie in attitudes of terror, some with a hand across their eyes as if to hide out the dreadful sight, some on the point of flight, having hastily taken off their outer clothing. One girl has yet a ring on her finger, while there is a dog still lying as he lay seventeen hundred years before. As a German poet has said—

The unearthing of Pompeii has revealed much of the ancient habits and customs of the Romans of old in their pleasure-loving days. It has taught us about their houses, their amusements, their clothes, their food. Here are their bake-houses, their loaves of bread, their money, their ornaments; and as we stand in the now deserted streets, looking up to the treacherous mountain above, and away to the blue bay on the other side, we can realise what the old Roman life must have been.

Paul Revere Warns Of British March Toward Lexington & Concord
From the Life of Paul Revere

The first fatal military operation of the American Revolution began at ten p.m. on the night of April 18, 1775, when eight hundred British infantrymen suddenly departed from Boston in rowboats. After rowing across the moonlit Charles River, the British Regulars started marching toward an American militia depot at Concord, Massachusetts, about twelve miles distant.

This nighttime movement of the British army alarmed members of an American spy ring in Boston. Several American spies prepared to leave Boston and travel by various routes to Concord, to warn the militia that the British were coming.

One of the spies, a silversmith named Paul Revere, was assigned to travel to Concord by way of Charlestown and Lexington. While passing through Lexington, Revere would pause to alert two rebel leaders, Samuel Adams and John Hancock, who were staying there.

Unfortunately for Revere, British General Thomas Gage had anticipated that an American spy might use Revere's route to carry a warning from Boston to Concord. The general had already sent parties of mounted British soldiers to wait in ambush along the highways that Revere would be riding.

Unaware of the danger he faced, Paul Revere began his secret mission by arousing several friends to assist him. One friend he sent to light signal lanterns in the belfry of the North Church in Boston, to alarm the Sons of Liberty across the river in Charlestown. Revere told his friend to light two lanterns, to signal that the British were leaving Boston by rowing across the Charles River. If the British had left Boston by land, marching up the south bank of the river, then the signal would have been only one lantern.

While his friend went to the North Church to light the signal lanterns, Revere went home and pulled on his riding boots. He then hurried with two different friends to a dock in the north part of Boston, where he kept a rowboat.

Revere wanted to cross the river a short distance downstream from the place where the British were still completing their own crossing. It was a quiet night and the moon was rising. Revere feared that British sentries might notice the noise of oars working against the wooden thole pins of his boat, so he asked one of his companions to find some rags to muffle the oars. The young man dashed into the night, and soon returned with a petticoat, which was said to be "yet warm from the body of a fair Daughter of Liberty, who was glad to contribute to the cause."

With the oars silenced, Revere's two friends rowed him across the river to Charlestown. On landing they were greeted by the local patriots, who had already been alarmed by the two signal lanterns burning in the belfry of the North Church.

319

Revere borrowed a fast horse from a friend in Charlestown. Before mounting, Revere heard a disturbing report that British officers, heavily armed and well mounted, had passed through Charlestown earlier that day, traveling up the road toward Lexington.

The moon was bright when Revere began his ride toward Lexington and Concord. "It was then about eleven o'clock and very pleasant," he later recalled.

After passing Charlestown Neck, Revere neared a place where the bones of a convicted murderer had hung in chains for many years. Revere wrote, "Nearly opposite where Mark [the murderer] was hung in chains, I saw two men on horseback, under a tree. When I got near them, I discovered they were British officers. One tried to get ahead of me, and the other to take me. I turned my horse very quick, and galloped towards Charlestown Neck, and then pushed for the Medford road. The one who chased me, endeavoring to cut me off, got into a clay pond, near where the new tavern is now built. I got clear of him, and went through Medford, over the bridge, and up to Menotomy. In Medford, I awakened the Captain of the Minute Men; and after that, I alarmed almost every house, till I got to Lexington."

Arriving at the house where John Hancock and Samuel Adams were sleeping, Revere found the place guarded by eight militiamen. The sergeant in charge of the guard told Revere to stop making so much noise. The sergeant was afraid that Revere would awaken the family of Reverend Clark, whose house it was.

"Noise!" shouted Revere." You'll have noise enough before long! The Regulars are coming."

The whole household was awake when Revere made his report to Hancock and Adams.

About half an hour after Revere's arrival, a second member of Revere's spy ring came galloping up to the house. This was William Dawes, who had set out from Boston by a different route. Revere and Dawes joined forces to complete their mission by carrying the alarm to Concord. As they rode side by side up the moonlit highway, they were overtaken by a young man who identified himself as Dr. Samuel Prescott, of Concord. The young doctor, who was headed home after visiting a lady, said that he was a Son of Liberty. When he heard that the British were coming, he volunteered to assist Revere and Dawes in spreading the alarm. He said that most of the homes along the road belonged to militiamen, so the three riders began making plenty of noise, shouting the warning and waking the inhabitants of almost every house they passed.

When the riders had traveled about halfway from Lexington to Concord, Revere later recalled, "Mr. Dawes and the doctor stopped to alarm the people of a house. I was about one hundred rods ahead, when I saw two men." In the moonlight, Revere recognized the holsters and cockades of British officers. Since Revere saw only two enemies, and since he was accompanied by two friends, Revere thought the odds were in his favor. He called to his companions to come up and help him capture the British officers.

As Dr. Prescott rode up in answer to Revere's summons, more mounted soldiers suddenly emerged from the night. "In an instant I was surrounded by four," Revere wrote. "We tried to get past them; but they being armed with pistols and swords, they forced us into the pasture."

Doctor Prescott, who knew the ground, jumped his horse over a low stone wall and escaped. William Dawes, who turned and galloped back down the road toward Lexington, also got away from the British. Revere, spurring his horse across the pasture, was not sure which way to turn. He wrote, "I observed a wood at a small distance, and made for that. When I got there, out started six officers, on horseback, and ordered me to dismount."

Revere decided to surrender. After he dismounted, an officer rode up to him and began asking questions:

`"Sir, may I crave your name?" the officer asked.

"Paul Revere."

"What! Paul Revere?"

"Yes. I am Paul Revere."

The officers seemed to recognize Revere's name. Several of them cried that Revere was a spy and ought to be hung on the spot. Another officer, however, assured Revere that nobody would kill him if he cooperated.

Revere admitted that he was a rebel. He warned his captors, "I have alarmed the country all the way up, and I shall have five hundred men here soon." One of the officers retorted that his side had fifteen hundred men coming, but he looked worried Revere thought.

One of Revere's captors wheeled his horse and rode off to report to his commander, Major Mitchell. The major soon came dashing up to Revere at full gallop. Reigning to a halt Major Mitchell clapped a pistol to his prisoner's head and said, "Revere, I am going to ask some questions, and if you do not give true answers, I shall blow your brains out."

Revere promised to cooperate. He later wrote, "I told him I esteemed myself a man of truth, that he had stopped me on the highway and made me a prisoner. I knew not by what right; I would tell him the truth; I was not afraid.

After Revere had answered many questions truthfully, the major seemed satisfied. Holstering his pistol, the major ordered Revere to mount his horse.

When Revere obeyed, the major seemed annoyed. He snatched the reins from Revere's hands, saying, "By God, sir, you are not to ride with the reins I assure you. He then gave the reins to an officer riding to the right of Revere.

At the major's command, more British soldiers suddenly appeared from bushes, together with four Americans who had been taken prisoner earlier that night. The major ordered all the prisoners to mount their horses; then he rode up to Revere and said, "We are now going towards your friends in Lexington. If you attempt to run, or we are insulted, we will shot you."

The group rode toward Lexington at a brisk trot. The British officers directed many violent threats at Revere, calling him a rebel and a traitor.

The sergeant who held Revere's reins told him, "You are in a critical situation."

Revere answered, "I am sensible of it."

When the group was about half a mile from Lexington, they heard a gun fired in the distance. The major asked what the gunfight signified, and Revere told him that militiamen were firing their guns to alarm the country.

The major then ordered the other four prisoners to dismount. When they obeyed, one of the officers cut the saddles and bridles off their horses, and drove their horses away.

"Now you may go about your business," the major told the four prisoners.

Revere said that he would also like to go about his business, but the major was reluctant to release a confessed spy.

Revere and the British officers rode on toward Lexington until they heard a volley, fired as an alarm signal by the militia at Lexington Meeting House. The major, realizing that he was approaching a large enemy force, asked Revere if there was another route he could follow back toward the British arm, that would allow him to detour around Lexington.

Revere advised him to take the road through Cambridge. He gave the major an honest description of the route, which was likely to lead the British safely back to their army.

When Revere had finished giving his helpful advice, the major turned to the sergeant who held the reins of Revere's horse.

"Is your horse tired?" the major asked.

The sergeant, a big man on a small horse, replied that his horse was very tired.

"Take the prisoner's horse," said the major.

Revere dismounted, and the sergeant took his horse. The officers cut the bridle and saddle from the sergeant's horse, then they rode off toward Cambridge, leaving Revere standing alone on the dark road.

Stagecoach Robbed

The following article was first published in the National Police Gazette on September 29, 1883.

County Clerk George H. Webb, of Louisville, Kentucky, tells the thrilling story of how he and his wife and five other passengers were robbed on a California stagecoach on the 13th of August. The stage was on its way from Madeira to the Yosemite Valley, a two days' ride over the mountains. The passengers besides Mr. and Mrs. Webb were Captain Murray of the British Army, a Mr. Ray and his sister of Buffalo, New York, and the Captains Clayton and Johnson of Fort Smith, Arkansas, and the driver, Bill Stevens, who had made many a trip before without having been compelled to "throw up his hands."

About 11 o'clock in the morning of the second day out, and when the stage was nearing the Yosemite Valley, the horses had just pulled the lumbering wagon to the top of what is known as the highest point of the road, being an elevation of 6,000 feet, and overlooking a tremendous abyss. The passengers were commenting on the grandeur of the scenery, when just as they made a short turn in the road, they were confronted by three masked men armed with shotguns, pistols, and dirks.

"Throw up your hands, every darn one of you!" ordered the leader of the band.

As if by instinct Bill Stevens dropped the reins and put up his hands.

The ladies screamed and one of the robbers said. "Scream away, my pretties, no one will hear you up here."

Mr. Webb, raised in Kentucky and well accustomed to the use of firearms, went back to his hip pocket, but when he looked out the hind end of the stagecoach, he found a gun leveled at his head.

Back went the pistol into his pocket and up went his hands.

"Now then, we will just take you one at a time," one of the villains said. 'This way, my little daisy," and he seized Mr. Webb by the arm and jerked him out of the coach. "Just stand still a few moments and we'll fix you up in a hurry." With his hands in the air Mr. Webb allowed himself to be robbed of his valuables-three hundred dollars in cash and a gold watch.

"We'll take the old gentleman with the cream-colored parasol next," said the leader of the band. "Step this way, please," and Captain Murray, who had fought in several wars and knew no such thing as fear, stepped out and submitted to the relieving process. Two hundred and fifty dollars was the extent of his loss.

Then came Mr. Ray who was held up for three hundred and twenty-five dollars and a fine watch. The two captains from Arkansas came next. Their valuables consisted of primarily drafts and checks. These were taken and shoved down in a big pocket of the leader's coat along with the other plunder.

Up to this time the ladies had not been molested, but while the men were being searched Mrs. Webb slipped off a diamond pin and slipped it into bosom. She was as cool as a refrigerator.

The robbers turned their attention to Bill Stevens. "Now, my hearty," said one of the gang, 'just cut them thar hosses loose and set 'em adrift." Bill was slow about complying, for he had an object in view. He knew that the stage coming from the Yosemite Valley was almost due, and by his "killing" time, assistance might arrive.

"Cut them horses loose, and be darn quick about it," repeated the leader of the robbers, "or there won't be enough of you left to make a mincemeat pie!" Bill saw that they meant business and commenced unhitching, but so slow was he about it that two of the gang drew their dirks and slashed the harness.

Bang! bang! went a couple of pistols in the hands of the villains, and away went four horses at breakneck speed around the curve and down the road.

When the horses were cut loose the coach began to roll back down the hill, and Miss Ray screamed for someone to help her off. Captain Murray requested the bandits to let him assist the lady.

"You are too polite, entirely," was the reply.

After the wagon had come to a stop by itself, one of the robbers, whose dialect indicated that he was a Mexican, noticed that Mrs. Webb had a handsome satchel on her arm. "Ah Senorita," said he, "hand out the bag."

"Here, take it, you old villain," said Mrs. Webb, as she spitefully threw the satchel at the robber's head. He picked it up and then the trio of highwaymen bade the travelers adieu and were off like a flash.

"You don't know how it feels to be gone through by stage robbers until you have passed through it, and then you are glad you got off with your life," said Mr. Webb later. "A man who has never been robbed by a party of mountain bandits always thinks he will show fight and shoot. After he has gone through it he is only too glad someone else didn't shoot."

Vigilante Justice • In California

On America's western frontier, pioneers often organized illegal vigilante movements to establish order in lawless areas. The leaders of these vigilante groups were usually respectable businessmen. William Tell Coleman, who helped to organize the vigilante movement in San Francisco, California, was the owner of an importing business. He was twenty-seven years old in 1851, when the city of San Francisco experienced a crime wave. The city's population was growing explosively as a result of the California Gold Rush, and the small established police force was unable to maintain law and order.

Discussing the problem with other local merchants, Coleman found that most of them opposed the idea of enlarging the police force, since that would mean raising taxes. The merchants also complained that the court system was unreliable, often setting criminals free because of legal technicalities.

On June 10, 1851, Coleman and two hundred other businessmen organized a Committee of Vigilance. They all signed an agreement "to watch, pursue, and bring to justice the outlaws infesting the city, through the regularly constituted courts, if possible, but through more summary process, if necessary."

At the end of their first meeting, the committeemen arranged to meet again in emergency session whenever a member gave a special signal- three taps of the fire-bell. They then adjourned.

William Tell Coleman later wrote:

"Scarcely half an hour had passed before the bell was tapped. On reaching the headquarters I found a number of gentlemen, and soon after (some members] brought in a very large, rough, vicious-looking man called Jenkins, an ex-convict from Sydney, Australia who had been caught in the theft of a safe from a store. He was well known as a desperate character who had frequently evaded justice. The committee was organized immediately into a court, and Jenkins was tried for the offense within an hour. The evidence was overwhelming; he was promptly convicted and sentenced to be hanged that night.

"Jenkins's bearing throughout the trial was defiant and insulting, and he intimated that his rescue by his friends might be expected at any moment. We were notified by our officers that already the roughest and worst characters throughout the city were mustering in force to resist the committee. At the same time, scores of our best citizens came forward and enrolled themselves as members, while others pledged their support in anything we might do.

"I strenuously resisted the proposition to hang Jenkins that night, as I held it cowardly to hang him in the dark in such hot haste. I proposed that he should be held until morning and then hanged in broad daylight as the sun rose."

Coleman's proposal to wait until daylight was put to a vote, and a majority of vigilantes voted to hang Jenkins immediately. According to Coleman:

Seeing that he must be hanged at once, I moved that the prisoner have the benefit of clergy. This was granted, but when the minister was left with him, the hardened criminal heaped the vilest insults upon his venerable head. This hastened his doom, and his career was quickly closed.

"The next morning the work of the Vigilance Committee was hailed throughout the state and hundreds of citizens came forward and tendered their approval of our acts and asked to be enrolled in our ranks. The unexpected arrest and quick execution of Jenkins spread consternation among all his class.

The Governor [of California] issued a proclamation denouncing vigilante violence and maintained a nominal opposition to our committee, but took no active measures against it. Many arrests were made of desperate characters, and where clear proof of murder within the state was lacking, it was decided that banishment or corporal punishment should be the penalty. During the active operations of the committee, four men were hanged, and about thirty were banished."

The Vigilance Committee operated for thirty days, then "finding that the country had been purged of a goodly number of the worst people," it suspended operations. It did not disband, but remained ready to respond to any emergency.

At least two hundred similar vigilante movements were organized throughout the American West during the latter half of the nineteenth century. Between 1860 and 1909, western vigilantes illegally executed at least 511 suspected criminals. Most vigilance committees operated quite openly. One Indiana vigilante group held an annual parade under banners that read, "No expense to the county."

Louis Pasteur Seeks Cure for Rabies
John Risser

When Louis Pasteur was a little boy in the late 1820s, he and the other inhabitants of Arbois in eastern France were terrified by a mad wolf which suddenly appeared in the streets of their village. Its mouth foaming with saliva, the wolf attacked any people it came near, biting them and infecting them with the fatal disease of rabies. Pasteur never forgot that ferocious wolf whose jaws had brought death to his friends and relatives. Throughout his life he would recall the shrieks of the wolf's victims.

When he grew up, Louis Pasteur achieved fame by discovering the part played by microscopic organisms in fermenting wine and in causing diseases in farm animals. By discovering the germs that caused some diseases in chickens and sheep, Pasteur was able to prevent or cure these diseases. Because of his achievements in microbiology he was appointed Director of Scientific Studies at the Ecole Superiure Normale in Paris, France.

As he studied the germs which caused illnesses among animals, his mind often went back to the horrible day in .Arbois when, as a child, he had witnessed the disease of rabies being transmitted from beast to human beings.

Pasteur felt sure that rabies was caused by a germ. He often thought that if he could discover this germ and learn how to tame it, he might be able to prevent or cure one of the most mysterious and terrifying diseases known to mankind. At age sixty in 1882 Pasteur began his search for the rabies germ.

The first step in his quest was to procure some mad dogs in which the germ resided. Since rabid dogs were usually killed as soon as their condition was diagnosed, it was not easy for Pasteur to obtain live rabid animals for study in his laboratory. Eventually he enlisted the help of dog catchers who supplied him with a few infected dogs which he housed in cages next to his laboratory.

As soon as he acquired rabid dogs, Pasteur began to look for the germ which caused rabies. He thought that the most likely place to find it was in the saliva which frothed at the mouths of these dogs.

In obtaining saliva from a dog's mouth, Pasteur needed the assistance of two strong laboratory assistants who held the dog's jaws apart while Pasteur sucked its saliva into a small tube. During this operation Pasteur's face was only inches away from the dog's fangs. He had to be careful to stop sucking before the dog's lethal saliva reached his own mouth.

327

When the lower end of the tube was filled with saliva, Pasteur dropped some of it onto a slide for microscopic examination. He also examined saliva from human patients who were dying from rabies.

After peering into his microscope for several days at specimens of rabid dogs' saliva, Pasteur thought he had probably found what he was looking for. In each specimen of rabid saliva that he inspected he found a minute creature which was shaped like the figure-8. His elation at having found the germ so easily, however, ended abruptly when he and his assistants found the figure-8 creature in the saliva of healthy human beings.

After continuing his microscopic search for several weeks, Pasteur began to despair of ever finding the rabies germ. He gradually came to believe that the germ was too small to be seen even under his powerful microscope. He started referring to it as the rabies "virus," a vague term at that time for any poisonous substance.

Since Pasteur had failed to find the rabies germ, he was unable to advance to the second stage in his study. He had planned that, after finding the germ, he would start a living culture of it which he could use in experiments. Without such a culture he had only one source of the rabies virus: the saliva of his caged mad dogs. Since the rabid dogs usually died from the disease in several weeks, his dog cages were soon empty, leaving him without any of the virus which he needed for his research.

His failure to find a rabies germ, plus his difficulty in keeping a supply of living rabid dogs, greatly discouraged him. For a while he thought that he would have to terminate his study of rabies. His desire to master this mysterious and terrifying disease, however, was strong, and he resolved to overcome the obstacles he had encountered.

In order to obtain more rabies virus, Pasteur had a mad dog lassoed and dragged to his laboratory. It was put into a cage with healthy dogs and was allowed to bite them. The supply of rabid animals was also increased by injecting rabbits and guinea pigs with saliva from mad dogs. Because of the mortality of rabid animals, their numbers had to be constantly replenished.

Pasteur observed that most of the injected animals showed the first symptoms of the disease after an incubation period of two weeks. He also observed that some of the injected rabbits never became rabid. Pasteur came up with a theory to explain both the two-week incubation period and the apparent immunity of some rabbits to the disease.

He had come to believe that rabies was a disease which attacked the nervous system including the brain. He believed that after he and his assistants had injected rabid saliva into healthy animals, it took two weeks for the virus to make its way through the body of an injected animal to its nervous system. He also believed that some viruses got lost in the body of the injected animal and never found their way to the nervous system.

Pasteur, who had been trained as a chemist, not as a physician or biologist, did not trust his own knowledge of physiology or neurology. He consulted with his assistant, Dr. Pierre-Paul-Emile Roux, who was a physician. Pasteur told Roux about his theory that the rabies virus attacked the central nervous system.

Pasteur told Roux that if his theory was correct, then an injection of rabid saliva directly into the brain of a healthy dog would quickly cause it to succumb to rabies.

Roux listened with interest to what Pasteur-was saying. He told Pasteur that it would be simple to introduce saliva directly into a dog's brain. "I can drill a little hole in his skull-without hurting him-without damaging his brain at all. It would be easy," said Roux.

Pasteur, who was no doctor, did not know how simple Roux' s proposed operation was and objected strenuously to Roux's suggestion. "What? Bore a hole right through a dog's skull? Why, you'd hurt the poor beast terribly. You would damage his brain. You would paralyze him. No! I will not permit it."

But Roux, who was taken by Pasteur's idea of injecting rabies virus directly into the brains of laboratory dogs, was unwilling to abandon the idea without testing it. Roux secretly disobeyed Pasteur by chloroforming a dog and drilling a hole through its skull. Roux then inserted a needle through the hole into the dog's brain. With a squeeze of the syringe attached to the needle, Roux injected into the dog's brain, not rabid saliva, but the ground-up remains of the brain of another dog which had just died of rabies.

The next day Roux confessed to Pasteur what he had done. "What?" exclaimed Pasteur. "Where is the poor creature?" When Pasteur saw the dog it was happy and frisky, suffering no ill effects from Roux's operation. Within two days, however, it became rabid and after several weeks it was dead. By transferring the virus from the brain of a dog which had died from rabies, directly into the brain of a healthy dog, Roux had corroborated Pasteur's theory that rabies was a disease of the central nervous system.

Pasteur repeated Roux's experiment far more often than required for scientific proof. Holes were drilled in the skulls of dogs. Diseased neural tissue was injected into the dogs' brains. Dog after dog expired.

Pasteur's assistants complained to him about what they perceived as pointless repetition, which added nothing to their knowledge of rabies. Without giving his assistants any reason for repeating the experiment, Pasteur, nevertheless, urged them to continue doing it. Grudgingly, his assistants obeyed their Director's orders.

Then after several monotonous months there was a break in the repeated routine. One of the dogs came down with the disease as all the other dogs had, but this dog, instead of dying, began to improve a week after being injected. In a month it appeared to be perfectly healthy. Was it now immune? Pasteur wondered. He gave it a shot of neural tissue from a dog which had just died of rabies. Then he carefully watched the recovered dog for the first signs of a recurrence of the disease.

One week passed, then two, and still the dog showed no symptoms of rabies. There was no doubt in Pasteur's mind that this dog was immune. Pasteur knew he was on the verge of success and was jubilant. He knew that if one dog could achieve immunity, so could other dogs.

"We must find a way to *tame* the virus," he said, "so that it is too weak to cause rabies." To weaken the virus, Pasteur's assistants took a small section of the spinal cord of a rabbit which had died of rabies. They dried this bit of spinal cord in a sterilized bottle for fourteen days. When they inoculated healthy dogs with this aged, dried substance, the dogs did not become rabid.

Pasteur said, "Now we'll try drying other pieces of this virulent stuff for shorter periods of time. Since the pieces will have dried less, they will be more virulent than the pieces dried for longer periods."

Pasteur worked out a schedule whereby a dog would be injected first with a weakened, well dried-out bit of the spinal column from a rabid animal. On each succeeding day the dog would be injected with an increasingly more virulent dose. The treatment would continue for fourteen days. On the fourteenth day, the dog would be injected with the most lethal dosage. In following this procedure of gradually increasing the virulence of the doses, Pasteur hoped to slowly build up the dog's resistance to rabies.

When Pasteur administered his fourteen-day treatment to healthy dogs, not one of them showed any of the symptoms of rabies. Next came the supreme test, which Pasteur dreaded administering to the dogs. Roux drilled holes in the skulls of four dogs. Two of these dogs had received the repeated inoculations; two had received no inoculations. Roux then shot the most virulent virus in the laboratory directly into the brains of all four dogs.

A month after Roux had administered his deadly shots, the two inoculated dogs were lively and normal; the two dogs which had not been inoculated were dead. Pasteur had proved that he could immunize dogs against rabies. Presumably, although he had not yet demonstrated that it could be done, people as well as dogs could be immunized.

So far, Pasteur had shown that he could protect dogs against rabies *before* they were infected. He had not yet demonstrated that he could also protect them from the disease *after* they had been bitten by a rabid animal. Pasteur believed that he could prevent the disease from occurring if the animal would be treated during the two-week incubation period following the bite and preceding the onset of the disease in the animal's central nervous system.

In order to test Pasteur's hypothesis, his assistants allowed a mad dog to bite healthy dogs confined in a cage. The bitten dogs were then given the fourteen-day treatment consisting of an initial shot of very weakened virus followed by shots of increasingly greater virulence each day. None of the bitten animals which received the fourteen-day treatment came down with rabies.

Pasteur was almost certain that people bitten by a mad dog could also be saved by his fourteen-day treatment, provided it was administered before the disease had invaded the nervous system.

He knew that many people who might be saved by his treatment were dying daily, but he was not absolutely positive that his treatment would work with human beings. He was afraid to test his treatment with people. He was afraid that something might go wrong, that a patient he would treat would die, that he would be called a murderer.

His dilemma was solved for him when a Mrs. Meister from Alsace burst into his laboratory without an invitation. With her was her nine-year-old son, Joseph, who two days previously had been bitten repeatedly by a mad dog. Because of his wounds Joseph vas barely able to walk.

"Save my boy, Mr. Pasteur," said Mrs. Meister.

"Come back at five," Pasteur told her.

He immediately went to see one of the outstanding physicians in France, a man who was familiar with Pasteur's work with rabies. Pasteur brought the eminent physician to his laboratory to see Mrs. Meister and Joseph. After examining   Joseph, the physician said to Pasteur, "If you do nothing, he will surely die."

The day was July 6, 1885, when the first anti-rabies shot was given to a human being. Joseph received the fourteen experimental shots and then returned to his home in Alsace; he never showed a sign of having rabies.

The news of Joseph Meister's successful treatment by Pasteur spread. People recently bitten by mad dogs turned up at Pasteur's laboratory from all over Europe, hoping that Pasteur could save their lives. Many foreigners who came to his laboratory knew only one French word, "Pasteur."

From Russia came nineteen peasants who had been bitten by a mad wolf nineteen days previously. Since the rabies virus seemed to reach the brain of an animal fourteen days after the animal had been bitten, there was little hope for the survival of these peasants. Because Pasteur's fourteen-day treatment was getting a delayed start, Pasteur gave two injections to each of the peasants every day for seven days. All but three of the peasants survived.

In gratitude for Pasteur's saving the peasants' lives, the Tsar of Russia sent Pasteur the diamond Cross of St. Anne, the highest honor the Russian court could confer. The Tsar also sent Pasteur a hundred thousand francs with which to establish a new research laboratory in Paris, called the *Institut Pasteur*.

The Story Of An Eyewitness
Jack London,

Collier's special Correspondent

Collier's, the National Weekly May 5, 1906

Upon receipt of the first news of the earthquake, Colliers telegraphed to Mr. Jack London—who lives only forty miles from San Francisco—requesting him to go to the scene of the disaster and write the story of what he saw. Mr. London started at once, and he sent the following dramatic description of the tragic events he witnessed in the burning city:

The earthquake shook down in San Francisco hundreds of thousands of dollars worth of walls and chimneys. But the conflagration that followed burned up hundreds of millions of dollars' worth of property. There is no estimating within hundreds of millions the actual damage wrought. Not in history has a modern imperial city been so completely destroyed. San Francisco is gone. Nothing remains of it but memories and a fringe of dwelling-houses on its outskirts. Its industrial section is wiped out. Its business section is wiped out. Its social and residential section is wiped out. The factories and warehouses, the great stores and newspaper buildings, the hotels and the palaces of the nabobs, are all gone. Remains only the fringe of dwelling houses on the outskirts of what was once San Francisco.

Within an hour after the earthquake shock the smoke of San Francisco's burning was a lurid tower visible a hundred miles away. And for three days and nights this lurid tower swayed in the sky, reddening the sun, darkening the day, and filling the land with smoke.

On Wednesday morning at a quarter past five came the earthquake. A minute later the flames were leaping upward. In a dozen different quarters south of Market Street, in the working-class ghetto, and in the factories, fires started. There was no opposing the flames. There was no organization, no communication. All the cunning adjustments of a twentieth century city had been smashed by the earthquake. The streets were humped into ridges and depressions, and piled with the debris of fallen walls. The steel rails were twisted into perpendicular and horizontal angles. The telephone and telegraph systems were disrupted. And the great water-mains had burst. All the shrewd contrivances and safeguards of man had been thrown out of gear by thirty seconds' twitching of the earth-crust.

The Fire Made its Own Draft

By Wednesday afternoon, inside of twelve hours, half the heart of the city was gone. At that time I watched the vast conflagration from out on the bay. It was dead calm. Not a flicker of wind stirred. Yet from every side wind was pouring in upon the city. East, west, north, and south, strong winds were blowing upon the doomed city. The heated air rising made an enormous suck. Thus did the fire of itself build its own colossal chimney through the atmosphere. Day and night this dead calm continued, and yet, near to the flames, the wind was often half a gale, so mighty was the suck.

Wednesday night saw the destruction of the very heart of the city. Dynamite was lavishly used, and many of San Francisco proudest structures were crumbled by man himself into ruins, but there was no withstanding the onrush of the flames. Time and again successful stands were made by the fire-fighters, and every time the flames flanked around on either side or came up from the rear, and turned to defeat the hard-won victory.

An enumeration of the buildings destroyed would be a directory of San Francisco. An enumeration of the buildings undestroyed would be a line and several addresses. An enumeration of the deeds of heroism would stock a library and bankrupt the Carnegie medal fund. An enumeration of the dead-will never be made. All vestiges of them were destroyed by the flames. The number of the victims of the earthquake will never be known. South of Market Street, where the loss of life was particularly heavy, was the first to catch fire.

Remarkable as it may seem, Wednesday night while the whole city crashed and roared into ruin, was a quiet night. There were no crowds. There was no shouting and yelling. There was no hysteria, no disorder. I passed Wednesday night in the path of the advancing flames, and in all those terrible hours I saw not one woman who wept, not one man who was excited, not one person who was in the slightest degree panic stricken.

Before the flames, throughout the night, fled tens of thousands of homeless ones. Some were wrapped in blankets. Others carried bundles of bedding and dear household treasures. Sometimes a whole family was harnessed to a carriage or delivery wagon that was weighted down with their possessions. Baby buggies, toy wagons, and go-carts were used as trucks, while every other person was dragging a trunk. Yet everybody was gracious. The most perfect courtesy obtained. Never in all San Francisco's history, were her people so kind and courteous as on this night of terror.

A Caravan of Trunks

All night these tens of thousands fled before the flames. Many of them, the poor people from the labor ghetto, had fled all day as well. They had left their homes burdened with possessions. Now and again they lightened up, flinging out upon the street clothing and treasures they had dragged for miles.

They held on longest to their trunks, and over these trunks many a strong man broke his heart that night. The hills of San Francisco are steep, and up these hills, mile after mile, were the trunks dragged. Everywhere were trunks with across them lying their exhausted owners, men and women. Before the march of the flames were flung picket lines of soldiers. And a block at a time, as the flames advanced, these pickets retreated. One of their tasks was to keep the trunk-pullers moving. The exhausted creatures, stirred on by the menace of bayonets, would arise and struggle up the steep pavements, pausing from weakness every five or ten feet.

Often, after surmounting a heart-breaking hill, they would find another wall of flame advancing upon them at right angles and be compelled to change anew the line of their retreat. In the end, completely played out, after toiling for a dozen hours like giants, thousands of them were compelled to abandon their trunks. Here the shopkeepers and soft members of the middle class were at a disadvantage. But the working-men dug holes in vacant lots and backyards and buried their trunks.

The Doomed City

At nine o'clock Wednesday evening I walked down through the very heart of the city. I walked through miles and miles of magnificent buildings and towering skyscrapers. Here was no fire. All was in perfect order. The police patrolled the streets. Every building had its watchman at the door. And yet it was doomed, all of it. There was no water. The dynamite was giving out. And at right angles two different conflagrations were sweeping down upon it.

At one o'clock in the morning I walked down through the same section. Everything still stood intact. There was no fire. And yet there was a change. A rain of ashes was falling. The watchmen at the doors were gone. The police had been withdrawn. There were no firemen, no fire-engines, no men fighting with dynamite. The district had been absolutely abandoned. I stood at the corner of Kearny and Market, in the very innermost heart of San Francisco. Kearny Street was deserted. Half a dozen blocks away it was burning on both sides. The street was a wall of flame. And against this wall of flame, silhouetted sharply, were two United States cavalrymen sitting their horses, calming watching. That was all. Not another person was in sight. In the intact heart of the city two troopers sat their horses and watched.

Spread of the Conflagration

Surrender was complete. There was no water. The sewers had long since been pumped dry. There was no dynamite. Another fire had broken out further uptown, and now from three sides conflagrations were sweeping down. The fourth side had been burned earlier in the day. In that direction stood the tottering walls of the Examiner building, the burned-out Call building, the smoldering ruins of the Grand Hotel, and the gutted, devastated, dynamited Palace Hotel.

The following will illustrate the sweep of the flames and the inability of men to calculate their spread. At eight o'clock Wednesday evening I passed through Union Square. It was packed with refugees. Thousands of them had gone to bed on the grass. Government tents had been set up, supper was being cooked, and the refugees were lining up for free meals.

At half past one in the morning three sides of Union Square were in flames. The fourth side, where stood the great St. Francis Hotel was still holding out. An hour later, ignited from top and sides the St. Francis was flaming heavenward. Union Square, heaped high with mountains of trunks, was deserted. Troops, refugees, and all had retreated.

A Fortune for a Horse!

It was at Union Square that I saw a man offering a thousand dollars for a team of horses. He was in charge of a truck piled high with trunks from some hotel. It had been hauled here into what was considered safety, and the horses had been taken out. The flames were on three sides of the Square and there were no horses.

Also, at this time, standing beside the truck, I urged a man to seek safety in flight. He was all but hemmed in by several conflagrations. He was an old man and he was on crutches. Said he: "Today is my birthday. Last night I was worth thirty-thousand dollars. I bought five bottles of wine, some delicate fish and other things for my birthday dinner. I have had no dinner, and all I own are these crutches."

I convinced him of his danger and started him limping on his way. An hour later, from a distance, I saw the truck-load of trunks burning merrily in the middle of the street.

On Thursday morning at a quarter past five, just twenty-four hours after the earthquake, I sat on the steps of a small residence on Nob Hill. With me sat Japanese, Italians, Chinese, and Negroes—a bit of the cosmopolitan flotsam of the wreck of the city. All about were the palaces of the nabob pioneers of Forty–nine. To the east and south at right angles, were advancing two mighty walls of flame.

I went inside with the owner of the house on the steps of which I sat. He was cool and cheerful and hospitable. "Yesterday morning," he said, "I was worth six hundred thousand dollars. This morning this house is all I have left. It will go in fifteen minutes. He pointed to a large cabinet. "That is my wife's collection of china. This rug upon which we stand is a present. It cost fifteen hundred dollars. Try that piano. Listen to its tone. There are few like it. There are no horses. The flames will be here in fifteen minutes."

Outside the old Mark Hopkins residence a palace was just catching fire. The troops were falling back and driving the refugees before them. From every side came the roaring of flames, the crashing of walls, and the detonations of dynamite.

The Dawn of the Second Day

I passed out of the house. Day was trying to dawn through the smoke-pall. A sickly light was creeping over the face of things. Once only the sun broke through the smoke-pall, blood-red, and showing quarter its usual size. The smoke-pall itself, viewed from beneath, was a rose color that pulsed and fluttered with lavender shades Then it turned to mauve and yellow and dun. There was no sun. And so dawned the second day on stricken San Francisco.

An hour later I was creeping past the shattered dome of the City Hall. Than it there was no better exhibit of the destructive force of the earthquake. Most of the stone had been shaken from the great dome, leaving standing the naked framework of steel. Market Street was piled high with the wreckage, and across the wreckage lay the overthrown pillars of the City Hall shattered into short crosswise sections.

This section of the city with the exception of the Mint and the Post-Office, was already a waste of smoking ruins. Here and there through the smoke, creeping warily under the shadows of tottering walls, emerged occasional men and women. It was like the meeting of the handful of survivors after the day of the end of the world.

Beeves Slaughtered and Roasted

On Mission Street lay a dozen steers, in a neat row stretching across the street just as they had been struck down by the flying ruins of the earthquake. The fire had passed through afterward and roasted them. The human dead had been carried away before the fire came. At another place on Mission Street I saw a milk wagon. A steel telegraph pole had smashed down sheer through the driver's seat and crushed the front wheels. The milk cans lay scattered around. All day Thursday and all Thursday night, all day Friday and Friday night, the flames still raged on.

Friday night saw the flames finally conquered, through not until Russian Hill and Telegraph Hill had been swept and three-quarters of a mile of wharves and docks had been licked up.

The Last Stand

The great stand of the fire-fighters was made Thursday night on Van Ness Avenue. Had they failed here, the comparatively few remaining houses of the city would have been swept. Here were the magnificent residences of the second generation of San Francisco nabobs, and these, in a solid zone, were dynamited down across the path of the fire. Here and there the flames leaped the zone, but these fires were beaten out, principally by the use of wet blankets and rugs.

San Francisco, at the present time, is like the crater of a volcano, around which are camped tens of thousands of refugees At the Presidio alone are at least twenty thousand. All the surrounding cities and towns are jammed with the homeless ones, where they are being cared for by the relief committees. The refugees were carried free by the railroads to any point they wished to go, and it is estimated that over one hundred thousand people have left the peninsula on which San Francisco stood. The Government has the situation in hand, and, thanks to the immediate relief given by the whole United States, there is not the slightest possibility of a famine. The bankers and business men have already set about making preparations to rebuild San Francisco.

The 8.3 magnitude earthquake that shook San Francisco on April 18, 1906, at 5:13 am, left 3,000 people dead, 225,000 homeless and 28,000 buildings gutted.

Wreck Of A Slave Ship
Thrilling Narratives Of Mutiny, Murder And Piracy,
A Weird Series Of Tales Of Shipwreck And Disaster,

From The Earliest Part Of The Century To The Present Time,

With Accounts Of Providential Escapes

And

Heart-Rending Fatalities.

The following extract of a letter from Philadelphia, dated November 11th, 1762, gives an account of the melancholy disaster that befell the Phœnix, Capt. M'Gacher, in latitude 37 deg. N. and longitude 72 deg. W. from London, bound to Potomac, in Maryland, from the coast of Africa, with 332 slaves on board.

"On Wednesday the 20th of October 1762, at six o'clock in the evening, came on a most violent gale of wind at south, with thunder and lightning, the sea running very high, when the ship sprung a leak, and we were obliged to lie-to under bare poles, the water gained on us with both pumps constantly working. 10 P. M. endeavored to put the ship before the wind to no purpose. At twelve the sand ballast having choked our pumps, and there being seven feet water in the hold, all the casks afloat, and the ballast shifted to leeward, cut away the rigging of the main and mizen masts, both of which went instantly close by the deck, and immediately after the foremast was carried away about twenty feet above. Hove overboard all our guns, upon which the ship righted a little. We were then under a necessity of letting all our slaves out of irons, to assist in pumping and baling.

"Thursday morning being moderate, having gained about three feet on the ship, we found every cask in the hold stove to pieces, so that we only saved a barrel of flour, 10 lbs. of bread, twenty-five gallons of wine, beer, and shrub, and twenty-five gallons of spirits. The seamen and slaves were employed all this day in pumping and baling; the pumps were frequently choked, and brought up great quantities of sand. We were obliged to hoist one of the pumps up, and put it down the quarter deck hatchway. A ship this day bore down upon us, and, though very near, and we making every signal of distress, she would not speak to us.

"On Friday, the men slaves being very sullen and unruly, having had no sustenance of any kind for forty-eight hours, except a dram, we put one half of the strongest of them in irons.

On Saturday and Sunday, all hands night and day could scarce keep the ship clear, and were constantly under arms.

339

"On Monday morning, many of the slaves had got out of irons, and were attempting to break up the gratings; and the seamen not daring to go down in the hold to clear the pumps, we were obliged, for the preservation of our own lives, to kill fifty of the ringleaders and stoutest of them.

"It is impossible to describe the misery the poor slaves underwent, having had no fresh water for five days. Their dismal cries and shrieks, and most frightful looks, added a great deal to our misfortunes; four of them were found dead, and one drowned herself in the hold. This evening the water gained on us, and three seamen dropped down with fatigue and thirst, which could not be quenched, though wine, rum, and shrub were given them alternately. On Thursday morning the ship had gained, during the night, above a foot of water, and the seamen quite worn out, and many of them in despair. About ten in the forenoon we saw a sail; about two she discovered us, and bore down; at five spoke to us, being the King George, of Londonderry, James Mackay, master; he immediately promised to take us on board, and hoisted out his yawl, it then blowing very fresh. The gale increasing, prevented him from saving anything but the white people's lives, not even any of our clothes, or one slave, the boat being scarcely able to live in the sea the last trip she made. Capt. Mackay and some gentlemen, passengers he had on board, treated us with kindness and humanity."

Remarks By Miss Susan B. Anthony

Debate on woman suffrage in the Senate of the United States, 2d session, 49th Congress, December 8, 1886, and January 25, 1887, by Senators H. W. Blair, J. E. Brown, J. N. Dolph, G. G. Vest, and Geo. F. Hoar

Miss Anthony:

I wish I could state the avocations and professions of the various women who have spoken in our convention during the last three days. Do not wish to speak disparagingly in regard to the men Congress, but I doubt if a man on the floor of either House could have made a better speech than some of those which have been made by women during this convention. Twenty-six states and Territories are represented with live women, traveling all the way from Kansas, Arkansas, Oregon, and Washington Territory. It does seem to me that after all these years of coming up to this Capitol an impression should be made upon the minds of legislators that we are never to be silenced until we gain the demand. We have never had in the whole thirty years of our agitation so many States represented in any convention as we have had this year.

This fact shows the growth of public sentiment Mrs. Duniway is here all the way from Oregon, and you say, when Mrs. Duniway is doing so well up there, and is so hopeful of carrying the State of Oregon, why do not you all rest satisfied with that plan of gaining the suffrage? My answer is that I do not wish to see the women of the thirty-eight States of this Union compelled to leave their homes and canvas each State school district by school district. It is asking too much of a moneyless class of people disfranchised by the constitution of every State in the Union. The joint earnings of the marriage co-partnership in all the states belong legally to the husband. If the wife goes outside the home to work, the law in most of the States permits her to own and control the money thus earned. We have not a single State in the Union where the wife's earnings inside the marriage co-partnership are owned by her. Therefore, to ask the vast majority of women who are thus situated, without an independent dollar of their own, to make a canvass of the States is asking too much.

Mrs. Gougar:

Why did they not ask the Negro to do that?

Miss Anthony:

Of course the Negro was not asked to go begging the white man from school district to school district to get his ballot. If it was known that we could be driven to the ballot-box like a flock of sheep and all vote for one party, there would be a bid made for us; but that is not done because we cannot promise you any such thing; because we stand before you and honestly tell you that the women of this nation are educated equally with the men, and that they too have political opinions. There is not a woman on our platform, there is scarcely a woman in this city of Washington, whether the wife of a Senator of a Congressman--I do not believe you can find a score of women in the whole nation--who have not opinions on the pending Presidential election. We all have opinions; we all have parties. Some of us like ne party and one candidate and some another.

Therefore we cannot promise you that women will vote as a unit when they are enfranchised. Suppose the Democrats shall put a woman-suffrage plank in their platform n their Presidential convention, and nominate an open and avowed friend of woman suffrage to stand upon that platform; we cannot pledge you that all the women of this nation will work for the success of that party nor can I pledge you that they will all vote for the Republican party if it should be the one to take the lead in their enfranchisement. Our women will not toe a mark anywhere; they will think and act for themselves, and when they are enfranchised they will divide upon all political questions, as do intelligent, educated men.

I have tried the experiment of canvassing four States prior to Oregon and in each State with the best canvass that it was possible for us to make we obtained a vote of one-third. One man out of every three men voted for the enfranchisement of the women of their households, while two voted against it. But we are proud to say that our splendid minority is always composed of the very best men of the State and I think Senator Palmer will agree with me that the forty thousand men of Michigan who voted for the enfranchisement of the women of his State were really the picked men in intelligence, in culture in morals, in standing, and in every direction.

It is too much to say that the majority of the voters in any State are superior educated, and capable, or that they investigate every question thoroughly, and cast the ballot thereon intelligently. We all know that the majority of the voters of any State are not of that stamp. The vast masses of the people, the laboring classes, have all they can do in their struggle to get food and shelter for their families. They have very little time or opportunity to study great questions of constitution law.

Because of this impossibility for women to canvass the States over and over to educate the rank and flue of the voters we come to you to ask you to make it possible for the Legislatures of the thirty-eight States to settle the question, where we shall have a few representative men assembled before whom we can make our appeals and arguments.

This method of selling the question by the Legislatures is just as much in the line of States' rights as is that of the popular vote. The one questions before you is, will you insist that a majority of the individual voters of every State must be converted before its women shall have the right to vote or will you allow the matter to be settled by the representative men in the Legislatures of the several States? You need not fear that we shall get suffrage too quickly if Congress shall submit the proposition, for even then we shall have a hard time in going from Legislature of Legislature to secure the two-thirds votes of three-fourths of the States necessary to ratify the amendment. It may take twenty years after Congress has taken the initiative step to make action by the State Legislature possible.

I pray you, gentlemen, that you will make your report to the Senate speedily. I know you are ready to make a favorable one. Some of our speakers may not have known this as well as I. I ask you to make a report and to bring it to a discussion and a vote on the floor of the Senate.

You ask me if we want to press this question to a vote provided there is not a majority to carry it. I say you, because we want the reflex influence of the discussion and of the opinions of Senators to go back into the States to help us to educate the people of the States.

Senator Lapham:

It would require a two-thirds vote in both the House and the Senate to submit the amendment to the State Legislatures for ratification.

Miss Anthony:

I know that it requires a two-thirds vote of both Houses. But still, I repeat, even if you cannot get the two-thirds vote, we ask you to report the bill and bring it to a discussion and a vote at the earliest day possible. We feel that this question should be brought before Congress at every session. We ask this little attention from Congressmen whose salaries are paid from the taxes; women do their share for the support of this great Government. We think we are entitled to two or three days of each session of Congress in both the Senate and House. Therefore I ask of you to help us to a discussion in the Senate this session. There is no reason why the Senate, composed of seventy-six of the most intelligent and liberty-loving men of the nation, shall not pass the resolution by a two-thirds vote. I really believe it will do so if the friends on this committee and on the floor of the Senate will champion the measure as earnestly as if it were to benefit themselves instead of their mothers and sisters.

Gentlemen, I thank you for this hearing granted, and I hope the telegraph wires will soon tell us that your report is presented, and that a discussion is inaugurated on the floor of the Senate.

Abraham Lincoln

Abraham Lincoln, the sixteenth president of the United States, was the son of poor parents, and his childhood and youth were full of trial and hardship.

His father, Thomas Lincoln, was a pioneer farmer in Kentucky; and there, in a one-roomed log cabin of the poorer sort, Abraham Lincoln was born on February 12, 1809.

His mother was Nancy, the daughter of Joseph Hanks, a neighbor who was also trying to earn a livelihood out of the soil. Abraham had also one sister, of whom not much has been recorded.

As there was little to encourage his stay in Kentucky, Abraham's father moved into Indiana, and built a log cabin in the midst of the forest at Pigeon Creek. Here most of Lincoln's boyhood was passed.

In 1818, Mrs. Lincoln died, and Abraham Lincoln was left motherless.

Eighteen months later his father married Mrs. Sarah Bush Johnston, a widow who had been a neighbor in Kentucky. She was a good woman and treated Abraham with the same care and tenderness which she showed to her own children.

Abraham Lincoln formed a strong attachment for his step-mother, which lasted all through his life. She was really able to do more for him than his own mother had been. He was not only better clothed and better fed; but he also had considerable help in his struggle for an education.

By the time he was ten he was working hard to help his father to clear some land and turn a little piece of the forest into a farm. He had little or no schooling. He once said, later on in life, that he did not think that all his schooling as a lad amounted to more than six months.

He learned to write by using a charred stick for a pencil, and a piece of board for a slate. There were no books in his home excepting a Bible, a catechism and a spelling book.

But he would walk miles to borrow a book, and he read with great care everything that he could find. He thus gathered a store of information that was of service to him throughout his wonderful career.

At sixteen years of age he had almost reached the height of six feet and four inches for which he was noted in after years.

His bodily strength was very great, and his services were very much in demand. He did everything he could to help his parents.

In 1830 the Lincoln family moved into Illinois and from that time their fortunes began to improve.

Lincoln was now twenty-one. One who knew him well at that time, thus describes his personal appearance: "He was tall, angular, and ungainly, and wore trousers made of flax and tow, cut tightly at the ankles and loosely at the knees. He was very poor, but was welcome in every house in the neighborhood."

He built a flatboat, with his father's consent, and carried a load of farm produce down the river to market. It was on this trip that he earned his first dollar by carrying two gentlemen and their trunks out to a steamer on the Ohio, a fact of which he was very proud and of which he often spoke in after years.

He afterwards made other trips as a boatman and was very successful in them. It was on one of these trips that he witnessed, in New Orleans, the brutality of the slave trade. This led him to say, "If ever I get a chance to hit that institution, I'll hit it hard."

He next entered the employ of a Mr. Offutt who put him in charge of a general store at New Salem.

While tending this More, Lincoln once sold to a woman goods for which she paid the amount of two dollars, six and a quarter cents. He discovered later that a mistake had been made, and that the store owed the customer the six and a quarter cents. After he had closed the store that night, he walked several miles in the darkness to return the amount.

At another time a woman bought a pound of tea. Lincoln discovered the next morning that a smaller weight was on the scales. He at once weighed out the remainder, and walked some distance before breakfast to deliver it.

It was by such deeds as these that he earned the name of "Honest Abe." He gained the good will of his neighbors who called upon him to settle their disputes, and always found him fair and upright in his decisions.

Misfortune overtook Mr. Offutt and Lincoln entered the service of the state of Illinois in what is known as the Black Hawk War. He was elected captain of the company, but neither he nor his men were called upon to do any actual fighting.

At the close of the war he returned to New Salem, and was urged to become a member of the legislature of Illinois; but he failed to be elected.

Like Washington he took up the business of a surveyor. In 1833 he was made postmaster of New Salem. In the following year, 1834, another election of the members of the state legislature took place, and this time he was successful and became a member for Sangamon County.

The two political parties were then known as the Democrats and the Whigs, and Lincoln belonged to the Whigs.

He was still so poor that he was obliged to borrow money with which to purchase suitable clothing before he could take his seat in the House.

His entering the legislature was an important event in his life. The capital of the state was soon afterwards changed from Vandalia to Springfield; and Lincoln who was rapidly rising into fame took up the study of law.

As a lawyer he was decidedly successful. He formed several partnerships with lawyers of eminence, and his days of biting poverty were over.

He still continued his general studies and became one of the best informed men in the state. He gave his first legal fee to his step-mother in the shape of one hundred and sixty acres of land, in memory of her great kindness to him as a boy.

In November, 1842, Abraham Lincoln married Miss Mary Todd, of Lexington, Kentucky, and the next ten years were the happiest of his whole life. In 1846 he was elected a member of the United States Congress. He took his seat in the House of Representatives at Washington on December 6th, of that year.

His first important speech in Congress was one in which he denounced the war then being carried on between the United States and Mexico; a speech in which he dealt the pro-slavery party a severe blow.

At the end of his first term in Congress Mr. Lincoln determined not to seek re-election. He therefore returned to Springfield and resumed the practice of law.

When, in 1854, a bill was passed which put aside the Missouri Compromise and gave greater powers to the friends of slavery, Lincoln again entered politics. He became a candidate for the Illinois legislature and was elected.

Mr. Stephen A. Douglas was then at the height of his power, and was bitterly opposed to Lincoln.

In 1860, with Douglas as his most formidable competitor, Mr. Lincoln was elected president; and in February 1861, he left Springfield for Washington and was duly inaugurated in March of that year.

In the election of Abraham Lincoln as president the South feared that the institution of slavery was in the gravest danger; and they put forth every possible effort for its defense.

Some of the Southern states voted to secede from the Union, Fort Sumter was fired upon, and the terrible Civil War began.

Lincoln called for men, and readily obtained them. It is to the honor of Mr. Douglas that when he saw the real danger in which the country stood, he acknowledged himself in the wrong and became one of Lincoln's friends and supporters.

This war, sometimes called the "War of the Union," lasted from 1861 to 1865. It was the saddest event in the history of our land; and every American boy and girl should make a careful study of its details from the fall of Fort Sumter to the surrender of General Lee at Appomattox.

These were trying days for President Lincoln; and at times his sufferings were intense. But he never flinched from what he felt to be his duty; and he was warmly supported by the generals, the army, and the people of the North.

During the progress of the war, after due warning, he issued his famous Emancipation Proclamation; and on January 1, 1863, most of the slaves in the South were declared free.

In 1864, the year before the close of the war, Abraham Lincoln was again elected president; and on March 4, 1865, he entered upon his second term of office. His majority at his second election was the largest ever given to any president up to that time.

When the war closed there was great rejoicing; and on April 11, two days after Lee's surrender, Lincoln made a speech in Congress in which he strongly urged that the states which had seceded should be treated with leniency and restored to their proper relations to the central government as quickly and as quietly as possible.

On April 14, 1865, the fourth anniversary of the fall of Fort Sumter, a general holiday was observed; and in the evening the President attended a special performance in Ford's theatre.

During the progress of the performance a retired actor gained access to the president's box and, placing a pistol over Lincoln's chair, shot him through the head.

The assassin escaped amid the general confusion, but was discovered, a few days later, in lower Maryland while hiding in a barn. He refused to surrender, and was shot dead by one of the soldiers who had been sent to capture him.

Lincoln's Assassination

Day Of The Assassination

Lincoln's day started well for the first time in a long time; he woke up cheerful. Senator James Harlan remembered taking a drive with the Lincolns only days before the president's assassination, and found him transformed. "His whole appearance, poise and bearing had marvelously changed. He was, in fact, transfigured. That indescribable sadness which had previously seemed to be an adamantine element in his very being, had been suddenly exchanged for an equally indescribable expression of serene joy as if conscious that the great purpose of his life had been achieved." Hugh McCulloch, the new Secretary of the Treasury, remarked that on that morning, "I never saw Mr. Lincoln so cheerful and happy". Edwin M. Stanton said: "At the earliest moment yesterday, the President called a cabinet meeting, at which Gen. Grant was present. He was more cheerful and happy than I had ever seen him. He rejoiced at the near prospect of a firm and durable peace at home and abroad, which manifested in a marked degree the soundness and honesty of his disposition, and the tender and forgiving spirit that so eminently distinguished him." No one could miss the difference. For months, the President had looked pale and haggard. Lincoln himself told people how happy he was. This caused First Lady Mary Todd Lincoln some concern, as she believed that saying such things out loud was bad luck. Lincoln paid her no heed. Lincoln told members of his cabinet that he had dreamed that he was on a "singular and indescribable vessel that was moving with great rapidity toward a dark and indefinite shore." He also revealed that he'd had the same dream repeatedly on previous occasions, before "nearly every great and important event of the War" such as the victories at Antietam, Murfreesboro, Gettysburg and Vicksburg.

At around noon while visiting Ford's Theatre to pick up his mail (Booth had a permanent mailbox there), Booth learned from the brother of John Ford, the owner, that the President and General Grant would be attending the theatre to see *Our American Cousin* that night. Booth determined that this was the perfect opportunity for him to do something "decisive". He knew the theater's layout, having performed there several times, as recently as the previous month.

That same afternoon, Booth went to Mary Surratt's boarding house in Washington, D.C. and asked her to deliver a package to her tavern in Surrattsville, Maryland. He also requested Surratt to tell her tenant who resided there to have the guns and ammunition that Booth had previously stored at the tavern ready to be picked up later that evening. She complied with Booth's requests and made the trip, along with Louis J. Weichmann, her boarder and son's friend.

This exchange, and her compliance in it, would lead directly to Surratt's execution three months later.

At seven o'clock that evening, John Wilkes Booth met for a final time with all his fellow conspirators. Booth assigned Lewis Powell to kill Secretary of State William H. Seward at his home, George Atzerodt to kill Vice President Andrew Johnson at his residence, the Kirkwood Hotel, and David E. Herold to guide Powell to the Seward house and then out of Washington to rendezvous with Booth in Maryland. Booth planned to shoot Lincoln with his single-shot Derringer and then stab Grant with a knife at Ford's Theatre. They were all to strike simultaneously shortly after ten o'clock that night. Atzerodt wanted nothing to do with it, saying he had only signed up for a kidnapping, not a killing. Booth told him he was in too far to back out.

Booth Shoots President Lincoln

Contrary to the information Booth had overheard, General and Mrs. Grant had declined the invitation to see the play with the Lincolns, as Mrs. Lincoln and Mrs. Grant were not on good terms. Several other people were invited to join them, until finally Major Henry Rathbone and his fiancée Clara Harris (daughter of New York Senator Ira Harris) accepted.

Lincoln told Speaker Schuyler Colfax, "I suppose it's time to go though I would rather stay." He assisted Mary into the carriage and they took off.

There is evidence to suggest that either Booth or his fellow conspirator Michael O'Laughlen, who looked similar, followed Grant and his wife Julia to Union Station late that afternoon and discovered that Grant would not be at the theater that night. Apparently, O'Laughlen boarded the same train the Grants took to Philadelphia in order to kill Grant. An alleged attack during the evening took place; however, the assailant was unsuccessful since the private car that the Grants were riding in had been locked and guarded by porters.

The Lincoln party arrived late and settled into the Presidential Box, which was actually two corner box seats with the dividing wall between them removed. The play was stopped briefly and the orchestra played "Hail to the Chief" as the audience gave the president a rousing standing ovation. Ford's Theatre was full with 1,700 in attendance. Mrs. Lincoln whispered to her husband, who was holding her hand, "What will Miss Harris think of my hanging on to you so?" The president smiled and replied, "She won't think anything about it. Those were the last words ever spoken by Abraham Lincoln, although Lincoln reportedly later told her he desired to visit the Holy Land, with the president's last words being, "There is no place I so much desire to see as Jerusalem."

The box was supposed to be guarded by a policeman named John Frederick Parker who, by all accounts, was a curious choice for a bodyguard. During the intermission, Parker went to a nearby tavern with Lincoln's footman and coachman. It is unclear whether he ever returned to the theatre, but he was certainly not at his post when Booth entered the box. Nevertheless, even if a policeman had been present it is questionable at best as to whether he would have denied entry to the Presidential Box to a premier actor such as John Wilkes Booth - Booth's celebrity status meant that his approach did not warrant any questioning from audience members, who assumed he was coming to call on the President.

About 10:25 pm, a man came in and walked slowly along the side on which the "Pres" box was and I heard a man say, "There's Booth" and I turned my head to look at him. He was still walking very slow and was near the box door when he stopped, took a card from his pocket, wrote something on it, and gave it to the usher who took it to the box. In a minute the door was opened and he walked in.

Upon gaining access through the first door of the entry to the Presidential Box, Booth barricaded the inward-swinging door behind him with a wooden stick that he wedged between the wall and the door. He then turned around, and looked through the tiny peep-hole he had carved in the second door (which granted entry to the Presidential Box) earlier that day.

Although he had never starred in the play itself, Booth knew the play by heart, and thus waited for the precise moment when actor Harry Hawk would be on stage alone to speak what was considered the funniest line of the play. Booth hoped to employ the enthusiastic response of the audience to muffle the sound of his gunshot. With the stage to himself, Asa Hawk responded to the recently departed Mrs. Mountchessington, "Don't know the manners of good society, eh? Well, I guess I know enough to turn you inside out, old gal; you sockdologizing old man-trap!" Hysterical laughter began permeating the theatre.

Lincoln was laughing at this line when he was shot.

Booth opened the door, crept forward and shot the President at point-blank range, mortally wounding him. The bullet struck the back of Lincoln's head behind his left ear, entered his skull, fractured part of it badly and went through the left side of his brain before lodging just above his right eye almost exiting the other side of his head. Lincoln immediately lost consciousness. Lincoln slumped over in his rocking chair, and then backward. Mary reached out, caught him, and then screamed when she realized what had happened.

Upon hearing the gunshot, Rathbone thought Booth shouted a word that sounded like "Freedom!" He quickly jumped from his seat and tried to prevent Booth from escaping, grabbing and struggling with him. Booth dropped the pistol on the floor and drew a knife, stabbing the major violently in the left forearm and reaching the bone. Rathbone quickly recovered and again tried to grab Booth as he was preparing to jump from the sill of the box. He grabbed onto Booth's coat causing Booth to vault over the rail of the box down to the stage below (about a twelve-foot drop). In the process, Booth's right boot struck the framed engraving of Washington, turning it completely over and his riding spur became entangled on the Treasury flag decorating the box, and he landed awkwardly on his left foot. He raised himself up despite the injury and began crossing the stage, making the audience believe that he was part of the play. Booth held his bloody knife over his head, and yelled something to the audience.

While it is widely believed that Booth shouted "*Sic semper tyrannis!*" (the <u>*Virginia*</u> state motto, meaning "Thus always to tyrants" in Latin) in the box, or when he landed on the stage, it's not actually clear whether the traditionally-cited quote by Booth is accurate. There are different "earwitness" accounts of what he said. While most witnesses recalled hearing Booth shout "Sic semper tyrannis!" others — including Booth himself — claimed that he only yelled "Sic semper!" Some didn't recall hearing Booth shout anything in Latin.

What Booth shouted in English is also muddied by varying recollections. Some witnesses said he shouted "The South is avenged!" Others thought they heard him say "Revenge for the South!" or "The South shall be free!" Two said Booth yelled "I have done it!"

While the audience were yet to realize what had happened, Maj. Joseph B. Stewart, a lawyer, rose instantly upon seeing Booth land on the stage and he climbed over the orchestra pit and footlights, and started pursuing Booth across the stage. Mary Lincoln's and Clara Harris' screams and Rathbone's cries of "Stop that man!" caused the rest of the audience to realize that Booth's actions were not part of the show, and pandemonium immediately broke out.

Some of the men in the audience chased after him when they noticed what was going on, but failed to catch him. Booth ran across the stage just when Rathbone shouted and exited out the side door. On his way, he bumped into William Withers, Jr., the orchestra leader, and Booth stabbed at Withers with a knife.

Upon leaving the building, Booth approached the horse he had waiting outside. Booth struck Joseph "Peanuts" (also called "Peanut Johnny")[1] Burroughs, who was holding Booth's horse in the forehead with the handle of his knife, leaped onto the horse, apparently also kicking Burroughs in the chest with his good leg, and rode away.

Death of President Lincoln

Charles Leale, a young Army surgeon doctor on liberty for the night, and attending the play, made his way through the crowd to the door at the rear of the Presidential box when he saw Booth finish his performance to the audience and saw the blood on Booth's knife. The door would not open. Finally, Rathbone saw a notch carved in the door and a wooden brace jammed there to hold the door shut. Rathbone shouted to Leale, who stepped back from the door, allowing Rathbone to remove the brace and open the door.

Leale entered the box to find Rathbone bleeding profusely from a deep gash in his chest that ran the length of his upper left arm as well as a long slash in his arm. Nonetheless, he passed Rathbone by and stepped forward to find Lincoln slumped in his chair, held up by Mary, who was sobbing and could not control herself. The President was paralyzed, and barely breathing. Leale lowered the President to the floor believing that Lincoln had been stabbed in the shoulder with the knife. A second doctor in the audience, Charles Sabin Taft, was lifted bodily from the stage over the railing and into the box.

Taft and Leale cut away Lincoln's blood-stained collar and opened his shirt, and Leale, feeling around by hand, discovered the bullet hole in the back of his head right next to his left ear. Leale attempted to remove the bullet, but the bullet was too deep in his head and instead Leale dislodged a clot of blood in the wound. Consequently, Lincoln's breathing improved. Leale learned that if he continued to release more blood clots at a specific time, Lincoln would breathe more naturally. Then Leale saw that the bullet was lodged in Lincoln's skull. Leale finally announced that it made no difference: "His wound is mortal. It is impossible for him to recover."

The Petersen House

Leale, Taft, and another doctor from the audience, Albert_King, quickly consulted and decided that while the President must be moved, a bumpy carriage ride across town to the White House was out of the question. After briefly considering Peter Taltavull's Star Saloon next door, they chose to carry Lincoln across the street and find a house. The three doctors and some soldiers who had been in the audience carried the President out the front entrance of Ford's Theatre. Rain fell down upon the crowd that carried Lincoln outside the theater.

Across the street, a man was holding a lantern and calling "Bring him in here! Bring him in here!" The man was Henry Safford, a boarder at William Petersen's boarding house known today as the Petersen House. The men carried Lincoln into the boarding house and into the first-floor bedroom where they laid him diagonally across the bed because his tall frame would not fit normally on the smaller bed.

A vigil began at the Petersen House. Using a probe, Barnes located some fragments of Lincoln's skull and discovered the bullet was still in his skull. Robert Lincoln, home at the White House that evening, arrived at the Petersen House after being told of the shooting at about midnight. Tad Lincoln was not allowed to go to the Petersen House, although he was at Grover's Theatre when the play was interrupted to report the news of the President's assassination.

Secretary of the Navy Gideon Welles and United States Secretary of War Edwin M. Stanton came and took charge of the scene. Mary Lincoln was so unhinged by the experience of the assassination that Stanton ordered her out of the room by shouting, "Take that woman out of here and do not let her in here again!" While Mary Lincoln sobbed in the front parlor, Stanton set up shop in the rear parlor, effectively running the United States government for several hours, sending and receiving telegrams, taking reports from witnesses, and issuing orders for the pursuit of Booth. For most of the night, Leale held the president's hand, and afterwards said that "sometimes, recognition and reason return just before departure. I held his hand firmly to let him know, in his blindness, that he had a friend."

Lincoln died at 7:22:10 a.m. on April 15, 1865. He was 56 years old. According to Lincoln's secretary John Hay, at the moment of Lincoln's death, "a look of unspeakable peace came upon his worn features".

Mary Lincoln was not present at the time of his death and neither were his children. The crowd around the bed knelt for a prayer. When they were finished, Stanton made a statement, though there is some disagreement among historians as to what exactly the statement was. All agree that he began "Now he belongs to the ..." with some stating he finished with *ages* while others believe he finished with *angels*. Hermann Faber, an Army medical illustrator, was brought into the room immediately after Lincoln's body was removed so that Faber could visually document the scene.

Though some experts have disagreed, Dr. Leale's treatment of Lincoln has been considered good for its time. He was honored for his efforts to save the President by participating in various capacities during the funeral ceremonies.

The Battle Of Gettysburg

The day after Jackson was wounded the battle of Chancellorsville continued, and ended in a second victory for the Confederates. On the 4th and 5th the fighting was again renewed. Then the Federals retired across the Rappahannock to their former camping ground unmolested, the Confederates being too exhausted to pursue them.

After Fredericksburg the Confederates had rejoiced. After Chancellorsville they rejoiced still more, and they made up their minds to carry the war into the northern states. So leaving part of his army under General J. E. B. Stuart to prevent the Federals pursuing him Lee marched into Pennsylvania. But General Stuart was unable to hold the Federals back, and they were soon in pursuit of Lee.

At Chancellorsville Hooker had shown that although he was a splendid fighting general he was a poor commander-in-chief, and towards the end of June, while the army was in full cry after the foe, General George Gordon Meade was made commander-in-chief. Meade continued the pursuit, and Lee, seeing nothing for it, gave up his plans of invasion, and turned to meet the foe.

The two forces met near the little town of Gettysburg in Pennsylvania, and a great three-day' battle took place.

The fighting began on the first of July when the Federal army was still widely scattered through the country, and Meade himself far in the rear, and again the Confederates triumphed.

Late that night General Meade arrived upon the field, and began to make preparations for the struggle on the morrow. On both sides the commanders and armies seemed to feel that a great turning point of the war had come, and they bent all their energies on winning. Both camps were early astir, yet each side seemed to hesitate to begin the fearful game, and put fortune to the test. So the morning passed quietly, the hot silence of the summer day being broken only now and again by fitful spurts of firing.

Late in the afternoon at length the Confederates attacked, and soon the battle raged fiercely. The fight swung this way and that, first the one side and then the other gaining ground here, losing it there. When night came the position was little changed. The advantage still lay with the Confederates.

Next day there was no hesitation. Both sides knew that the deadly duel must be fought to the close, and at dawn the roll and thud of cannon began. From hill to hill gun answered gun, shells screamed and hissed, and the whole valley seemed to be encircled with flame and smoke. But the Confederates gained nothing. The Federals stood firm.

At length Lee determined to make a mighty effort to smash the center of the Federal line, and split it in two. Collecting about a hundred and fifty guns he massed them along a height named Seminary Ridge, and with these he pounded the Federals on Cemetery Hill opposite. For two hours the terrible cannonade lasted. At first the Federal guns replied vigorously, then they almost ceased. They ceased, not because they had been put out of action, not because ammunition was running short, but because Meade was reserving his strength for the infantry attack he knew must come.

In the Confederate camp there was strained anxiety. Lee had determined to make the attack, but General Longstreet was against it. He did not believe that it could succeed. It was, he felt sure, only the useless throwing away of brave lives, and his heart was wrung with sorrow at the thought. But Lee insisted, and General George E. Pickett's division was chosen to make the attempt.

So Longstreet gave way. But when Pickett came to him for last orders he could not speak; he merely nodded his head, and turned away with a sob.

Pickett, however, knew neither hesitation nor fear.

"Sir," he said firmly, "I shall lead my division forward."

Again Longstreet gave a sign, and Pickett, gallant and gay, rode off "into the jaws of death." Erect and smiling, his cap set rakishly over one ear, his brown-gold hair shining in the sun, he seemed, said Longstreet long after, more like a "holiday soldier" than a general about to lead a desperate and almost hopeless attack.

The Federal lines were a mile away. Towards them, towards the bristling row of guns, the men marched steadily, keeping step as if on parade, their banners fluttering gaily, and their bayonets glittering in the sunshine. Confident and elated they swept on. They were out to win not merely the battle but the war, and they meant to do it.

Half the distance was covered. Then the Federal guns spoke. Crashing and thundering they tore great gaps in the approaching column. Still the men moved on steadily, resistlessly, until they came within musket range. Then on a sudden the whole Federal line became as it were a sheet of flame and smoke, and the first line of the advancing Confederates seemed to crumble away before the fearful fusillade. But the second line came on only faster and yet faster, firing volley after volley, scattering frightful death as they came.

Nothing could stay their impetuous charge. On they came right up to the rifle pits. In a rush they were across them, and over the barricades. Then with a yell of victory they threw themselves upon the guns, bayoneting the gunners. Leaping upon the barricade a man held aloft the Confederate flag, waving it in triumphant joy. The next instant he fell mortally wounded, and the flag, bloodstained and torn, was trampled underfoot.

The Confederate success was only the success of a moment. The handful of heroic men who had reached the Federal guns could not hope to hold them. They died gallantly. That was all.

A storm of shot and shell tore its way through the still advancing ranks. It became an ordeal of fire too great for even the bravest to face. The lines at length wavered, they broke, and the men were scattered in flight. Thousands lay dead and dying on the field, many surrendered and were taken prisoner, and of the fifteen thousand gallant soldiers who had set forth so gaily, only a pitiful remnant of thirteen hundred blood-stained, weary men at length reached their own lines.

This gallant and hopeless charge brought the battle of Gettysburg to an end. It brought victory to the Federal side, and the Confederates slowly retired into Virginia once more.

Yet the victory was not very great nor in any way decisive, and the cost of life had been frightful. Indeed, so many brave men had fallen upon this dreadful field that the thought came to the Governor of the state that it would be well to make a portion of it into a soldiers' burial place and thus consecrate it forever as holy ground. All the states whose sons had taken part in the battle willingly helped, and a few months after the battle it was dedicated. And there President Lincoln made one of his most beautiful and famous speeches.

Gettysburg Address

Abraham Lincoln, given to John Nicolay

It has been claimed that Lincoln gave the earliest draft to his private secretary John Nicolay. The Nicolay copy is often called the "first draft."

Four score and seven years ago our fathers brought forth, upon this continent, a new nation, conceived in liberty, and dedicated to the proposition that "all men are created equal"

Now we are engaged in a great civil war, testing whether that nation, or any nation so conceived, and so dedicated, can long endure. We are met on a great battle field of that war. We have come to dedicate a portion of it, as a final resting place for those who died here, that the nation might live. This we may, in all propriety do. But, in a larger sense, we can not dedicate—we can not consecrate—we can not hallow, this ground—The brave men, living and dead, who struggled here, have hallowed it, far above our poor power to add or detract. The world will little note, nor long remember what we say here; while it can never forget what they did here.

It is rather for us, the living, to stand here, we here be dedicated to the great task remaining before us—that, from these honored dead we take increased devotion to that cause for which they here, gave the last full measure of devotion—that we here highly resolve these dead shall not have died in vain; that the nation, shall have a new birth of freedom, and that government of the people by the people for the people, shall not perish from the earth

Gettysburg Address

Abraham Lincoln, given to John Hay

This draft was given to Lincoln's secretary John Hay. The Hay copy, which is sometimes referred to as the "second draft", was made either on the morning of its delivery, or shortly after Lincoln's return to Washington.

Four score and seven years ago our fathers brought forth, upon this continent, a new nation, conceived in Liberty, and dedicated to the proposition that all men are created equal.

Now we are engaged in a great civil war, testing whether that nation, or any nation, so conceived, and so dedicated, can long endure. We are met here on a great battle field of that war. We are now have come to dedicate a portion of it as the a final resting place of for those who here gave their lives that that nation might live. It is altogether fitting and proper that we should do this.

But in a larger sense we can not dedicate—we can not consecrate—we can not hallow this ground. The brave men, living and dead, who struggled here, have consecrated it far above our ^poor power to add or detract. The world will little note, nor long remember, what we say here, but can never forget what they did here. It is for us, the living, rather to be dedicated here to the unfinished ^work which they have, thus far, so nobly carried on. It is rather for us to be here dedicated to the great task remaining before ^us—that from these honored dead we take increased devotion to the that cause for which they here gave gave the last full measure of devotion—that we here highly resolve that these dead shall not have died in vain; that this nation shall have a new birth of freedom; and that this government of the people, by the people, for the people, shall not perish from the earth.

Gettysburg Address

Abraham Lincoln, given to Edward Everett

Mr. Edward Everett was collecting the speeches given at the Gettysburg dedication into one bound volume to sell for the benefit of stricken soldiers at New York's Sanitary Commission Fair. The Everett copy, also known as the "Everett-Keyes" copy, was sent by President Lincoln to Edward Everett in early 1864.

Four score and seven years ago our fathers brought forth upon this continent, a new nation, conceived in Liberty, and dedicated to the proposition that all men are created equal.

Now we are engaged in a great civil war, testing whether that nation, or any nation so conceived, and so dedicated, can long endure. We are met on a great battle-field of that war. We have come to dedicate a portion of that field, as a final resting place for those who here gave their lives, that that nation might live. It is altogether fitting and proper that we should do this.

But, in a larger sense, we cannot dedicate—we cannot consecrate—we cannot hallow—this ground. The brave men, living and dead, who struggled here, have consecrated it far above our poor power to add or detract. The world will little note, nor long remember, what we say here, but it can never forget what they did here. It is for us the living, rather, to be dedicated here to the unfinished work which they who fought here, have, thus far, so nobly advanced. It is rather for us to be here dedicated to the great task remaining before us—that from these honored dead we take increased devotion to that cause for which they here gave the last full measure of devotion—that we here highly resolve that these dead shall not have died in vain—that this nation, under God, shall have a new birth of freedom—and that, government of the people, by the people, for the people, shall not perish from the earth.

Gettysburg Address

Abraham Lincoln, given to George Bancroft

Mr. George Bancroft requested this copy for inclusion in "Autograph Leaves of Our Country's Authors", which he planned to sell at a Soldiers' and Sailors' Sanitary Fair in Baltimore. However it was unacceptable for "Autograph Leaves" as it was written on both sides of the paper, and Lincoln was asked to produce a more suitable copy.

Four score and seven years ago our fathers brought forth, on this continent, a new nation, conceived in Liberty, and dedicated to the proposition that all men are created equal.

Now we are engaged in a great civil war, testing whether that nation, or any nation so conceived, and so dedicated, can long endure. We are met on a great battle-field of that war. We have come to dedicate a portion of that field, as a final resting-place for those who here gave their lives, that that nation might live. It is altogether fitting and proper that we should do this.

But, in a larger sense, we can not dedicate—we can not consecrate—we can not hallow—this ground. The brave men, living and dead, who struggled here, have consecrated it far above our poor power to add or detract. The world will little note, nor long remember what we say here, but it can never forget what they did here. It is for us the living, rather, to be dedicated here to the unfinished work which they who fought here have thus far so nobly advanced. It is rather for us to be here dedicated to the great task remaining before us—that from these honored dead we take increased devotion to that cause for which they here gave the last full measure of devotion—that we here highly resolve that these dead shall not have died in vain—that this nation, under God, shall have a new birth of freedom—and that government of the people, by the people, for the people, shall not perish from the earth.

Gettysburg Address

Abraham Lincoln

The Bliss copy, once owned by the family of Colonel Alexander Bliss, Bancroft's stepson and publisher of "Autograph Leaves", is the only manuscript to which Lincoln affixed his signature.

Address delivered at the dedication of the cemetery at Gettysburg.

Four score and seven years ago our fathers brought forth, on this continent, a new nation, conceived in Liberty, and dedicated to the proposition that all men are created equal.

Now we are engaged in a great civil war, testing whether that nation, or any nation so conceived and so dedicated, can long endure. We are met on a great battle-field of that war. We have come to dedicate a portion of that field, as a final resting place for those who here gave their lives that that nation might live. It is altogether fitting and proper that we should do this.

But, in a larger sense, we can not dedicate—we can not consecrate—we can not hallow—this ground. The brave men, living and dead, who struggled here, have consecrated it, far above our poor power to add or detract. The world will little note, nor long remember what we say here, but it can never forget what they did here. It is for us the living, rather, to be dedicated here to the unfinished work which they who fought here have thus far so nobly advanced. It is rather for us to be here dedicated to the great task remaining before us—that from these honored dead we take increased devotion to that cause for which they gave the last full measure of devotion—that we here highly resolve that these dead shall not have died in vain—that this nation, under God, shall have a new birth of freedom—and that government of the people, by the people, for the people, shall not perish from the earth.

November 19, 1863.

Abraham Lincoln

Gettysburg Address (1922)

by Abraham Lincoln

This is the version of the text inscribed on the walls at the Lincoln Memorial in Washington D.C.

FOUR SCORE AND SEVEN YEARS AGO OUR FATHERS BROUGHT FORTH ON THIS CONTINENT A NEW NATION CONCEIVED IN LIBERTY AND DEDICATED TO THE PROPOSITION THAT ALL MEN ARE CREATED EQUAL •

NOW WE ARE ENGAGED IN A GREAT CIVIL WAR TESTING WHETHER THAT NATION OR ANY NATION SO CONCEIVED AND SO DEDICATED CAN LONG ENDURE • WE ARE MET ON A GREAT BATTLEFIELD OF THAT WAR • WE HAVE COME TO DEDICATE A PORTION OF THAT FIELD AS A FINAL RESTING PLACE FOR THOSE WHO HERE GAVE THEIR LIVES THAT THAT NATION MIGHT LIVE • IT IS ALTOGETHER FITTING AND PROPER THAT WE SHOULD DO THIS • BUT IN A LARGER SENSE WE CAN NOT DEDICATE~WE CAN NOT CONSECRATE~WE CAN NOT HALLOW~THIS GROUND • THE BRAVE MEN LIVING AND DEAD WHO STRUGGLED HERE HAVE CONSECRATED IT FAR ABOVE OUR POOR POWER TO ADD OR DETRACT • THE WORLD WILL LITTLE NOTE NOR LONG REMEMBER WHAT WE SAY HERE BUT IT CAN NEVER FORGET WHAT THEY DID HERE • IT IS FOR US THE LIVING RATHER TO BE DEDICATED HERE TO THE UNFINISHED WORK WHICH THEY WHO FOUGHT HERE HAVE THUS FAR SO NOBLY ADVANCED • IT IS RATHER FOR US TO BE HERE DEDICATED TO THE GREAT TASK REMAINING BEFORE US~THAT FROM THESE HONORED DEAD WE TAKE INCREASED DEVOTION TO THAT CAUSE FOR WHICH THEY GAVE THE LAST FULL MEASURE OF DEVOTION~THAT WE HERE HIGHLY RESOLVE THAT THESE DEAD SHALL NOT HAVE DIED IN VAIN~THAT THIS NATION UNDER GOD SHALL HAVE A NEW BIRTH OF FREEDOM~AND THAT GOVERNMENT OF THE PEOPLE BY THE PEOPLE FOR THE PEOPLE SHALL NOT PERISH FROM THE EARTH

The Slaves Are Made Free

The Federals rejoiced greatly at the successes of Grant and the navy, and indeed they had need of success somewhere to keep up their spirits, for on the whole things did not go well. George McClellan was commander-in-chief, and although he drilled his army splendidly he never did anything with it. He was a wonderful organizer, but he was cautious to a fault, and always believed the enemy to be far stronger than he really was.

He was at last dismissed, and was succeeded by one commander-in-chief after another. Not none proved truly satisfactory. Indeed it was not until the last year of the war, when Ulysses Grant took command, that a really great commander-in-chief was found.

At the beginning of the war no matter who was leader the long campaigns in Virginia ended in failure for the Federals. On the Confederate side these campaigns were led first by Joseph E. Johnston, and then by the great soldier, Robert E. Lee.

Lee came of a soldier stock, being the youngest son of "Light Horse Harry Lee," who had won fame during the War of the Revolution. He was a noble, Christian gentleman, and when he made his choice, and determined to fight for the South, he believed he was fighting for the right.

With Lee was Stonewall Jackson, his great "right hand," and perhaps a finer soldier than Lee himself. His men adored him as they adored no other leader. Like Cromwell he taught them to pray as well as to fight. He never went into battle without commending his way to God, and when he knelt long in prayer his men might feel certain that a great fight was coming. He was secret and swift in his movements, so swift that his troops were nicknamed "Jackson's foot cavalry." Yet he never wore his men out. He thought for them always, and however urgent haste might be he called frequent halts on his flying marches, and made the men lie down even if it were only for a few minutes.

To conquer such leaders, and the men devoted to them, was no easy matter, and it was not wonderful that the campaigns in Virginia marked few successes for the Federals. At length the long series of failures ended with a second, and for the Federals, disastrous, battle of Bull Run. This was followed two days later by the battle of Chantilly, after which the whole Federal army fell back to Washington.

Lee, rejoicing at his successes in Virginia, made up his mind then to invade Maryland, which state he believed would readily join the Confederacy. But he was disappointed. For if the Marylanders had not much enthusiasm for the Union cause they had still less for the

Confederate, and the invaders were greeted with exceeding coldness. Their unfailing good fortune, too, seemed to forsake the Confederates, and the battle of Antietam, one of the fiercest of the war, although hardly a victory for the Federals, was equal to a defeat for the Confederates. For fourteen hours the carnage lasted, and when at length night put an end to the slaughter thousands lay dead on either side. Next day, having in a fortnight lost half his army, Lee withdrew once more into Virginia.

Lincoln's chief object in carrying on the war was not to free slaves, but to save the Union.

"My first object is to save the Union," he wrote, "and not either to save or destroy slavery. If I could save the Union without freeing any slave I would do it. If I could save it by freeing all the slaves I would do it. And if I could save it by freeing some, and leaving others alone I would also do that." Gradually, however, Lincoln began to believe that the only way to save the Union was to free the slaves.

Many people were impetuously urging him to do it. But Lincoln would do nothing rash. It was a tremendous step to take, and the question as to when would be the right moment to take it was, for him, one of tremendous importance. So he prepared his Proclamation of Emancipation and bided his time. Following his own good judgment and the advice of one of his Cabinet he resolved not to announce it so long as things were going badly with the North lest it should be looked upon as the last measure of an exhausted government, a cry for help. It was not to be sent forth into the world as "a last shriek in the retreat," but as a companion to victory.

But victory was slow in coming. At length the great battle was fought at Antietam. It was scarce a victory, for the Federals had lost more men than had the Confederates. Yet it had to pass for one. And a few days after it Lincoln issued his Proclamation of Emancipation. In this he declared that in every state which should be in arms against the Government on the 1st of January, 1863, the slaves should be free forever more. This gave the rebel states more than three months in which to lay down their arms and return to their allegiance.

Meanwhile the war went on. In November General Ambrose E. Burnside was appointed commander of the army of the Potomac. He accepted the post unwillingly, for he did not think himself great enough to fill it. It was soon proved that he was right.

On December 13th a great battle was fought at Fredericksburg in Virginia. The weather had been very cold and the ground was covered with frost and snow. But on the morning of the 13th, although a white mist shrouded the land, the sun shone so warmly that it seemed like a September day. Yet though the earth and sky alike seemed calling men to mildness and peace the deadly game of war went on.

The center of the Confederate army occupied some high ground known as the Maryes Heights, and Burnside resolved to dislodge them. It was a foolhardy attempt, for the hill was strongly held, the summit of it bristled with cannon. Yet the order was given, and with unquestioning valor the men rushed to the attack. As they dashed onward the Confederate guns swept their ranks, and they were mowed down like hay before the reaper. Still they pressed onward, and after paying a fearful toll in dead and wounded they at length reached the foot of the hill. Here they were confronted by a stone wall so thick and strong that their fire had not the slightest effect on it, and from behind which the Confederates poured a deadly hail of bullets upon them.

Here the carnage was awful, yet still the men came on in wave after wave, only to melt away as it seemed before the terrible fire of the Confederates. "It was like snow coming down and melting on warm ground," said one of their leaders afterwards.

Never did men fling away their lives so bravely and so uselessly. A battery was ordered forward.

"General," said an officer, "a battery cannot live there."

"Then it must die there," was the answer.

And the battery was led out as dashingly as if on parade, although the men well knew that they were going to certain death.

At length the short winter's day drew to a close, and darkness mercifully put an end to the slaughter.

Then followed a night of pain and horror. The frost was intense, and out on that terrible hillside the wounded lay beside the dead, untended and uncared for, many dying from cold ere help could reach them. Still and white they lay beneath the starry sky while the general who had sent them to a needless death wrung his hands in cruel remorse. "Oh, those men, Oh, those men," he moaned, "those men over there. I am thinking of them all the time."

Burnside knew that he had failed as a general, and in his grief and despair he determined to wipe out his failure by another attempt next day. But his officers well knew that this would only mean more useless sacrifice of life. With difficulty they persuaded him to give up the idea, and two days later the Federal army crossed the Rappahannock, and returned to their camp near Falmouth.

With this victory of Fredericksburg the hopes of the Confederates rose high. They believed that the war would soon end triumphantly for them, and that the South would henceforth be a separate republic. There was no need for them, they thought, to listen to the commands of the President of the North, and not one state paid any heed to Lincoln's demand that the slaves should be set free.

Nevertheless on New Year's Day, 1863, Lincoln signed the great Proclamation of Freedom.

He had first held a great reception, and had shaken hands with so many people that his right hand was trembling. "If they find my hand trembling," he said to the Secretary of State, as he took up his pen, "they will say, 'He hesitated,' but anyway it is going to be done."

Then very carefully and steadily he wrote his name. It was the greatest deed of his life. "If my name is ever remembered," he said, "it will be for this act, and my whole soul is in it."

And thus slavery came to an end. From the beginning of the war there had been a danger that France and Britain might help the South. Lincoln had now made that impossible by making the war one against slavery as well as one for Union. For both France and Britain were against slavery, and could not well help those who now fought to protect it.

Now that they were free, many Negroes entered the army. At this the Southerners were very angry, and declared that any negroes taken prisoners would not be regarded as soldiers, but simply as rebellious negroes, and would be punished accordingly. But in spite of their anger many black regiments were formed, and proved themselves good soldiers. And before the end of the war the Confederates, too, were making use of Negro Soldiery. But this was cutting the ground from under their own feet, and showing the injustice of slavery. For as a Southerner said, "If a negro is fit to be a soldier he is not fit to be a slave."

Emancipation Proclamation
By the President of the United States of America:
A PROCLAMATION

Whereas on the 22nd day of September, A.D. 1862, a proclamation was issued by the President of the United States, containing, among other things, the following, to wit:

"That on the 1st day of January, A.D. 1863, all persons held as slaves within any State or designated part of a State the people whereof shall then be in rebellion against the United States shall be then, thenceforward, and forever free; and the executive government of the United States, including the military and naval authority thereof, will recognize and maintain the freedom of such persons and will do no act or acts to repress such persons, or any of them, in any efforts they may make for their actual freedom.

"That the executive will on the 1st day of January aforesaid, by proclamation, designate the States and parts of States, if any, in which the people thereof, respectively, shall then be in rebellion against the United States; and the fact that any State or the people thereof shall on that day be in good faith represented in the Congress of the United States by members chosen thereto at elections wherein a majority of the qualified voters of such States shall have participated shall, in the absence of strong countervailing testimony, be deemed conclusive evidence that such State and the people thereof are not then in rebellion against the United States."

Now, therefore, I, Abraham Lincoln, President of the United States, by virtue of the power in me vested as Commander-In-Chief of the Army and Navy of the United States in time of actual armed rebellion against the authority and government of the United States, and as a fit and necessary war measure for supressing said rebellion, do, on this 1st day of January, A.D. 1863, and in accordance with my purpose so to do, publicly proclaimed for the full period of one hundred days from the first day above mentioned, order and designate as the States and parts of States wherein the people thereof, respectively, are this day in rebellion against the United States the following, to wit:

Arkansas, Texas, Louisiana (except the parishes of St. Bernard, Palquemines, Jefferson, St. John, St. Charles, St. James, Ascension, Assumption, Terrebone, Lafourche, St. Mary, St. Martin, and Orleans, including the city of New Orleans), Mississippi, Alabama, Florida, Georgia, South Carolina, North Carolina, and Virginia (except the forty-eight counties designated as West Virginia, and also the counties of Berkeley, Accomac, Morthhampton, Elizabeth City, York, Princess Anne, and Norfolk, including the cities of Norfolk and Portsmouth), and which excepted parts are for the present left precisely as if this proclamation were not issued.

And by virtue of the power and for the purpose aforesaid, I do order and declare that all persons held as slaves within said designated States and parts of States are, and henceforward shall be, free; and that the Executive Government of the United States, including the military and naval authorities thereof, will recognize and maintain the freedom of said persons.

And I hereby enjoin upon the people so declared to be free to abstain from all violence, unless in necessary self-defence; and I recommend to them that, in all case when allowed, they labor faithfully for reasonable wages.

And I further declare and make known that such persons of suitable condition will be received into the armed service of the United States to garrison forts, positions, stations, and other places, and to man vessels of all sorts in said service.

And upon this act, sincerely believed to be an act of justice, warranted by the Constitution upon military necessity, I invoke the considerate judgment of mankind and the gracious favor of Almighty God.

CPSIA information can be obtained
at www.ICGtesting.com
Printed in the USA
BVOW07s1520150416
444365BV00006B/16/P